DANGER on the
DOORSTEP

DANGER on the

DOORSTEP

ANTI-CATHOLICISM AND AMERICAN PRINT CULTURE IN THE PROGRESSIVE ERA

JUSTIN NORDSTROM

University of Notre Dame Press
Notre Dame, Indiana

Manufactured in the United States of America

Danger on the Doorstep was designed by Jane Oslislo and Wendy McMillen;
Composed in 10/13.2 ITC New Baskerville by Four Star Books;
printed on 60# Williamsburg Recycled paper by Versa Press, Inc.

Library of Congress Cataloging-in-Publication Data

Nordstrom, Justin.
Danger on the doorstep : anti-Catholicism and American print culture in
the progressive era / Justin Nordstrom.
p. cm.
Includes bibliographical references and index.
ISBN-13: 978-0-268-03605-8 (pbk. : alk. paper)
ISBN-10: 0-268-03605-5 (pbk. : alk. paper)
1. Anti-Catholicism—United States.   2. Press—United States.
3. Publicity—United States.   4. United States—Church history—
20th century. I. Title.
BX1770.N67   2006
305.6'827309041—dc22

                                        2006017249

Contents

Acknowledgments

Academic writing is almost never produced in isolation, and this book is no exception. Without the insight, mentorship, patience, and suggestions of numerous individuals, I could never have seen this project through to completion. In particular, I owe a tremendous debt of gratitude to the faculty at three outstanding universities that have shaped my intellectual and professional development in ways large and small. The University of Rochester is an inspiring place, made even more exceptional by the outstanding mentors I first met more than a decade ago. I am grateful to Daniel Borus, Curt Cadorette, Emil Homerin, Anne Meredith, Robert Westbrook, and other faculty in history and religion at the University of Rochester, my undergraduate alma mater. Special thanks to Joan Rubin for serving as my undergraduate advisor for her continued guidance and accessibility throughout the years.

Indiana University proved to be an engaging environment for historical studies, particularly under the guidance of John Bodnar, a prolific scholar and exceptional mentor. Professor Bodnar's kindness and assistance were boundless in guiding me through the formative steps of my graduate career. This book began several years ago as a doctoral dissertation, and I'm pleased to thank members of the dissertation committee: Wendy Gamber, Dave Nord, and Mary Jo Weaver. Each provided helpful comments throughout my graduate training and helped me conceptualize anti-Catholic literature within broader historical frameworks. I am also grateful to other exceptional teachers and mentors at Indiana University: Mike Grossberg, Leah Shopkow, Steve Stowe, Barbara Truesdell, and, from the *American Historical Review*, Moureen Claver and the late Allyn Roberts.

The Pennsylvania State University has been similarly hospitable. I have been fortunate to work with exceptional scholars, librarians, and staff members at several campuses. At the Hazleton campus, where I am fortunate to teach, I am grateful to Suzanne Bahrt, William Ellis, Joseph Fennewald, Monica Gregory, Deidre Jago, Michael Kattner, John Madden, Shannon Richie, David Smith, Lisa Swenson, and Elizabeth Wright.

Scholars at other institutions have been supportive and helpful as well. For assistance on earlier drafts and versions of the research presented in this book, I am grateful to Christopher Kauffman, Deborah Dash Moore, Bob Orsi, and Jonathan Sarna. Several former graduate students have provided ongoing support and advice long after our classes together were over. I am indebted to Tom Lappis, Margaret Puskar-Pasewicz, and Steve Sheehan for sharing perspectives on teaching and research. I also wish to thank close friends Karla and Wes Horne for their optimism and encouragement.

I am grateful for generous financial assistance provided by Indiana University—not merely in offering funding throughout my graduate training, but in providing additional support through the Department of History's McNutt Fellowship. I also wish to thank several librarians and archivists who helped me identify historical sources. Fr. Walter Gagne, Barbara Martire, and Sister Hildegard Varga assisted me in locating records from *The Antidote*. The staff of Duquesne University assisted me in retrieving reports from the Knights of Columbus, and librarians at Indiana University, Purdue University, and Penn State University helped me with dozens of loan requests for nativist texts. Special thanks to the John Hay Library at Brown University for copying anti-Catholic texts that illustrate this book's appendix, and to the Penn State Library for their assistance in locating lenders of anti-Catholic ephemera. I am particularly grateful to Kevin Cawley at the University of Notre Dame for his helpful comments on reading anti-nativist texts.

The University of Notre Dame Press also deserves recognition as an exemplary publisher. My sincere thanks to the Press for its interest in this project and its constant support. Particular thanks go to Lowell Francis and Barbara Hanrahan for their guidance through the publishing process. I am also grateful to two anonymous reviewers who provided invaluable assistance in earlier manuscript drafts and helped me to improve my treatment of the anti-Catholic crusade. My sincere thanks to Beth Wright for her exemplary editing of the manuscript.

My family has brightened my life in countless ways and provided unsolicited support. I am grateful to George and Gloria Freeman for their enthusiasm and encouragement. My grandparents and, especially, my parents Harold and Mary Jo Nordstrom are a source of immense love, and many thanks to Angela and Chris Jennings for their support and sense of humor. Above all, my greatest source of admiration and encouragement has been my wife, Alicia, whose love and generosity have never wavered. Alicia has encouraged and motivated me in large and small ways to be a more insightful scholar and a better person. This book is dedicated to her.

Introduction

ANTI-CATHOLICISM AND
THEORIES OF NATIONALISM

In January 1916, two opposing groups squared off in the U.S. District Courtroom in Joplin, Missouri. On one side of the room sat the defendants, members of the Menace Publishing Company who had waged a five-year journalistic war against America's Roman Catholic hierarchy, proclaiming it "the greatest menace to our liberties and our civilization." In the pages of their landmark newspaper *The Menace,* writers and editors called upon their hundreds of thousands of loyal readers to recognize, challenge, and attack the dangers posed by Catholic conspiracy and duplicity. On the opposite side of the room were their accusers, members of the U.S. District Attorney's Office alongside high-ranking members of the Catholic fraternal organization, the Knights of Columbus, and heads of other prominent Catholic agencies. Wary that the paper's resounding popularity might trigger long-standing anti-Catholic animosities, lay and clerical Catholic leaders had spent months scouring the pages of *The Menace* and similar periodicals, providing clippings for federal prosecutors to use as evidence.[1]

This legal clash had been coming for some time. Catholic officials had attacked *The Menace* for years, arguing that its vituperative articles misrepresented Catholics' true loyalty and patriotism. The real danger to national unity and American society, the plaintiffs believed, were not the nation's Catholic parishioners, but their critics, who divided America with unfounded and bitter attacks. In effect, the adversaries on either side of

the courtroom were engaged in two trials at once. At its most factual level,
the case accused *The Menace* and its editors of violating federal law by printing lewd descriptions of priestly immorality in their exposés of Catholic
confessionals. Evoking the type of sexualized anti-Catholic rhetoric popular since the 1800s, *Menace* writers had insisted that priests posed sugges-
tive and titillating questions to female penitents in order to seduce and hu-
miliate innocent women and children within the confines of confessional
booths (abuses that, anti-Catholic writers would also maintain, occurred
in convents, rectories, and other Catholic circles with appalling regu-
larity). On the legal merits of the case, anti-Catholics clearly won the day,
as the paper was acquitted of all seven charges of sending obscene material through the mail, and the editors went on to print weekly diatribes
against their accusers for several years.

But everyone in the room knew that the case wasn't strictly about the
minutia of "obscenity" charges, their ambiguity in federal law, or even the
application of First Amendment freedoms (though this latter point was
often evoked by the defendants). On a more crucial level, members of the
Menace Publishing Company and their Catholic opponents were debating
several fundamental issues: Which posed a greater danger to the American
public—Catholicism, or its converse, anti-Catholicism? Was the Catholic
Church in need of governmental protection, or did it simply manipulate
the national government to squash opposition and serve its own sinister
ends? What (if anything) could plaintiffs or defendants do to illustrate the
sincerity of their convictions or the importance of their position? With
these debates formulating the background of the Joplin trial, one thing
was clear: in the minds (and weekly diatribes) of the anti-Catholic press, the
wrong group was on trial—the real criminals, xenophobic writers loudly
maintained, were the legions of foreign-minded priests intent on undermining the nation's ideals.

Ultimately, though, the legal clash between Catholic apologists and
anti-papal crusaders in 1916 was simply one facet of a more pervasive and
drawn-out war during the years leading up to America's entry into World
War I and continuing until the dawn of the 1920s. For the most part, the
battle between defenders and critics of American Catholicism was fought
not in courtrooms, but in the pages of the burgeoning periodicals industry. Each side churned out dozens of publications and spilled oceans of
ink to argue their position on one critical question: could Catholics be
loyal Americans? Thus, despite their vindication in the Joplin trial, *Menace*

writers continued to face off against Catholic foes in the more important battle for readership in the arena of Americans' own consciousness. And acquittal on the legal indictment did not translate into enduring national acceptance—shortly after winning their court case, *The Menace* faced financial burdens and a shrinking circulation base. By 1919, the paper, and dozens of anti-Catholic sheets like it, had ceased publication.

This book examines the enormous rise of anti-Catholic literature in the years leading up to, and immediately following, the Joplin trial, as well as the foundational issues and motivations that informed anti-Catholic writers and their "Romanist" opponents. As *The Menace* case illustrates, from 1910 to the end of World War I, American society witnessed a tremendous outpouring of books, pamphlets, journals, and, especially, newspapers espousing virulently anti-Catholic themes and calling on readers to emerge from their myopic state and recognize Catholicism's danger to the American republic. Using the rhetoric of patriotic militarism, anti-Catholic writers, editors, and publishers lambasted their Romanist opponents as disloyal, backward-thinking, and intellectually stunted conspirators whose dedication to a corrupt priestly hierarchy rendered them unable to grasp or appreciate the tenets of American liberties and, thus, unworthy of national belonging or citizenship. During a decade in which Catholics themselves began to enumerate their significant sacrifices for and positive contributions toward the nation's well-being, anti-Romanist writers scoffed at Catholic claims, branding their "papist" counterparts as naïve at best or, more often, incipient agents intent on dismantling America's traditions and undermining the government itself.

Moreover, this book explores the critical overlap between anti-Catholicism and nationalism during the 1910s, demonstrating that an understanding of the former is incomplete if not rooted in the latter. In what follows, I argue that the anti-Catholic literature that enjoyed such a prominent place in the American cultural landscape in the early twentieth century derived its popularity by infusing the emerging themes of progressivism, masculinity, and nationalism, central to print culture immediately prior to and during World War I, within the broader framework of America's long-standing anti-Catholic traditions. In several respects, the anti-Catholic statements of the early twentieth century were far from unique. Warnings of Catholic depravity, deception, and rebellion have found resonance within nearly every episode in American history—from the Colonial Era, through the antebellum years, and into the Gilded Age—although it was in the Progressive Era that these voices received the broadest circulation and loudest pitch, with the largest and most powerful anti-Catholic newspapers reaching thousands, even millions, of American readers every week.

Despite references and similarities to earlier epochs, anti-Catholicism in the Progressive Era also embodied significant differences from its predecessors, particularly its exclusively rural character that sought to locate small-town values at the center of America's democratic tradition and feared encroachment by Catholic agents emanating from distant cities. Alongside claims of unpatriotic Romanism, anti-Catholic print culture in the years surrounding World War I revealed a recognition of and abiding concern for fundamental changes confronting American society. Within the pages of anti-Catholic texts, Catholicism emerged as the manifestation and, to a large degree, scapegoat for the excesses of modernity—including rampant urbanization, political corruption, and the proliferation of "trusts" or illicit power conglomerates. Root out Catholic conspirators, dismantle priestly authority, expose the stockpiles of weapons and subversive literature, these journalists promised to readers, and the dangers of modern life would evaporate. Thus, anti-Catholic writers embody a paradox—employing metaphors, accusations, and symbols of Catholic corruption that resembled those of prior generations, but updating and revising these anti-Catholic clichés to resonate with a new, twentieth-century audience. This blending of familiar anti-Catholic diatribes with new accusations that speak directly to Progressive-Era concerns is what made anti-Catholic literature such a prevalent cultural force in the mid 1910s, and is the focus of the chapters that follow.

As I began to write this book, I was struck by two contemporary events that both captivated the popular media and reflected critical aspects of this project. The first was the growing sexual abuse scandal in the Catholic Church, which revealed dozens of cases of pedophilia that were kept out of the public eye by Catholic leaders and raised serious questions about priestly transgression, misconduct, and criminality. The second was the recent publication of the book *The Death of the West,* a scathing indictment of current demographic and cultural trends put forward by archconservative Pat Buchanan, bemoaning a perceived loss of "western" values and "civilization" in America. Hitting the talk-show circuit as his book hit the shelves, Buchanan called for such diverse policies as massive reductions in immigration, economic and political isolationism, new governmental incentives for higher marriage and birthrates, and improved history teaching—steps necessary, Buchanan argued, to counteract the effects of "un-American" immigrants from outside Western Europe, whose nonwhite, non-Christian culture threatens to supplant America's "traditional" values.[2]

These recent events underscore two central and interrelated themes critical to the study of early twentieth-century anti-Catholicism. First, both contemporary reporters and their Progressive-Era counterparts faced the alarming discovery (and its promulgation in public media) that Catholics constituted a threat to America's safety because of misused clerical power, conspiratorial cover-ups, and attacks on the most vulnerable members of American society, particularly children. Second, Buchanan's words demonstrate how an illiberal vision of American citizenship can seek to depict segments of the nation's population as out of sync with American culture and traditions and, therefore, unfit for national belonging. Of course, ironies abound in these comparisons—anti-Catholicism in the 1910s, for instance, was generally the product of extensive exaggeration if not outright fabrication, while contemporary reports of priestly abuse seem frighteningly germane. And Buchanan's remarks derive not from xenophobic anti-Catholicism, but from his own conservative Catholic beliefs. Such a comparison of contemporary and Progressive-Era media offers few direct parallels, but it does illustrate that the issues of Catholic authority and restrictive visions of nationalism were as central a century ago as they are today.

Nationalism and Anti-Catholicism

Although Roman Catholicism has been America's single largest religious denomination for well over a century, critics have frequently and openly questioned whether it is possible to be both a devout Catholic and a loyal American—a compatibility question that church leaders have usually (though not always) attempted to answer in the affirmative. As the noted historian Charles Morris states, Catholicism in the United States has "always been defined by its prickly apartness from the broader, secular American culture—*in* America, usually enthusiastically *for* America, but never quite *of* America."[3] The questions of when and to what extent Catholics have experienced inclusion in American society (if, indeed, they ever have) have underscored most of the historiography of the American

Catholic Church—and dozens of texts in sociology, history, and literary criticism.[4] While putting these often-debated questions to rest goes beyond the scope of this book, the gaps between what might be termed "mainstream" white Protestant America and Roman Catholicism, and attempts to lengthen or transcend them, are critical to an exploration of American xenophobia.

Before delving further into the conflicts between "Romanists" and their opponents, however, I want to draw attention to the arena in which the debates over Catholic inclusion were carried out—particularly theories of American nationalism. For well over a century, historians and other scholars have put forth explanations on the development, spread, and attraction of nationalism—most, though not all, indicating that nationalism emerged alongside modern phenomena of western capitalism and technological innovations, such as printing and industrialization. One of the most salient issues in modern nationalist theory has been how to chart patterns in nations' development and differentiate criteria nations use to distinguish members of a particular nation from nonmembers. Toward this end, historians have attempted to construct a series of typologies of nationhood, which, despite key differences, indicate that national inclusion or exclusion hinges on either common ideological and institutional traits, shared hereditary (ethnic, racial, linguistic) attributes, or some combination thereof. Ernest Gellner, for instance, suggests that nations tend to identify members either by "cultural" or "voluntaristic" criteria (with the former based on shared ideas and associations and the later rooted in meaning attached to "shared attributes" of language, geography, or heredity).[5] Miroslav Hroch's recent study of European nationalism reveals that national identity is rooted in a "collective consciousness" manifested in three "irreplaceable" ties that bind members of a nation together. Two of these—"'memory' of some common past" and "a density of linguistic or cultural ties"—might stand in opposition to the third category, "a conception of the equity of all members of the group organized as a civil society." The first two traits offer a restrictive vision of national membership, in which citizenship is limited to only those descendants of a certain genealogy or speakers of a certain language, while the third embraces all that share a common government and vision of equity.[6]

Likewise, Rogers Brubaker's study of national minorities presents a distinction between political affinity (citizens' "legal citizenship") and their "ethnonational affinity," and it illustrates how these often conflicting loyalties can lead to tension, particularly in newly developing states.[7] Perhaps the most articulate examination of this critical overlap between ethnic and civil strains of nation building is Liah Greenfeld's influential study *Nationalism: Five Roads to Modernity*, which juxtaposes civic nationalism (wherein membership is based on attachments to shared political and legal institutions) against Europe's more recent arrival, ethnic nationalism (in which membership is limited to a particular ethnic or racial group). Greenfeld's work indicates that civic nationalism predominated in Britain and, later, the United States, where abundant internal distinctions precluded the restrictive rhetoric of ethnic nationalism, which would find adherents in Germany, central Europe, and elsewhere. Central to Greenfeld's analysis is an explicit correlation linking inclusion and tolerance with "civic" images of nationalism on the one hand and xenophobia, intolerance, and restrictivism with "ethnic" forms of nationalism on the other.[8] Michael Hechter's recent volume *Containing Nationalism* echoes this typology—suggesting that scholars have taken pains to "distinguish the liberal, culturally inclusive (Sleeping Beauty) nationalisms characteristic of Western Europe from the illiberal, culturally exclusive (Frankenstein's Monster) nationalism more often found elsewhere."[9]

Each of these typologies, at their most fundamental level, states that nationalism can be based on two features—how people *look* (their *ethnic* and racial features) or how people *think* (their *civic* or ideological similarities). Greenfeld maintains that the United States, among all western countries, went furthest to promote civic nationalism and demonstrates how America (along with France and Britain) modeled citizenship on common understandings of "liberty" as opposed to narrow definitions of race.[10] Other scholars, however, are less convinced. As Eric Foner has pointed out, "Nationalism, in America at least, is the child of both of these beliefs. . . . American nationalism has long combined both civic and ethnic definitions. For most of our history, American citizenship has been defined by blood as well as political allegiance."[11] And as Rogers Smith's study of citizenship law makes clear, America has exhibited not only conflicting civic and ethnic understandings of nationhood but differing degrees of tolerance and openness. For Smith, previous generations of scholars (particularly Louis Hartz, who saw American nationalism as the outgrowth of English liberal philosophy) have failed to take into account the influence of political philosophies that saw citizenship rooted in gender and hereditary factors (and occasionally other factors such as religion). These illiberal

voices, which Smith terms "inegalitarian ascriptive traditions of Americanism" clashed with broader, more fully democratic ones over the legal, political, and cultural questions of citizenship from the Revolution through
the early twentieth century, with each side occasionally winning an upper
hand, until the inegalitarian ascriptive forces began to coalesce and pre-
dominate in the Gilded Age and Progressive Era.[12]

American nationalism has occupied a protean place on the two overlapping dichotomies most used by scholars—civic versus ethnic forms
of nationalism on one hand and the often concomitant scales of liberal/
democratic versus illiberal/inegalitarian ascriptive on the other. Since
civic and liberal visions of nationalism often go hand in hand and ethnic
and inegalitarian conceptions of citizenship likewise concur on scholarly
typologies, twentieth-century anti-Catholicism, predicated on a staunchly
exclusivist and inegalitarian scope of nationalism, seeking to deny membership to millions of citizens who, collectively, made up the country's
largest and most visible religious body, would therefore seem to follow an
ethnic approach toward Catholic persecution. Under this logic, we should
expect to see anti-Catholic writers using eugenicist or racially charged arguments to brand their opponents as physically or genealogically unfit
for full citizenship. We would expect to see arguments for a "pure" Anglo-
Saxon, Protestant vision of national belonging in which all "true" (i.e.,
racially pure) Americans shared similar ancestry (or at least appeared outwardly to do so) and that challenged Catholics on the basis of impure
bloodlines, racial characteristics, or adherence to European languages.

Indeed, when I began my research on twentieth-century anti-Catholic
literature, I anticipated finding these arguments, and scores of ethnic
and racial caricatures, portraying Catholics as dangerous to America because their "mongrelized" racial stock put them at odds with Protestants,
who were intent on presenting themselves and their nation as ethnically
"pure." Instead, what I found is that anti-Catholic writers virtually never
refer to racial stereotypes or ethnic slurs and were remarkably reserved
in criticizing Catholicism's multilingual and multinational population.
What writers were denouncing, however, was Catholics' perceived inability
to embrace American civic virtues—insisting that their adherence to
priestly hierarchies made Catholics unable to accept American values of
egalitarianism, individualism, and tolerance. This approach is extremely
significant for a number of reasons. First, it illustrates a significant limita-
tion in the prevailing typologies of nationalism, which generally equate

civic forms of nationalism with libertarianism, not xenophobia. While the dichotomies put forth by Greenfeld, Foner, Smith, and others allow for this form of "civic" xenophobia, it seems far more common for "ascriptive" or illiberal advocates to take a racial or eugenic approach. Furthermore, the ideological bent of the early twentieth century distinguishes that generation's anti-Catholicism from variations that prevailed prior and since, which generally pursued an anti-immigrant, eugenicist, or racial-purity agenda concomitant to their anti-Romanist crusade. In contrast, writers during the 1910s were far more concerned with Catholics' perceived inability to comprehend American dogma and traditions and their alleged threats to subvert civic institutions from within. Finally, the ideological and civic motives of anti-Catholic writers reveals a fundamental irony in their approach: by questioning Catholics' capacity to abide by the American ethos of toleration, open-mindedness, and democracy, anti-Catholic writers gave themselves license to abridge these values. In exposing Catholics' lack of open-mindedness, anti-Catholic writers were remarkably intolerant; accusing Catholics citizens of threatening American democracy, anti-Catholic writers truncated the boundaries of democracy itself.

THE ANTI-CATHOLIC GENRE

With an eye toward elaborating on this historiography by examining an under-studied episode of anti-Catholic radicalism, this book presents a textual and historical criticism of ten anti-Catholic newspapers active from 1910 to 1919, all of which articulated nearly identical portrayals of the Roman Catholic Church and its membership. Wary that the church had become more numerous, attained more political power, and above all had begun to establish itself as a prominent, respectable, and contributing aspect of American social life during the Gilded Age and Progressive Era, each of these anti-Catholic papers condemned the church as hurtful and destructive to American civilization itself. These papers exhibited significant differences in longevity, duration of their anti-Catholic focus, and circulation. The smallest anti-Catholic printing enterprises had a parochial and limited circulation, reaching less than two thousand nearby subscribers, while more successful anti-Catholic sheets boasted national circulations in the hundreds of thousands, vastly exceeding mainstream newspapers more familiar to historians of the Progressive Era. By 1915, the most successful anti-Catholic newspaper of this decade, aptly named *The Menace,* boasted over 1.6 million weekly readers, a circulation three times greater than the largest daily papers in Chicago and New York City combined, while others lagged far behind.[13] (As I demonstrate in chapter 2, existing publication directories support the circulation figures reported in the most successful anti-Catholic periodicals.) Anti-Catholic papers of the Progressive Era were strikingly similar in their location, content, rhetoric, and tone. Based in rural hamlets and small towns, predominantly in the Midwest and upper South, the anti-Catholic editors and writers who produced these sources looked to distant cities as the seat of Romanism's power and the center of anti-American attitudes and threats. Anti-Romanist newspapers shared an inflammatory, even militaristic tone reflective of the "investigative" and exposé-minded journalists of the early twentieth century.

This Progressive-Era emphasis on uncovering destructive secrets and uprooting corruption was conveyed throughout anti-Catholic columns and in the publications' titles themselves. Newspapers with names such as *The Peril, The Crusader, The Liberator,* and *The Menace* conjured images of anti-Catholic writers and editors as heroic defenders against sinister enemies. Not mere scribblers or paper pushers, writers who warned of impending Catholic attacks positioned themselves as courageous, masculine defenders of the nation's precious institutions and vulnerable citizens, and they called on a galvanized "army" of determined readers to do the same. The mastheads and headlines of these papers—blaring messages such as "Roman Catholicism, the Deadliest Menace to Our Liberties and Our Civilization," "Cry for Help from Convent Walls," "Rome's Inquisition at Work Again," "Roman Catholic Designs on the American Nation," and "Military Maneuvers Start" reveal significant fears by early twentieth-century writers that America was under attack—literally and figuratively—from Catholic forces, a claim that seems paranoiac and pushes the envelope of credibility for contemporary readers.[14] Indeed, many of the sensationalized exposés of Catholic corruption that flooded the American literary landscape seem to have been complete fabrications, gross exaggerations, or deliberately skewed portrayals of Catholic activities and motivations.[15] But as large circulation figures demonstrate, these claims also found credence with an American public relying on the power of information to make sense of a changing world around them and willing to extend America's legacy of anti-Catholic hostility well into the twentieth century.

Yet while several of the most prolific anti-Catholic papers had tremendous public appeal and staggering circulations during the mid 1910s, all prominently anti-Catholic periodicals of that decade rapidly disintegrated as the decade came to a close, abruptly suspending circulation or fading into obscurity by the dawn of the 1920s. In many respects, this rapid decline illustrates the effectiveness of Catholic mobilization, as clerical and lay spokespeople nationwide wrote rebuttals to anti-Catholic attacks, waged legal battles charging publishers with civil and criminal charges for defamatory remarks, generated large sums of money to counteract anti-Catholic propaganda, and wrote a torrent of letters to secular and even anti-Catholic papers themselves, vocally upholding Catholics' loyalty to and prominent place within American society. However, anti-Catholicism's rapid, albeit temporary, relegation to literary obscurity had more to do with developing wartime conditions than Catholic agitation. America's entry into World War I increased paper and printing costs and, more importantly, shifted readers' attention from internal Catholic threats to external tensions overseas. Following 1919, anti-Catholicism took a remarkably different direction, vested in the vigilante actions and pageantry of the Second Ku Klux Klan on one hand and, increasingly as the twentieth century wore on, in literary intellectuals on the other.

One of the most unfortunate commonalities among all Progressive-Era anti-Catholic newspapers is a frustrating lack of any extant business records or correspondence within or between papers. Since anti-Catholic newspapers quickly went out of business by the late 1910s or shortly thereafter, leaving behind no subscription lists, I've had to rely purely on some scattered published letters, nearly all of which were glowing endorsements of anti-Catholic journalists and their crusading efforts. Nevertheless, limited source material prevents me from following a "reader-response" approach to the study of Progressive-Era xenophobia in print culture or to draw firm conclusions about the locations, professions, or identities of subscribers who filled circulation rolls. Furthermore, available copies of anti-Catholic newspapers themselves fluctuate widely—ranging from several hundred extant copies of *The Mountain Advocate, Watson's Magazine, The Yellow Jacket,* and others, to a few dozen issues of *The Jeffersonian, The Crusader,* and *The Peril,* and only a couple scattered issues of *The Woman's Witness, The*

Rail Splitter, or *The Liberator.* Over a dozen Progressive-Era anti-Catholic papers are completely lost from the historical record. For this reason, I've been forced, in some cases, to sketch patterns in anti-Catholic periodicals based on fragmented and imperfect documentary sources.

Another important caveat is that this book focuses on "anti-Catholicism" in its political, social, cultural, and literary manifestations and not on the theological arguments surrounding Catholic religiosity. The journalists who wrote anti-Catholic articles vehemently denied criticizing Catholicism's "strictly religious" tenets; rather, they asserted that they were attacking the hierarchical, oligarchical, and politicized clerical structure that undermined America's traditional ideals. In fact, while anti-Catholic publishers expressed proudly that their papers were well received by Protestant ministers throughout the nation, the rhetoric of anti-Catholic xenophobia was meant to appeal to readers as concerned citizens and patriotic Americans—not dyed-in-the-wool Protestants.

DANGER ON THE DOORSTEP?

This book's title plays on a double entendre that highlights the fierce debate between anti-Catholic writers, lecturers, and publishers on the one hand and Catholics and their supporters on the other. From anti-Romanists' perspective, the "danger on the doorstep" through the early twentieth century was the growing presence, population, influence, and power of the American Catholic Church and its agents, parish priests, nuns, the Jesuit order, and individual Catholic parishioners themselves. Anti-Catholic writers and printers insisted that these sinister forces were infiltrating and corrupting American homes, particularly by threatening vulnerable women and children, and served as a hazard to the nation as a whole. Catholics countered that the "danger" appearing, quite literally, on America's doorsteps was in fact anti-Catholic papers themselves. Such papers, Catholics contended, were dangerous because they divided Americans against each other, misrepresented Catholic loyalties, and poisoned readers with ignorance and unfounded slander.

At stake in this debate, which raged in newspapers and courtrooms until the 1920s, was whether Catholics had made sufficient contributions and sacrifices to American social development to be considered patriotic citizens or whether their activities were actually a conspiratorial plot to mask

their antipathy for American values and institutions. One of the most striking aspects of Progressive-Era anti-Catholic literature, repeated on an
almost weekly basis, is its condemnation of Catholic historical figures
(whom the church praised as patriotic role models) and the denunciation
of Catholic charitable work, which anti-Catholics dismissed as merely a
front for child slavery. "Sham" charity and insincere patriotism, asserted
Catholic opponents, siphoned money out of the public treasury and into
papal coffers and, worse yet, duped Americans into believing that Romanists were a benign, even beneficial force in daily life. Not coincidentally,
the intense outburst of anti-Catholic hostility that emerged in the 1910s coincided with Catholics' earliest concerted attempts to assert and demonstrate full membership in American society—a process that continued
unevenly through the late twentieth century.

Denying and denouncing Catholics' overt claims to national belonging
became one of the primary goals of anti-papal writers in the early twentieth century, a task they carried out with an intensity that would have
been unnecessary and irrelevant in previous manifestations of American
anti-Catholicism. Because they argued that Catholic historical figures had
helped secure America's progress in the past and that selfless charity allowed Catholic lay and clerical workers to contribute to its well-being in
the present, Catholics were viewed as infringing on what their opponents
considered critical ideological territory. In some respects, this makes anti-
Catholics' newspapers appear as if their priorities are out of sync, since
some papers dedicated more attention to seemingly trivial issues—such
as Catholic celebrations of Columbus Day—than more severe issues such
as a priest's cold-blooded murder of his illicit lover, accounts of torture
in convents, or the Knights of Columbus's immanent overthrow of the
American government itself.

In what follows I attempt to explore this contested ground of national
respectability, outlining the efforts Catholics took to secure it, and the arguments their opponents made to keep the mantle of full citizenship at
arm's length from their foes. In chapter 1 I delve into competing understandings of nativism to explore the historiographical debates surrounding this term and position Progressive-Era anti-Catholicism within the long
tradition of American anti-Romanism. While early twentieth-century forms
of anti-Catholicism borrowed heavily from their antecedents, I argue that
Progressive-Era xenophobia was unique in its reliance on civic or ideological forms of nationalism to motivate its anti-Romanist agenda. Anti-Catholic

print culture of this era was steeped in the language and symbolism of a glorified American past and conjured a pantheon of historical figures to represent and demonstrate its commitment toward American loyalty and patriotism. I develop these connections with prominent historical figures and explore how anti-Catholic writers not only focused on the nation's founders to substantiate their own movement but consistently undermined Catholic efforts to do the same. While Catholic leaders pointed to Christopher Columbus, Commodore John Barry, and other figures in America's historical development as proof of Catholicism's compatibility with American values and dedication to the American nation, their opponents sneered, attempting to demonstrate that these figures were either disreputable and insincerely patriotic or not Catholic at all.

The second chapter explores the distinct rural character of early twentieth-century anti-Catholicism, which likewise distanced it from its predecessors. While previous episodes of American anti-Catholic agitation grew out of urban environments, in which nativists frequently encountered their Catholic foes, Progressive-Era anti-Romanism emerged from predominantly rural areas with negligible Catholic populations. As outposts in America's rural heartland, anti-Catholic writers could freely expound on the dangers of Catholicism, while newspapers in America's urban centers, anti-Catholic writers maintained, had been corrupted by Catholic populations and an oppressive Church hierarchy, making mainstream newspapers unable or unwilling to speak the "truth" about papist corruption. As Robert Wiebe illustrates in his landmark study *The Search for Order*, the decade leading up to the U.S. entry into World War I marked the end of a transition of power away from America's relatively isolated small towns (or so-called island communities) to bureaucratized, industrialized urban centers.[16] Much of the anti-Catholic literature of the 1910s can be seen as a belated response to this shift, as journalists reacted to the marginalization of small-town communities and lashed out at the power of urban influence.

Moreover, this chapter positions anti-Catholic literature within the broader context of Progressive-Era investigative or so-called muckraking journalism, arguing that anti-Catholic journalists demonstrated the same exposé style and the same faith in the power of information to rectify social ills that characterize more familiar Progressive-Era writers. Despite its crusading rhetoric of reform, historians have frequently shown that progressivism was a somewhat conservative movement that attempted to mollify more radical reforms while pursuing an agenda that entrenched the status quo, albeit in a slightly altered form. Like other Progressive-Era writers, anti-Catholic journalists sought to use an agenda of reform to assert and galvanize their own influence, control and moderate the explosive changes surrounding them, and counteract the most egregious aspects of modern life. Setting anti-Catholic literature within this context suggests that the papers emanating from rural towns in the 1910s saw Catholics as emblematic of and even responsible for the decline of small-town American life, as well as the prestige and influence of anti-Catholic editors and the communities they hoped to lead.

In chapter 3 I explore how anti-Romanists rebutted Catholic philanthropic and charitable efforts. Though initially lagging behind their Protestant counterparts, Catholic benevolent associations blossomed in the early twentieth century, prompting a flood of challenges alleging that this "sham" charity deluded an ignorant public into accepting Catholic advances. Rather than accepting their opponents' claims that they were contributing to the nation's public welfare, anti-Catholic writers asserted that their enemies targeted the "weakest" members of society—women, the elderly, the sick, the insane, and children—for graft, corruption, and violence, urging male readers to wage a crusade against the defilers of innocence and American virtue. Arguing that their Catholic opponents were unmasculine and uncharitable, nativist writers could, in turn, label Catholics as enemies of the nation's common good and exclude them from the ranks of respectable citizenship. Conversely, nativist journalists depicted their own movement as thoroughly masculine—and invested their papers and their subscription drives with a militaristic flair, insisting that anti-Catholicism both protected women and femininity and provided an outlet for expressions of manly responsibility and duty.

Taken together, these three initial chapters attempt to explain the dramatic rise of anti-Catholic print culture in the 1910s by illustrating how xenophobic texts tapped into several of the decade's most salient themes—the rise of patriotism, Americana, and public memory; progressivism and anxieties surrounding encroaching modernity; and fluctuating masculine gender conventions. Anti-Catholic texts proved popular in the 1910s because their writers both evoked traditional anti-Catholic tropes that had a proven track record of notoriety and financial success and used these popular tropes to address pressing social and cultural concerns in the early twentieth century. At the height of the anti-Romanist movement,

American readers purchased over two million anti-Catholic periodicals every week. Much of this circulation, I argue, stems from anti-Catholicism's ability to fuse several prominent but divergent cultural streams into a single text.

Chapter 4 takes a somewhat different tact, focusing on Catholics' vigorous and highly organized counterresponse to journalistic attacks in the 1910s, ranging from lawsuits and indictments to widespread public relations campaigns in parochial and popular media. Just as anti-Catholic writers addressed themes of nationalism, masculinity, and progressivism in mounting attacks against Romanists' opponents, Catholics and their supporters relied on remarkably similar tropes in challenging the anti-Catholic agenda. As anti-Catholic periodicals became increasingly popular and vocal, clerical and lay leaders within the American church developed a series of strategies and bankrolled an extraordinarily expensive campaign to combat their opponents' efforts, leading to the establishment of a Committee on Religious Prejudices by the Knights of Columbus in 1914. Ironically, the chief weapon used in this counterresponse was a thorough exegesis of anti-Catholic newspapers themselves, which anti-defamation leaders within the church combed for inconsistencies, inaccuracies, and misinformation. This allowed Catholics both to discredit their opponents in print and to wage successful legal battles to enforce criminal penalties and punitive damages on rival journalists. Anti-Catholic writers, however, adopted the same tactics, scouring parochial papers for evidence of Romanists' wrongdoing and using information gleaned from Catholic texts to bolster their legal defense. The war of words carried out by Catholic writers and their opponents hinged on circular and almost paranoiac readings of rivals' texts, using opponents' words against them in courtroom and propaganda battles that waged throughout the 1910s.

While these battles stunted the growth of some of the largest anti-Catholic newspapers, America's involvement in World War I signaled a rapid though temporary decline in anti-Catholicism's authoritative voice in American print culture. While Catholics pointed to wartime service and sacrifice as illustrations of national belonging and sincere patriotism, chapter 5 concludes the project by describing journalistic efforts to denounce these claims. Anti-Catholics insisted that their opponents served as spies for enemy forces, sabotaged wartime operations, and formed a mysterious fifth column, seeking to overthrow the American government while the nation was distracted by campaigns oversees. The unraveling of anti-

Catholic print literature by the decade's end and the growing public presence of American Catholicism as the twentieth century wore on suggest that Catholic claims to national belonging and full citizenship had trumped opponents' assertions of conspiracy. Yet Catholic progress toward full national acceptance did not proceed unchecked, as revivals of anti-Catholic print culture continued to gain in popularity, as evidenced by the persistence of anti-Catholic thought by such prominent twentieth-century intellectuals as John Dewey and the tremendous success of writers like Paul Blanshard, who continued to rail against the encroachment of "Catholic Power" and its attacks on American democracy well into the Cold War era, a topic I address at the close of chapter 5.[17]

Nativists' persistent and ongoing efforts to denounce and discredit Catholics' Americanism, along with contrary claims to Catholics' patriotism and loyalty, demonstrate an aspect of what sociologist Benedict Anderson has termed "imagined communities," in which national identity is based less on geographic residency than shared ideologies and myths disseminated through print culture. Anderson's understanding of nationalism fits well into studies of cultural or religious conflict, as he demonstrates that the advent of widespread literacy and vernacular printing sparked the spread of anti-clericalism in Reformation Europe.[18] But Anderson's theory of nationalism is perhaps most important in suggesting that nationalisms are inherently subjective and malleable phenomena that are continually contested and reinvented. The "imagined" and subjective nature of nationalism allows for divergent, even competing explanations of who belongs to a nation and deserves the enfranchisement, rights, or status awarded to citizens. Critics have contended that Anderson's definition of nationalism is far too broad, but for my purposes, its generality is critical, illustrating how various factions of early twentieth-century Americans could imagine their country in vastly divergent—even contradictory—forms.[19]

Twentieth-century claims of Catholic subversion, immorality, and danger to the nation can thus be understood as illustrating an "imagined" community of rural Anglo-Saxon Protestants valiantly defending the nation from threats by an internal, foreign, and sinister force invading American cities. Romanist attempts to win the American public's support and respect were extremely dangerous because they threatened this idyllic imagined depiction of American nationalism. Yet Catholics and their supporters likewise held a vision of America, one in which loyal, hard-working,

and patriotic citizens had contributed to American progress only to be attacked by ignorant and vicious opponents. Wartime sacrifice, philanthropic
service, and the actions of historical figures became invested with heightened meaning through their attempts to support this imagined representation of national belonging. Exploring these competing understandings,
or imagined representations, of Americanism and their corresponding influence on American print culture and social views will form the foundation of my successive chapters.

CHAPTER ONE

"Utterly Incompatible Are Romanism and Americanism"

IDEOLOGICAL NATIVISM, ANTI-CATHOLIC
TRADITION, AND AMERICAN PATRIOTISM

On June 22, 1912, the fledgling anti-Catholic newspaper *The Menace* broadcast a stunning headline: "Knights of Columbus Storm Washington." Alarming prose told readers that over one hundred thousand Catholics, under the direction of Jesuit leaders, had descended on the American capital and threatened "all civic bodies" in the city. In many respects this shocking headline seems to represent the culmination of two centuries of invective, sometimes paranoiac, rhetoric decrying the threat of armed Catholic rebellion in America and insisting that a Catholic coup was close at hand. In fact, this early twentieth-century article, with its stern warnings of Catholic uprising, was remarkably similar to other anti-Catholic texts of the antebellum era—in which violent clashes between Catholic and Protestant residents were strikingly commonplace in America's streets. Under the aegis of liberating girls held prisoner by sinister Catholic nuns, working-class Protestants in Charleston, Massachusetts, raided and burned the Ursuline convent in 1834. Fears that meddling Catholics would keep Protestant hymns and prayers out of public schools sparked an outbreak of violence in Philadelphia in 1844 that claimed the lives of Catholics and Protestants alike, and similar waves of violence spread throughout American cities during the nineteenth century, a time in which fraternal organizations, political parties, and even vigilante groups stood ready to demonstrate and counteract perceived Catholic aggression.[1]

Although the article that graced the front page of *The Menace* reflected traditional themes of Catholic subversion, it did so in ways that would appeal to twentieth-century readers while making significant elaborations on anti-Catholic conventions. The Catholics described in the 1912 article were not "storming Washington" to wage overt rebellion against the U.S. government or start a bloodbath of violence. Instead, they were assembling to dedicate a statue to Christopher Columbus, an occasion many Catholics saw as a clear demonstration of Roman Catholicism's participation in and dedication toward America's national development. By proclaiming and celebrating that one of the earliest architects of settlement in America was a devoted Catholic, lay and clerical leaders hoped to assert full membership in American citizenry and illustrate that efforts to denounce Catholic patriotism were misguided and misdirected. Writers of *The Menace* and similar newspapers, however, would have none of this alleged Catholic patriotism, and dedicated their journals to exposing the errors of Catholic Americanism in general and Columbus veneration in particular. *The Menace* condemned organizers of the Columbus assembly as duplicitous when they claimed that Columbus manifests Catholic unity with the American nation while excluding non-Catholics from participating in the unveiling. *The Menace* lambasted the ceremony, insisting that "it was an occasion when 'No Protestant or non-Catholic need apply,'" with the sole exception of a small band of American soldiers who were purely window dressing, trotted out "to lend important [*sic*] and an air of nationality to this purely Catholic occasion and 'fete day.'"[2]

This example demonstrates one of the most prominent themes in anti-Catholic writings of the early twentieth century: influential Romanists knew the power and importance of outward signs of patriotism and would often evoke them for selfish, even anti-American purposes. In this case, Catholics invited soldiers, political dignitaries, and politicians to participate in an event that *Menace* writers insisted "was entirely a function of the Catholic church" and even arranged for President Taft to deliver the unveiling speech. But Catholic sham patriotism, xenophobic writers asserted, had an insidious motive—masking the truth of Catholic greed and lust for influence behind a pleasant veneer of respectable Americanism. *Menace* writers wondered out loud, "If you please, can you tell us what the ceremonies attending the unveiling of the Columbus statue were if not an entering wedge toward effecting the union of the Catholic church with the state in this country?" What further outraged *Menace* reporters was the coverage the Columbus unveiling received in secular daily newspapers, which glamorized the celebration and praised it as "the nation's tribute to its discoverer!" Unwilling to be duped or manipulated by Catholic pageantry or deception, *The Menace* insisted that it understood the true ways of Catholic conspiracy and concluded the article by outlining the extent of Romanism's duplicitous patriotism:

> It is estimated that there were more than 100,000 visiting Catholics in Washington on that great fete day of the church, and every one of them, as well as every Catholic who lives in Washington, turned out with little American flags in their hands—undoubtedly by the instigation of the Jesuit Fathers. Every little movement has a meaning of its own, and the meaning of this flag movement was the "Jessywhitticle" design of trying to fool "non-Catholics" into the belief that Catholics are devoted to the principle of the American republic, and love its flag;—and this on the very day when they had flagrantly violated one of the first principles of our government by openly and defiantly making a strictly Catholic event of an occasion which should have been a truly national affair.

At issue in early twentieth-century Catholicism, which this article brings into relief, is the extent to which Catholics should or could demonstrate— or "prove"—their national belonging and patriotism. One of the leading scholars of anti-Catholicism, the noted historian John Higham, has suggested that, while resentment toward Catholicism has been endemic since the Protestant Reformation, anti-Catholicism has taken on distinctly American characteristics and was fundamental to the formation of American nativism—the belief that an insidious, foreign presence threatens the nation's well-being from within.[3] In what follows, I examine the theory of nativism itself to find a forum for exploring conflicting understandings of Catholic national belonging and to extend several arguments about nationalism and citizenry that prove integral to Progressive-Era anti-Catholicism. I then turn my attention to the concomitant rise of outwardly visible, public forms of Catholicism and the rise of the "patriotic cult" in the late nineteenth and early twentieth centuries. In these contexts, symbolism and imagery become important cultural currency, helping to explain why anti-Catholic newspapers achieved such a wide popularity and why debates over Catholic historical figures in America, Columbus in particular, reached such a high pitch.

TWO VIEWS OF NATIVISM

The term "nativism" and its derivatives have often been used by historians in the study of xenophobia, ethnicity, and interreligious hostility in general and anti-Catholicism in particular. But exactly what this term means and how it should most effectively be applied to the study of American society have been matters of considerable historiographical debate for decades. One of the most innovative and influential voices in the study of nativism comes from John Higham's path-breaking book, *Strangers in the Land: Patterns of American Nativism,* which provides a crucial entrée into the study of xenophobic sentiment. Still in print (and widely cited) nearly a half century after its initial publication in 1955, *Strangers in the Land* remains one of the leading and most enduring resources for the exploration of internal conflicts within divergent segments of the American population during the nineteenth and early twentieth centuries. While originally a pejorative term connoting bigotry, the label "nativist" has been widely applied to xenophobic groups throughout the world, yet Higham contends that the term had a distinctly American root and specifically "should be defined as intense opposition to an internal minority on the grounds of its foreign (i.e. 'un-American') connections."[4] Throughout this book I intend to borrow from Higham's definition and understanding of nativism: vigorous resentment of and attacks upon one segment of the American population (in this case, American Catholics) because of perceived foreign identity. But I also hope to nuance and expand on Higham's presentation of nativism, exploring ways in which his depiction of this crucial dynamic falls short of fully explaining twentieth-century anti-Catholicism.

Higham asserts that nativism is more than a simple "ethnocentric habit of mind" or resentment of foreigners but rather was initially the product of mid nineteenth-century culture, first centering on the vehemently anti-Catholic American Party (or so-called Know-Nothing Party) in antebellum politics. Significantly, Higham links early usage of the term "nativism" with American anti-Catholicism, noting that "the oldest and—in early

America—the most powerful of the anti-foreign traditions came out of the shock of the Reformation" and "Protestant hatred of Rome."[5] In fact, Higham points out that anti-Catholicism and nativism had similar roots and have often been used interchangeably—a tendency that, he notes, obscures the crucial ethnic (as opposed to a more tepid and limited theological) basis of American anti-popery. In particular, Higham contends that "Anti-Catholicism has become truly nativistic, however, and has reached maximum intensity, only when the Church's adherents seemed dangerously foreign agents in the national life."[6] For Higham, nativism is a response to immigrant ethnicity—not a religious argument per se.

Higham notes that the Civil War momentarily dispelled American nativism by "absorbing xenophobes and immigrants into a common cause," but he illustrates how these positive feelings and America's open-door policies toward European immigration quickly shifted in the face of stiffening nativistic attitudes in the early twentieth century.[7] Higham bookends *Strangers in the Land* with the attitude of tolerance of newly arrived immigrants in the late 1860s on one hand and the enactment of federal immigration restrictions and restrictive immigrant quota systems in the mid 1920s on the other. For this reason, his analyses of anti-immigrant and anti-Catholic sentiment often become conflated. Higham's focus on Americans' changing attitudes toward immigrants suggests that Catholic and immigrant "foreigners" were one and the same—a belief supported by some, though not all, nativist activists and opposed by Catholics themselves. Higham's work is noteworthy for its illustration of anti-immigrant sentiment, but one of its largest limitations is its overemphasis on the ethnic and racial dimensions of American anti-Catholicism. His discussion of immigration legislation and restrictions suggests that ethnic differences were a barometer for an immigrant group's exposure to nativist attack and eventual acceptance into the American mainstream. His analysis, therefore, hinges on the racial and ethnic distinctions between immigrants and their nativist counterparts, who, readers assume, were white Anglo-Saxon Protestants intent on preserving a place of dominance in American society for themselves and their children.

Higham makes this point explicit in an article he wrote shortly after the initial publication of *Strangers in the Land*. Writing in 1958, Higham conceded that, at its broadest level, nativism was "an ideological disease," but he largely eschews this categorization, which, he writes, "proved serviceable only for understanding the extreme and fanatical manifestations

of ethnic discord."[8] Instead of offering a thorough examination of political or ideological factors contributing to nativism, Higham prefers to explore "status rivalries," which, he contends, were "all of the activities . . .
in which men of different ethnic backgrounds have competed for prestige and for favorable position in community life." Status rivalries, Higham
continues, "have not arisen from irrational myths but rather from objective conditions; they have not usually reached the point of hatred or hys-
teria; they have not depended upon ideological expression."[9] Arguing
that nativist attacks rest on "ethnic cleavage" and "the slow process of ethnic integration," Higham consistently downplays ideological or cultural
differences as the root of nativist or anti-Catholic sentiment in favor of
racial and ethnic explanations.

In some respects, Higham's work anticipates some of the most prominent strains of American historiography in the late twentieth century, particularly theories of "whiteness" and the social and cultural construction
of ethnicity put forth by eminent immigration historians. Scholars such
as George Lipsitz, David Roediger, Karen Brodkin, and numerous others
have demonstrated critical links between Americans' understanding of
race in general and "whiteness" in particular and the ebb and flow of European immigration. Noel Ignatiev, for instance, has illustrated that Irish
Catholics used their familiarity with the English language and their white
complexions to their advantage—distancing themselves from other European ethnic groups and embracing America's racial dichotomies to attack blacks, while hoping to win the acceptance of Anglo-Saxon neighbors. Scholarship on "whiteness" repeatedly demonstrates how immigrants
prompted nativists to reassess and rearrange their hierarchical understandings of racial superiority. Matthew Frye Jacobson, for instance, notes that
during the late eighteenth century, whiteness—that is, visible traits of European ancestry—proved a necessary and sufficient condition for immigrants to receive full acceptance into American citizenry. Immigration
regulations and social integration, which provided only minor obstacles
to newcomers in the colonial and revolutionary eras, became increasingly
stringent with the influx of Catholic immigrants, largely from Ireland and
Germany, in the antebellum decades. The arrival of racially suspect immigrants in large numbers signaled a shift in Americans' racial attitudes
from a unified platform, in which all "white" races were viewed as citizens,
to a two-tiered approach, distinguishing bona fide whites of Nordic, Anglo,
and Germanic races from "probationary" whites of eastern and southern

European descent. Jacobson illustrates how this racial approach, which contended that "probationary" whites must be contained, monitored, and supervised before receiving full citizenship, shifted once again during the Civil Rights conflicts in the mid twentieth century, returning to a bifurcated understanding of race that distinguished simply between white and "nonwhite" in determining a group's place in American society.[10]

Thus, whereas Higham argued that ethnic "status rivalries" are "not dependent on ideological expression" or "ideological warfare," more recent studies of ethnicity have suggested exactly the opposite. While historiography of the last ten or fifteen years has heightened the importance of racial and ethnic characteristics in shaping the contours of American nativism, writers such as Davis, Ignatiev, and Lipsitz have viewed race not as a static reality but as inherently linked to immigrant and mainstream cultural and ideological negotiation and therefore as constantly debated, contested, and reassessed. Avoiding ideological explanations for American nativism leaves Higham to conclude that Catholics were the subject of nativist attacks because they were immigrants, without leaving open the possibility that the opposite could also be true—that certain immigrants were singled out for attack because of their Catholic identity.

One of Higham's contemporaries, the distinguished historian David Brion Davis, examined similar episodes of anti-Catholic nativism but reached vastly different conclusions from those put forth in Higham's accounts. Davis's essay "Some Themes of Counter-Subversion" examines anti-Catholic, anti-Mormon, and anti-Freemasonic literature in the early to mid nineteenth century, asserting that these strains of nativistic literature shared a common desire to expose criminal conspiracies, protect the American nation, uncover licentious sexuality, and disintegrate incipient cells of dissention before they dismantled the young American republic. Davis equates nativism with "counter-subversion," insisting that the rhetoric and imagery of anti-Catholic, anti-Mormon, and anti-Masonic groups was largely similar: "as the image of an un-American conspiracy took form in the nativist press, in sensational exposés, in the countless fantasies of treason and mysterious criminality, the lines separating Mason, Catholic, and Mormon became almost indistinguishable."[11]

In Davis's account, nativism hinges not solely on external, ethnic, racial, or ancestral traits but also on ideological, internal, hidden, even esoteric characteristics, which nativists believed separated genuine republicans from the nation's subversive traitors. Davis writes, "Obviously, the literature of counter-subversion reflected concrete rivalries and conflicts of interest between competing groups, [but] it is important to note that the subversive bore no racial or ethnic stigma and was not even accused of inherent depravity. . . . This suggests that counter-subversion was more than a rationale for group rivalry and was related to the general problem of ideological unity and diversity in a free society."[12] Davis's study suggests that anti-Catholic nativism was intimately linked to questions of national belonging, loyalty, and patriotism. Hence the notion of counter-subversion rests on individuals' ability to abide by national ideals more than claim to ethnic or racial superiority. In fact, Davis points out, "it is precisely the absence of distinguishing outward traits that made the enemy so dangerous, and true loyalty so difficult to prove."[13] Opponents charged that, despite their differences, Catholics, Mormons, and Freemasons were essentially similar subversive forces because their esoteric structures were predicated on "unconditional loyalty to an autonomous body." The very fact that their rituals, leadership, and pageantry were shrouded in secret made subversives both fascinating and dangerous in the minds of American nativists; their covert actions begged the question, "In a virtuous republic, why should anyone fear publicity or desire to conceal activities, unless those activities were somehow contrary to the public interest?"[14]

Davis's study is also crucial for exploring why counter-subversion proved to be such an influential and long-standing feature of American cultural history. Like subsequent authors such as John Demos and Jenny Franchot, Davis illustrates that exposing alleged sedition allowed nativists to galvanize diverse elements of the American cultural landscape into a common crusade. However, exploring the carnal aspects of Catholic, Mormon, or Masonic activity also provided a venue to legitimize Protestant desire and sensuality. Motivated by feelings of "personal insecurity" and "adjustment to bewildering social change," Davis illustrates that "nativist literature conveyed a sense of common dedication to a noble cause and sacred tradition. . . . The exposure of subversion was a means of promoting unity, but it also served to clarify national values and provide the individual with a sense of high moral sanction."[15] Although Davis's study primarily examined the antebellum era, his "themes of counter-subversion" resonate with subsequent examples of American xenophobia, particularly anti-Catholic antagonism in the early twentieth century. Both episodes of nativism sought to unify vigilant defenders of the American nation in a cause that transcended self-interest and upheld the public good—evoking the language of American nationalism to justify and glorify their anti-Catholic agenda. Both used print culture as a means of exposing conspiratorial threats, but both antebellum and twentieth-century nativism revealed the writers' own anxieties as well. In particular, Davis remarks that counter-subversive literature served a "subtle function" beyond its nationalistic and unifying rhetoric—namely, the legitimization of pseudo pornographic literature under the guise of respectable cautionary tales. As Davis demonstrates, counter-subversive writers "projected their own fears and desires into a fantasy of licentious orgies and fearful punishments," and "while nativists reaffirmed their faith in Protestant monogamy, they obviously took pleasure in imagining the variety of sexual experience supposedly available to their enemies. . . . Licentious subversives offered a convenient means for the projection of guilt as well as desire."[16]

Ultimately, Davis suggests, nativist counter-subversion proliferated rapidly in American print culture because fanciful tales of "an evil group conspiring against the nation's welfare" provided an arena in which "the nativist could style himself as the restorer of the past, as the defender of a stable order against disturbing changes," while simultaneously orchestrating a vision of the future.[17] In subsequent chapters I will address nativists' evocation and defense of imagined visions of a glorified, bucolic past that they believed were under attack by menacing Romanist forces. I also explore the consistent use of sexualized tropes of captivity and male aggression, popular in anti-Catholic literature from the eighteenth century through the early twentieth. These issues aside, Davis's essay is critical because it underscores the essential ideological and cultural dimension of twentieth-century nativist print culture, which proved far more prominent, popular, and influential than racial or ethnic arguments.

When I began research on twentieth-century nativism, I had expected anti-Catholic texts to rely on broadcasts of traditional immigrant and ethnic stereotypes—drunken Irishmen, simple-minded Poles, and so forth. Instead, what I discovered in reading anti-Catholic newspapers of the 1910s was their reliance on more ideologically and politically charged arguments intent on discovering, in the words of one newspaper, "Rome's Ripening Conspiracy" and, as another loudly declared, "Roman Catholic Designs on the American Nation." Whereas Higham's account delineates the restrictionist movement in American immigration history, throughout the 1910s, anti-Catholic papers that I examined demonstrated far less concern over "shutting the gates" or sealing off America's shores to undesirable

newcomers. Rather, they were much more intent on undermining what
they saw as Romanism's sophisticated hierarchical and political machinery
already present on American soil.

"Poor Misshapen Intellects":
The Contours of Ideological Nativism

At issue in the divergent depictions of nativism put forth by
Higham and Davis is the extent to which writers in the 1910s sought ideological rationales, rather than ethnic tropes, to justify and promulgate
their anti-Catholic message. While Higham is no doubt correct in presenting ethnic "status rivalries" and rampant immigration as causes for alarm,
leading America to enact stringent legislation a decade later, during the
period under consideration here, anti-Catholic journalists were much
more concerned with embracing the language of counter-subversion outlined by Davis and espoused by previous generations of anti-Catholic authors. During the Progressive Era, anti-Catholic writers consciously linked
their sensationalized depictions of Catholic corruption and criminality
with prior episodes of nativism, such as the American Protective Association of the late nineteenth century, or with "Know-Nothing" or alleged
"escape nun" literature, which circulated widely prior to the Civil War.
Davis's account is persuasive both because it provides a more suitable
framework to contextualize twentieth-century anti-Catholicism with its antecedents and because it provides more nuanced and compelling explanations for the motivations and fears imbedded within nativist texts. Like
their nineteenth-century counterparts described in Davis's account, publishers, editors, and writers of anti-Catholic periodicals in the early twentieth century used highly sexualized and alarmist depictions of supposed
Catholic threats and were intent on presenting their counter-subversive
movement as exposing Catholic conspiracy as well as safeguarding traditional American values in the face of rapid social change.

The contested understandings of nationalism in Higham's and Davis's
accounts underscore distinct views of nationalism and national belonging
itself. Scholars have generally distinguished between *ethnic* forms of nationalism, based on common hereditary characteristics, and *civic* dimensions of nationalism, in which members of a nation are united by political
institutions and, moreover, the perception of shared values, beliefs, and

traditions. Higham's reliance on ethnic "status rivalries" speaks to an ethnic understanding of American nationalism, whereas Davis's use of counter-subversion resonates with a civic pattern of nationalism, in which American traditions and institutions are threatened from Catholic conspirators. Anti-Catholics' reliance on these intellectual, cultural, or semantic boundaries of Americanness (which I will term "ideological nativism") during the early twentieth century represents a departure from historians' conventional schemas of nationalism and citizenship. Whereas ethnic conceptions of nationalism are generally considered restrictive—limiting full participation in the nation to residents of a particular ethnicity, race, or lineage—scholars usually view civic nationalism as inclusive—inviting all members of society to participate in a common culture shaped by a shared tradition and vocabulary of civic involvement. In this case, however, proponents of anti-Catholicism eschewed ethnic categorizations in favor of attacks that portrayed Catholic opponents as out of sync with the basic tenets of American culture and society. While civic concerns trumped ethnic ones, anti-Catholic journalists espoused the same restrictive and exclusive visions of citizenship found among their eugenicist contemporaries.

Anti-Catholic periodicals are riddled with exclamations of this form of ideological nativism. One outspoken commentator in *The Peril* voiced objection to Catholic claims that priests represent upright lawfulness and rarely, if ever, violate American laws. Instead, the article maintained, "the priesthood of the Catholic church have their dupes so hoodooed that such a statement can be made and the latter [lay Catholics] will swallow it for the truth. This is why Catholic hoodlums will obey the priesthood and mob patriotic speakers. This is why Catholics will join in a boycott at the command of a priest."[18] In contrast to soft-minded and brainwashed Catholics, nativist papers represent genuine Americans as aware of and resistant toward Romanist duplicity and deception. *The Liberator* explains that legions of priests have attempted to storm America, intent on filling Americans' minds with falsehoods, "but the thing that fools them is the intelligence of the Americans."[19] Contrasting Catholic moral depravity, deference to "priestcraft," and lack of individuality and tolerance on the one hand with nativists' intellectual vigor and independence of thought on the other is perhaps the most powerful trope in the pages of Progressive-Era anti-Catholicism, illustrating that Catholic mentality is wholly incompatible with Americanism. *Watson's Magazine* lambastes Catholic radicalism and extremism, arguing "to be a good Catholic, all the eloquence, wit, wisdom and patriotism of American history is a lost land, for the deadly brand of heresy lays upon the whole of it. . . . The whole outfit, from Washington the Episcopalian, to Jefferson, the infidel, and Thomas Paine, the Deist, were rank heretics, deserving to be burnt." The article concludes, "What sort of intelligence would a good Catholic have if he should obey the rules" dictated by conniving priests?[20]

In a subsequent article, the magazine's editor, noted Populist Senator Thomas Watson, refutes and criticizes Catholic claims to patriotism. Written as an "Open Letter to Cardinal Gibbons" of New York, Watson's essay begins by citing Gibbons's claim (and the assertion of most Catholic leaders) that American Catholics "love their country. They prefer its form of government before any other. They admire its institutions and the spirit of its laws. They accept the Constitution without reserve." American Catholics, in Gibbons's view, aspired to civic forms of nationalism, sharing the institutions, government, laws, and admiration for their homeland with their compatriots. Watson, however, refutes these aspirations by criticizing Catholics' "slavish doctrine of Papal infallibility which chains *your* mind to an Italian's mind, chains *your* conscience to the alleged conscience of an Italian." While they claim allegiance to America's laws and Constitution, Watson contends that Catholics actually revere "a decrepit Italian whose intellect never did rival yours in native power."[21]

Viewing Catholics as intellectually, mentally, and emotionally unfit for American citizenship, *The Silverton Journal* maintained, "There is no doubt that this 'inner circle' of the great Catholic Church, in its confessional schools has set itself to destroy the sovereign principles on which the government of this great republic was founded and on which it still rests. These poor misshapen intellects, warped and stunted by early teachings of superstition and priestcraft, in turn seek to implant in the souls of children irremediable misunderstandings, destined to cleave our country into factions of the worst warring character." Ultimately, Catholic slavish devotion to priestly demagogues and inability to weigh the virtues of American tradition for themselves produce generations of Romish slaves who are "plotting to over throw our republic and to make it an ecclesiastical monarchy."[22] Warning of "Roman Catholic designs on the American nation," *Watson's Magazine* challenged "any liberty-loving, free-thinking American [with] doubts as to what the Church of Rome would do to our glorious Republic, should she ever make good her promise to the present

Pope—that is, to 'Capture America for the church in this generation'"
to "realize the menace and danger the Roman Catholic Church is to our
country and the whole world." Contrasting the manipulative and diaboli-
cal authority of the clergy with the witlessness of their unquestioning followers, the article continued, "The leaders of the Roman Catholic Church,
the priests, the Paulist fathers, and so forth, and the Jesuits are among the
most talented and best educated men on earth. This only makes them
more dangerous. . . . The only way they can hold their power is through
superstition and ignorance, and therefore they are an enemy to all progress, liberty of thought, and enlightenment." The Catholic Church, the
essay concludes, "has marshaled her cohorts" into an unthinking army
and "hates and has always hated America for the liberty and enlightenment for which she has stood."[23]

Echoing this sentiment, the nativist sheet *The Yellow Jacket* proclaimed
that "the honest dupe of Rome is not at all to blame. His birth, training
and environment have made him what he is. The majority of the slaves of
Rome are born slaves of the Papal system." As such, "the unfortunate dupe
may imagine that he can be true to America and Rome at the same time,
but he cannot. . . . They are as far apart as the poles."[24] Repeated depictions of "papists" as "dupes" without the ability to see priestly deception or
recognize American values helped nativists countermand Catholics' claims
of patriotism and belonging as simply tools for underhanded clerics to trick
their own followers—and any non-Catholics foolish enough to listen—
into ignoring the dangers of Catholic conspiracy.

Nativism, Nationalism, and Catholic Power

Adopting Davis's ideological and "conspiratorial" understanding of nativism is also useful because it provides a window through which
to examine twentieth-century anti-Catholicism within the broader context
of Progressive-Era patriotism, which profoundly shaped American culture
at the dawn of the twentieth century. Expressions of patriotism and public
memory formed not simply an arena of conflict between anti-Catholics
and their Romanist foes but a landscape of cultural meanings for a newly
industrializing America. Scholars have recently demonstrated that the late
nineteenth and early twentieth centuries formed a watershed era in the
creation, formulation, and transformation of American nationalistic ritual,

symbolism, and pageantry. Stuart McConnell, for instance, addresses the "patriotic cult" surrounding the increased visibility and sacrosanct status afforded to the American flag at the close of the 1800s. Arguing that "in little more than a decade, the United States saw the invention—or at least the major retooling—of many of its patriotic traditions," McConnell explores the possible motivations and rationales for America's heightened patriotic rhetoric.[25] He demonstrates that the omnipresence of American flags in public buildings, schools, and community events amounted to more than a simple knee-jerk reaction by white elites attempting to calm their anxieties over the social unrest brought on by immigration, labor clashes, and the Spanish-American War. He contends that such patriotic actions "show native-born whites groping toward a new definition of what 'American' meant. In so doing, they moved away from earlier, paternalistic readings of national loyalty, readings that had been tied to family, locality, and historical incident and toward an abstract national vision that was at once more and less flexible than the particularisms that proceeded it."[26] Replacing older localized understandings of national belonging with more pervasive national readings of Americanness served to reinforce nativist claims—as established native-born community leaders could keep disloyal or suspect Americans from fully enjoying the fruits of national citizenship.[27]

Celia O'Leary likewise demonstrates how the Gilded Age and Progressive Era witnessed a heightened veneration and rearticulation of the Civil War experience, through voluntary associations, fraternal organizations, monuments, and historical reenactment. Emphasizing the "valor" of both Confederate and Union soldiers while bracketing out any discussion of racial inequality provided a means of uniting northerners and southerners in a common understanding of wartime masculinity and heroism, while overlooking both historic issues of slavery and enduring Jim Crow segregationism, an overlap between masculinity and Civil War public memory also emphasized by Gerald Linderman and Mark Kann.[28] Michael Kammen's influential study *The Mystic Chords of Memory* similarly traces the heightened pitch of American nationalism in the early twentieth century, noting that the sudden demand for Americana crafts, the search for genuine and "traditional" American forms of art and literature, and, in particular, entrepreneur-sponsored manifestations of public memory (such as John Rockefeller's Colonial Williamsburg and Henry Ford's Deerfield Village) underscored the appeal and influence of outward manifestations of

American traditionalism. Moreover, both Kammen and subsequent scholars such as James Lindgren suggest that early twentieth-century public memory sought to reinforce an understanding of American tradition and history that placed Yankee Protestants in a central and privileged place in the nation's progress and development. Taken together, these studies demonstrate both the popularity and the utility of patriotism and public memory, which became vociferous elements of turn-of-the-century American culture in part because they served as a means of articulating and safeguarding white native-born privilege.[29]

As John Bodnar, David Glassburg, and others have demonstrated, however, attempts at supplanting local, ethnic, or individual understandings of American nationalism have rarely experienced complete, long-standing success. Rather, as Bodnar illustrates, expressions of public memory underscore an inherent tension between pervasive "official" explanations of the past—which generally validate the authority of leaders and seek to preserve the status quo—and various "vernacular" interests—which represent the concerns of neighborhoods, families, ethnic or racial communities, religious groups, and individuals and are frequently at odds with official culture and each other.[30] While the early twentieth century witnessed an outpouring of nationalism intent on expressing a vision of American development that emphasized the achievements of Yankee Protestants, the decades leading up to World War I also highlighted a new visibility among American ethnic groups in general and American Catholics in particular. As Eric Hobsbawm and Terence Ranger's explorations of "invented" or manufactured tradition illustrate, many of the "traditions" ascribed to long-standing European roots were actually twentieth-century innovations produced in the diaspora.[31] Scholarship by Kathleen Conzen, Gerald Gjerde, Roy Rosenzweig, Thomas Spencer, and numerous other historians suggests that localized, religious, neighborhood, class-based, or ethnic celebrations not only endured efforts to subsume vernacular loyalties to more overarching cultural forms but actually proliferated and expanded into highly visible public forms. In particular, as David O'Brien's presentation of the growing public presence of the American Catholic Church, Jay Dolan's depiction of urban Catholicism, Christopher Kauffman's study of fraternal organizations and the burgeoning Knights of Columbus, and, in particular, Robert Orsi's analysis of Catholic processionals and celebration in Italian-American urban neighborhoods all convincingly assert, American popular Catholicism began to exert a powerful public

presence that coincided with a simultaneous movement by nativists to
buffer and limit vernacular displays of affiliation.[32]

Within the prevailing though contentious mood of early twentieth-
century patriotic nationalism on the one hand and America's ongoing tradition of counter-subversion, exposé journalism, and ideological nativism
on the other, it is not surprising that anti-Catholic nativism adopted a vocal
defense of American traditions and that attacks on its opponents formed
newspapers' most insistent message to readers. Likewise, however, American Catholics themselves embraced the language and symbolism of Americanism to defend their place within the nation. Just as the 1910s witnessed
an outpouring of nationalistic sentiment, so too this decade saw a tremendous intensification, organization, and mobilization of Catholic resources and influence. Pointing to the demographic increase in its membership and the growth of Catholic churches and schools from the late
nineteenth and throughout the twentieth centuries, Catholics could rea-
sonably claim that they were securing a place within the American landscape. By the early twentieth century, American Catholics began to enumerate their contemporary contributions to America's well-being (notably
their charitable and philanthropic institutions, which blossomed in the
years following the Civil War) and, like their Protestant counterparts,
to reroject their American patriotism by honoring Catholic heroes, like
Columbus, who had added to the nation's founding and prosperity. The
church's burgeoning influence and population were of grave concern for
nativists, and in subsequent chapters I address anti-Catholics' efforts to
undermine Catholic claims of charity and philanthropy. For our purposes
here, however, the most critical aspect of nativistic literature was maintaining public patriotism as nativists' exclusive preserve—condemning Catholic attempts at Americanness as poaching on white Anglo-Saxon Protestant
terrain.

POLITICS, PRINT CULTURE, AND PARANOIA: THE ANTI-CATHOLIC LEGACY

While anti-Catholic ideological nativism was predicated on depicting Romanist foes as intellectually, morally, and patriotically bankrupt,
anti-Catholic writers were just as quick to warn readers to be vigilant and
support nativist efforts, otherwise they risked becoming "dupes" or slaves

to Romish machinations themselves. This sentiment runs consistently through America's long anti-Catholic tradition—as Franchot reminds us, warnings of "backsliding" or complicity with Catholic schemes were commonplace in the American cultural landscape beginning in the Colonial period, when anti-Catholic agitation was linked to threats of attack from Native Americans or their Catholic allies in French or Spanish territories. Throughout the eighteenth and nineteenth centuries, Franchot argues, Catholicism occupied a paradoxical place within the American Protestant imagination. On the one hand, it was seen as alien, foreign, and "other"— incompatible with and inferior to the perceived purity and vitality of American Protestant culture. Franchot contends, "profoundly familiar yet rendered foreign by the Reformation, Romanism was a force that threatened to disrupt the American self."[33] Ironically, on the other hand, antebellum Catholicism also exerted an attraction, even fascination, for American Protestants, aided by the newfound availability of steamship travel to Catholic Europe and, closer to home, by the proliferation of Catholic institutions and, above all, popular novels and literature that brought the imagery (however stilted, commodified, and sensationalized) of Catholic ritual to Protestant readers.

Franchot argues that, while Protestant "encounters with Catholic culture, specifically with architecture and liturgical rites, created a nexus of troubled sensations that argued against Protestant . . . supremacy," Americans also "experienced an ardent, even dependent, attraction" to "decayed" or allegedly corrupt Catholicism.[34] During the Colonial and Revolutionary eras, Catholicism was equated with the supposed savagery and brutality of Native American cultures, which, collectively, posed a threat to American settlement. As Richard Slotkin illustrates, the captivity of white settlers, particularly white women, at the hands of Indian aggressors forms one of the most prevalent themes in frontier mythology, particularly the conquest and "taming" of frontier savagery by the victorious white rescuer and the return of femininity to the protective outposts of civilization.[35] Moreover, as Demos's depiction of Puritans held captive by French and Iroquois invaders illustrates, American colonists feared the "spellbinding" powers of Jesuit priests as much as the strength and guile of their tribal companions—as both represented the degeneration of Puritan culture and a descent into savagery.[36]

As Native American "removal" and forced relocation became more prominent in the Jacksonian Era, Americans were distanced from the

perceived Indian threat that had once occupied a dominant place in popular literature and captivity genre. In its absence, American writers heightened the threat of Catholic captivity, making priestcraft, convent abductions, and the sinister power of Catholicism the stand-ins for Native
aggression. Franchot argues that "Anti-Catholic narratives, while developing the conventional but still compelling association of the violent, the
exotic, and the hidden that had structured the Indian captivity genre,
moved . . . from the forest to the parochial school, the nunnery, and the
confessional."[37] The threat of victimized womanhood, religious ensnare-
ment, and mesmerizing savagism that had once been relegated to distant
peripheries, as a means of juxtaposing Protestant settlement and civility
with the barbarism of outsiders, had become more immanent in the early
nineteenth century. Worried that Catholic priestcraft would "contami-
nate" the purity and vitality of Protestant culture and, worse, that Protestants would be spellbound and mesmerized into complicity by the sensuousness of Catholic art and ritual, Protestant writers, journalists, and
readers actively engaged in a barrage of anti-Romanist literature, centering on the destructive, alien, and sinister forces of Catholicism and their
threat to American life in the nineteenth century.[38]

Two of the earliest and most successful books in a litany of texts trans-
posing Catholic convent imprisonment for earlier tropes of Native abduction were Rebecca Reed's *Six Months in a Convent,* published in 1835, and
The Awful Disclosures of Maria Monk, published in 1836. Both accounts told
stories of young innocent women who unwittingly entered convent life
and reported on tortures, sexual licentiousness, and cold-blooded murders that Protestant readers feared were commonplace behind convent
walls. Both were also ghostwritten by male literary agents who used the
alarmist tone and sexualized content of the abduction stories as a way of
generating unprecedented sales and notoriety. Reed's account was written
in the aftermath of the looting and burning of an Ursuline convent (which
had served as a Catholic "finishing school" for well-to-do Bostonians, predominantly Protestants, in nearby Charlestown, Massachusetts) and was
published shortly after the arsonists were acquitted of all charges. The
editors of *Six Months in a Convent* begin by voicing their intention to "open
the eyes of Protestants, so as to convince them of the impropriety of in-
trusting the education of their daughters to a secret and superstitious community of Catholic Priests and Nuns."[39] Calling "the ascetic austerities" of
convent life "destructive of all domestic and social relations," Reed's ac-

count outlines beatings and maltreatment at the hands of priests but worries most that the "daughters of republicans" would be undermined by celibate convent life and seek alternatives to their prescribed roles of motherhood and marriage.[40] I discuss this theme further in chapter 3.

The Awful Disclosures expands on the themes raised in Reed's account, but, in the words of historian Nancy Lusignan Schultz, it "moves beyond Reed's [account] to a level of pseudo-pornography."[41] Maria Monk's exposé of the Hotel Dieu Nunnery in Montreal is riddled with priestly orgies, made even more macabre by the murder of children born of "unholy unions" between priests and initiate nuns. Monk's level of detail in outlining the convent grounds (including subterranean passages used for priestly trysts and lime pits for burying strangled infants) and her presumed precision in recounting initiation rites seem to support a thorough exposé of convent life and the claim that the Catholic Church is "a deviant, dangerous institution that should not be permitted to exist in a democracy." In fact, however, later explorations of her work revealed that Monk was not an initiate at all, but a Quebec prostitute and patient in a Catholic insane asylum. Nineteenth-century Catholic writers and subsequent historians have routinely denounced Monk's account as a complete fabrication. Nevertheless, The Awful Disclosures became an overnight literary success, selling hundreds of thousands of copies; revised editions were published well into the twentieth century.[42]

Taken together, Monk's and Reed's works illustrate what Franchot terms America's "trope of incarceration," in which devious Catholics often surround, contain, and attack their Protestant betters, representing an inversion of Protestants' idealized social roles.[43] However, nativist fears of Catholic advances sparked not only a literary outpouring but political activism as well. Tyler Anbinder's discussion of the "Order of the Star Spangled Banner" (better known as the "American" or "Know-Nothing" Party) illustrates the efforts of northern politicians to leverage anti-Catholic attitudes and transform nativist sentiment into political clout. Before splintering over the contentious slavery issue in the late 1850s, the party galvanized support from the working and middle classes into a movement that virtually controlled the U.S. Congress, as well as the executive and legislative branches of several state governments.[44] Following the Civil War, nativism again took on a political slant, most distinctly in the emergence of the American Protective Association (APA), predicated on ousting Catholics from political office, school boards, and civil service positions. Convinced

that Catholic deception had infiltrated American politics, the APA gar-
nered the support of middle- and working-class voters, becoming a national movement by the early 1890s and swelling the ranks of the Republican Party. Shortly thereafter, however, the APA movement fell apart. Like
their Know-Nothing predecessors, the anti-Catholic rhetoric of APA organizers was insufficient to transcend burning political questions—in this
case Free Silver and the support for McKinley. Although the movement
limped on through the first decade of the twentieth century, its influence
had dwindled by 1900, and the collapse of the movement was completed
with the death of its founder, Henry Bowers, in 1911, just as a more influential wave of anti-Catholicism began to spread through the American
landscape.[45]

Historian Les Wallace has noted that the APA's brief success in joining
a "wide spectrum of individuals" from the middle and working classes derived from its patriotic and nationalistic rhetoric—members "accepted
the movement out of a feeling of American dedication. . . . The organization sensed that its strength derived from the ordinary citizen."[46] The attention to plainspoken Americanism, belief in the language of patriotism
to unite disparate supporters, and abiding concern for ousting Catholic
conspirators and political meddlers, which collectively formed the back-
bone in the short-lived APA, would find resonance in its successor, the
anti-Catholic journalistic movement of the Progressive Era. Like their predecessors, nativist organizers developed lurid stories of Catholic abductions and affronts to Protestant women, pledging to undo Romanist corruption and restore what they viewed as traditional American values, but
they did so with few of the overt political platforms that had divided anti-
Catholic movements of the nineteenth century. Instead, as I will illustrate
in my next chapter, for anti-Catholic publishers, reading and circulation
themselves were described as forms of political activism, and circulation
was the arena in which the war against popery was to be fought.

Extending the Anti-Catholic Legacy

In addressing the pervasiveness of anti-Catholic nativism in
America, Higham has argued "the idea that papal minions posed a subversive threat to national freedom was so deeply entrenched in myth and
memory that it needed relatively little objective confirmation."[47] Indeed,

by the 1910s, nativist writers were able to draw on America's already substantial anti-Catholic traditions as an entrée and foundation for their own work. While Progressive-Era anti-Catholicism exhibited less vigilantism than its antebellum antecedents and muted the overtly politicized rhetoric of its APA forerunners, it valorized the architects of nineteenth-century anti-Romanism as stalwart pioneers and glorified their work as the impetus for the current patriotic crusade against the Catholic threat. Progressive-Era newspapers dedicated a substantial amount of space and energy to "proving" the accuracy of nineteenth-century escaped nun stories, maintaining that evidence of Catholic wrongdoing in the past would demonstrate the Romanist threat in the present. A headline in a 1919 issue of *The Menace* proclaimed the "Maria Monk Story Confirmed" and outlined the "great pains [that] have been taken by the Jesuits to discredit the story . . . but notwithstanding, the story persisted; it gripped the hearts of Christian people and the attention of the reading public." While Catholics claimed "Maria Monk was a myth," *Menace* reporters described a visitor to their office, who told them "My Mother [*sic*] now in her ninety-eighth year heard the story from the lips of Maria Monk before the story was printed." The article concluded, "This evidence comes after years without solicitation and is additional proof of convent cruelty."[48]

Likewise, in *Watson's Magazine,* his weekly newspaper, *The Jeffersonian,* and, in particular, a monograph entitled *Maria Monk and Her Revelation of Convent Crimes,* Tom Watson routinely sought to validate the stories put forward by Maria Monk, Rebecca Reed, and other nineteenth-century anti-Catholic pioneers. Watson published letters from Montreal residents that asserted not only that Monk's remarks were absolutely true but that Catholics remodeled the interior of the nunnery "in order that they might disprove her description of the rooms in case an investigation was ever made" and that "when the sewers of the Hotel Dieu [nunnery] were cleaned out, there were scores of infant skulls and bones found, proving beyond a shadow of a doubt that she only published the truth in her book."[49] Watson goes on to argue that well into the twentieth century, Catholic priests continued to use nuns or "housekeepers" for illicit sex, which "proves" that not only was Monk's story accurate but the scandal she outlines had continued into the present.[50] *The Yellow Jacket* published similar validations of Monk's book, including a long quotation from *The Awful Disclosures* and a rejoinder that Catholic authorities have never been able to successfully deny any of its contents.[51]

Nativist writers of the early twentieth century understood their work to be an extension of and, in some cases a tribute to, prior generations of anti-Catholic agitation and journalism. Shortly after the death of APA founder Bowers, *The Menace* printed a glowing eulogy, hoping to "awaken interest in the principles of that organization." *The Menace* announced, "The Organization may have gone out of business, but the spirit will incarnate itself" in the future, announcing "A.P.A.ism is not Dead," because its powerful work will be continued by a subsequent generation of anti-Catholic writers and their patriotic readers.[52] Other newspapers reprinted the nativist depictions of Thomas Nast as inspiration for their contemporary work in the twentieth century.[53]

But despite references to, and sincere veneration for, previous episodes of anti-Romanism, twentieth-century anti-Catholic journalism embodied several features that, if not unique to the Progressive Era, were certainly brought into broader relief during the 1910s than in previous episodes of anti-Catholicism. In particular, denunciations of Catholic convent abductions were couched in the emergent language of post–Civil War patriotism and public memory. As O'Leary demonstrates, by the early twentieth century, architects of American public memory shifted the emphasis and content of Civil War commemoration away from potentially divisive issues such as sectionalism and slavery and toward a common vision of "heroism," in which northern and southern soldiers could reflect on a common experience of masculine valor. Progressive-Era nativists took this transformation a step further, using imagery and rhetoric from the Civil War, as well as previous chapters of American history, to embroil their readers in a fierce rhetorical war against their Catholic adversaries. This is particularly apparent in nativist use of the term "slavery," which referred to either physical bondage in Romanist "institutional slave pens"—convents, confessionals, or Catholic schools—or ideological slavery that would capture the minds of Americans if they failed to realize the dangers of Rome's political power.[54] Numerous articles labeled Catholic priests "slave catchers," who rounded up girls for the dangerous and torturous drudgery of convent life. One writer outlined the conditions of a Cincinnati convent in which "youth and innocence are hounded from city to city by the tools of Rome" and "captured" girls were treated like pre–Civil War slaves by their arrogant and demonic masters.

Other writers similarly linked their anti-Catholic crusade with heroes from America's past. *Watson's Magazine* stated, "Our forefathers created

this self-governing Republic as an escape from the foul, debasing part-
nerships of Popes and Kings. Our ancestors fled from the Old World to establish a government which would not be cursed by your [that is, Catholic]
despotic methods" and concludes by asserting that the Catholic Church
is denounced by "the voice of patriots, scholars, soldiers, lovers of humanity and liberty, choking with blood."[55] *Watson's Magazine* also included
a long article that evoked the language of George Washington's "Farewell
Address" of September 17, 1796, and James Monroe's influential speech
before Congress on December 2, 1823 (the so-called Monroe Doctrine)—
two famous statements that reiterate America's independence from and
hostility toward European encroachment. Applying these tenets of Americanism, the magazine asserted, "Every sisterhood is a foreign colony, not
only un-American. . . . The cruelties, the tragedies, and the indecencies
enacted, behind nunnery doors and walls defy description. . . . Utterly incompatible are Romanism and Americanism."[56] Within the pages of anti-
Catholic periodicals, Lincoln, Monroe, Washington, and others are evoked
as symbols of actual Americanism, contrasted with Catholics' phony and
insincere patriotism, meant to ensnare, or even destroy, the nation. Anti-
Catholic writers and readers, these papers hoped to make clear, were carrying out important, even heroic, work, by extending America's tradition
of toppling slave catchers or resisting aggression. And by their efforts,
anti-Catholic writers sought, as *The Silverton Journal* maintained, "to assist
the sleeping people in realizing that the truth is that the Roman Catholics are praying, without ceasing, to be able to take the United States for
Rome . . . and that the liberty and freedom of this country is in immediate danger."[57]

Anticipating accusations of hypocrisy from their critics, anti-Catholic
publications were quick to point out that their "patriotic" nativist message did not run counter to the freedom of religion safeguarded in the
First Amendment. Anti-Catholic newspapers in the Progressive Era often
attempted to distinguish between the religious views of individual Catholic parishioners and the political, organizational, and bureaucratic powers of the institutional Church. Tom Watson included a disclaimer before a series of vehemently anti-Catholic articles, explaining "The Roman
Catholic *organization* is the object of my profoundest detestation—*not*
the beliefs of *the individual*," and likewise wrote, "I do not claim that there
are no Roman Catholics who love their country—our great Republic; God
forbid. But I do claim that any man who allows himself to become a slave

to the dogma of the Roman Catholic Church will find it incompatible and
even impossible for him to remain a true American."[58] With only a handful of exceptions, anti-Catholic writers asserted that Catholics were not ill-
suited for American citizenship because of inborn characteristics, but
became so because of the corrosive effects of Catholic education and the
destructive agency of priestcraft. While anti-Catholic papers on rare oc-
casions cited examples of Catholics who stubbornly refused to listen to
priestly authority and acted in accordance with what nativist writers considered appropriate Americanism, more often Catholicism was seen as
completely antithetical to American values. As *The Mountain Advocate* maintained, "when anyone seeks by the machinery and organization of any
creed, regardless of its name, to control this government of the United
States, then we oppose to the fullest extent of our ability."[59]

In this article, as in hundreds of others, anti-Catholic writers attempted
to chronicle attempts by the Catholic Church to infiltrate, corrupt, and
destroy the American Republic. In fact, this objective could well be seen
as the raison d'être for anti-Catholic publishing in the Progressive Era, as
virtually any Catholic activity, regardless of how innocuous its function
appeared to be, from raising funds for orphanages to monument dedi-
cations, was seen as a deceptive plot that fundamentally threatened the
American nation. *The Liberator* called its readers "patriots who desire to
preserve the state and the nation from the encroachments of the enemies
of the Republic," and *Watson's Magazine* called "the bold movements of
the Roman Catholic Church here in the United States, trying to undermine our fundamental national laws" nothing short of "a Modern Inquisition."[60] *The Peril* echoed these sentiments, asserting, "After a heroic
struggle this government was founded upon the principles of Civil and
Religious Liberty, but the republic is in deadly peril of having these blood-
bought principles set aside by the Roman hierarchy. . . . Thus, it would set
up in the United States a vast, heartless, soulless papal political system that
has cursed every nation in which it has obtained a foothold. It is this deadly
peril to American Liberty and Civilization that this paper is fighting."[61]

As the article illustrates, nativist papers considered themselves valiant,
often solitary, defenders of American values against the dangers of Catholic encroachment. Their mission, as writers frequently maintained, was
to "wake up" complacent readers. While *The Menace* frequently employed
the headline "Rome Never Sleeps," the paper contrasted Catholic fanatical vigilance with Protestant indifference.[62] *The Silverton Journal* warned

"Silence Is Treason" and stated, "because of Rome's quiet, underground, secret workings, many who love liberty most are led to think that such papers as *The Silverton Journal* exaggerate and that after all there is no immediate danger. Friends of this great republic, beware of this attitude. Eternal vigilance is still the price of liberty and we must advance or fall back."[63] Warning "An American Pope Is Probable" and insisting "We wish to be of service to humanity while we have a chance," writers of *The Silverton Journal,* like other anti-Catholic periodicals, served as agents of what Davis might term "counter-subversion," enlightening the American nation to the dangers of an organized conspiracy bent on its destruction. And since "the Roman Catholic Church stands for principles which spell ruin to America and her institutions," nowhere was the need to inform, convince, and educate readers about the extent of Catholic duplicity seen as more urgent or necessary than in exposing Romanists' insincere and conspicuous display of patriotism and national solidarity.[64]

The most dangerous and untenable consequence of American complacency was the rise of Catholic "so-called patriotism," which used lavish pageantry and haughty words to dupe spectators into accepting Catholic Americanism. Anti-Catholic journalists, they insisted, knew better, and sought to disprove Catholic attempts at public demonstration of national fidelity. Warning that "liberty is never fully appreciated until it is lost," writers conjured nightmarish scenarios of papal rule in America to contrast Catholic claims of support for the American government.[65] In denouncing the duplicity of the Church, *Watson's Magazine* wrote, "To make herself [that is, the Catholic Church] popular, she must rend the air as it were, with cries of Liberty. . . . 'Long live the Constitution.' . . . 'We are for Free America and her free Institutions!' Not only in this, but there are many other ways she has for fooling the credulous Yankee into the belief that she is The One and Only Holy Religion."[66]

One of the most striking depictions of nativist contempt for Catholic Americanism is shown by a woodcut illustration that was the frontispiece of *Watson's Magazine* in July 1912. The woodcut advertised the book *Out of Hell and Purgatory,* in which Watson published the exposé writings of an ex-priest who was familiar with the inner workings of the Catholic Church. Like accounts by Maria Monk and Rebecca Reed, *Out of Hell and Purgatory* was meant to alert readers to Catholicism's dangerous power and the depths of its debauchery. In advertising the book to his readers, Watson chose an overtly political tact—placing a drawing of the Statue of Liberty in the drawing's left corner. Surrounding the statue and symbolically obscuring American freedom and traditions are billows of smoke, inscribed with the words "Hypocrisy," "Greed," "Strife," "Superstition," and "Ignorance." The source of the smoke is a bursting cauldron in the center of the drawing, representing the Catholic Church, which is surrounded by an assortment of skeletons. The imagery of the drawing presents another opportunity to explore the ideologically and intellectually rooted basis for Progressive-Era anti-Catholicism. While other portrayals of the Statue of Liberty could assert the cohesive power of American institutions and iconography to transcend differences and thus represent a civic form of nationalism, this image shows just the opposite. (For a visual representation of Statue of Liberty iconography in American anti-Catholicism, see the Appendix.) Catholicism's perverted superstition, ignorance, and hypocrisy make it ideologically and mentally incompatible with and threatening toward American values. Once again, Catholics were not singled out as racially, ethnically, or biologically unfit for full citizenship but blocked by the smoke of their own ideology, which also literally choked the life out of America itself.

"Let Us Keep History Straight": The Defense of Nationalistic Iconography

In contrast to the insincere and corrosive assertions of patriotism by Catholic foes, nativist writers filled the pages of their newspapers with a litany of genuine Protestant heroes, who glorified and advanced the purpose of the American nation and spoiled the connivings of Romanism. This is particularly true of references to Abraham Lincoln, which virtually deified the martyred president. As *The Mountain Advocate* put it, "the philosophy of a life like Lincoln's takes hold upon millions; it shines in the hearts and minds of men; it influences nations; it inspires whole races. In comparison with it what other is worth while?"[67] Anti-Catholic texts went out of their way to illustrate the political legacies, critical national contributions, and noble character of America's stalwart founders, pointing out personal anecdotes to give their heroic icons a "personal side" as well.[68] Yet nativist writers contended that Catholic meddlers distorted "true" history and tarnished the image of venerable symbols of American patriotism. *The Yellow Jacket,* for instance, reprinted an article from the Catholic newspaper *The Catholic Western Watchman,* which recounted a story of George Washington entering Boston in 1775 and denouncing the practice of "Pope's Day," in which Bostonians ridiculed Catholics and burned an effigy of the Pope. *The Catholic Western Watchman* reported that Washington rebuked the revelers, saying, "instead of offering the most remote insult, it is our duty to address public thanks to our Catholic brethren, as to them we are indebted for every late success." This, the Catholic paper continued, illustrates the contributions of American Catholics to the cause of independence and freedom: "Here, then, we have the highest authority for asserting that our coreligionists have already rendered signal service to the cause of liberty."[69]

After citing the article, *The Yellow Jacket* wasted no time in striking down Catholic arguments. Washington could not have been present in Boston in the fall of 1775, since the city was under British control until March 1776, *The Yellow Jacket* asserted, meaning that the story was "a Romish lie pure and simple." The article concluded, "Washington was in Boston . . . in Catholic imagination only. Let us keep history straight!"[70] This text illustrates two critical aspects of anti-Catholic journalism in the Progressive Era. First, the author deliberately reprinted sections or, as in this case, the entire text from a Catholic source. This was a common technique among anti-Catholic publishers—and was usually accompanied by annotations, commentaries, or postscripts designed to illustrate the duplicity and danger of what Catholic sources were trying to convey. (Ironically, Catholic supporters used a similar tactic in denouncing nativist papers—reprinting and refuting nativist arguments in periodicals designed to combat Catholic defamation, generating a somewhat circular exchange between pro- and anti-Catholic newspapers. I address this subject in chapter 4.)

Second, *The Yellow Jacket* article illustrates that, while nativist writers evoked American leaders and symbols to justify and extend their own agenda, they were intent on denying this opportunity to their Catholic opponents. An accurate reading of American history, this article suggested, would seal Catholics' fate, rather than provide their vindication. The same message appeared on the front page of *The Menace,* in an article entitled "Praising Lincoln," which began by citing a clipping from the *Minneapolis Tribune,* in which a Minnesota priest lauded the martyred president. *The Menace* lambasted Catholic priests for having the nerve to praise Lincoln and raise funds to build a monument in his honor, since, the paper reasoned, Catholic were responsible for conspiring to assassinate the heroic

American leader.[71] *The Silverton Journal* likewise reported that radical Catholics "at the most critical time of the great rebellion" circulated stories accusing Lincoln of being born, baptized, and raised Catholic, to "brand [Lincoln's] face with the ignominious mark of apostasy" and orchestrate his assassination. The article concluded, "The whole story will never be known, but there is enough know to brand the hierarchy with the foulest names in the English language—traitor and assassin."[72]

Evoking Lincoln's assassination and contradicting Catholic interpretations of history were two of the most common strategies by nativist periodicals in refuting displays of patriotism and loyalty. When these proved insufficient, anti-Catholic texts would simply accuse Catholics of insincerity and pandering to observers in a futile display of reverence. In June 1912, the Knights of Columbus presented the pennant of the Battleship Maine to the Spanish War Veterans of Chicago, a display that *The Menace* called ostentatious, since Catholic organizers "were anxious to make a show of themselves and connect up with some far away patriotic incident." This gesture, rather than demonstrating patriotism, evidenced Catholic deception: "Catholic manipulation has served great opportunities for papists to make capital, and announce themselves to the public . . . to appear patriotic—to get rid of the suspicion of disloyalty."[73]

Nowhere was the assertion of Catholic duplicity more germane than in the coverage given to Columbus celebrations in the anti-Catholic press. Catholics upheld Columbus, who hailed from Catholic Italy and whose voyage was financed by Catholic Spain, as emblematic of Catholics' role in American settlement, colonization, and national progress. Yet nativists contended that, while their papers properly honored American accomplishments, Romanists had become obsessed with Columbus, who was more of a villain than a bona fide hero and opposed, rather then epitomized, actual American values. Their fanatical hero worship expressed Catholics' misplaced desire to manifest a veneer of respectability through insincere patriotism. In several respects, nativist criticism of Columbus veneration anticipated many arguments that would seem familiar today. First, anti-Catholic texts questioned the claim that Columbus "discovered" America at all. Under the headline "Columbus Day Might Suffer Competition at Hands of Chinese," *The Menace* reported that Chinese explorers landed on the West Coast a millennium prior to Columbus, bringing "the religion of Buddha at various places from Alaska to Mexico"—a missionary effort that also explains why inept Jesuits were able to easily convert the West, since the minds of natives living there were already weakened by Chinese philosophy. The article rebuked Catholic efforts to profit from politicizing the celebration of Columbus, stating, "Alas, how are the mighty fallen! For years Catholic priest and writers have boasted of the discovery of America by Catholics and claimed the right to occupy and rule this part of the world by virtue of said alleged discovery, in spite of Leif Erickson's prior voyages to the continent proper. Exposure is generally the fate of pretenders and our bombastic Romanist friends must again face the inevitable." The article cited academic research that "proves conclusively from official Chinese records" that Columbus was a latecomer to American shores and that Catholic arguments to the contrary were nothing more than fraud.[74] One of the critical aspects of this article is the language of "proof," "exposure," and unearthing "official" evidence to contradict the actions of "pretenders," expressions that show how Progressive-Era muckraking journalism influenced anti-Catholic periodicals as much as their mainstream counterparts—a subject I will take up in chapter 2. But this language of investigation and evidence also speaks to the tremendous importance placed on exposing Catholics' "sham" patriotism, which carried significant political weight during the Progressive Era in general and on the pages of nativist texts in particular.

The passing reference to Leif Erickson's prior journey to North America, which anti-Catholics were quick to point out predated Columbus by centuries, echoed the sentiment in several articles that American exploration and settlement should be matters of Protestant pride rather than Catholic pageantry. *The Jeffersonian* attacked New Jersey governor Woodrow Wilson for joining in a New York banquet to celebrate the establishment of Columbus Day, stating, "Governor Wilson is a scholar and therefore knows that the mainland of North America was not discovered by an Italian Catholic but by an English Protestant, Sebastian Cabot. North America was not only discovered by Protestants, but was taken possession of and colonized by English, Dutch, and French Protestants." Wilson's appearance, the article concluded, was nothing more than a disgraceful bid "for the Romanist votes of New York City."[75] Elsewhere, nativists similarly denied that the term "America" derived from Amerigo Vespucci, a Catholic navigator, but told readers it sprang instead from either a Native village in South America or a European town from which early European settlers departed for the New World.[76]

Even if nativists grudgingly accepted Columbus's role in settling America, they vocally disputed his depiction as grandiose champion of liberty or opportunity. Instead, like many contemporary revisionists, na- tivists painted Columbus as a slave catcher, robber, and common pirate, focused primarily on his own wealth and aggrandizement. *Watson's Maga- zine* put the matter bluntly: "The real character of Christopher Columbus has been so industriously misrepresented, veneered and varnished over by the Roman Church, that the portrait of the discoverer . . . appears dif- ficult to recognize." Columbus, the article continued, was nothing more or less than a thug: "No sooner had Columbus taken formal possession of the island of Hispaniola than he asked the wondering natives for gold," after which he enslaved native tribes, shipping many back to Spain to offset the cost of his expedition. The article concludes by pointing out "the cruelty of the gold-hunters, and the terror they inspired in the natives."[77]

Some anti-Catholic texts even took their criticism of Catholic venera- tion for Columbus a step further. Even if Columbus's role in discovering the New World were to go unchallenged, and even if the American pub- lic could overlook his atrocious misdeeds, readers were asked to call into question whether Columbus was genuinely Catholic in the first place. In an article titled "The Pope Didn't Believe in Columbus," *The Yellow Jacket* pointed out that Catholic leaders in the fifteenth century rejected the very idea of a western hemisphere and tried to prevent its discovery, "but the king of Spain thought more of the scientific knowledge of Columbus than he did of the bull-necked stupidity of Pope Zachary, and handed over the coin to old Chris." Thus, Columbus's accomplishments came in spite of, rather than because of, his Catholic identity.[78]

In *Romanism: A Menace to the Nation,* one of the most widely printed and best-selling anti-Catholic books of the early twentieth century, Jere- miah Crowley made this point even more explicitly. Crowley, whose claim of being an ex-priest was hotly contested and eventually refuted in a se- ries of court battles, sold his writings to the Menace Publishing Company for printing, marketing, and distribution, and in their capable hands the book sold thousands of copies in the 1910s. One of his most intriguing chapters is titled, "Christopher Columbus a Jew," in which Crowley as- serted that Columbus commemorations were absurd, since their only pur- pose was to allow "the Roman Church, with all the pomp, trappings and circumstances" to assemble together and:

parade the streets with all the gaudy robes and vestments and other insignia of the Roman Church in order to impress Americans with the sense of their power. Among the methods which the Roman Catholic prelates, priests and politicians are using the 'make American dominantly Catholic' is that of extolling those supposed to be of their faith who were active in the discovery, colonization and settlement of America; and among these by far the most important stands Christopher Columbus.[79]

Yet, Crowley asserted, "the latest investigations tend to support the view that he was a Jew at heart," and much of Crowley's text is dedicated to an exegesis of Columbus's writings and genealogy to show that he was a Jewish Spaniard who at most paid lip service to Catholicism.[80]

In addition to Columbus, nativist writers sought to preempt other forms of Catholic nationalistic celebration, going out of their way to discredit Catholic contributions toward America in any form. *Watson's Magazine* denounced Catholic claims that one of their coreligionists, Commodore John Barry, should be recognized as the "father of the American Navy" and the first to fly the naval flag or engage the enemy in combat. Arguing that two Protestant commanders should share that honor instead, *Watson's Magazine* wrote, "It is an outrage upon historical integrity and upon American patriotism that the powerful Roman Catholic organizations of the present day should pull down the two Protestant heroes and set up a Romanist in their place."[81] *The Menace* expressed similar antipathy for Catholic "heroes" and uncertainty at the building of a statue in Barry's honor, yet the paper took a somewhat different tact, similar to the strategy evoked in the above example of Columbus. Pointing out that "what has made the monument business pretty nearly a scandal is not that men like Barry and Columbus and Marquette were men to be honored in their day and generation, for what they were really worth, but that they are specially great because they were Catholics," *The Menace* labeled all expressions of commemoration, public memory, or patriotism on the part of their Romanist foes as insincere political posturing. In Barry's case, like Columbus's, the papers continued, "there is doubt, possibly, whether he was a Romanist, but if he were, that was not what moved him to espouse the cause of the colonies. He did it in spite of Catholicism which at that time was the acknowledged foe of liberty, of free thought and action, of free religion in a free state."[82]

Nativists similarly rebuffed claims that Catholic figures such as Galileo and Copernicus made innumerable contributions to the western world; they pointed out the hostility to scientific discovery by popes and other clerical leaders and argued that General Lafayette, whom Catholics praised as a symbol of their dedication to America, was hostile to and openly condemned the Church — acting for the good of America in spite of, rather than in conjunction with, his Catholic upbringing.[83] Anti-Catholic papers likewise ridiculed Catholics for honoring trivial figures, purely on the basis of their alleged Catholic identity, and using dedication ceremonies to siphon money from the public treasury for purely Romanist ends.[84]

The Menace recounted with pride the groundbreaking of the Washington Monument in 1848 and described a significant act that occurred in 1854, as the monument was being completed. Late at night, a group of men stormed the building site when they heard that a carved block of marble had been sent from Rome as a gift from the Pope to commemorate Washington and provide a sign of goodwill toward the United States. Looking unfavorably on the pontiff's gift, the men stormed the monument, subdued the watchman, hacked out the block, and flung the marble slab into the Potomac River. Rather than condemn the vandalism of a public monument, of course, *The Menace* lauded the vigilantes' actions in preserving the sanctity of American public commemoration and went on to note, "Today Catholicism is employing the same tactics as in the days of the building of the Washington Monument. By plausible statements and actions she seeks to ingratiate herself into the confidence of the American people. She claims to be the conservator of liberty, and to be in harmony with our republican institutions." In this article, and in dozens of others, nativists sought to present Catholic commemoration activities as disingenuous, while maintaining their role as arbiters of genuine patriotism and historical integrity.[85]

"Patriotism Begets Heresy!"

Throughout the 1910s, the refutation of Catholic claims to patriotism, heroism, and national service served as the bread and butter of the nativist press. When a Catholic wrote an angry letter to *The Yellow Jacket* exclaiming that Catholics had built and financed the Statue of Liberty and exemplified its values, the paper launched into an attack on the

horrors of convents, insisting that, with the bones from woman and infants murdered in nunneries, Romanists could build an even taller statue.
When Catholics pointed to wartime sacrifice, nativists countered with accusations of desertion by Catholic soldiers.[86] When the Catholic newspaper *Our Sunday Visitor* argued that "without Catholic aid the American
colonies could never have achieved their independence" and "The patriotism of Catholics is no idle boast. On the contrary, the past history of our
country shows Catholics to be head and shoulders above all other classes
of people in devotion to country," *The Peril* answered that Catholics had
the highest rates of mutiny among U.S. soldiers and had even joined fellow Catholic soldiers in Mexico in fighting *against* American troops in the
Mexican American War. The underlying message of virtually all nativist
texts was that allegations of Catholicism patriotism were not only unfounded but an affront to true national pride.[87]

Moreover, Catholics faced a double indictment—charged by the anti-
Catholic press of both insincere patriotism and skewing and misrepresenting facts, undermining the public's access to information, and distorting
history itself. Like many Progressive-Era news outlets, anti-Catholic newspapers placed a high premium on the power of journalism to enlighten
readers, an action they felt was a necessary and sufficient condition for social improvement. Exposing Catholic meddling in the Government Printing Office (an effort to keep accusations of priestly improprieties out of
the Congressional record and the public eye), *The Yellow Jacket* boasted "We
Keep History Straight." Safeguarding public information in the present
and representations of America's virtuous past were overlapping and self-
reinforcing agendas in anti-Catholic periodicals, ones that I will take up
in the following chapter.[88]

Nativists feared that, left unchecked, demonstrations of Catholic patriotism would obscure and overshadow Romanism's harmful impact on
America's sacrosanct institutions. Arguing that "Patriotism Begets Heresy,"
anti-Catholic papers attempted to convince readers not to fall victim to
Catholics' half-hearted patriotism, which amounted to little more than
smoke and mirrors.[89] "Double-faced," and "menacing" in their influence,
Catholic conspirators hoped to win the trust of genuine Americans while
simultaneously threatening to undo institutions in such disparate areas
as civil marriage, court oaths, business relations, and overseas econom-
ics.[90] Most important, Catholics overshadowed American electoral politics.
Incapable of thinking independently, Catholic voters formed a pliable

power bloc in the hands of conniving Jesuits, making political parties "mercenary in their bidding for the Catholic vote."[91] Flaunting their power, priests made demands that political candidates were powerless to resist.

Contrasting American traditions and institutions on one hand with Catholic depravity on the other, *The Liberator* wrote, "The American ballot box is the ark of liberty; the Roman Confessional box is the prison house of freedom. The ballot box stands for intelligence; the confessional box for dense ignorance. The ballot box stands for civic virtue; the confessional box stands for moral pollution. The ballot box represents elevated humanity; the confessional box is the degrader of humanity. . . . The ballot box stands for public freedom; the confessional box is the slaughter house of liberty."[92] This comparison is perhaps the most succinct description of the contours of ideological nativism. Unable or unwilling to accept American conventions, traditions, and institutions and, instead, trying to pervert or manipulate them for their own selfish ends, Catholics stood outside the symbolic and institutional bounds of true American nationalism. Anti-Catholic writers saw their mission as ensuring this boundary and preserving the virtues and traditions within from the corrosive effects outside.

"Help Us to Turn on More Light"

PROGRESSIVISM AND MODERNITY
IN THE NATIVIST PRESS

The Progressive "Information" Age

One of the most common labels applied to the late twentieth century and the beginning of our own is "the Information Age." With the rapid development of electronic communication, the internet, and computerized databases, as well as the omnipresence of twenty-four-hour cable news networks, Americans in the early twenty-first century often feel surrounded, even bombarded, with information. But a century ago, at the beginning of the 1900s, America was undergoing a similar information boom. New technologies in newspaper printing and distribution, newfound avenues of advertising revenue, higher literacy rates, and, above all, a previously unknown technique called "investigative journalism" had caused newspaper and magazine readerships to skyrocket. Contemporary America has become used to the idea of political scandals that decorate the pages of newspapers and weekly magazines, but a century ago, this journalistic convention was still being formulated. In the first two decades of the twentieth century, from 1900 until the close of World War I in 1919, American readers became enthralled by a new objective in reading and writing literature. Newspapers and magazines, which had once served largely to report on local events and provide novel entertainment, began to serve a much more engaging and, their publishers believed, loftier goal. During these two formative decades, periodicals sought to uproot corruption and

scandal, urge the nation to prosperity, and mitigate the most egregious instances of social discord and inequality. In fact, while our current mind-set
might be termed the "Information Age," the label most often applied to
the early twentieth century is "the Progressive Era," emphasizing its reliance on investigation, improvement, and journalistic innovation.

Reporters on the Progressive Era found themselves writing in a unique
period in United States history. Prior to the Civil War, America had been,
at best, a marginal economic power on the world scene: its production
was mainly limited to agricultural goods; the nation's economic capacity
was small and provincial; its transportation systems were localized; and
its cities, while growing, were dwarfed by their counterparts in Europe.
By the end of the nineteenth century, and increasingly in the decades that
followed, the United States had become a worldwide economic power with
an infrastructure and thirst for markets that spanned the continent and
reached across the globe. With this transition came a tremendous increase
in industrialization, urbanization, and corporations and, as a result, an increased polarization in wealth, political power, and social influence. Progressive writers sought primarily to address the injustices resulting from
these rapid changes sweeping the nation and to suggest reforms to moderate the effects of America's entry into industrial capitalism. Accordingly,
such writers were often termed "muckrakers"—a label first applied deroga-
tively by President Theodore Roosevelt—for their attempts at digging up
scandal and focusing on the bleakest aspects of twentieth-century society.[1]

While most scholars recognize progressivism's influence in the early decades of the twentieth century, the direction and foundation of Progressive-
Era thought have served as fodder for numerous historiographical debates.
In fact, the very term "Progressive Era" is itself problematic, as historians
commonly disagree over the impetus and duration of America's reform
impulse. Several writers have argued that progressivism declined rapidly
at the dawn of the 1920s, while others posit a continuation of pre–World
War I reform throughout the twentieth century.[2] Likewise, historians have
long debated whether progressivism served to alter the fundamental nature of American politics and society or whether early twentieth-century
reform was a mere panacea to stave off more radical change. Most observers of the decades leading up to U.S. involvement in World War I, however, have adopted a balanced approach, suggesting, as one recent biography of a leading Progressive-Era journalist noted, that progressivism
straddled "a line between reform and radicalism," allowing reformers to

"still maintain credibility with establishment forces and act as an effective agent of social change."[3]

Determining precise delineations of progressivism or which actors "count" as bona fide progressives is an almost impossible feat in an era dominated by vocal writers with differing agendas. In fact, in a recent review of progressive scholarship, historian Colin Gordon compares the "search for progressivism" with "the American historical profession's version of a snipe hunt"—a practical joke in which children convince their unsuspecting peers to search for a mysterious creature that doesn't really exist. Gordon continues: "We watch those engaged in the pursuit, even participate ourselves on occasion, but never fail to shake our heads ruefully at those who claim to have 'seen it' or 'found it.'"[4] Moreover, as Glenda Gilmore has recently pointed out, determining precisely who progressives were or what they were striving for may be matters of perpetual historiographical debate.[5]

Exacting definitions of progressivism thus go beyond the scope of this essay. For my purposes, it will suffice to say that the Progressive Era was a period in the very late nineteenth and early twentieth centuries that was characterized by the prevailing rhetoric and mood of reform and social amelioration to be brought about by the collection, analysis, and dissemination of information to the public. As a working definition, then, those actors who used the power of information to enact change on the communities around them could be said to be "progressives." At the risk of further muddying the already cloudy category of progressivism, it is critical to examine the significant intersection between anti-Catholic literature and Progressive-Era print culture in general and anti-Catholic nativism's contribution to the Progressive-Era information boom in particular. Anti-Catholic periodicals represent an important, though relatively understudied, dimension of the outpouring of print literature that descended on the American cultural landscape in the early twentieth century.

CIRCULATIONS OF EXTANT PROGRESSIVE-ERA
ANTI-CATHOLIC PERIODICALS WITH CIRCULATIONS
OF MAINSTREAM PERIODICALS[6]

Tables 1 and 2 rely on data from the *Ayer Directory of Publications*, a resource designed primarily for advertisers inquiring about the relative

TABLE 1. Anti-Catholic Periodicals

Title of Periodical	Place of Publication	*1911* Circulation	*1913* Circulation	*1915* Circulation	*1917* Circulation
The Liberator	Magnolia, Arkansas	Not Available	Not Available	15,000	Not Available
The Jeffersonian	Thompson, Georgia	43,043	45,000	Not Available	61,000
The Mountain Advocate	Barbourville, Kentucky	1,200	1,200	1,200	1,200
The Menace	Aurora, Missouri	Not Available	Not Available	1,469,400	1,250,000
The Peril	Wilkesboro, North Carolina	Not Available	Not Available	38,500	Not Available
The Yellow Jacket	Moravian Falls, North Carolina	Not Available	Not Available	Not Available	200,000
Watson's Magazine	Thompson, Georgia	16,000	80,000	Not Available	15,000

Not Available—Indicates that no listing or circulation figures for that periodical appeared in the corresponding bi-annual edition of *The Ayer Directory of Publications*.

No circulation figures were available for the following publications: *The Rail Splitter* (Milan, Illinois), *The Woman's Witness* (Anderson, Indiana), *The Crusader* (Iola, Kansas), and *The Silverton Journal* (Silverton, Oregon).

scope of periodicals. The first table above provides a brief sketch of the anti-Catholic periodicals that circulated in the United States between 1910 and 1919 that can be found in the historical record, noting the circulation of each where available. The second table lists the circulation rates for some of America's most influential and widely known periodicals of the Progressive Era. As the tables illustrate, while some anti-Catholic newspapers had a broader reach than some of the decade's most notable journalistic enterprises, most had more modest or uncertain circulation rates. Nevertheless, periodicals such as *The Menace* and *Watson's Magazine* boasted huge financial success, large publishing plants and distribution networks, and a significant employee payroll, rivaling more conventional journalistic outlets of the Progressive Era.

The question these tables provoke, and the one that has guided my research on American anti-Catholic literature for several years, is, How did nearly two million copies of fervently anti-Catholic periodicals find their way into American homes during the 1910s? Surely, as I discuss in chapter 1, part of the answer rests in anti-Catholics' use of the patriotic

TABLE 2. Other Progressive-Era Periodicals

Title of Periodical	1911 Circulation	1913 Circulation	1915 Circulation	1917 Circulation
Harper's Weekly	70,000	70,000	75,000	102,360
The Atlantic Monthly	30,000	30,000	32,071	51,278
Ladies Home Journal	1,305,030	1,714,202	1,602,263	1,543,048
McClure's Magazine	450,000	400,000	533,805	559,513
Saturday Evening Post	1,425,072	1,885,289	1,950,565	1,825,205
Good Housekeeping	302,162	310,972	350,000	389,773
Collier's	571,768	500,000	642,390	842,126
Cosmopolitan	440,000	750,000	1,000,000	1,055,245
Everybody's Magazine	508,918	600,000	600,000	505,744

imagery and iconography that were emerging as a powerful cultural force in the early twentieth century. But just as nativists mapped their message onto the prevailing language of patriotism and public memory, they also tapped into the language of progressive crusades and reform to bolster their anti-Catholic agenda and enhance the appeal of the anti-Catholic movement. Nativist writers employed the rhetoric of Americanism to present themselves as valiant defenders of the nation and likewise evoked the alarmist tone, investigatory models, and language of "the common good" to position themselves as champions of reform and enlightenment in the face of Catholic depravity and destruction.

MUGWUMPS AND ISLANDS

Like their mainstream progressive counterparts, anti-Catholic writers were at times ambivalent about and, more often, repulsed by the sweeping changes wrought by industrial modernity. Not surprisingly, nativist texts saw Catholics as responsible, or at least scapegoats, for the excesses and aftereffects of American modernity, including urban sprawl, corruption, graft, violence, labor unrest, and other social ills. Like other journalists of the Progressive Era, anti-Catholic nativists targeted overcrowded cities as the site where reform was desperately needed and where the disproportionate wealth and abuse of illicit power were most acute. But here

we see a deep irony: whereas prior instances of anti-Catholic activism resonated from urban areas, where nativists lived almost shoulder-to-shoulder
with their Catholic foes, anti-Catholic journalism in the early twentieth
century emanated from distant rural locales and small towns that contained virtually no Catholic or foreign-born residents. And while other
Progressive-Era reformers relied on personal observation as the basis for
investigative journalism, anti-Catholic writers remained remarkably insu-
lated from their Catholic foes.

The question then becomes how to reconcile anti-Catholics' rhetoric
of reform and enlightenment on the one hand with their hostility toward
modernism (in fact, their considerable conservatism) on the other. On a
related note, how are we to understand anti-Catholic small-town localism
and opposition to distant urban sources of corrupt authority? The key to
addressing each of these points is to see anti-Catholic writers acting to preserve America's small-town pastoral values in the face of dramatic social
upheaval. Throughout this chapter, I argue that, by depicting the Catholic
Church as the symbol of decadent modernity, not only could anti-Catholic
publishers tap into America's long-standing anti-papal legacy, they could
also fight to preserve the integrity of small-town life, which was in danger
of slipping away. Editors, reporters, and publishers, who occupied positions of considerable, though jeopardized, influence in the small communities where they worked, could maintain their status and leadership if and
only if they could galvanize resistance to the growing power of far-flung
cities. Most of all, by lumping urban corruption, the excesses of modernity,
and their Catholic rivals together as a common enemy, nativist texts could
argue that their pastoral communities represented a repository of genuine Americanism, untainted by priestly or urban corruption, and that this
pure heartland held the power to redeem the nation as a whole.

Critical to this analysis of small-town traditionalism at odds with the en-
croaching forces of modernity are two pioneering studies of Progressive-
Era reform, Richard Hofstadter's *The Age of Reform* and Robert Wiebe's
The Search for Order. While early observers of progressivism such as Charles
Beard and Frederick Jackson Turner lauded the era primarily as a populist and democratic movement, by the mid twentieth century, historians
had eschewed these facile depictions, noting that most progressive actors
instituted reform movements to advance their own social and political
influence in the face of corporate expansion. Hofstadter's classic work,
The Age of Reform, envisioned the early progressive movement as a "status

revolution" in which "Mugwumps"—old-order professionals, gentry, merchants, and small manufacturers—felt their political and communal influence dwarfed by newer captains of industry and government. Stripped of their previous clout and determined to cling to their inherited positions of community leadership, Mugwumps embarked on progressive reform campaigns both to attack the source of their status rivalry and to attract support for their position within their community. By curtailing the power of corporate trusts, Mugwumps hoped to demonstrate their continued commercial, economic, and social influence in the face of rapid social change.

In contrast, Robert Wiebe's subsequent study asserted that progressive ranks were bolstered with up-and-coming businessmen who sought to use a new emphasis on efficiency and reform to attain their individual goals. Wiebe insisted, unlike Hofstadter, that progressivism was a reform movement driven by the newer middle class, descended not from the elite gentry but from individuals of more modest means who attempted to forge a "sense of order" amid the chaotic dissolution of small-town life.[7] While Hofstadter saw progressivism emerging from America's older cities, where Mugwumps competed with their new corporate rivals, Wiebe illustrated that progressivism sprang from what he termed "island communities"— small towns that were once relatively isolated from the world around them. With the advent of railroads, improved communication channels, and national markets, these communities began to lose their unique identity, as they were drawn into the broader nation. Progressives' "search for order" came as a way to stave off the rapid disappearance of small-town "island communities" and limit the reach and influence of the business interests that would ultimately destroy island communities themselves.

Although Wiebe, Hofstadter, and their supporters draw opposing conclusions about the motivations and objectives of progressive reformers, their accounts suggest that progressives were primarily white, middle-class businessmen intent on shaping the social climate to further their own ends. Subsequent observers take issue with this approach, however, expanding historical understandings of progressive activism. Katherine Aiken, Camilla Stivers, Rebecca Edwards, Maureen Flanagan, and numerous others have demonstrated how gendered understandings of social roles and women's leadership have profoundly shaped the goals and directions of progressive reform. James Connolly, Shelton Stromquist, and Elizabeth Sanders have noted that working-class men and women were not simply passive recipients of progressive philanthropy but also directed progressivism and influenced its course. Mary Neth and David Berman have illustrated the rural character of early twentieth-century social change, arguing that progressivism was not limited to America's largest cities. Jacqueline Moore, Glenda Gilmore, and others have demonstrated the influence of race on America's progressive ethos, and Daniel Rodgers's recent study even looks beyond America's shores to study the roots of progressive political and charitable reform in Europe and its manifestation across the Atlantic world.[8] These limitations aside, Hofstadter and Wiebe are invaluable for their analysis of the overlapping features of progressivism and social change. Despite their differences, Hofstadter and Wiebe share a common understanding that progressivism emerged as a means of maintaining or achieving middle-class social status and influence and preserving the status quo in communities that were increasingly threatened by external forces of modernity. Although Wiebe and Hofstadter reach different conclusions on whether progressives constituted an "old" or "new" middle class, they agree on one critical ingredient: progressives believed that their communities and their own way of life were jeopardized by powerful, sometimes secretive forces that needed to be challenged. Progressive reform had as much to do with middle-class fears of loss (loss of their community and the social interactions that held it together) than it did with social amelioration.

This conclusion is critical for a thorough understanding of American anti-Catholicism in the first decades of the twentieth century. Nativist writers, like Hofstadter's Mugwumps, saw their influence waning—a decline they attributed not to corporate trusts but to the corrosive forces of Roman Catholicism and the gigantic daily newspapers under the church's control. Like Wiebe's depictions of "island communities," anti-Catholic writers feared that the small towns they inhabited and lead would disintegrate under the weight of rampant urbanization or, worse yet, through the more insidious introduction of modern entertainments that would corrupt traditional values. Championing the overlapping values of small-town traditionalism and American patriotism, nativist writers battled their Romanist enemy with the same energy and employed virtually the same rhetoric and imagery as other Progressive-Era activists. Although the enemies they singled out differed, anti-Catholic writers and reformers outlined in Hofstadter's and Wiebe's texts shared common goals: preserving their influence and the integrity of their communities in the face of new-found uncertainty and instability endemic to the modern era.

THE "PRINCESS OF TRUTH":
BATTLING MODERNITY FROM AFAR

The June 1913 issue of *Watson's Magazine* contained one of the most concise descriptions of anti-Catholicism's dominant message throughout the Progressive Era. In an "Open Letter to Cardinal Gibbons," the magazine's editor, Tom Watson, addressed the influential Catholic archbishop of New York City, boasting that the nativist crusade would spell the end of the Catholic Church's influence in the United States. In illustrating the power of the nativist press to curb Catholic advances, Watson wrote, "The grandest of all music today, is the voice of independent Thought. Its battle-axe rings upon the castle gate, and the chained Princess of Truth *must* be freed. Its all-seeing eye is the sungleam into all the dungeons of superstition."[9] In several respects, this article underscored the ideological nativism that ran throughout early twentieth-century anti-Romanist texts. Incapable of "independent Thought" and bound by "the dungeons of superstition," Catholics were unable to support or participate in America's institutions and thus could not be trusted or welcomed as citizens. But this article, and countless ones like it, also embodied several crucial facets of anti-Catholic progressivism as well. The article's crusading, hyperbolic tone was characteristic of nativist texts in this era, which evoked images of battle and combat to describe circulation drives and criticism of the Catholic enemy. Moreover, Watson's reliance on the power of "truth," disseminated by the nativist press, to overthrow Catholic tyranny is emblematic of the anti-Romanist stance, which claimed that the power of information and the printed word could undo centuries of Catholic abuses.

In several respects Watson's article is somewhat inaccurate. If the "battle axe" of anti-Catholic agitation would attack the Romanist "castle" of corruption and falsehood, it would only be from afar. Despite its rhetoric of confrontation and militarism, twentieth-century anti-Catholicism emerged far from the alleged urban strongholds that served as the perceived locus of Catholic power. Instead, they had small-town roots and thrived in communities with few, if any, Catholic residents.

In *Strangers in the Land,* John Higham illustrates this point by describing the geographic shifts in anti-Catholic ideology, noting: "What had issued from Boston, New York, and Philadelphia in the 1840s, radiated from the smaller cities of the Middle West in the 1880s and finally found its most valiant champions among the hicks and hillbillies. . . . In the twentieth century, [anti-Catholicism] reemerged most actively in rural America, where adherents of the hated faith were relatively few. This shift tied in with a trend already underway in the late nineteenth century: the extrusion of religious nativism from the citadels of middle-class culture."[10] Higham's observations are helpful in illustrating the alterations in anti-Catholic ideology. In the nineteenth century, anti-Catholic agitation was led by urban residents, who competed with Catholic opponents for access to housing, jobs, and political influence. These confrontations often led to violent outbursts by rivals living in close proximity to one another.[11] By the early twentieth century, however, the contours of anti-Catholicism had changed. As Higham points out, America's anti-Romanism had become increasingly removed from both the greatest concentrations of Catholic population and its own urban roots.

However, Higham's classification of rural anti-Catholicism presents a fairly inaccurate portrait of twentieth-century nativism as a whole. By labeling anti-Romanists "hicks and hillbillies," Higham implies that opponents of Catholicism were completely out of touch with prevailing national trends and, moreover, unsophisticated and inarticulate in their writing. He suggests that their periodicals were not embraced by the American mainstream and held little influence beyond the realm of country bumpkins. And by announcing nativism's "extrusion" from "the citadels of middle-class culture," Higham suggests that anti-Catholic writers were not themselves middle class but relegated to a lower social order.

To formulate a more accurate description of anti-Catholic texts and the communities in which they were written, I assert that each of these points is incorrect. While anti-Catholic papers surely cultivated a rustic image of small-town Americanism, they owed much of their popularity to their insight and sensitivity toward prevailing national trends and successfully tapped into the prevailing language of patriotism, progressivism, and gendered expectations to attract a broad readership. Higham's contrast of "the important urban newspaper" with "rustic journals" presents a false dichotomy, overlooking the fact that the most successful anti-Catholic papers exerted a long reach over their audience, and what little evidence of anti-Catholic readership exists suggests that the largest anti-Catholic sheets drew a majority of subscribers from urban areas.[12] Regardless of size, anti-Catholic periodicals reflected national concerns and anxieties, and they echoed the language of reform and progress seen in larger, more mainstream documents. Higham's last point is especially problematic because, as I hope to show, anti-Catholic writers considered themselves a fundamental part of middle-class life in their local communities. Pointing out that their periodicals were essential to the stability of the towns in which they were produced, nativist editors took pride in the natural beauty and vitality of their communities as well as their own local leadership and prestige, both of which they saw as increasingly threatened.

Higham's dismissive tone toward early twentieth-century anti-Catholicism's influence does little to explain how over two million readers bought these newspapers every week, but he does illustrate an important point about the emergence of anti-Catholicism's rural roots in the 1910s. Examining federal census records produces a similar profile of the communities in which anti-Catholic texts emerged during the second decade of the twentieth century. As the following tables indicate, the counties in which extant anti-Catholic documents were produced contained exceptionally low rates of Catholic residents.[13]

The tables are drawn from several census documents. Table 3 illustrates the relative population and population growth of counties producing extant anti-Catholic periodicals during the 1910s. Using census data in 1900, 1910, and 1920, it suggests that counties producing anti-Catholic texts tended to be small, with modest population expansion. This conclusion is strengthened by contrasting the relative urban population of these counties in 1910, indicating that, with the exceptions of *The Rail Splitter,* published outside of Moline, Illinois, and *The Woman's Witness,* produced in Anderson, Indiana, these periodicals were produced in predominantly rural communities. (Unfortunately, rural and urban population by county was not measured in the 1920 census, so this analysis is incomplete.[14] Moreover, there are only a tiny handful of extant copies of *The Woman's Witness* or *The Rail Splitter,* making it impossible to juxtapose the content of rural-based periodicals with more urban ones.)

Table 4 contrasts the county populations reported in the 1910 and 1920 censuses with the 1916 Census of Religious Bodies, which allows us to examine the Catholic population of the counties in which nativist periodicals were produced in the early twentieth century. Since prior and subsequent

TABLE 3. Populations of Counties Producing Extant Anti-Catholic Texts, 1910–20

Periodical	Place of Publication	State	County	County Population, 1900	County Population, 1910	County Population, 1920	County Urban Population/Percent of total, 1900	County Urban Population/Percent of total, 1910
The Liberator	Magnolia	Arkansas	Columbia	22077	23820	27670	0/0	0/0
The Jeffersonian/Watson's Magazine	Thompson	Georgia	McDuffie	9804	10325	11509	0/0	0/0
The Rail Splitter	Milan	Illinois	Rock Island	55249	70404	92297	36741/66.5%	51199/72.7%
The Woman's Witness	Anderson	Indiana	Madison	70470	66224	69151	40349/60.9%	38600/55.8%
The Crusader	Iola	Kansas	Allen	21728	27640	23509	7193/33.1%	11580/41.8%
The Mountain Advocate	Barbourville	Kentucky	Knox	17372	10791	27172	0/0	0/0
The Menace	Aurora	Missouri	Lawrence	31662	26583	24211	6191/19.6%	4148/15.6%
The Peril/The Yellow Jacket	Wilkesboro/Moravian Falls	North Carolina	Wilkes	26872	30282	32644	0/0	0/0
The Silverton Journal	Silverton	Oregon	Marion	27713	39780	47187	4258/15.4%	14094/29.9%

TABLE 4. Relative Catholic Populations of Counties Producing
Anti-Catholic Texts

Periodical	County Population, 1910	County Population, 1920	Mean of Population 1910–20	Catholic population, 1916	Catholic population as percentage of total
The Liberator	23820	27670	25745	11	< 0.1%
The Jeffersonian/ Watson's Magazine	10325	11509	10917	0	0
The Rail Splitter	70404	92297	81350.5	10316	12.7%
The Woman's Witness	66224	69151	67687.5	3701	5.5%
The Crusader	27640	23509	25574.5	504	2.0%
The Mountain Advocate	10791	27172	18981.5	30	0.2%
The Menace	26583	24211	25397	1383	5.4%
The Peril/The Yellow Jacket	30282	32644	31473	0	0
The Silverton Journal	39780	47187	43483.5	7201	16.6%

censuses did not include county-by-county analyses, we are left with a
simple comparison of the relative Catholic population of "nativist" counties, which precludes a longitudinal study that measures increase or decrease of Catholic residents over time. Furthermore, census timing is problematic, since the 1916 Census of Religious Bodies straddles the usual
timeline of census population records. For Table 4, I took the mean of the
1910 and 1920 county populations to approximate the populations at mid-
decade. I then contrasted this number with the relative Catholic population to find the approximate percentage of Catholic residents in counties
producing nativist texts.

Taken together, these census records suggest that the Catholic enemies
denounced in nativist periodicals held little if any influence in the predominantly rural areas where anti-Catholic texts were written and produced. On the national level, Catholic populations swelled by almost
11 percent from 1906 to 1916, and by another 18.3 percent in the subsequent decade, yet these increases had virtually no direct impact on the
populations that most vocally denounced Catholic advances.[15] The snapshot afforded by the census data suggests that twentieth-century anti-
Catholic writers were not lashing out at enemies in their own midst, as

their predecessors had done in the nineteenth century. Romanists were not "Menacing" Aurora, Missouri, nor did they "Imperil" Wilkesboro, North Carolina. Instead, nativists believed that the rural communities they led were facing a more insidious danger from the encroachment of modernism itself, and they latched on to distant Catholic foes as a tangible representation of modernity's corrosive influence. In the Wiebian sense, anti-Catholicism can be seen more as a response to the jeopardization of local "island" communities than a direct representation of the community's population.

Several scholars have explored this relationship between urbanization and rural and small-town life in the early twentieth century, arguing that the boundaries between urban and rural communities were far more porous and far less defined than nativist periodicals of the time would have readers believe. Jane Adams's *The Transformation of Rural Life*, for instance, explores rural Union County, Illinois, through oral history, anthropology, and material culture; her premise is that individuals arrange their personal and community histories along dual "courses" of family history and the chronology of farming and land use. While arguing that farming required immense time and labor through World War II, Adams illustrates how rural communities were shaped by changing agricultural practices, electrification projects, innovations in equipment and consumer goods, and market demands. Adams does much to dismiss the myth of independent family farming, suggesting that tenants, servants, and renters often shared the home and housework with farm owners and that rural farmers were intimately tied to the networks of trade and commerce in nearby cities and the nation as a whole. In the crucial period from 1890 to 1920, Adams explains, the social hierarchy between "landowning businessmen" and wage-earning "laborers" who provided labor and wealth for property owners, intensified. Growing pressure from foreign markets and the concomitant need to invest in machinery to remain competitive changed the pace and level of economic investment in wheat farming in Illinois.

Though Adams's account stands in contrast to the picturesque and utopic depictions of agrarian life put forward in nativist texts, she does recognize, like anti-Catholic writers, that rural dwellers made sense of their communities through "the formal institutions of church, school, political party, and business enterprise, and the neighborhood bonds of reciprocity."[16] While nativist writers sought to juxtapose these "traditional" American values against the decadence of urban life, Adams illustrates that these institutions were in decline in Union County and other rural communities in the early twentieth century. Class stratification and the boom and bust of farming costs and produce added pressure and insecurity, placing strains on these conventional foundations of rural life. Far from an oasis of timelessness and virtue, Adams concludes that market forces and class conflict proliferated in the country, just as nativists argued that corruption ran roughshod through America's cities. Adams's account is also valuable for illustrating the tenuous grasp many middle-class citizens held in leading rural communities as increased economic and commercial tensions threatened to unravel the social hierarchy upon which local institutions and personal interactions were based. This point is further illustrated by David Danborn's survey of American rural life, *Born in the Country*, which reflects the changing relationships between rural and urban producers and markets, illustrating a growing closeness between the two, particularly in the twentieth century. David Blanke's recent study of farming in the Midwest and Mary Neth's examination of women farmers both point out the availability and influence of consumer goods, as catalog sales and postal delivery provided affordable goods for farmers and therefore a growing reciprocity in markets and goods between farms and cities.[17] Robert Barrows's essay "Urbanizing America" takes this a step further, arguing that Progressive-Era writers who came of age in the late nineteenth century often looked upon the towns of their youth with nostalgia and rose-colored glasses. Thus many progressive writers viewed current conditions as deplorable in large part because they corrupted the "homelike" and "leisurely" communities of their youth, which were largely based on the writers' memories and imaginations.[18]

As Barrows contends, progressive writers often yearned for a "simpler time," and nowhere was this more apparent than nativists' romanticization of the bucolic communities they hoped to lead against Catholic opposition. Despite scholars' evidence to the contrary, editors and writers of nativist texts went to great lengths to illustrate dichotomies between pristine small-town life and corrosive urban modernity, by praising the citizens and landscape of the former and condemning the latter. *The Silverton Journal* praised "the inhabitants of this picturesque little city, situated along the banks of Silver Creek."[19] The front page of one issue depicted a smiling child, the "Fresh Air Kiddie" of Silverton, "who deserves the courtesy of a hearty welcome amongst us, with all the good things at our command, and especially that costless yet priceless product of Silverton, which

is a necessity for life, liberty and the pursuit of happiness—fresh air."[20]
Here, the writer combined Americanist rhetoric from the Declaration of
Independence with endorsement of Silverton's natural conditions and
pristine landscape. Likewise, *The Silverton Journal* printed a long poem extolling the natural beauty of the town's countryside: "O Silver Stream,
your waters pure / Bring life and hope and joy divine. / Let gold be sought
in desert sands; / Here's home for me and mine."[21]

Similarly, *Watson's Magazine* printed a laudatory poem extolling the surrounding Georgia countryside in which "the soft breeze stirs the blossoms /
Of the purple passion vines; / And the fragrant oleanders / Star the dusk-
light of the pines."[22] *The Mountain Advocate* ran a short article titled simply
"The Mountains," which boasted of the town of Barbourville and its majestic scenery: "How beautiful are the Mountains of old Kentucky when the
trees have put on their summer wraps of green. . . . Oh! Isn't it paradise?
How many of us realize it? If not all, we should."[23] In these articles, and several others, anti-Catholic writers praise their rural communities as havens
of tranquility and splendor—a direct contradiction of their portrayals of
city life. As Adams's account reminds us, "we are implicated in the construction of the landscape not only through the way we physically alter its
contours and uses, but also through the meanings we find in it."[24] In the
case of nativist journalists, repeated calls to observe and realize the pristine
environment served to galvanize support for local institutions and the individuals that directed them and contrast simple small-town life, with urban
disorder and corruption.

Anti-Catholic writers praised their surrounding communities not simply
as sites of natural beauty but as the source of refinement, culture, and
efficiency as well. *Watson's Magazine* reported on efforts to expand rural
libraries as the center of learning in small towns.[25] Praising Silverton, Oregon, as "one of the finest home cities in the world,"[26] *The Silverton Journal*
went on to extol the community's "Happy Family . . . made so by the loyalty, industry, and wisdom of the parents and the politeness, obedience,
and harmonious conduct of the children."[27] Nativist texts venerated not
only their communities' natural surroundings but also their residents—
people of education, civility, and camaraderie. Calling its hometown of
Barbourville "the Athens of the Mountains," *The Mountain Advocate* boasted
"scores of cultured men and women" that made the community "a leader
in enlightenment. It is a beacon luminary for a vast and resourceful territory. It is a city, set upon a hill to charm, beautify, strengthen an entire

commonwealth."[28] Working to counteract stereotypes of rural dwellers as ignorant rustics, nativist texts insisted that the tradition of "enlightenment" was not exclusively the work of urban metropolises but was carried on in America's hinterland.

This focus on displaying the community's sophistication and enlightenment reflects broader concerns for local boosterism that thrived in the early twentieth century. Like other writers in the Progressive Era, nativists were anxious to extol the efficiency and business virtues of their surrounding communities to help attract investments and residents to their neighborhoods.[29] Just as *The Silverton Journal* praised the "Fresh Air Kiddie" to showcase the community's wholesome health benefits and natural splendor, it also included a woodcut entitled "A Scene in Silverton," which illustrated "Fischer's Flouring Mill which is one of our best industries." Fischer's Mill is nestled among "wavering branches and the sweet scent of the pear and cherry blossoms and spring flowers," suggesting that industry and nature operate in harmony within rural communities.[30] Loudly proclaiming Silverton an "Up-To-Date Business-Like City," a similar article boasted "the quaint old Silverton . . . is not the hustling, up-to-date city of the present." Public works projects, "paved streets, new and up-to-date water and sewer systems, new business blocks, thriving enterprises, many new and attractive homes and a fast increasing population" made Silverton a promising site for businesses and residents.[31] A subsequent article entitled "Silverton and Progress" restated the point simply: "There is probably no more progressive little city, of two thousand people with a most excellent surrounding country, than is Silverton, Oregon."[32]

Likewise, *The Mountain Advocate* boasted of new railroad routes in Kentucky that would allow residents to harness the tremendous power of local resources. Showcasing the "remarkably, productive country" of Appalachia, *Mountain Advocate* producers organized an exposition to "impress upon the people at home and abroad important facts" related to the region's virtues in mining, industry, and agriculture. Writers urged local citizens to promote the town's businesses in order to improve the region.[33] Outlining "A Receipt for a Good Town," the newspaper listed boosterism as a key ingredient; when describing the local community: "Talk about it, Write about it. . . . Speak well of it. . . . Help to improve it." Tellingly, *The Mountain Advocate* listed an additional requirement for improving the town: "Advertise in its paper. . . . Speak well of the public-spirited men."[34]

One of the primary elements in anti-Catholic journalism, then, was the notion that the fate of rural communities rested in the hands of local newspapers and that the writers, editors, and producers of nativist periodicals should serve as the leaders of their surrounding towns. The same article that promoted the progressive spirit of Silverton went on to outline the growth opportunities afforded by nativist publishing. *The Silverton Journal* looked to the example of *The Menace* in Aurora, Missouri, showing how the latter paper's success represents the tremendous commercial opportunities afforded by anti-Catholic periodicals in rural communities.

> A little paper started up a short time ago in a little town in Missouri. They had one clerk in the post office at that time and now they have eight. Can't you see what that means to you and to our city? Suppose this paper gets as many subscribers as the Missouri paper has at present. . . . Think of the advertising it would give this city and the army of people it would put to work, and the great good it would do by getting the people all over the world to thinking along progressive lines and into action to bring about better things. Every merchant in Silverton will be benefited by our success.[35]

Here *The Silverton Journal* maintained that the newspaper was critical in both promulgating progressivism on the macroscopic level and promoting the success of small towns on the local level. Newspapers are the critical ingredient to the community's economic and commercial foundation, and the individuals who lead newspapers should, in turn, receive the support and admiration of their neighbors, particularly in the remote areas where anti-Catholic texts proliferated.

The Yellow Jacket likewise sang the praises of *The Menace* in illustrating the collaboration between anti-Catholic periodicals and small-town life. After *The Menace* successfully weathered a storm of federal indictments (and charges of libel by Catholic opponents), the citizens of Aurora, Missouri, turned out in throngs to celebrate the four editors, "heroes of free speech and the victims of Rome's relentless hatred," who returned home from the trial with great fanfare and ceremony. Prior to the trial, "the brave women were praying the Lord on High from the Protestant churches of Aurora, for the release of the four editors," and, after their release "they were met by a huge assembly of men, women and children, more than 2,000 in number, who rent the air with their cheers while the Aurora band played the national anthem."[36] The message in this article is critical for two reasons. First, it illustrates the cross-promotion common among anti-Catholic periodicals. As I will demonstrate shortly, showcasing the successes and activities of like-minded newspapers was a routine part of anti-Catholic texts. Far from rivals, anti-Romanist writers considered themselves a group of activists fighting for a common cause and dedicated to promoting each others' work.

Second, tying the fortunes of the community to those of the local nativist paper was a common technique in illustrating local veneration for and dependence upon anti-Catholic papers and their editors. Local townspeople were depicted as actively following and being personally invested in the activities of anti-Catholic newspapers. Moreover, the papers and their readers regarded anti-Catholic editors as emblematic of the town itself, vested with the influence to shape the community's development. Like Hofstadter's Mugwumps, anti-Catholic publishers were the traditional leaders and supporters of their local communities, and they looked upon their position with pride, taking the responsibility of shepherding their small towns seriously. *The Yellow Jacket* made this point explicitly, announcing: "It is often the case that travelers who stop in to see The Yellow Jacket shop ask us why we don't move to the city where we might enjoy better advantages in newspaper work. Our reply is that we love the country and we are trying to make the farmers see that if a newspaper can be run in the country that maybe it would be better for more of the farmers to try to run their business in the country instead of flocking to town."[37] Neglecting the potential gains in circulation and revenue, *The Yellow Jacket* editor argued that he could revive the village of Moravian Falls, North Carolina, and demonstrate the vitality of rural communities. In part, this argument clearly springs from the emigration of rural residents to larger cities and towns—what Wiebe would call the dissolution of "island" communities. Proclaiming "The Drudgery of Farm Life a Thing of the Past," *The Mountain Advocate* urged readers to invest in modern equipment and farming techniques, to make farming a viable career option for youngsters, one filled with more economic opportunities and leisure time than distant cities. Demanding that residents "Keep the Boys at Home," the paper hoped to jumpstart the formation of agricultural clubs "that they may find themselves in a larger and finer manhood and womanhood, that will make our country life into something better than it ever has been in the past."[38]

But centering community life around anti-Catholic periodicals also
served to generate prestige and social influence for their editors, at a time
when historians have shown that political, economic, and social power was
increasingly becoming centralized in urban metropolises. The influence
of railroad infrastructure, the growing reach of mail-order consumerism, tremendous fluctuations in agricultural goods and costs, and concentration of political influence combined to curtail the once-significant autonomy of small towns, connecting them to once-remote markets. In turn,
these forces limited the social power of local elites, who once held sway
in their small towns but rapidly lost power to corporate giants in America's
burgeoning cities. Local bourgeoisie (such as shop owners, businessmen,
well-to-do landowners, and, as their literature suggests, newspapermen)
thus fought a losing battle to retain the social status and local influence
they once possessed. This point is critical because it allows us to connect the
historiography of progressivism, and anti-Catholics' use of progressive
rhetoric, with their espousal of small-town values in their ongoing conflict
with Catholic opponents.

"THE RISING VOLCANO": CATHOLICISM AND THE THREAT OF URBAN MODERNITY

Whereas nativist texts portrayed their immediate surroundings
as centers of productivity and splendor, urban locales were described in
less glowing terms. In fact nativists depicted America's cities as the fulcrum
of Romanism's insidious invasion of the nation—by dominating city life,
nativists argued, Catholics had placed the U.S. in a stranglehold and could
extend their influence indefinitely. *Watson's Magazine* demonstrated that
Catholics amounted to a relatively small part of the nation's population:
"It is only in the cities where they are organized that they have control;
and they would not control in the cities were it not for the cowardice and
the venality of our editors and politicians."[39] Watson argued that city congestion led to a breakdown of rural values and the abandonment of farming and rural life and threatened to undo American progress and accomplishment. Concentrating their power and population in urban centers,
Catholics "have produced conditions that militate against their own and
their country's best interest." While nativist texts routinely condemned ur-
banism for enticing rural residents away from their traditional communi-

ties with empty promises of opportunity and sophistication, Watson's article goes a step further, arguing that cities held the real possibility of overt rebellion and revolution. "Here and there may be heard already the rumbling of the rising volcano that rages beneath, whose outbreak is inevitable, if not warded off while yet we may."[40] Catholic conspiracy, which had crippled and corrupted America's cities, threatened to spill over into a force that could destroy the entire nation, if America's rural heartland allowed this corruption to continue unabated.

Along with their nearly universal condemnation of city life, anti-Catholic papers shared an antipathy toward new forms of education, entertainment, and culture that threatened to encroach on what they depicted as America's traditional values. Here we find a paradox in anti-Catholic writing. While nativist journalists generally embraced the language of boosterism and progressivism to illustrate the potential and bounty of their rural communities, they simultaneously rejected new cultural forms and yearned for a return to "good old times." One issue of *The Silverton Journal,* for instance, denounced resistance to progressivism and modern industrialism, insisting, "There is no bigger fool on earth than the mule man who is so balky that he won't advance, but wants things to remain forever the same. These times require real citizenship. . . . These conservatives are so shallow as to even think that the evils swooping down upon us, are brought about by the very reformers who are rallying, organizing, preaching and fighting to counteract them. . . . The enemies of today are as dangerous as the red coats were in 1776. Join the revolution against King George III in what ever guise the principles of tyranny he represents comes."[41] On a superficial level, then, the writer identifies modernism as essential to contemporary life, even in small communities. In an important sense, however, this article clearly delineated aspects of progressivism that it deemed beneficial and noteworthy—new business practices, infrastructure developments, factory construction, and other innovations in "political, and economic conditions"—without mentioning new forms of entertainment, culture, social organization, literature, or education. In the very same issue, *Silverton Journal* writers criticized tobacco, alcohol, and even seemingly innocuous activities such as roller skating as "Modern Witches," capable of destroying individuals and entire communities. Warning that "in the old days people feared imaginary spirits of evil, but now we are up against the real thing," the article explicitly links modernism with the corrosive and destructive effects of contemporary culture: "They do not only kill, but worse than that, they often drag down their hosts to a state of imbecility or stimulate them to a frenzy."[42] While effective business and industrial progressivism were advantageous to the community as a whole, the paper suggests, cultural modernism, as applied to individual tastes, should be avoided at all costs.

Although in some cases patriotism and progressivism were intimately linked, more commonly Americanism was cast as adherence to customs and traditions that were in danger of slipping away, and readers were warned to distance themselves from representations of contemporary culture. *The Yellow Jacket* began one of its frequent diatribes against modernism by stating, "In the good old times men raised their boys about the home and farms and churned into them liberal doses of common sense, and a large per cent of them amounted to something. But in this day and time the fathers raise their boys to live on the street corners and side walks. They lie around soda fountains and drinketh nothing but slop and hookworm germs. They grow up with nothing in their minds except smoking cigarettes and cussing." Young people, the article continued, were being raised without the strict work ethic and dedication to community that had kept small towns together, replacing these traditional values with consumerism and fascination with fine clothing. While previous generations were based on pragmatism and common sense, the young man of today "sits up late at night writing poetry and yet he knows no more about the multiplication table than a blind rooster. His mind turns to the vanities of life."[43] Here modernism is connected not with business innovation and economic expansion, but with the negative effects of individualism, vanity, excess, and ephemeral pursuits. This point is reinforced in descriptions of motion pictures and theatres that corrupt sabbatarian efforts and young minds alike.[44] Modern "fool" fashions, nativism writers maintained, undo traditional values of thrift and humility. As one author concluded, "there never was a dress designed . . . that is half so beautiful as a young girl's modesty."[45] Likewise, writers denounced popular music styles. *The Yellow Jacket* went so far as to condemn the very introduction of the word "jazz" into the American vocabulary and its effect on young children, saying, "It is a mystery why anyone . . . should want to listen to it. . . . Like the cancerworm of the scriptures that 'spoilith and fleeth away' it has attacked the finest flowers of our civilization."[46]

As Kathy Peiss, Roy Rosenzweig, Michael Kimmel, and other scholars of working-class life have demonstrated, the early twentieth century witnessed a host of new forms of entertainment and recreation. While accepting transitions in the business world, nativist writers roundly condemned these new artistic or cultural forms. In part, this reflects writers' efforts to position themselves as stewards of community life and champions of small-town values in the face of changing social pressures. It also demonstrates the nativist strategy of defending allegedly vulnerable individuals, notably children, from opportunistic enemies that would use their naïve nature to infiltrate the community (a point I discuss in detail in chapter 3).[47]

Alongside their criticism of modern fashion, entertainment, music, and social values, nativists frequently condemned new attitudes toward consumption, education, and religion—ideologies that likewise challenged firmly held values. Echoing their criticism of consumerism and lavish fashion, nativists rejected installment-plan purchases and modern tendencies to live beyond one's means. More significant, anti-Catholic writers repudiated the teachings of Darwinism and employment of biblical criticism, declaring that scholarly investigations of biblical origins warped the Gospel truth and misdirected readers and insisting that readers avoid these ideas in favor of traditional Christian teachings.[48] Praising "Old Time Religion," *The Yellow Jacket* noted, "If the present day spirit of unrest had done nothing else, its creation of a lack of reverence for the lowly faith of our fathers would stand as a monument to its unutterable folly."[49] Taking this a step further, a subsequent *Yellow Jacket* article remarked that Darwinists were even more objectionable than Catholics and even more dangerous to the American republic. Insisting "a Godless country is never a free country," *The Yellow Jacket* maintained, "we would rather take our chances in the Vatican of Rome than with a set of Sabbath-wrecking law breaking, rubber necking bipeds who say men's great-grandfather was a monkey and that our genealogy begins where theirs leaves off."[50]

Nativists thus approached modernity from a double standard, selectively appropriating technological developments that improved rural life while shielding their fiefdoms from the hallmarks of a Progressive-Era corporate and modern order, characterized by the embrace of capitalism, urbanization, mechanized assembly, and new educational, religious, and recreational standards. Beneath the rhetoric of boosterism and applause for progressive innovation, nativist texts' reference to a trembling "volcano" of modernity belied a deep anxiety that their "island communities" and social prestige were in jeopardy, which prevented anti-Catholics from full engagement in the American mainstream or interacting with urban audiences, particularly their Catholic foes, on a common ground. Nativists' fears, and those of their readers, prompted them to construct an alternate culture and sense of American nationalism that imagined the nation as departing from its traditional, rural foundations. The nation's past and future, anti-Romanists maintained, were both rooted in small-town communities. Progressive innovations that were consistent with this vision could be tolerated, but the Progressive-Era's concomitant social transformation and modern attitudes and entertainments could not.

In effect, nativists' fears prompted them to forge a distinct subculture, one that demonized emerging social change in general and Catholic harbingers of modernity in particular, while simultaneously preventing any genuine engagements with these groups. This reflects a trajectory outlined by political theorist Richard Dees, whose recent study attempts to explain why interreligious tolerance emerged in Britain while the same experiment failed miserably in nearby France. Dees recognizes that toleration between competing social groups is inherently ephemeral and fragile, initially emerging as a temporary standoff, when both groups feel unable to overwhelm the other. Using game theory and social analysis, Dees concludes that England's incipient attitudes toward proto-democracy, capitalism, and individual autonomy set the stage for interpersonal interaction between rivals that brought opponents together in economic and political environments (such as the marketplace and legislature) on an even footing. These opportunities for common ground were largely absent in France, where Huguenots instead established a "state within a state" that kept Catholics and Protestants separated and heightened tensions between these groups. Each faction, Dees reasons, worried that the other would grow too powerful and topple the delicate balance of power that perpetuated national toleration.[51]

Largely retreating from the modern world, nativists likewise feared that social change and political Romanism would corrode their power and support. Revering their neighbors for providing an oasis of civility and "old time" religion, nativists also depicted their communities as a bastion of genuine Americanism, contrasting rural patriotism with urban squalor and decay. One of the most telling descriptions of nativists' rural Americanism comes from *The Menace*'s account of its own trial and vindication in federal court. Indicted on charges of libel, the newspaper secured a mistrial, and the editors returned triumphantly to their small town of Aurora,

Missouri. The trial's location in the nearby small city of Joplin, Missouri, was heightened to almost mythic importance; *Menace* writers claimed that the city's rejection of papal corruption and vindication of truth and freedom gave the small community a "claim to immortality." Boasting of their victory, *Menace* pundits compared Joplin to Harper's Ferry, Marathon, Greece, and Lexington, Massachusetts: "All of these places would have been forgotten, or innocent of interest, had it not been for events of historic importance. . . . Such deeds of daring, marking crucial moments in the annals of nations or the history of civilization, make indelible impress upon the ages. These are dear to history; so Joplin henceforth will live in story." Obviously, this passage elevates a relatively minor court case to the level of a civilization-altering event and places *The Menace* and its editors on equal footing with the greatest actors of history. But this hyperbole also suggests that history's greatest accomplishments were often performed in peripheral, rural areas. The most pivotal events in American history, the passage implies, took place in the nation's small towns, making them essential to America's development and character.[52]

Other articles extended this metaphor, illustrating that close-knit communities provided a repository of American values and patriotism in danger of slipping away. Describing the surrounding community of Barbourville, Kentucky, a poem in *The Mountain Advocate* depicted the town's "glorious hills" and majestic courthouse but went on to illustrate an even more important facet of community life—the town's solidarity and patriotism. "Lifting 'Old Glory' to the skies / In Barbourville, My Barbourville, / Our hearts are loyal, brave, and true, / We love, and we'll defend thee too. / All Hail! All Hail! Red, White, and Blue, / Shouts Barbourville, My Barbourville!"[53] *The Mountain Advocate* also published frequent examinations of the life of Abraham Lincoln, insisting that his rural upbringing and backwoods character made him suitable to lead the nation through crisis. Most notable for their connections between America's "wilderness" and her later destiny, these stories and poems presented Lincoln as an archetype of rural, pristine Americanism, ready to serve his nation.[54]

The Yellow Jacket also embraced these "backwoods" values, maintaining that rural values of honesty and dedication were responsible for the paper's success and readership. Implicitly distancing his paper from urbane and sophisticated periodicals in the nation's cities, the *Yellow Jacket* editor proclaimed, "The editor of the Yellow Jacket is a home-grown,

corn-fed, hand-spanked North Carolina clodhopper who never saw over
18 months training inside the school room." Filling the paper with "backwoods classics" and rustic truthfulness proved a popular approach, and
readers eagerly filled subscription rolls.[55] Highlighting the importance of
rural culture, nativist periodicals urged the preservation of folklore societies and called farmers "custodians of the nation's morality." Stressing
a Jeffersonian yeoman ideal, nativist papers insisted that "the farm is the
power-house of all progress and the birthplace of all that is noble. The
Garden of Eden was in the country and the man who would get close to
God must first get close to nature."[56] Defenders of American values and
appropriate Christianity, farmers and their rural neighbors needed to be
strengthened and unified by the powerful influence of the rural press.
Concerned that rural news was underreported or, worse, misrepresented
by powerful city papers "who seek to profit from the story," *The Mountain
Advocate* urged readers to subscribe to their local newspaper: "no home
should be without it." By supporting community periodicals, farmers would
find more sources of accurate local reporting. "The local paper is part of
the community life and the editor understand the farmer's problems. It is
the local press that will study the local problems and through its columns
deal with subjects of most vital importance to local life." Whereas "the city
problems are blazon upon the front pages of the metropolitan dailies,"
the struggles of rural communities would be eased and understood by
like-minded periodicals and their editors.[57]

Echoing this praise for the rural press and its leaders, one particularly
noteworthy article detailed a traveler's visit to the Menace Publishing Company's office in Aurora, Missouri. Like other nativist texts, this article
straddled a fine line; it praised the office's efficiency and modern publishing equipment, but not without stressing the periodical's plain-spoken
language and rural roots. The visitor "was first shown the poor, humble
little wooden building where it [the newspaper] started three brief years
ago" and then saw in contrast to these modest beginnings the contemporary bustling printing plant, predicated on "neatness, modern equipment
and perfection of organization in every department." Impressing on their
visitor the immense leaps in subscriptions, Menace staff members compared their tremendous growth (to well over a million subscribers by the
time the article was printed) with less successful mainstream papers. Critics and imitators of *The Menace* "achieved little or nothing because they
chose rather to use elegant diction and scholarly phrases than language

adapted to dealing appropriately with the unsavory record of Romanism, past and present." Moreover, *The Menace* owed its success, the visitor insisted, to inspiration and hard-working editors and writers: "These Menace people are too wise in their day and generation not to know, first, that to make their paper a power, it was necessary to have a great circulation. . . . They realized that they must first get the ear of the general public and that a certain element of sensationalism is necessary in order to build up that required circulation." This statement is critical because it represents the only admission within nativist texts that writers used hyperbole or outright exaggeration to communicate their anti-Catholic message. Elsewhere, anti-Catholics frequently reiterated that their journals represented complete accuracy and that the chilling accounts of Catholic murder, rape, theft, or corruption only *seemed* exaggerated because they illustrated the full measure of Catholic depravity.

Yet rather than denounce *Menace* editors for sensationalized reporting (as Catholics themselves did), the visiting reporter in Aurora praised them for spreading the message of Rome's destructive nature. Emphasizing the importance of this work, the article concluded: "These men do not pose so much as makers of public sentiment as expressers of sentiment already existing among the more intelligent element of the American people. They had the courage of their convictions to walk boldly out, like the brave and conscientious patriotic men that they are and fight the people's battles and the people have unqualifiedly expressed their approbation."[58]

"THIS MIGHTY AND RAPIDLY GROWING ARMY": ANTI-CATHOLIC NETWORKS

The sentiment expressed in *The Menace*'s account of a visit to Aurora embodies several critical facets of early twentieth-century anti-Catholicism, particularly its praise of small-town values and its insistence that editors embody the attitudes and wishes of the population at large and thus deserve the community's respect and admiration. To preserve America's traditional rural values and the status of newspapermen that supported and enriched them against the overlapping forces of Catholicism and contemporary culture, nativist writers banded together to form a network of anti-Catholic writers, publishers, and readers. Nearly every anti-Catholic newspaper from the early twentieth century spoke of its readers in glorious, crusading words, describing loyal readers or "subscription hustlers" that filled the circulation rolls as an army, brigade, "firing line," or other militaristic term. The efforts of newspapers to promote readership and generate subscription revenue is hardly surprising, since the Progressive Era witnessed a sharp increase in periodical circulation and, consequently, competition for readers and advertisers. In fact, subscription drives and promotion of readership were commonplace advertising strategies among publishers of all stripes. But what is more surprising, given the Progressive Era's environment of competition among different journals, is the extent to which anti-Catholic periodicals joined forces to cross-promote, collaborate, and share information with one another. While individual nativist journals frequently sought to boost their own circulation, they were just as intent on assisting like-minded papers in spreading their antipathy for Romanism.

Anti-Catholic periodicals frequently printed glowing reviews of books, pamphlets, and lectures generated by other nativist sources and even ran full-page advertisements for other anti-Catholic papers. Editors often wrote columns inspired by other anti-Catholic newspapers and circulated letters of support and encouragement to one another. Rather than distinguish themselves individually, nearly all anti-Catholic periodicals sought to lump themselves into the larger body of nativist agitation and to describe the anti-Catholic crusade as a unified movement. Rather than competing fragments, anti-Romanist writings were described as "the present anti-Catholic cyclone that has struck the country."[59] *Watson's Magazine* listed several anti-Catholic periodicals and "the millions of aroused readers of and earnest workers for such publications" who worked as one in showing "that the Roman Catholic Church is the deadliest enemy to American institutions. . . . Can this mighty intensely alive and rapidly growing army of citizens be all wrong . . . ?"[60] Instead of trying to drive readers away from would-be rivals, anti-Catholic editors and publishers encouraged readers to purchase subscriptions in other nativist journals and praised one another for promoting the anti-Catholic message, rather than sliding into backbiting or jealousy.

While anti-Catholic writers advocated cooperation among "patriotic or Rome-fighting periodicals" to form a unified movement, nearly all newspapers recognized that *The Menace,* as the most successful and far-reaching anti-Catholic text of the time, stood as an inspiration and in some sense a representation of the nativist movement itself. Virtually all of the extant anti-Catholic literature of the Progressive Era expresses support and admiration for *The Menace* and often imitated the successful anti-Catholic sheet in their tone, rhetoric, and fervor. The fact that *The Menace* got its name from a series of articles printed by Thomas Watson—"Romanism: The Deadliest Menace to Our Liberties and Our Civilization"—and published in *The Jeffersonian* suggests the extent to which anti-Catholic publishers read and borrowed from each other's work.[61] When critics lambasted smaller periodicals for their association with such a fervently anti-Catholic newspaper, nativist writers turned these accusations on their head, expressing intense pride in their participation in the anti-Catholic crusade. *The Mountain Advocate,* for instance, reprinted an editorial from a Louisville newspaper, criticizing the tiny *Mountain Advocate* for its affiliation with *The Menace,* to which the paper abruptly replied: "It will be observed that the editor of the Mountain Advocate is called an apt student of the Menace, which is one of the greatest anti-Catholic papers in the world; and at the outset we desire to thank the author of this article for the comparison. We consider that the greatest honor you could have conferred on us. To do battle for so noble and glorious a cause is indeed a pleasure to us, for we believe there is no greater or more important issue confronting the American people today than that of the Catholic Church."[62] Likewise, *The Peril* attempted to deflect and invert condemnation it received in the Catholic press for the formulation of "the Menace-Peril clique," a partnership between the powerful *Menace* and the far more limited and provincial *Peril.* Rather than sidestep its partnership in anti-Catholic networks, *The Peril* insisted, "This condemnation . . . is the very highest political compliment that the gentleman could have paid" the humble newspaper.[63]

Perhaps one of the reasons smaller anti-Catholic periodicals lauded *The Menace* was the latter paper's tendency to promote other nativist sheets, particularly in their first year of production. Both Thomas Watson and Wilbur Phelps (editor of *The Menace*) dedicated substantial space in their columns to efforts of other editors. Embracing a framework of mutual support and publicity, nativist writers frequently reiterated one another's viewpoints or reprinted entire articles. *The Menace* took pains to point out Catholic corruption in distant Oregon and efforts by *The Silverton Journal* to curb Romanism's pernicious effects. Likewise, *The Silverton Journal* reprinted *Menace* articles and urged readers to order subscriptions.[64] *The Crusader* printed editorials thanking Watson and Phelps for their support, praising its "elder brother" for the "warm welcome" into the

ranks of anti-Catholic print culture.[65] Although *The Liberator* is all but lost
to the historical record, with only a handful of articles currently extant, far
more articles are available to historians because they were paraphrased or
reprinted entirely by other nativist papers.[66] Moreover, what little information we have suggests that the *Liberator* shared with *The Menace* not only
an inflammatory style but identical advertisements and a common admiration for anti-Catholic crusaders. While virtually all anti-Catholic periodicals fell out of circulation by the end of the 1910s, a couple continued
to produce scattered issues into the 1920s and beyond. Even in this fragmented and muted state, the few stalwart anti-Catholic newspapers that
persisted continued to share information and reprint articles, suggesting
that the ties between these journals were pervasive indeed.[67]

NOTES FROM THE "FIRING LINE":
SELF-PROMOTION AND BUSINESS TECHNIQUES

During their heyday in the 1910s, anti-Catholic periodicals constituted a solid network, supporting one another by sharing information,
articles, sponsorship, and, in extreme cases, financial support.[68] Nevertheless, these papers did demonstrate slight differences, notably on the duration and durability of their anti-Catholic outlook. While several of the
decade's most prominent nativist papers, such as *The Jeffersonian, Watson's
Magazine,* and *The Menace,* began publication early in the decade and were
exclusively anti-Catholic in their orientation from their inception, others appeared as latecomers to the anti-Catholic party, shifting their attention to Romanism only when it had become fashionable (and financially
profitable) to do so. And while most of the staunchly anti-Catholic papers
ceased publication when the nation's attention shifted from domestic anti-
Catholicism to foreign conflicts in Europe after America's entry into World
War I, some of the more tepid voices of anti-Catholic agitation successfully
shifted their focus away from anti-Catholic issues and continued publication well into the 1920s. *The Silverton Journal,* which published dozens of
scathing articles against the forces of Romanism, was one example of such
ephemeral anti-Catholicism. The small Oregon paper began publication
in the late nineteenth century reporting primarily on local events in Silverton, such as issues before the local school board, efforts to improve
the town's industry, and social gatherings (it also published some occa-

sional serialized novels in the early twentieth century). Provincial in nature, *The Silverton Journal* engaged in local boosterism on a pro-temperance platform.

The paper had been in print for decades before the first mention of anti-Catholicism, which occurred on June 13, 1913, more than two years after the initial publication of *The Menace*, at a period when the latter paper enjoyed a circulation of approximately one million. Reprinting a *Menace* article condemning Catholicism's destructive influence on public schools, *The Silverton Journal* wrote: "If these are true quotations and if they express the general sentiment of the catholic church, then it is time that every true American wakes up, or blood will again run in another silly religious war." Although the paper initially expressed a desire to serve as a forum for "a fair justification by both sides" of the debate over American Catholicism, this objectivism quickly shifted to adamant nativism a few weeks later, when the paper reported on rape and captivity in nearby convents and accounts of murdering priests and made pleas to readers for additional subscriptions to fight the anti-papal crusade—themes that had become the bread and butter of similar anti-Catholic periodicals during the Progressive Era.[69] Within a few months of publishing its first anti-Catholic critique, the entire content and tone of *The Silverton Journal* had shifted radically.

In one sense, the paper retained its localist viewpoint. Whereas *The Menace, Watson's Magazine,* and other large-scale anti-Catholic periodicals were national in scope, *The Silverton Journal* retained some of its local character, reporting primarily on convent captivity and abuse in the nearby town of Mount Angel. On one occasion, *The Silverton Journal* objected to local critics who spoke of "The [Silverton] Journal-Menace Clique," retorting, "There is really no clique with us at all. The Catholic priesthood is really a clique and a most dangerous one at that."[70] But in nearly every respect, *The Silverton Journal* mirrored the rhetoric, style, and journalistic conventions of its more successful counterparts. Beginning in 1913, the Oregon paper began printing "Stickers"—short one-sentence sayings that were usually quick jabs at the Catholic enemy, such as "There are many other mysteries in Mt. Angel besides the mystery of holiness" and "Think of the suffering millions!" These pithy sayings echoed a common convention among anti-Catholic periodicals of the decade. Called "Stingers" in *The Yellow Jacket* and "Notes from the Firing Line" in *The Menace,* and cropping up in the margins of similar newspapers, these witty comments suggest a common journalistic style that can be traced to a common root in the socialist *Appeal to Reason* in the early twentieth century, which provided early training and funding for writers and editors of *The Menace*.[71]

The Silverton Journal imitated *The Menace* not merely in journalistic layout and style but in tone and rhetoric as well. What had once been a largely isolated paper now embraced the wider community of anti-Catholic readers and writers. Within a few months of publishing its first anti-Catholic article, *The Silverton Journal* sought "to compel every liberty loving citizen to become an active agent in the anti-Catholic campaign, which seems to be sweeping this county from coast to coast and from the Lakes to the Gulf."[72] Participation in the anti-Catholic crusade produced not only a new format and emphasis for *The Silverton Journal* but new demand and revenues as well. Shortly after joining the anti-Catholic bandwagon, the paper reported, "Last week's issue of The Silverton Journal aroused more interest than any other issue ever published. Long after our thirty or forty extra copies were sold a steady stream of anxious would-be purchasers called at the office, hailed us on the streets, and wrote to us from distant places. Some wanted one copy, but many wanted a half dozen copies or more to send to their friends."[73] A similar article stated, "We are very sorry that it is impossible to fill the enormous list of orders we had for our issue of August 1st, containing the account of the escape of the nun from Mt. Angel. All this week the orders came steadily pouring in. . . . The best we can do, friends, is to put the whole thing in a little booklet, which will be ready in a few days. . . . Order now if you want one."[74] Increased attention to anti-Catholicism carried a huge financial incentive and offered once obscure papers increased readership and, by cross-promotion, a share of the national limelight anti-Catholic periodicals enjoyed during the middle of the 1910s. This pattern can be seen in other newspapers as well. Initially the Republican weekly for Knox County, Kentucky, *The Mountain Advocate* had been in circulation for several decades before reprinting anti-Catholic articles and poems from *The Menace* in January 1914. In less than three months, the paper's circulation had nearly doubled.[75]

Preexisting newspapers such as *The Mountain Advocate* and *The Silverton Journal* shifted from an agenda of Republicanism (in the case of the former) or temperance (for the latter), of which Catholics could easily be seen as adversaries. Yet their muted or tacit anti-Catholicism emerged only with the circulation and financial successes of larger, more consistent nativist outlets. Likewise, several new periodicals began publication during anti-Catholicism's heyday and in direct imitation of *The Menace*, when the latter had already paved the way for anti-Catholic readership. *The Crusader* began publication in January 1914, building a base of eight thousand readers in the first three months. This short-lived paper emulated the same club-based model of subscribers and, moreover, the same patriotic rhetoric as its counterparts—vowing to continue publication "while the flag is threatened by a conspiracy against all that it represents."[76] Shortly after its initial publication, however, the paper began to report a slump in subscribers—a trend that continued until the paper ceased publication in the late 1910s—suggesting that *The Crusader* experienced not only the rapid rise but also the concomitant decline of its anti-Catholic peers.[77] A similar trend can be seen in *The Peril*, which urged readers to "join the Patriots on the firing line."[78] Like *The Crusader*, *The Peril* began in the 1910s to capitalize on the anti-Catholic craze; after an initial boom in circulation that peaked at over 30,000, the paper rapidly faded into obscurity.

Although anti-Catholic papers exhibited differences in longevity, readership, and circulation, these papers were remarkably similar in their commercial practices, anti-Romanist message, and boom-and-bust production cycle.[79] Addressing the business strategies of Progressive-Era anti-Catholic periodicals is problematic, since no records or correspondence exists. But one plausible way of exploring the internal workings of the most dominant anti-Catholic sheet, *The Menace* (and, in turn, of understanding its imitators), is by studying its progenitor—the well-known socialist paper *The Appeal to Reason*. As David Nord, Elliot Shore, and Aileen Kraditor have shown, *The Appeal* provided inspiration, training, and start-up funds to Phelps's fledgling *Menace*, though the latter paper eschewed overt socialism in favor of staunchly anti-Romanist rhetoric.[80] In his study of *The Appeal*, Dave Nord points out two critical elements of the paper's circulation base that have a direct bearing on its later, anti-Catholic descendants. First, Nord states that one crucial facet of *The Appeal* "was its continuous self-promotion and its incessant hustle for circulation." Nord writes that the largest component of stories and articles were "about the Appeal itself, usually pleas for more circulation, descriptions of circulation contests, promotion of special issues, and items about 'the Appeal Army,' a dedicated band of thousands of readers who hustled subscriptions for their 'Little Old Appeal.'"[81] Alongside this explicit self-aggrandizement was another feature of *The Appeal*'s short-lived success. As Nord points out "The Appeal always operated expansionisticly. . . . Subscription prices were so

low (twenty five cents a year for many years) that the paper always needed
more and more new subscribers every day just to cover current operating
expenses."[82] Nord's assessment of *The Appeal* suggests that the paper operated much like a modern pyramid scheme — using up the proceeds from
yearly subscriptions to buy equipment or cover the expenses of publicizing
and printing a single issue, leaving almost nothing in reserve. This meant
that even more subscribers were needed for the next publication, creating
a cycle of incessant demand for new readers to support the paper. While
this method allowed for rapid expansion, as publishers could offer very
inexpensive subscription rates and dedicate their efforts to wholesale self-
promotion, it also spelled disaster if the paper experienced a downturn
or even a leveling of new subscriptions.

The rhetoric and expansion cycle of anti-Catholic newspapers suggest
that *The Menace* and its followers faithfully embraced this model of subscription and self-promotion. Like *The Appeal, The Menace Army* served the
anti-Romanist crusade by rallying new subscribers. Publishers organized
"Bundle Brigades" to solicit subscribers from friends and coworkers by
handing out sample copies of the paper.[83] Other papers used similar militaristic rhetoric and organizational schemes to promote their circulations
in the quest for new subscribers. After embracing the anti-Catholic agenda,
The Silverton Journal took on the movement's thirst for subscriptions, telling readers "Don't Tire! Fire!!!" and praised "the firing line" for their efforts at promoting the paper.[84] Warning subscribers that a drooping circulation base would put the paper out of business, the *Journal* demanded,
"Every one of our readers, secure us one subscriber . . . or send us a club
of four or more subscribers. . . . This is the fight of every true American.
Let us stand by our guns!"[85] Tom Watson echoed this message, maintaining that "spreading the Jeff[ersonian] Circulation is the Best Way to Fight"
against Romanist corruption.[86]

THE ANTI-CATHOLIC PERSONA:
WILBUR PHELPS AND TOM WATSON

While there are several explanations for the intense outburst
of nativist literature in the 1910s, much of its brief success stems from the
publicity and crusading mentality generated by anti-Catholicism's two leading proponents — Tom Watson of Georgia and Wilbur Phelps of Missouri.

In effect, Watson and Phelps represent the two most successful (and there-fore most identifiable) proponents of American anti-Catholicism in the Progressive Era, and in some sense they proved strange bedfellows in the anti-Catholic movement, given Phelps's early start as a printer with *The Appeal* and Watson's vocal condemnation of socialism. Nevertheless, the two editors shared, along with their open disdain for Catholicism's en-croaching power, a staunchly anti-corporate and anti-industrialist stance and a strong belief that America's glorious traditions and future direc-tions were rooted in rural communities. In Phelps's case, this translated into a widespread antipathy for urban life, particularly city newspapers, which extended the reach of modern life and were themselves awash in Catholic lies. Phelps's entire journalistic career, in fact, was spent moving from one small-town paper to another across the Plains states and the upper South. Some of his ventures, like *The Appeal* and *The Menace,* en-joyed national recognition and readership, though subsequent sheets, as I illustrate in chapter 5, had an extremely limited lifespan and were ig-nored altogether.

Watson shared Phelps's concern that agrarian life in the South was under attack, and he believed that determined readers could expose and undo Catholic deception and preserve American traditions. In other re-spects Watson's career was remarkably different from Phelps's, shaped primarily by the vicissitudes of political aspiration and failure in Watson's home state of Georgia. Throughout his life Watson championed the inter-ests of farmers over against the actions of industrialists, railroad magnates, and other post-Reconstruction proponents of the urbanized, mechanized "New South." As the exemplary biographer C. Vann Woodward has noted, this produced something of a split personality in Watson, since his ini-tial enthusiasm for racial equality, integration, and solidarity among social classes gave way to bigoted hate-mongering, social discord, and narrow-mindedness when Watson's Progressive Party aspirations were crushed by Democratic rivals. Watson began his career as a U.S. Congressman in 1890 but feared the splintering of the Democratic Party between factions of businessmen (industrialists and corporate architects of New South urban life) on the one hand and farmers (who, Watson concluded, were increas-ingly marginalized in state and national politics) on the other.

Essentially, Watson's early work in organizing the Farmer's Alliance Platform—an offshoot of the Democratic Party—was predicated on racial cooperation and tolerance, including sharp condemnation of lynchings and promoting the efforts of black farmers. Ultimately, Watson abandoned the Democrats, forging a populist agenda that was framed as a class-based party for farmers (and, to a lesser extent, working-class city dwellers) who would find no support, Watson maintained, under the prevailing Republican (or "Bourbon" industrialistic) Democratic leadership. Yet Watson's experiment at populism and racial harmony ended in failure when Southern industrialists proved more effective in galvanizing support, owing, Watson claimed, to his rivals' "machine politics" and courting of the "black vote."

Writing just a decade after Watson's death, Vann Woodward illustrates that, initially, "In his battle against industrial capitalism, Watson sought to align in his ranks all agrarian forces, whether landowners tenants, or laborers," but the "corruption" of black votes and their mobilization by political rivals pushed Watson further from the reins of political power and stymied his national political aspirations.[87] Watson's condemnation of Catholics, like his latter racist mind-set, thus seemed to have been motivated by his contempt for electoral subterfuge, anxiety over social transformation that would undermine farming communities, and, ultimately, personal defeats at the hands of industrialists and "machine" politics. In some respects, Watson's critique of American Catholics was remarkably different from the racist and segregationist views he developed latter in life, since Watson made no mention of Catholics' ethnic, linguistic, or immigrant affiliations in singling out this group as dangerous to American institutions. But Watson expressed fear that, like black voters, Catholics' superstition and limited intellect would be easily enticed by industrialists and corporate trusts occupying positions of influence in distant urban centers and would be easily manipulated into destroying the very fabric of American society.

Wary that his political autonomy (and that of his farmer constituents) was being eclipsed by the South's new Bourbon Democrats and industrialists, Watson became, in Vann Woodward's classic term, an "Agrarian Rebel" (a label that would apply equally well to Phelps and other anti-Catholic editors in the early twentieth century)—staunchly championing rural ways of life in the face of rampant social change.[88]

Ultimately, Watson's message of "backwoods" traditionalism, Jeffersonian idealism, the dangers of urbanized and mechanized expansion, and concern that ignorant Catholics and other groups threatened the contours of rural life stands as the hallmark of anti-Catholic nativism in the 1910s (and in some respects persists for several decades thereafter). While less is known about the writers and editors of other papers, who lacked Watson's place in the spotlight of national politics but not his outspoken critique of industrialized modernity, the rapid proliferation of anti-Romanist texts in the early twentieth century and their insistent veneration of farming and rural life suggests that Watson's message of Catholic complicity in undermining American traditions found fertile soil among readers anxious about the nation's increasingly corporate social order.

While Phelps and Watson were certainly influential, the staggering circulation rates enjoyed by the most successful Catholic periodicals reflect not only flagrant self-promotion and editors' attitudes and ambitions but Progressive-Era innovations in printing, distribution, and marketing of print media itself. The late nineteenth and early twentieth centuries constituted a boom time for the American press writ large. Extending second-class mailing privileges to magazines, developing free rural delivery in the 1880s and extending the service in subsequent decades, and tightening copyright laws allowed the federal government to stimulate periodicals' circulation. Moreover, the growth of literacy, more accessible secondary education, and the corresponding demand for reading material contributed to the swell in newspapers and popular literature. New technological innovations in printing, such as the linotype machine, "half-tone" photo engraving (to replace traditional woodcuts), and eventually color images, which started to gain in popularity with America's entry into the Spanish-American War, allowed publishers to meet readers' demands—producing more detailed texts in larger quantities and at faster rates. A concomitant decrease in paper and printing prices and increased possibilities for advertising revenues (by 1900, two-thirds of all publishing revenue came from advertising contracts, as opposed to subscription costs), meant that newspapers could be run more efficiently, with greater circulations, and new opportunities for profitability than previously expected. Greater advertising revenue, in turn, called for greater publisher accountability, sparking the creation of circulation review boards and advertising bureaus. In a somewhat circular fashion, unprecedented newspaper circulation and reach generated additional advertising dollars, which, in turn, put still greater pressure on publishers to ensure and maintain lengthy subscriber lists.[89] In part, the tenor and scope of anti-Catholic circulation reflected a broader trend in early twentieth-century journalism as a whole.

"An Indictment of American Character": Themes in Progressive-Era Print Culture

Along with similarities in circulation drives and self-promotion, anti-Catholic papers of the Progressive Era expressed a dramatic uniformity in their nativist agenda. In particular, by the heyday of anti-Catholic periodicals in the mid 1910s, each of these papers was extremely similar in its desire to combat Catholic encroachment on American institutions, use the power of the press to preserve genuine Americanism, and demonstrate the duplicity of Catholic adversaries. The bombastic, militant, and patriotic tone and fervent embrace of one or more of these goals became the cornerstone of thousands of anti-Catholic articles throughout the Progressive Era that were written with such strikingly similar style and content that, in all probability, the masthead of one newspaper could have been exchanged for the other and readers would scarcely have been able to discern a difference. Rather than competing, anti-Catholic writers worked in common to promote each other's periodicals and share the latest news of Catholic aggression. In one particularly telling article, Wilbur Phelps explained that his greatest trouble in editing *The Menace* is keeping up with a tremendous flood of correspondence. Phelps wrote, "Thousands of people send us news clippings every day. We appreciate these, and it is from them that we grind the grist that makes the Menace. . . . The same is true of manuscripts. A man in a distant state will send in a manuscript of which, in his mind, depends the salvation of the Menace and the movement it espouses. . . . To publish them all would require a forty page daily the size of the Menace."[90] Rather than an isolated paper, then, *Menace* publishers saw their paper as a giant clearinghouse of anti-Catholic information and support—a way of galvanizing momentum and ammunition for their crusade against the evils of Rome.

Anti-Catholic publishers thus formed a network of like-minded writers united in their common distribution practices and ideology. But the most salient factor that united these writers was the importance they attributed to the written word itself. Anti-Catholic writers praised their movement for bringing truth to their readers—something "Romanized" daily papers in the nation's larger cities could never accomplish. The foundation of the nativist crusade was the belief in the power of information to curb Catholicism's influence and preserve the nation. With this emphasis on the transformative power of information, anti-Catholic writers echoed the mantra of their Progressive-Era contemporaries, just as they shared a rhetoric for urban reform and a hatred for illicit conspiracy. A complete understanding of early twentieth-century nativism, then, requires an elaboration of how anti-Catholic writers mirrored the prevailing language of Progressivism within their pages. In the stories they wrote, the often shrill tone in which the stories were written, and, above all, the meanings they attached to the work of journalistic writing, anti-Catholic writers bore a strong resemblance to their Progressive-Era counterparts working for more mainstream and familiar journalistic outlets.

The meaning and influence of Progressive-Era thought, its longevity, and its conservative or transformative nature have served as fodder for numerous historiographical debates. The issue, then, is how to identify the most common strains and attitudes of progressive writers—which is not an easy feat in an era dominated by vocal writers with differing agendas—and how to relate these to the anti-Catholic message in the early twentieth century. One possible way of isolating key components of progressive concerns and relating them to the anti-Catholic outlook is to examine a pivotal moment in the formation of progressive literature and ideology.

One such moment occurred in January 1903, when *McClure's* magazine, one of the leading voices of the progressive movement and one of the pioneering muckraking journals, published three articles—"The Shame of Minneapolis," "The History of the Standard Oil Company," and "The Right to Work," by Lincoln Steffens, Ida Tarbell, and Ray Baker, respectively—that would go on to become Progressive-Era landmarks and would launch the careers of these three writers, whose work would form the foundation of mainstream progressivism. This issue provided a touchstone in Progressive-Era print culture, outlining key topics and setting a rhetorical tone that would be echoed by dozens of other writers in daily newspapers, anti-Catholic sheets, and other muckraking organs for almost two decades thereafter. Although it would be difficult to identify a canon of classics in Progressive-Era literature, and harder still to pinpoint progressivism's starting point, these articles deserve consideration on both counts.

In a brief editorial introduction to these articles, the magazine's editor, S. S. McClure, called them "an indictment of American character" that "should make every one of us stop and think."[91] McClure, not surprisingly, raised the tone and tenor of these articles to almost mythical status, insisting that his magazine and writers would banish corruption and inequity

from America and herald the arrival of a new era in U.S. society, dominated by the oversight of an observant and benevolent public press. Traditional channels of American authority and justice—such as the law,
churches, and colleges—were unable or unwilling to defend the "public
good," McClure contended, and instead were looking out for their own
interests. Since intellectuals, industrialists, and the clergy were either too
aloof or too corrupt to rectify American society, McClure argued that only
the "public at large" could address social abuses. In language reminiscent
of traditional Republican rhetoric, McClure condemned the proliferation of "special interests" that placed the demands of the few above the
needs of the greater public good: "We forget that we all are the people;
that while each of us in his group can shove off on the rest the bill of today,
the debt is only postponed; the rest are passing it on back to us. We have
to pay in the end, every one of us. And in the end, the sum total of the
debt will be our liberty."[92] McClure praised the articles in his magazine
as monitors of America's "public good," suggesting that journalists had
become the public's new champions and that the private interests of the
few could not be given more weight than the public good that affects
everyone.

The first article in the series was Lincoln Steffens's "The Shame of Minneapolis," which described the career of Albert Ames, who climbed from
minor office holder to four-time mayor of that city. In this office, Steffens
contended, Ames "set out on a career of corruption which, for its deliber-
ateness, invention, an avarice has never been equaled."[93] Steffens outlines
how Ames charged kickbacks to allow brothels to operate with impunity,
hired his own dishonest friends to run the corrupt police force, and allowed the spread of opium in exchange for healthy extortion payments—
most of which found their way into the mayor's pockets. Steffens's article
outlines how Mayor Ames and his crime ring were investigated and brought
down by the foreman of the city's grand jury and district attorney, who, he
maintained, applied "simple business sense to the problems" of Minneapolis. Ames was betrayed by his own friends and replaced by the squeaky-
clean new mayor of Minneapolis, Percy Jones, who was "convinced by an
exposure of a corrupt municipal council" to enter the political arena and
who remained unswayed by the threats of gambling houses, brothels, and
liquor traffickers and left Minneapolis "clean and sweet" without any hint
of impropriety.[94]

Steffens's article, which would go on to become the foundation for his monumental book, *The Shame of the Cities,* was followed by the equally path-breaking essay by Ida M. Tarbell, "The History of the Standard Oil Company." Tarbell's article, part of a serialized exposé commissioned by *Mc-Clure's,* described the activities of a mysterious company of oil producers known as the South Improvement Company, which had secured preferential rates on railroad freight shipments in Pennsylvania, threatening to force rival companies, who were forced to pay higher rates, out of business. In outlining these events, Tarbell wrote, "On every lip there was but one word, and that was conspiracy."[95] Investigators scrambling to uncover the workings of the company were shocked to learn that it was a national conglomerate that worked completely in secret in a variety of industries and territories to enrich a hidden cabal of stockholders. While undercutting competitors was problematic, Tarbell stressed that the company's conspiratorial dealings and secretive origins were even more alarming because they threatened the public's access to information and allowed a mysterious agency to operate with impunity. Tarbell said that the esoteric workings of the South Improvement Company posed a risk not merely to competing oil producers but to the American public at large, insisting, "It is responsible to no one, makes no reports of its acts or financial condition; its records and deliberations are secret; its capital illimitable; its objects unknown." She called the company's oligarchical rulers "landsmen granted perpetual letters of marquee."[96]

Although Tarbell asserted that the origins of the South Improvement Company "had always remained in darkness," investigators learned that Standard Oil owned a controlling stake in the company and, in many respects, the latter corporation was simply the inconspicuous arm of the former, granting Standard Oil license to "prey on all commerce everywhere" without fear of public attention. Ultimately, John D. Rockefeller's Standard Oil succeeded in securing preferential rates that sparked what Tarbell called "The Oil War," in which a large, secret corporation preyed upon smaller ones, destroying competitors and threatening America's welfare in the process.[97]

The final article in this trio was Ray Baker's "The Right to Work," which told the heartbreaking story of division and discord in a rural community during a coal mining strike. Baker paid particular attention to the non-striking workers, "examining firsthand the evidence of their difficulties and dangers, recording exactly the reasons they gave for continuing to work, securing corroboration and further light from all sources."[98] Baker outlined the vandalism, beatings, robbery, arson, and even murder inflicted on so-called scab workers, giving biographical sketches of these ostracized workers. Thus, although he often employed a detached rhetoric, describing "the many cases I investigated," Baker's article has a very human feel.[99]

"We Keep History Straight": Anti-Catholicism, Progressive Attitudes, and the Power of Information

Taken together, these essays illustrate several of the most poignant elements of progressive thought. McClure's discussion of the paramount importance of the public good and the press's role in preserving it, Steffens's exposure of urban political graft and corruption, Tarbell's discovery of conspiracy and secret power, and Baker's focus on investigation, evidence, and "light" present critical facets of the muckraking and progressive genre. But these same factors that served as the cornerstone in dozens of progressive texts were also the basis of countless articles written in the early twentieth century documenting the sinister and destructive power of the Catholic Church in America.

Watson's Magazine shared McClure's concern for safeguarding America's public good and denouncing those who put their own advancement above the nation's. Watson announced that the Catholic Church was engaged in a "modern crusade" against American principles that threatened all citizens. Mesmerized by Catholic pageantry and power, American leaders "obsequiously bow down" to clerical leaders who constitute "the Political and Ecclesiastical despotism known as the Roman Catholic Church." Arguing that Catholicism was "ruling and ruining" U.S. society by its insidious control of the political process and bought elections, *Watson's Magazine* warned, "This government, this Republic, is being delivered body and soul to Romanism by political demagogues for votes."[100] A similar theme ran through the pages of *The Mountain Advocate* under the title "Is Popery in Power in Washington?" The newspaper scolded readers for not recognizing Catholicism's impending danger, asserting that most Americans were too absorbed in luxury and commercialism to care about the threats facing the nation from the Catholic menace. Such indifference, writers warned, "is the result of selfishness—or self absorption. Men are so eager for money and for pleasure that they give no thought to the weal of the nation to which they profess allegiance." Citizens' shortsightedness was responsible for Catholic gains, which threatened the very life of America itself and struck at the very heart of the nation. The paper concluded, "The city of Washington—the capital of our nation—has a population which is but one-third Roman Catholic, but the Romanists rule the city just as effectively as if they were a great majority." Prosperity and self-interest were doubly dangerous because they made readers indifferent to or unaware of Catholic aggression—attitudes that anti-Catholic writers sought to correct by brushing the dust from "the lenses of our myopic friends."[101] Likewise, in language evoking classic republican rhetoric and echoing McClure's admonition, *The Peril* illustrated that readers had an obligation to embrace the American press, just as the press had a duty to safeguard America's institutions. The paper declared, "Let your Patriotism reach your hearts and down to your pocket books. . . . Reader, will you resolve NOW to cut out some luxury or luxuries, and thus enable yourself to do something practical to save your country from the peril that it is facing?"[102] Part call to arms, part sales ploy, the message of this article—that donations to the paper are a measure of patriotism and that as the subscription lists grow, so did American liberty—was frequently repeated in anti-Catholic sheets, joining the newspaper and the reader in a common battle to guarantee American freedoms.

Thus, like S. S. McClure, anti-Catholic writers focused readers' attention on the need to preserve the "public good" against the dangers of self-interest. Catholics were branded as foreigners unable to understand or appreciate American liberties, while anti-Catholic journalists were elevated to the level of moral champions. Not mere scribblers or paper pushers, newspapermen who warned of Catholic threats considered themselves, as *The Liberator* reported, "patriots who desire to preserve the state and the nation from the encroachments of the enemies of the Republic."[103] The heightened role of literature and the preservation of the public good were both in keeping with Progressive-Era values and hyperbole. *The Jeffersonian* lauded the American press and its architects, such as Joseph Pulitzer, as ensuring "faith in humanity" and "the right of every man to his fair share in the good things of the world." It noted that newspapers must serve as "the champion and advocate of the oppressed." Hinting at the justification for the success of anti-Catholic literature, the article concluded, "The paper must be loyal to the people, wise, full of information, and so attractive that the casual reader must become a constant reader."[104]

Laying the blame for manufactured ignorance on the shoulders of "those educated and wealthier men who have, and are using their brains and money as tools for the most un-American force in our country," *The Menace* viewed its growing circulation as the remedy for mainstream papers that served as mere Catholic mouthpieces. Calling manipulation of the press "a crime equal to if not greater than that of America's first traitor, Benedict Arnold," *Menace* writers held out hope that "if the American people only knew the truth (and they will some day) they would at once lift up such an outcry of indignation as would forever silence these priestly voices, and put their press agents out of business."[105]

Like Steffens, anti-Catholic journalists maintained that securing the public good depended on routing out political scandal and exposing governmental abuses. *The Crusader* looked with disgust at "Romanized" courts, where the Church's influence helped criminals and thugs get minor sentences for grievous crimes. A subsequent article outlined how the political bosses of Boston and New York had helped Catholics secure nearly all public works jobs in those cities, while keeping this information out of the public eye and bilking Protestant taxpayers of millions of dollars every year. When this tactic fails, the author continued, Catholics would adopt phony charity schemes, which claimed to assist orphans, the sick, or elderly but actually filled the Church treasuries instead. Like Minneapolis in Steffens's account, Boston was condemned for political favoritism, governmental waste, and a corrupt boss—in this case John Fitzgerald—who harbored scandal and injustice.[106] Similar articles pointed to Catholic domination of civil servant jobs in New Orleans, Chicago, and Washington, D.C.[107]

This point was reinforced in an article entitled "America's Danger," which warned that "America's danger is the Roman Catholic Church in politics, and there is evidence on every hand that she is in politics. Her widely heralded battle cry . . . We must make America Catholic! is indicative of her intentions. For years her fake charity schemes have been bleeding the Protestant American public to the tune of tens of millions of dollars. She is now firmly entrenched behind a Gibraltar of wealth and is reaching out for Governmental control, so as to make her conquest complete. . . . It is high time for Americans to awake."[108] Nativist critics frequently warned that Catholics' concentration of wealth, population, and influence in America's largest cities was not mere coincidence but a way of consolidating and maintaining political control over both local affairs and the nation as a whole. Under the heading "Catholics Control Large Cities," the *Silverton Journal* warned that only concerted effort and a greater circulation of the "facts" about America's Catholic foe (read: increased subscription rolls) could stem this tide. The article presented statistics to demonstrate the "astonishing majority" of Catholic residents in America's cities and concluded by telling "every one from New York to San Francisco, and from the Lakes to the Gulf, buckle on the sword of true patriotism and go forth to battle for their God, their home and their native land."

Even more startling than Catholics' own deception and cunning was the ignorance, if not complicity, of Protestants bowing to Catholic power. Denouncing the waste and corruption brought on by Catholic control of Chicago, *The Jeffersonian* printed a letter supposedly written by a well-connected "ex-Catholic" and member of the city's police force. In language reminiscent of Steffens's essay, the anonymous writer maintains, "With the police force and sanitary inspectors, Catholics . . . can ruin a Protestant or independent Catholic who dares to criticize or protest against their underhanded persecution, which is often the lowest or meanest kind." Along with controlling all city services the Catholic Church made the city treasury an endowment fund for its support everywhere. Objecting to Catholic influence in city affairs, the author admitted, was nearly impossible, however, as critics could be victims of Catholic boycott, targets of frivolous arrests by the predominantly Catholic police force, or even singled out for Catholic vigilante violence. Moreover, Catholics attempted to deflect such criticism by employing Protestant "good fellows" "who can be used as tools of the Jesuit system, as by keeping them in employment, the low Roman Catholic politicians who rule our cities can have some proof that there is no favoritism. So well is the hand of the Roman Catholic clergy concealed that not a particle of evidence could be produced against them."[109] Exposing Catholic urban graft is, therefore, more challenging and more critical, because it entails rooting out non-Catholic sympathizers. *The Silverton Journal* notes that Catholicism's "wise-as-a-serpent hierarchy has learned that it pays better in the long run to use non-Catholics whenever it can to do its dirty work, and therefore many of our so-called Protestant officers are nothing but Catholic tools."[110]

While eager to adopt the prevailing tone and tenor of urban social reform, anti-Catholic nativists were also careful to insist that their opponents were indifferent, if not hostile, to the goals of progressivism. Editors contrasted "true" Americans' thirst for political openness with Catholic deception, pointing out that prominent Catholic leaders opposed electoral reform, the direct election of senators, and other progressive innovations, such as the referendum and the initiative.[111] Anti-Catholic newspapers frequently argued that Catholics had corrupted legal proceedings and that secretive oaths sworn by Catholic laypeople and clergy would make them unable to carry out the demands of public office. *The Menace* bemoaned the candidacy of a Catholic sheriff, stating, "You could not easily prosecute a criminal priest or bishop in a court that had a Roman sheriff and judge. Besides, these priests who dominate county officers must obey the church first when church interests and county or state or individuals are in conflict with Roman interests."[112] By failing to embrace Progressive tenets, Catholics were a roadblock to genuine reform. Reading like a page out of Steffens's *The Shame of the Cities,* the temperance-minded *Woman's Witness* cast its spotlight on the small city of Terre Haute, Indiana—"a city of splendid possibilities" but one whose "future is clouded by the low level of public morals." Chief among Terre Haute's stumbling blocks was its domination by Catholic councilmen, described as no more than "gangsters" who insisted on keeping Terre Haute "wet" and embracing saloon owners. Under the influence of Catholic control, "vice and lawlessness have not only flowered but have gone to seed."[113]

Along with a desire to implement Steffens's call for urban reform and to present Catholicism itself as the "shame" of America's cities, anti-Catholic crusaders shared Baker's rhetoric of enlightenment and investigation. *The Silverton Journal* asked readers to "help us turn on the light" and in so doing preserve "civilization itself."[114] A similar passage noted "Catholicism always works in the dark, there is a mystery connected with all their work. Their institutions are not open for investigation by the public."[115] Fearing that nuns were being enslaved, raped, or murdered and that priests were rehearsing plans to dissolve the American nation, anti-Catholic writers demanded to investigate, by force if necessary, Catholic properties off-limits to the public—including convents, seminaries, churches, and schools. Demanding this level of "investigation" allowed anti-Catholic writers to root out alleged conspiracies. Readers could join in this important work by increasing subscription rates and warning others of Catholic atrocities. Doing this would, in the words of one writer, "open the windows, help us to turn on more light."[116]

Calling "political Rome" America's greatest peril, nativist writers filled the pages of anti-Catholic periodicals with investigations of election fraud, manipulation of juries, crooked police forces, inept public works departments, illegal saloons, brothels, or prostitution rings, and countless other instances of urban impropriety, all of which served as examples of Catholic licentiousness and power. Investigating these issues, *The Menace* concluded that Romanism's "methods may change, but her purpose, never. There is scarcely a city or hamlet of any importance where its misrule has not been painfully felt. . . . You will find this churchly influence wedging itself into every crevice."[117] Perhaps the most pervasive—and ironic—indictment of Catholic graft and deception was nativists' criticism of "sham" charities, allegedly providing philanthropic aid, comfort, and relief to America's cities but actually draining city funds and Protestant pockets while enriching wealthy priests. Praising "patriotic" communities who "refused to be blackmailed" by Catholic frauds, *The Menace* urged readers to rid cities of Catholic pseudo-progressivism. One telling cartoon depicts a street scene with an austere Catholic friar standing on a sidewalk beside a collection box labeled "sweet charity." Unsuspecting passersby notice the box and, moved by the man's apparent compassion, drop donations into it. Unknown to the donors, however, the "charity" box is actually a chute, funneling the money to a subterranean chamber below the city street, where it is collected in a huge barrel labeled "Political Corruption Fund." Presiding over the overflowing barrel are two bloated priests, grinning at Rome's ill-gotten gains.[118]

As historians have frequently demonstrated, this image of Catholics lurking in secret passages to prey on unsuspecting citizens and induce corruption was a prevalent trope throughout American nativism, and it proved to be exceptionally popular as Catholic charitable work increased in the early twentieth century.[119] Moreover, the illustration of Catholics hidden from the public eye and scheming to corrupt America from the inside out resonates with Tarbell's depiction of Progressive-Era conspiracy. Exposing what *The Silverton Journal* termed "Rome's Ripening Conspiracy," nativist papers declared that Catholicism served as a dangerous "trust" working to consolidate power in secret, just as other monopolies had done, but doing so under the guise of benevolence.[120] Just as Tarbell had blown the whistle on the conspiracy and secret deals of powerful oil companies, wary journalists claimed to see similar maneuvers in the American Catholic Church. *The Crusader* warned that Chicago's police force, nearly all of whom were Catholic, were stockpiling weapons to overthrow the United States and install a papal appointee as America's sovereign king. The article explained that the only reason why most Americans were unaware of this danger was that dissenters who refused to follow the Church's orders or who told others of the Church's secret mission in America were kidnapped or murdered. The time for intense bloodshed, *The Crusader* warned, was not far off.[121]

Not content to ruin America from the inside, Catholics were criticized at the end of the 1910s for plotting to assist America's enemies in World War I or orchestrating the conflict itself. One anti-Catholic writer observed that World War I's "causes are secret and hidden. . . . Its real causes run back into history and exist in the Secret Diplomacy and the plots and plans of Royal Ruffians who deem and Openly Assert that nations are their estates."[122] The root cause of the Great War, anti-Catholics often asserted, was the scheme of the Church to retain power and influence over a changing European society. Directing world activities in secret, the Church sought to control the press, universities, and even individual minds, to minimize resistance to its sinister plans. Blaring headlines that read "There Is a Modern Inquisition," *Watson's Magazine* insisted that the inquisition "is not an open, public one, but a secret, unrelenting, powerful, religious organization, jesuitically managed in the dark for the aggrandizement of the Roman Catholic Church."[123]

While rumors of Catholic insurrection and inquisition were prevalent in nativist publications prior to and during World War I, the most common and vocal criticism of Catholic conspiracy centered on the suppression of anti-Catholic periodicals themselves. The front page of *The Jeffersonian* asked "Is a Conspiracy Possible?" and outlined readers' complaints of missing issues from anti-Catholic newspapers. Watson condemned Catholic postal authorities, taking pains to "show how well planned the conspiracy must be to work so thoroughly" to suppress nativist voices, and pledged to "keep my publications going as long as there is breath in my body."[124] Warning subscribers to "Watch your Catholic Postmasters," nativist sheets accused their enemies of stealing and destroying anti-Catholic texts, to "exclude critics" and avoid the publicity of Catholic wrongs.[125] *The Menace* issued a front-page article to report on a single subscriber who had requested a copy of the press's book *Romanism: The Deadliest Menace to Our Civilization* but whose order never arrived, suggesting Catholic foul play.[126] Asking "Is the American Press to Be Muzzled?" *The Crusader* lambasted

Catholicism's control of the secular press and interference in the work of "patriotic" anti-Catholic publishers. Concluding that "the person who wishes to have papers suppressed evidently has something to hide," nativist journalists urged subscribers to "let the light shine" and "write your letters now" to support federal investigation of Romanist mail snatchers.[127] Anti-Catholic writers also reasoned that, when their opponents' overt tactics failed, Catholics and their supporters would attempt to impose legislation banning nativist papers from the mails, threaten boycotts of advertisers in "anti-Romanist" texts, even buy up copies of anti-Catholic documents to prevent their circulation—each tactic providing, as *The Yellow Jacket* maintained, "another stab at free speech."[128]

From a contemporary standpoint, this attention seems to have primarily self-serving aims. Why would anti-Catholic papers, particularly *The Menace*, with almost two million readers, dedicate so much press to one customer's single missed issue, particularly when doing so relegated stories that seem far more serious to the paper's margins and back pages? Shouldn't far more glaring examples of Catholic abuse, such as the abduction of young girls to serve as priest's concubines, plots to overthrow America and murder its leaders, or accounts of multimillion-dollar embezzlement claims get center stage?

For most anti-Catholic writers, the answer was generally no. Reports of intentionally damaged or misplaced newspapers or Catholic efforts to stop nativist propaganda were seen as the most vital issues writers could print. In part, this is because it preserved the paper itself, allowing it to continue its anti-Catholic crusade. Moreover, alerting readers to Catholic conspiracies aimed at purging the mail of nativist sheets ensured Americans' First Amendment rights to a free press, while further demonstrating the duplicity of their opponents. Above all, the efforts of anti-Catholic publishers to preserve a wide circulation demonstrated their commitment to the Progressive Era's faith in the fundamental and transformative power of information itself. Dedicating a great deal, if not the majority, of their columns to reporting their own papers' obstacles and achievements might seem like journalistic narcissism, but as William Thorn and Mary Pfiel point out, this self-referential approach was a common attribute throughout the turn-of-the century American press. Anti-Catholic and mainstream periodicals alike used headlines to broadcast circulation milestones, held rallies to boost subscriptions, and distributed prizes and trinkets to solicit sales, leading to what Thorn and Pfiel term the "circulation wars," as large publishing enterprises competed with themselves to gobble up smaller presses. But progressive journalism's obsession with promulgating facts, information, and "enlightenment" amounted to more than shrewd business practices. It signaled an ideological mind-set that saw disseminating information not simply as the prelude for political activism but as an end in its own right.[129]

Moreover, for anti-Catholic authors in the Progressive Era, reading and writing nativist texts were of paramount importance because the journalistic arena, even more than political debates or electoral politics, was the setting where conflicts with Catholic foes would be won or lost. *The Silverton Journal* made this point explicitly, calling journalism America's "Modern War." The paper contended:

> Animal man fought with clubs and spears, with bows and arrows, and finally with guns and swords. Modern warfare is on a higher plane, and soon the old idea of killing men to settle questions will entirely give way to killing false ideas and false systems. The modern warrior, or a true knight of the twentieth century, is the one who, with his bundle of propaganda, blows into atoms the false ideas that have enslaved his fellows. . . . Oh yes; we know the Catholic church is powerful. . . . But threats and boycotts, fines and imprisonment can not conquer us—can not stop our glad new song of liberty of thought nor our onward march to the promised land. Charge![130]

Nativist writers argued "We Keep History Straight" and publicized Romanist attempts to suppress or distort information, such as Catholic plots to infiltrate the government printing office and manipulate the Congressional record, or doctor court testimonies and legal records.[131] *The Menace* argued that Catholics not only attacked public schools but secretly worked with library boards, educators, publishers, and journalists to distort textbooks, encyclopedias, and periodicals, presenting Catholics in a highly favorable light. These Catholic actions showed "How the Light of History is darkened and the sources of knowledge are poisoned," proving that Romanists stood as "enemies of truth and enlightenment" who "poisoned the wells of knowledge and put lies for truth and falsity for fact." The article concluded by asking "what the friends of truth and history have been doing while the Jesuits have been blowing out the lights of history?"[132]

The hyperbolic insistences on "light," "fact," and "truth" were in keeping with prevailing progressive attitudes toward the nearly sacred status afforded to information and publicity. In the introduction to his study on Progressive-Era "social centers," which sought to open public schools as centers for adult learning and debate, Kevin Mattson highlights the importance progressives placed on informing "the public." Noting that muckraking writers "exposed the exploitative excesses" in American society, "encouraging an educated 'public' to correct the injustices of industrial capitalism," Mattson states flatly, "If people were allowed to know about corruption, these journalists believed, they would do something about it."[133] Glenda Gilmore points out that one of the few characteristics shared by Progressive reformers was the notion that "The main cure for society's ills . . . consisted of exposure to the light and air of public opinion."[134] This progressive reliance on information and the anti-Catholic incorporation of these notions to thwart Romanism might seem obvious and pedestrian. But the thirst for information and the open disclosures of Catholic aggression stand in contrast to many, though not all, anti-Catholic nativist campaigns prior or since (such as the antebellum burning of convents, the Philadelphia Bible Riots, and the influence of the second Ku Klux Klan), which relied on vigilantism, secret societies, and violence to uproot alleged Catholic conspiracy.

The Discovery that Catholicism Corrupts Politics

Early in this chapter, I posed the question of how two million anti-Catholic periodicals found their way onto Americans' doorsteps every week during the mid 1910s. Based on an examination of anti-Catholic sources themselves, several answers emerge. Nativist texts drew on advances in print technology and marketing strategy, they shared information and articles with one another, and they worked to actively cross-promote one another. But the most significant factor leading to anti-Catholicism's success in the literary marketplace of Progressive-Era America seems to be its ability both to build on traditional anti-Romanist tropes and imagery (which had already proven wildly successful and marketable in the nineteenth century) and to coalesce several prominent trends that dominated Progressive-Era culture. The absence of correspondence and business

records makes the task of deducing who anti-Catholics were, or what motivated their mission, a difficult one. But one thing seems abundantly clear:
early twentieth-century nativists were, first and foremost, remarkable syn-
thesists. Their success stemmed from their ability to weave together several themes that, while divergent, were profoundly salient to Progressive-
Era audiences.

As I've shown earlier, the groundswell of patriotism and public memory
coincided with nativists' treatment of appropriate and disingenuous uses
of the past and their frequent use of Americanist rhetoric and diligence
in denouncing Catholics' claims of national belonging. Furthermore, as
I will show in the next chapter, nativists spoke to the shifting gender concerns of the 1910s, using novel understandings of masculinity to generate
support for its movement. Likewise, nativists relied on the rhetorical style
and significant themes commonplace among classics of Progressive-Era
literature. They addressed growing concerns for the influence of modernity and were ambivalent about its effects on once autonomous rural communities. Moreover, opting into the language and concerns of progressivism allowed anti-Catholic writers to update the conventional iconography
of previous decades, packaging it in a form that would prove comprehen-
sible and immensely popular to subsequent readers.

Embracing the rhetoric, language, methods, and ideology that motivated scores of other Progressive-Era writers, anti-Catholic journalists can
best understood as embodying the attitudes, techniques, strengths, and
limitations historians routinely attribute to their contemporaneous muckrakers. *The Woman's Witness,* for instance, outlined its plan to undo urban
corruption by relying on the spread of information to rectify unjust situ-
ations, proposing "to let the sunlight of publicity in upon the operations of
this invisible government. I propose to print in plain, cold unimpassioned
type the real facts. I propose to let the light of day into the caucus . . . and
to sweep the veil of mystery from around these men."[135] As Richard McCormick has demonstrated, however, overriding faith in the power of information and publicity, shared by anti-Catholic and mainstream progressives alike, may also amount to a significant liability and limit long-term
political accomplishment.

In his classic essay "The Discovery that Business Corrupts Politics,"
McCormick argues that, in the first decade of the twentieth century, "a
remarkable number of cities and states experienced wrenching moments
of discovery that led directly to significant political changes. Usually, a

scandal, in investigation . . . exposed an illicit alliance of politics and business and made corruption apparent to the community."[136] The ultimate result of "the discovery that business corrupts politics" was the establishment and spread of industrial review boards, staffed by supposedly impartial experts installed to drive out corporate graft, who actually minimized and precluded more radical change while making only token gestures toward reform. McCormick suggests that constant searching and publicizing of "facts" and information impeded and distracted true Progressive reform and political engagement. Muckraking accounts, though "full of facts and revelations," were "also dangerously devoid of effective solutions."[137]

If, as McClure contends, the essential recipe for muckraking was the attempted exposure or awakening of a community to the indifference (or, more often, collusion) by governmental officials in an organization's efforts to subvert the public good for its own ends, then the anti-Catholic press was one of the most vocal and determined muckraking voices of the early twentieth century. While McCormick stresses Progressive-Era muckrakers' abhorrence of unjust business practices and influences, his argument holds for what nativists perceived as Catholicism's unlawful corporate and organizational structure, which bribed politicians, controlled the press, and hampered the public's right to information. Despite their eloquence, authors offered little in the way of practical solutions or strategies to overcome the Catholic foe. With the exception of occasional calls for legislation to authorize convent inspections, the only solution put forth by the nativist press to defeating Romanism was increasing the circulation of the newspapers themselves, making anti-Catholic publications seem more like modern-day computer viruses, predicated on the rapid spread of information, and less like concerted political platforms of decisive strategies.

Yet nativist papers were more than minor annoyances, and like other progressive actors, anti-Catholic publishers saw the spread of information as a political act in itself. Whereas other facets of American anti-Catholicism sought to oust Catholics from political office, impose strict immigration restriction, blacklist Catholics from employment, drive Catholics from positions in teaching and education, and even form vigilante mobs to repulse Catholicism's alleged threat, these formed, at most, peripheral concerns for Progressive-Era anti-Catholic writers. Instead, their fundamental goal was to spread information about Catholicism's wrongdoing and alert America's citizens to do the same. Reading and passing on anti-Catholic information became, in the minds of nativist writers, a necessary

and sufficient condition for genuine patriotism. Hoping that "the campaign of education will be carried on and the light flooded on the evil ambitions of the Hierarchy against our priceless liberties," anti-Catholic writers elevated nativist rhetoric to the level of patriotic devotion.[138]

Calling nativist periodicals "The Light from the Old North Church" and
asking readers to "Be a Paul Revere. Waken the neighbors. Call out the
minute men," *The Menace* linked Progressive-Era thirst for information
with Revolutionary ideology and patriotism.[139] This quotation is significant because it addresses several overlapping themes embedded in anti-
Catholic nativism of the 1910s. Its use of militaristic and historic imagery
is consistent with the dominant tropes of anti-Catholic journalism, and
its patriotic tone links reform and "light" with the struggles of America's
heroic past. Moreover, the work of "the minute men" in waking the neighbors and galvanizing the community to action against impending doom
suggests the centrality of local communities and ordinary citizens in the
anti-Catholic crusade. Generating support for traditional values and Americanism, anti-Catholic texts and their publishers sought to shield small-
town ways of life and the rural communities that preserved them from the
dual threats of modernity and Romanism. To "waken the neighbors" and
brighten "the Light from the Old North Church," nativists embraced the
dominant motifs and themes of Progressive-Era culture, further inflating
the efforts and social prestige of anti-Catholic writers and editors. Confident that anti-Catholic journalism was a political enterprise, nativist
writers had a moral task as well: safeguarding their vulnerable communities against Catholic forces bent on their destruction. Protecting the vulnerable members of society from Catholic depravity formed the basis of
masculine gender expectations and became a cornerstone of nativist literature during the 1910s, themes I will address in the next chapter.

CHAPTER THREE

"Rome Is the Jailer of Youth"

MASCULINITY, CHILDHOOD, AND
THE ANTI-CATHOLIC CRUSADE

When readers of *The Menace* walked to their doorsteps on April 15, 1914, they were greeted with an ominous message. The paper's front-page headline for that day read, "Girls Hunted by Slave Catchers," and the subsequent article described how two teenage girls had been held captive in a Santa Barbara convent and managed to escape. *The Menace* detailed the thrilling four-day chase that ensued between the girls and police, which ended when the "prisoners" collapsed from exhaustion and could be "recaptured." The article condemned the "torture and suffering inflicted upon innocent girlhood in these hell holes of iniquity" and called upon readers to defend childhood innocence from Catholic aggression. The article concluded by insisting on the dangers of convent captivity and warned readers not to let "the fairest maidens of the land [be] fed to the beast of lust that has the manhood of the American nation cringing at its feet in the dust. Would to God that we even had a hundred REAL men on American soil today!"[1]

Despite its shocking content and inflammatory tone toward Catholic adversaries and loyal readers alike, the article illustrates an extremely common theme that permeated the pages of anti-Catholic periodicals from their rise to prominence in the early 1910s to their rapid disintegration by 1920. *The Menace* and like-minded newspapers evoked various images of victimized childhood to elicit sympathy and support for their anti-Catholic crusade. By insisting that their Catholic opponents targeted weak members of Protestant communities—the sick, the elderly, women, and, especially, children—*Menace* writers could both demonize their opponents and send a rallying cry to Protestant men. This strategy of safeguarding children from a "Romanist peril" depended on a specific construction of childhood among anti-Catholic writers, one that saw children (or at least Protestant children) as inherently innocent and weak and defense of this innocence as a vital ingredient in both the nativist crusade and American masculinity itself. The message from this article and scores of others is that good Protestant children needed and deserved special protection from Catholic foes and it was the job of the anti-Catholic press to make sure that men granted this protection.

The goal of this chapter is to expand and elaborate upon this point by situating anti-Catholic periodicals within two overlapping contexts—literature on masculinity and gender norms during the Progressive Era and the small but growing research among historians and sociologists on childhood as an analytic category. Taken together, these perspectives illustrate a fundamental dimension of anti-Catholic literature. Just as writers used patriotic icons of American nationalism and the themes of Progressive-Era muckraking to elicit support for their anti-Catholic movement, they also tapped into the decade's emerging understanding of childhood vulnerability and masculine expectations.

As I outlined in chapter 2, while Progressive-Era anti-Catholicism exhibited some significant differences from earlier nativist forerunners, early twentieth-century architects of anti-Romanism's journalistic crusades clearly saw themselves as carrying on a tradition of defending American institutions against the corrosive effects of Catholic treachery. Anti-Catholic periodicals dedicated dozens of articles to substantiating and praising earlier anti-Catholic crusades, such as the Maria Monk affair or the American Protective Association.[2] Telling readers "APA-ism is not dead," for instance, *The Menace* lauded the work of its late nineteenth-century anti-Catholic antecedents and pledged to continue their inspired anti-papal legacy.[3] Often, however, the papers' connections with earlier examples of anti-Catholic activity were more subtle. In particular, anti-Catholic writers were careful to present their periodicals as exerting a particular form of masculinity—one that sought to protect the weak and vulnerable. In so doing, they built upon the long-standing rhetoric in American anti-Catholic literature that presented Catholic aggressors as preying upon individuals who were too weak or too naïve to defend themselves. Moreover, while this trope of manhood's defense of vulnerability capitalized on established anti-Catholic traditions, it was also particularly salient to Progressive-Era readers. Through their emphasis on masculine duty and valor, anti-Catholic papers echoed powerful cultural shifts within many facets of American society in the early twentieth century. Scholars have pointed out that the 1910s witnessed a dramatic masculinization of Protestant churches and an increased male attention to the duties of fatherhood. Furthermore, nativist writers co-opted the dominant language of rugged masculinity, "muscular" Christianity, and militarism, infusing their papers with accounts of vigilant "armies" whose strength would safeguard the weak and drive out the corrosive agents of Romanism. These "armies," in turn, depended on an understanding of masculinity in which women and children were archetypal victims, dependent for their survival on the actions of heroic men. In what follows, I demonstrate how anti-Catholic writers incorporated manhood's "defense of the weak" and positioned themselves within both a formidable nativist tradition and a timely cultural outlet in the early twentieth century.

PROTECTING INSTITUTIONS AND INDIVIDUALS

As historian Maureen McCarthy has pointed out, this perception of manhood's need to defend the weak and vulnerable sparked some of the most intense outbursts of anti-Catholicism in the antebellum era. In assessing the burning of the Ursuline convent in Charleston, Massachusetts, and the proliferation of "escaped nun" narratives in the early nineteenth century, McCarthy writes, "the themes of male rescue, female victimization, and Catholic 'Otherness' emerged again and again."[4] McCarthy demonstrates that in the turbulent antebellum era, protecting femininity from a common Catholic foe served to unify disparate groups of Protestant men. Thus opponents of Catholicism cast their anti-Romanist crusade "in explicitly gendered terms, as the male rescuer of defenseless womanhood."[5] McCarthy illustrates that throughout the nineteenth century, convents were seen as a conspicuous symbol of Catholics' difference from and presence within Protestant society. These institutions were considered suspect primarily because they instructed Protestant girls and young women. McCarthy demonstrates that most antebellum aggression toward Catholics stems from "a single narrative: an innocent woman was or had been subject to abuse within a convent, and needed the protection of Protestant men."[6]

This rhetoric of masculine defensiveness extended into the late nineteenth and early twentieth centuries, particularly through the activities of the American Protective Association (APA). The APA was formed in 1887 over a disputed mayoral election in the small town of Clifton, Iowa. Believing that a coalition of Roman Catholics had ruined his chances for election, the APA's founder, Henry Bowers, began an organization dedicated to removing Catholics from political power and denouncing Catholic institutions, particularly parochial schools. The APA coalesced with other nativist and nationalistic organizations in the early 1890s, and by 1893, the APA was a full-fledged national movement. APA members proved highly influential in state and local elections in 1894, although concerns of whether to support Republican candidates or run their own independent presidential campaign split the movement in 1896, after which the APA gradually faded out of existence.[7] Much like antebellum manifestations of anti-Catholicism, APA leaders saw their movement as protecting innocence in general and girlhood and womanhood in particular. One of the APA's typical targets was the Houses of the Good Shepherd, Catholic homes for girls and women convicted of crimes or left as public wards. In his study of the APA, Donald Kinzer points out that Houses of the Good Shepherd "were charged with being unfit places for the innocent, and lurid stories were repeated of priests taking advantage of the female inmates to satisfy their allegedly unlimited carnal appetites."[8] The APA's numerous newspapers and pamphlets, which proliferated in the early 1890s, presented themselves as "watchdogs," warning of Catholic cruelties, a pattern that was extended by the anti-Catholic press in subsequent decades.[9]

Other authors in the late nineteenth and early twentieth centuries evoked this same rhetoric, calling on Protestants to stand up to Catholic assaults upon innocence. An 1894 poem titled "A Woman's Plea for Her Country" asks Protestants, "Would you have the dear Bible thrown out of the schools?" and goes on to accuse Romanists of squandering public funds given by poor Protestant parents. The author asks if hard-working Protestants will allow papists "to build a grand church in the finest location / While your own little ones suffer and die of starvation." The poet goes on to indict "sleeping" Protestants, criticizing them for letting their children "go without shoes to their feet, / To keep out of the hard winter's cold and its sleet, / With nothing but rags to cover their bed, / While they shiver with cold and wish they were dead."[10] Similarly, anti-Catholic lecturer Margaret Shepherd denounced Catholic priestcraft, announcing that in the Catholic confessional, "motherhood, wifehood, womanhood are degraded. The priest stands between parent and child."[11] Another dimension of anti-Catholic sentiment was expressed in the poem "Raise a Flag O'er Every Schoolhouse," distributed in pamphlet form in 1915. The poem begins: "Raise a flag o'er ever school house / Beloved banner of the free, / Tell the children of its triumphs / On the land and on the sea." The poet continues, "Let all other nations see / Tho many have fallen neath Roman rule / We will maintain our liberty."[12]

It is important to note that, while each of these authors targets a particular dimension of Catholicism (such as political graft, the parochial school, or the confessional), each chose to articulate its message by demonstrating Catholicism's harmful effects on children. In so doing, they evoke an image of endangered innocence—one that demonizes Catholic aggressors and urges action on the part of Protestants. This depiction of the child threatened by Catholic evil, whether exploited by papist politics or captured in nunnery prisons, forms a powerful trope in the ongoing discourse of anti-Catholic literature. In fact, McCarthy's account suggests that the trope of the threatened child was so powerful in nineteenth-century anti-Catholicism that reports of Catholic aggression against adults were deliberately altered and represented as cruelties to children. McCarthy demonstrates that the event that triggered the burning of Charleston's Ursuline convent in 1834 was the report that a "young girl" named Elizabeth Harrison had been seduced into a convent and was being held (and possibly tortured) by nuns. Boston's papers repeated the story, charging that Catholics were targeting young Protestant girls for their convents. McCarthy insists, however, that "far from a 'young lady' [Harrison] was a woman in her thirties. She was not a young woman unable to make decisions for herself. Instead she was an adult who had lived within a convent for thirteen years."[13] The fact that this rhetoric of defending children's innocence pervaded nearly a century of American anti-Catholicism suggests that *The Menace*'s later condemnation of Catholic attacks on childhood found fertile soil among anti-Catholic readers in subsequent decades.

The notion of "defending" America and its citizens was a perennial theme running throughout nativist periodicals. This frequently meant exposing grandiose Catholic schemes to subvert American politics—such as

rigging elections, suppressing the mail, or siding with the Central Powers
during World War I. One such article warned readers of an impending
Catholic coup, saying, "Image the Pope of Rome Marching behind the
Stars and Stripes and to the tune of the Battle Hymn of the Republic!"[14]
Catholics were accused of spying for the Kaiser during Word War I, stockpiling weapons for a military attack, and even condemning the national
anthem.[15] Moreover, nativists condemned Catholic opponents for subvert-
ing America's most essential institutions by breaking up Protestant families
and undermining the public school system. Nativist writers commonly argued that Catholic convents enticed daughters to leave their families, neglecting their parents in old age. Newspapers also condemned juvenile
authorities and courts for separating children from their parents by placing minors in state institutions or, worse, Catholic convents, a point I will
return to later in this chapter.

Like earlier anti-Catholic organizations, anti-Catholic writers in the Progressive Era were also deeply critical of the parochial school system, insisting that Catholic schools undermined public education, the foundation of the nation's character and development. *The Yellow Jacket* called the
"Little Red Schoolhouse" the nation's "Cradle of American Patriotism"
and "The Safeguard of American Liberty," denouncing Catholics for threatening it. In praising public schools, the article concluded, "The 'Little Red
School House' has been again and again assaulted, maligned, and slandered . . . [yet] like the virtue of a pure woman is still spotless."[16] One of
nativists' most common complaints was that Catholics were unjustly influencing local school boards and using tax dollars to fund parochial education. Catholics were depicted as unpatriotic and subversive, cowardly
attacking "the bulwark of American citizenship" through corrupt politics.[17]
Another particularly vehement article used the language of World War I
militarism to condemn Catholicism's attacks on public education, saying,
"Our schools will not be protected by licking the boots of the entrenched
autocrats who are bombarding them with gas shells. . . . These schools
must be manned by crews that will not steer them into the danger of Vatican submarines."[18] Citing Catholic hypocrisy, *Watson's Magazine* remarked,
"Look how the Catholics refuse to send their children to our public schools,
and yet have the audacity to ask the government to support their parochial
schools, which are simply training camps for Popish perversion of the
coming generation."[19]

The article went on to illustrate an even more sinister motive for Catholic education—the indoctrination of Protestant children by duplicitous Catholic teachers. Warning that Catholic control of school boards meant the brainwashing of innocent children, *Watson's Magazine* continued, "If you want to strike at the very heart of a nation, then corrupt her youth. The Jesuit boasts, 'Give me a child until he is ten years of age, and the world may have him afterward. For, in that time, I will have planted the seeds of Roman Catholicism so deep in his soul, that it will be almost impossible to change him.' "[20] Thus perhaps the greatest danger in the minds of anti-Catholic writers was that Catholic teachers would instruct young Protestant students, thereby eroding young minds and placing Protestant children in harm's way. One such writer warned, "our schools are being Romanized just as fast as . . . terrorist tactics can be brought to bear on Protestant fathers and mothers."[21] Another article described a school system "cursed with the misfortune of having Catholic lay teachers in a surprisingly great number . . . teachers who were deliberately placed there for the purpose of giving Catholic sectarian instruction to the pupils."[22] By exposing the Catholic hierarchy's attack on American institutions, the nativist press hoped to "expose" Catholicism as unpatriotic and a suspect element of the American social landscape.

While intent on preserving American institutions, more often anti-Catholic journals saw their mission as protecting weak or naïve individuals from Catholic trickery aimed at defrauding or even destroying those who could not protect themselves. Much like the architects of the Ursuline convent riot or the Maria Monk affair, nativist journalists presented depictions of victimized women to illustrate for readers the enormity of papist cruelty. Catholic priests, these papers argued, continually degraded women both in overt ways, such as physical or sexual abuse, or through more subversive means, such as denying women political suffrage or equality. An article describing Romanist assaults on femininity insisted, "Nothing has been more trampled on, despised and maltreated by the Catholic Priest than women."[23] *Watson's Magazine* expanded on this point, noting that within the Catholic Church, "the idea of the inferiority of women and their unfitness for rule is naturally carried over from Church to State. Women should not, in their view, have more or very different privileges from what they now have,—especially nothing that would make them equal to men in power. Like laymen, they are to be ruled."[24] *The Peril* noted with disgust

the formation of the Daughters of Isabella, a Catholic women's organization similar to the Knights of Columbus. Citing Catholic duplicity, the article remarked on how Catholics initially opposed women's suffrage but,
when it seemed immanent, urged the Daughters of Isabella to muster at
the polls in support of Catholic candidates. The author continued, "The
principal function of the Roman Catholic Church is that of a political machine. Although it has been opposed to giving the vote to women, it now
follows its usual tactics, bows to the inevitable, and turns an apparent dis-
advantage into gain."[25] *The Liberator* likewise pointed out that Catholic
oppressors denied women both economic and political rights, and *The
Women's Witness* vowed to fight demeanors with "the burning scorn of the
awakened womenhood of the country."[26]

Along with political marginalization, nativists accused their Catholic
foes of targeting women with blatant violence, rape, and assault. A particularly graphic article details how a young nun was bound, gagged, whipped,
beaten, and repeatedly raped by a group of drunken priests. While raping
women outright is bad enough, priests were also accused of keeping young
women as "housekeepers," who actually served as mere concubines for
priestly lust.[27] This proved an especially common theme in anti-Catholic
writing. *The Peril,* for instance, echoed the classic Maria Monk narratives
in outlining how naïve nuns were "forced into prostitution," bearing ille-
gitimate children to sex-crazed priests.[28]

Nativists were quick to contrast Romanists' antipathy for women with
their own veneration of femininity. Anti-Catholic periodicals promoted
women's suffrage, hosted "women only" meetings, and, in one case, organized "women's auxiliaries" of their dedicated readers. By the end of
the 1910s, a portion of the nativist message was dedicated to informing
women of the dangers Catholicism presented to American femininity, urging women to seek a greater voice in politics and describing how to use
political activism to foil papist plots. Women readers, much like their male
counterparts, were often presented as "sleeping"—ignorant to Rome's
attacks on their physical bodies and political rights. One such article, entitled "Women and Priestcraft," contrasted women's treatment in Catholicism, where they "are sainted and worshipped *after they are dead,*" with Protestantism, which treats women with dignity and respect. Since the Catholic
Church regards women as "something less than human," women need to
be awakened to Catholic aggression—"Wake up, women and come out of
it!"[29] Likewise, a *Menace* writer asked women, "Are we going to let a foreign

country come in and take control of America?" and went on to insist that unless women "wake up and help the few men who are working this is what Rome will do."[30]

While nativists did form auxiliaries of women readers, women's participation in the anti-Catholic crusade was intended to be wholly secondary. The rhetoric, militant imagery, and repeated calls for a more vocal, vigilant, and galvanized American manhood far overshadowed the establishment of a "women's auxiliary." As I demonstrate later in this chapter, anti-Romanism tapped into pervasive cultural currents within turn-of-the century Protestantism that sought to instill masculine participation and rhetoric into American religion and society. Basing their movement on manhood's responsibility to defend victimized women and children, anti-Catholic leaders paid virtually no attention to their women readers until the movement began to decline after 1916. Tellingly, only *The Menace,* which survived into the late 1910s, called upon women readers, and it did so later, as the decade came to an end. Their late attention to women customers suggests that women were a mere afterthought, an attempt to revive a flagging circulation base when anti-Catholics' primary audience, Protestant men, had turned a deaf ear to the nativist message. Moreover, the rapid disintegration of anti-Catholic journalism by the dawn of the 1920s indicates that this half-hearted effort to court new readership failed by a wide margin.[31]

This is not to say that women were absent from the pages of nativist journalism. In fact, anti-Catholic writers frequently showcased the experiences of women who escaped Catholic imprisonment in convents and lived to tell the tale—insisting that, having seen the horrors of convent life, "escaped nuns" could reveal the truth about Catholic conspiracies.[32] Thus, women's treatment in the anti-Catholic press was paradoxical. On the one hand, their stories and firsthand accounts of convent life were invested with power (or at least potential power) capable of ridding America of corruption and evil; on the other hand, women were primarily depicted as the innocent victims of priestly abuse. Women assumed a largely iconographic status in the pages of anti-Catholic newspapers and existed not as agents of change in their own right but as a way of illustrating the need for manly defenders against the insidious papists. As Mary Ryan and other scholars have shown, the introduction of women icons serves important symbolic and political functions within a text, even as women themselves are prevented from directly participating or having any political agency.

Likewise, although relegated to secondary status within the nativist cru-sade, women served a symbolic role to galvanize male outrage.[33]

While highly concerned about abuses of feminine innocence, anti-Catholic papers also took pains to point out Catholic assaults on other weak or defenseless individuals. The sick and insane, for instance, often relied on Catholic hospitals for care and medical treatment. Nativist jour-nalists argued that while this might initially seem to be an illustration of Catholic morality, philanthropy, and compassion, these hospitals were ac-tually fronts for Catholic graft and deception. In fact, papers repeatedly in-sisted that Catholic charity was actually a sham—a way of providing care for Catholic patients that victimized sick Protestants and exploited non-Catholic taxpayers. One *Menace* writer reported, "It is too often the case that real charity cases, those who are in need of attention and care, are turned away from Rome's hospitals on one pretext or another and charity becomes a farce, a mockery, and a snare."[34] Another article recounted the story of a Cleveland man who, as a young boy, was struck by a streetcar and taken to a Catholic hospital. Once administrators found out that the boy was Methodist, they virtually ignored him, letting him suffer great pain. He was eventually treated by two "quack" doctors, "both half drunk," who insisted upon amputating his leg, although the procedure was com-pletely unnecessary. Although he "escaped" to a better institution and sub-sequently recovered, he recalled, later in life, "No care was given me by the hospital and the bones had slipped past and were not knitting at all. . . . Had I remained there I would have been a cripple for life."[35]

Nativist periodicals were intent on exposing these stories of Catholic atrocities on the sick and infirm but gave their accounts a political spin as well. Papers routinely pushed for "inspection" legislation that would allow civil authorities the right to investigate reports of graft and abuse in Catholic charitable institutions. A *Menace* article investigating Catholic hos-pitals reported, "The institutions are not open for inspection by the au-thorities of the law, and when patients are starved, frozen, or otherwise put to death by neglect, if not premeditatedly, friends or relatives of the de-ceased have no recourse."[36] Such legislation would allow loyal *Menace* read-ers both to demand fair treatment for Protestant patients and to check Rome's financial and political control over state and local governments.

This pattern of exposing graft and ensuring protection of the weak was also evident in the paper's treatment of the elderly. *The Menace* reported that, like hospital patients, residents of Catholic "Old Folks Homes" were subjected to abuse, deception, and even violent torture. While it might *seem* genuine, Catholic care for the elderly is another sham, a way to "take advantage of the weakness caused by disease or the condition of a dying man, to whisper Catholic propaganda into his ears for the purpose of securing a convert or a bequest in a deathbed will."[37] Other papers likewise chastised Romanists for brainwashing the sick for Catholic financial gain. *The Silverton Journal* reported a story of Mrs. Kate Ruddan, an affluent widow, who was visited by a priest who insisted on serving as her "spiritual advisor." The article asserts that "while acting as her spiritual advisor [Father Cooperman] drew up a will himself and caused her to sign it while she was on her deathbed. . . . Her spiritual advisor had complete dominion over her and . . . none of her kin was present."[38] *Watson's Magazine* echoed this warning, insisting that Jesuits received instruction from leaders of their order to seek out and befriend wealthy widows, preventing them from coming into contact with suitors so that they would remain unmarried and donate or will their property to the Jesuit Order. *The Jeffersonian* took this investigation a step further, illustrating how Catholic priests used the deathbed conversion of a woman with tuberculosis not only to steal her money but to railroad her four children into a Catholic orphanage, where they toiled as slaves.[39] As it was for its abuse of women and the sick, the Catholic Church was often indicted for attacking those least able to defend themselves, the frail and elderly. One infuriated *Menace* writer reported the story of a seventy-one-year-old woman who was taken to a Catholic "Home." There the Catholic staff members had "beaten [her] with sticks and straps," leaving "horrible marks on her body." A doctor later confirmed "she will never leave that bed alive," and the writer concluded, "Charity, love, religion! Such holy names should not be blasphemed by use in connection with such a hellish place."[40]

In large measure, nativists' critique of Catholic charity stems from Catholicism's own increased visibility and public presence in charitable and philanthropic efforts. As the anti-Catholic journalistic movement was gaining speed, American Catholics themselves had begun to embrace the Progressive-Era emphasis of reform and public outreach. Just as the 1910s witnessed an outpouring of nationalistic sentiment, so too this decade saw a tremendous intensification, organization, and mobilization of Catholic resources and influence. This was particularly apparent in the growth of Catholic churches and schools from the late nineteenth and throughout the twentieth centuries, leading to the American church's burgeoning infrastructure. Equally important, however, was the growth of Catholic charitable and philanthropic work in the years leading up to World War I. American Catholics founded more than 325 hospitals from the end of the nineteenth century to the 1910s, with the most vigorous rate of growth occurring in the later decade. During the 1910s, Catholic charitable organizations operated more than 285 orphanages, dozens of homes for the "aged poor," charitable homes for unwed mothers, and "Houses of the Good Shepherd" for the care of delinquent women and wards of the state. Catholics even emulated the work of Protestant reformers, developing "Settlement Houses" for newer Catholic immigrants; by 1915 over three dozen Catholic "settlement houses" were in operation in America's largest cities.[41]

Prior to the twentieth century, the institutional Church was standoffish, if not altogether hostile, to prominent reform efforts, judging (often rightly) that many philanthropic organizations were driven by "Social Gospel" evangelists, seeking to Protestantize and monitor their Catholic neighbors.[42] Joseph McShane has noted that Catholic clerical leaders entertained only "timid and ineffective" programs of reform in the nineteenth century, despite the dire straits of many of their working-class parishioners. Leaders feared more direct participation in worker relief, philanthropic organization, or advocating social policy would raise the ire of nativist writers and politicians, even though Pope Leo XIII's notable 1891 encyclical *Rerum Novarum* opened the door to at least moderate support for labor and the working poor. Carol Coburn and Martha Smith illustrate how Catholic and Protestant reformers clashed over evangelical grounds well into the nineteenth century.[43] By the early twentieth century, however, American bishops began to feel pressure from the prevailing mood of progressive activity and grew wary that continued neglect of social conditions could lead to Socialism or even more radical measures, pushing Catholic ecclesiastical leaders sluggishly toward a reform agenda.

Nevertheless, as David O'Brien has noted, if the institutional church were initially sluggish in accepting a greater emphasis on reform and "progressive" philosophy, individual Catholics, outspoken priests, predominantly Catholic labor unions, and lay and religious fraternal and philanthropic groups advanced prominently onto the American public stage. The rise of "liberal" Catholic figures, notably Cardinal John Ireland of Minneapolis and Bishop John J. Keane of Richmond, espousing the complete compatibility of Catholicism and American values and their public participation in high-profile ecumenical events such as the World Parliament of Religions in 1893 demonstrated a new "public" and less insular Catholic approach to and relationship with the broader American public. Catholic writers, educators, and critics began to influence a broader segment of American literature, and Catholic fraternal and service organizations began to emulate other progressive movements, efficiently mobilizing volunteers, donations, and public opinion. Philip Gleason has illustrated how Catholic wartime relief efforts eventually culminated in the establishment of the American Federation of Catholic Societies, which flourished from 1901 to 1919, forming an umbrella organization to guide Progressive-Era Catholic organizations. By 1919, even the Church's hierarchical leadership had warmed to the notion of reform, issuing the Bishop's Program of Social Reconstruction, a bold statement recognizing social inequity and calling for such measures as greater federal employment legislation, increases in wages and living standards among the nation's workers, government-subsidized housing for the poor, control of monopolies, and even old-age, unemployment, and health insurance for workers, paid for by employers and state grants. By the dawn of the 1920s, America witnessed what Jay Dolan has termed "Catholic triumphalism, Catholic Big at its best," as the American church continued its uneven and jerky transition from a passive force in the American social order to an advocate for greater Progressive action.[44]

One possible reaction on the part of nativists to Catholicism's turn away from insularism and toward a greater engagement with Progressive-Era culture would be to breathe a sign of relief and applaud Romanists for finally embracing prevailing American social values. Not surprisingly, this was not the case. In fact, Catholicism's heightened public presence was profoundly alarming to American nativists, who saw their opponents making significant inroads into American acceptance and respectability. The proliferation of anti-Catholic newspapers in the 1910s and the widespread appeal of many of these sheets suggest that Catholics' determined presence within American culture was not universally welcomed. Ultimately, nativist periodicals targeted Catholic philanthropy because it provided a way of articulating membership in and important contributions to American society. As Mary Oates states in her recent survey of American Catholic philanthropy, "In their struggle to contribute as a community to the social good, members of an outsider church became more confident of their place in American society."[45] Just as Catholic claims of public memory and patriotism trespassed on nativists' ideological territory (as I outlined in chapter 1), anti-Catholic writers greeted Catholic claims of philanthropy and reform with outrage, convinced that these were mere ploys to garner attention and distract Americans from Rome's conspiratorial plans. As the nativist backlash toward the proliferation of Catholic charities indicates, however, Catholic efforts at charitable reform only solidified nativist antipathy and condemnation. Moreover, nativists could (and often did) point to several official hierarchical pronouncements in the late nineteenth and early twentieth centuries as being out of sync, if not completely hostile to American values and institutions, such as Pope Pious IX's "syllabus of errors," which condemned public education, separation of church and state, and a nonsectarian press. While few American laypeople or clerical leaders abided by, or even knew about, these policies, their opponents found new ammunition in these statements.

In its treatment of the weak and vulnerable, the Catholic Church was thus doubly reproachable—first for inflicting physical cruelties and second for using so-called charity to turn a profit and extend its political influence and social acceptability. The examples cited here, and dozens of others, illustrate that the anti-Catholic press presented itself as a watchdog intent on exposing Catholics' abuse of both power and defenseless individuals. Although papers presented women, the sick, and the elderly as powerless victims of Catholic aggression, they reserved their most graphic and enraged comments for accusations of Catholic abuse inflicted on helpless children. As I will demonstrate, nativists' "trope of the child" extended journalists' indictment of Catholic sham charities and reinforced the image of Catholic aggressors assaulting those least able to defend themselves. Their treatment of children depended on a particular construction of childhood innocence: children were presented as easily tricked and even more easily injured by Catholic deception and therefore in special danger from Romanist attack. According to anti-Catholic writers, this Catholic exploitation was particularly destructive because it threatened Protestant children's bodies, minds, and innate purity.

Convents, Confessionals, and Nativist Eroticism

One of nativists' most frequent attacks on the "Romanist peril" consisted of reports of abuse and mistreatment of young girls and boys at the hands of Catholic priests and nuns. In fact, these papers consistently described, in graphic detail, how Catholic leaders lashed out mercilessly and often violently against innocent children. One such article, entitled, "Brutal Assault on an Innocent Girl," asserts that an eight-year-old girl was beaten with a rope by an enraged Detroit priest for attending the city's public schools. Although the child's injuries were severe, the Catholic hierarchy successfully pressured her parents and law enforcement officials not to bring charges against the offending priest.[46] A similar article recounts how John Stolz, a twelve-year-old Milwaukee boy, was beaten by a parish priest when he showed up late for parochial school. Describing the severity of Stolz's injuries, the writer reported that "the little boy's leg was broken, the arteries were in such shape that it was only by the heroic work on the part of the physicians that he was kept from bleeding to death." In this case as well, no charges were brought against the priest because Stolz's parents were threatened with excommunication if they reported the assault to the authorities.[47]

Children's physical abuse was frequently linked to sexual abuse as well. In January 1914, *The Menace* reported the story of a teenage girl working as a housekeeper for a Pennsylvania priest. The priest reportedly slapped the girl in the face, "otherwise mistreated her," and finally "committed a criminal assault upon her." The article went on to report that the teenager gave birth to a baby girl some time later, suggesting that the priest raped the housekeeper after attacking her.[48] Still another story described how a priest "seduced" a sixteen-year-old girl and, when he tired of the affair, refused to see her any longer. When the girl continued to pursue him, the priest escaped to Puerto Rico, leaving his "mistress" to fend for herself and their unborn child.[49]

While these horrific accounts of child abuse were commonplace in Progressive-Era anti-Catholic periodicals, Catholic convents were singled out as particular sites of danger to children and childhood innocence. Like the APA, *The Menace* and its imitators condemned Catholic orphanages and Houses of the Good Shepherd, calling them places of immorality and child slavery. One *Menace* article insisted that "the so-called Houses of the Good Shepherd are nothing more or less than industrial slave pens where female indigents and hapless victims are buried for years, and very often for life."[50] *The Silverton Journal* asked readers, "How Long Will These Prison Houses Run?" outlining how novices were deprived of contact with parents, families, and the outside world.[51] Once trapped within convent walls, children were subjected to virtually unimaginable pain, toil, and suffering. An examination of a "young girl" induced to enter a Mexico City convent told the story of how the mother superior forced children to stay awake all night reciting prayers. The writer insisted, "As the girl could not avoid dropping to sleep, the mother superior . . . fastened to each eyelid a steel spring attached to a chord in order to hold the lids open — something like a form of Chinese torture."[52] *The Jeffersonian* investigated a convent called "Little Sisters of the Poor," whose conditions were noticeably appalling. "Little Sisters of the Poor," the article noted, were simply murderous sites devoid of hope, "secret dens which imprison women for life" guarded by conspiratorial "priest keepers."[53] *Menace* writers suggested that convents were especially threatening to young bodies and minds because they deprived children of the safety and security of the broader community — seducing them into a world of Catholic cruelty. One angry writer, describing a fourteen-year-old girl's imprisonment in a Kansas City orphanage, proclaimed, "Rome is the Jailer of Youth" and called the Houses of the Good Shepherd an "altogether unjust place of imprisonment and commitment of girls."[54]

Like the convent, the confessional represented a traditional site of innocent victimization at the hands of Catholic attackers. A classic trope of imprisoned femininity, the practice of Catholic confession had been a lighting rod of criticism in the American press, and twentieth-century anti-Catholic writers earnestly extended this indictment. *Watson's Magazine,* for instance, asked, "What high-minded lady would allow a bachelor priest, by auricular confession, to tear asunder the veil of feminine modesty. . . . How many noble women continually suffer excruciating torture, ere they can bring themselves thus to allow a man to lay bare the most sacred precincts of their souls! The sacred veil of modesty was divinely given to every woman, and no man has the right to lift it."[55] Likewise, a subsequent article remarked, "Isn't it about time that Romanist laymen — fathers, husbands, brothers — withdraw their daughters, wives and sisters from that awful peril?"[56] This latter article suggested that Catholic men, unlike their Protestant counterparts, neglected their obligation to defend women and children, making the Romanist laity, along with the clergy, contemptible from a nativist standpoint. *The Liberator* called the confessional "conclusive proof of [Catholics'] own corruption,"[57] and Tom Watson put the issue of Catholic sexual depravity and confessional confinement bluntly by stating, "I put it to your common sense — how could a weak, passionate mortal refrain from a woman, who came to him of her own free will, and *alone with him* IN PRIVATE, *confessed that she wanted a man.* You know what we men are."[58]

As David Brion Davis has illustrated (and as I have argued in chapter 1), one of the leading arguments for the appeal of nativist literature is the justification and sanctification it provided for reading erotically charged material. As Nancy Schultz has indicated, "Readers of popular . . . convent literature read these titillating books under the guise of reading enlightening literature, but the books themselves offered access to violent and erotic literature, which was generally proscribed in this era."[59] Jenny Franchot expands this argument, noting that captivity tropes allowed readers both access to pseudo-pornographic material and a way of extending "imaginative control" over a chaotic environment, particularly in Jacksonian America.[60] Social historians have often debated the role and influence of "soft porn" on images and interpretations of femininity. In her article "Soft-Porn Culture," Ann Douglas discusses the proliferation of Harlequin romances and similar literature as a backlash against the women's movement. Noting how sales of mass-market romance literature exploded in the late 1960s and throughout the 1970s, Douglass discusses the remarkable uniformity of soft-porn texts: "The heroine, usually an immigrant from another less modern culture to the energized, bewildering terrain of the male, is literally in his power. . . . Her inevitable loss of control constitutes the Harlequin plot." Moreover, "The Harlequin girl must love the Harlequin man no matter how viciously he treats her. . . . The fantasy [is] obvious: women need men pitifully more than men need them."[61] Janice Radway's analysis of women romance readers, however, takes a far different view of Harlequin novels. Whereas Douglas views soft-porn romance as fundamentally harmful to women, Radway takes the opposite approach. Through conversations, questionnaires, and oral history interviews with women readers, Radway concludes that romance reading by middle-class women was a sign of "independence" and a challenge to patriarchy. While some readers stated that the romance served as a form of "escape" or "tranquilizer," most found the conventions of romance writing helpful in coping with daily struggles. Radway notes, "the meaning of the romance-reading experience may be closely tied to the way the act of reading fits within the middle-class mother's day and the way the story itself addresses anxieties, fears, and psychological needs resulting from her social and familial position."[62]

Despite their radically different interpretations of the meanings and significance of romance literature, both Douglas and Radway illustrate that
the soft-porn literary genre was highly formulaic. Radway notes that its
predictable plot and structure (in which readers could generally predict
the outcome of each chapter before opening the book) provided the
romance's chief appeal—even more so than its titillating content. Like
subsequent Harlequin novels, anti-Catholic publications in both the nineteenth and early twentieth centuries were highly formulaic and repeatable
with stock characters of sinister priests, mysterious nuns, beautiful and innocent children (usually girls), and indifferent or complicit police and
courts. The incredible overlap, hyperbole, and uniformity of language and
content from one newspaper to another and striking similarity of anti-
Catholic journalism week in and week out suggests that anti-Catholic readers, like romance enthusiasts later in the century, knew what they would
be reading before they walked to their doorsteps.

Creating and Preserving Childhood Innocence

Within the pages of the anti-Catholic press, nowhere was there
a more repetitive theme or frequently evoked trope than that of the endangered child. "Investigations" of convent captivity or confessionals gave
readers tantalizing glimpses of erotic scenes. Moreover, these tragic, almost
melodramatic accounts of imprisoned and endangered youth, repeated
in dozens of anti-Catholic texts, suggest that these papers consciously employed images of victimized childhood to elicit an emotional and direct
response on the part of readers and to further stigmatize and denigrate
their Catholic opponents. Since reports of child abuse in general and children's convent captivity in particular were part and parcel of the articulation of anti-Catholic sentiments, it is important to examine the period's
language and rhetoric about childhood, before assessing how the paper
applied it in stories of convent "prisons." In so doing, I will draw from the
burgeoning field of studies of children in religion to show how childhood is, in fact, a crucial analytic category, particularly when dealing with
intense expressions of nativism, such as those seen in Progressive-Era anti-
Catholicism.

One of the greatest challenges in employing childhood as an analytic
device is that societal representations of childhood are generally perceived

as "natural." As sociologists and historians who examine childhood point out, social representations and depictions of children are so deeply engrained in a particular culture that individuals fail to consider children as anything more than incipient adults. Sociologist Chris Jenks, for instance, illustrates that "most social theories, through their emphasis on a taken-for-granted adult world, spectacularly fail to constitute the child as an ontology in its own right."[63] Jenks also insists that, while societies tend to see their particular concept of childhood as "normal" or inherent, all experiences of childhood are shaped by a particular (adult) cultural mind-set. Jenks writes, "The widespread tendency to routinize and 'naturalize' childhood, both in common sense and in theory, serves to conceal its analytic importance behind a cloak of [the] mundane."[64] Thus, according to Jenks, "childhood is to be understood as a social construct," a malleable and illustrative expression of adult sentiments, and an analytic category capable of exploring adults' own fears and desires.[65]

Political scientist Ashis Nandy echoes Jenks's sentiments. Nandy, like Jenks, asserts, "There is nothing natural or inevitable about childhood. Childhood is culturally defined and created; it too, is a matter of human choice."[66] While confirming Jenks's assertion, Nandy goes a step further, illustrating how children often embody deep contradictions and serve as the projections of adults' own trepidation. Nandy writes, "The older generation are allowed to project into the child their inner needs and use him or her to work out their fantasies of self-correction or national or cultural improvement."[67] For Nandy, childhood acts as a "screen" onto which adults project their deepest fears and hopes—such as anti-Catholics' dread of Catholic aggression. Moreover, since the younger generation embodies both the anxieties and the fantasies of adults, children's cultural representations are often paradoxical. In Nandy's analysis, children are simultaneously praised for their "childlikeness"—positive qualities in the minds of adults—and condemned for their "childishness"—negative qualities that measure children as imperfectly formed adults. In this way, Nandy suggests, childhood's importance as an analytic category is heightened, for children can simultaneously manifest concepts that are contradictory in the adult world.

While historians have seldom recognized the importance of childhood as a cultural construct, a few works have employed childhood as a means of examining adult society. Philip Greven's landmark work *The Protestant Temperament*, for instance, uses child-raising practices and personal reflections

on childhood as a lens through which to explore deeper social and cultural trends in colonial America. For Greven, children serve as a crucial
link for differentiating and investigating three distinct streams of colonial
thought.[68] Greven's subsequent research studies the overlap of violence
and memory in children, exploring how abuse in children permeates the
subconscious memory of both individuals and society as a whole.[69]

Finally, art historian Anne Higonnet has demonstrated how visual images of childhood reflect the deep-seated values and anxieties of a given
culture. In particular, Higonnet illustrates that the "modern, western, concept of an ideally innocent childhood" is a relatively recent innovation,
dating back to the European Enlightenment. In her analysis, Higonnet
echoes the writings of one of the earliest historians to consider childhood
as a historical category worth of scholarly attention, Philippe Ariès, whose
influential study, *Centuries of Childhood,* argued that childhood itself did
not come about until the modern era. Previously, Ariès and Higonnet contend, high infant mortality rates and the need for child labor precluded the
parental warmth and close familial bonds that would characterize childhood in the post-Enlightenment Age—a notion that has been contested
by subsequent scholars.[70] As Higonnet argues, children had been "understood as faulty small adults, in need of correction and discipline."[71] With
the advent of Enlightenment reasoning, children were presented in idealized, Romantic forms. Higonnet insists, however, "Because it looks natural,
the image of childhood innocence looks timeless, and because it looks
timeless, it looks unchangeable. Yet that image was invented. . . . The Age
of Innocence began only about two hundred years ago."[72] For Higonnet,
this "innocent" child—modernity's "invented ideal" image of youth—has
permeated western culture to such an extent that youthful innocence is
perceived as both a logical and natural state of being. Employing these
theories alongside a study of nativist captivity narratives provides an opportunity to illustrate both how childhood can be employed as a category
for historical analysis and how writers employ a rhetoric of childhood to
tap into readers' fears and sympathies.

This theme of childhood innocence forms a powerful category and
trope within the pages of the anti-Catholic press. In fact, at one point,
The Menace seemed to imply that it deliberately evoked images of childhood innocence to boost circulation and denounce papist opponents. In
an article titled "Rome Robbing Chicago of Thousands through Merciless Child Traffic" the paper asserted, "In all the world there is nothing

which touches the human heart chords of gladness or sorrow as the happiness or misery of little children."[73] *Menace* writers and their nativist compatriots took youthful purity as the norm, often going to great lengths to show how it was being compromised by Catholic subversion. Reading these child theorists in light of the earlier discussion of children's convent captivity suggests that nativist writers concentrated much of their hatred toward Catholicism on alleged imprisonment and enslavement of children to underscore Romanist assaults on children's inherent innocence.

Much as Higonnet illustrates, anti-Catholic periodicals depicted Protestant children as invariably pure and virtuous. In fact, one of nativists' strongest incitements against Catholic convents was that children were placed there unnecessarily—without having committed any offense. An exposé of New Orleans convent life insisted, "It is rather appalling to think that a helpless little innocent of six, eight, or ten years, guiltless of anything but misfortune, may thus be committed for life to what is virtual imprisonment."[74] Writers presented captivity as an affront to children's natural innocence and condemned corrupt judges, "Romanized" police forces, and cowardly politicians, all of whom were complicit in Catholic schemes to imprison young boys and girls in Catholic "slave pens." To highlight children's "natural" innocence and illustrate Catholic political corruption, *Menace* writers reported stories of children sent to suffer in Houses of the Good Shepherd for the most trivial offenses. One article condemned convent slavery and pleaded for "the innocent little girl who may have been sent there by some Romanized Judge for the simple offense of playing marbles in the street."[75] A similar story described how three New Haven girls "ranging in age from 14 to 16" were taken "before a Romanist judge" and committed to a House of the Good Shepherd for playing "the innocent game of 'tag.'"[76] In other cases, Rome's political influence was presented as so enormous that children were railroaded into convents without committing any offense at all. One *Menace* writer insisted Catholic officials "drew up a bill to enable the juvenile court to pick up children indiscriminately and, without notice to parents or guardians, commit them to private prisons anywhere in the United States."[77] Similarly, an article entitled "Innocent Girl Committed to Roman Prison" reported that a twelve-year-old girl was sent to a House of the Good Shepherd although "no charge was, or could be made."[78]

While articles of this sort support Higonnet's argument about the prevalence and influence of childhood innocence in modern western society, they also demonstrate one of the principal dangers of convent captivity. Children, as innocent and helpless victims of Catholic aggression, were unable to defend themselves against Rome's trickery or political machinations and therefore were in need of protection and assistance from watchful Protestants. While nativist writers presented Protestant children as invariably innocent, their Catholic counterparts were more complicated. For instance, *The Menace* suggested that Catholic children, much like Protestant ones, were naturally innocent but that their innocence had been corrupted by papist dogma and superstition. One *Menace* article insisted, "It is likely that [a Catholic's] mind has become a receptacle for Romish superstitions from childhood. In the effort to become a dutiful child of the 'only true faith' he had renounced reason and become incapable of thinking for himself."[79] It is thus children's misplaced efforts to be "good Catholics" that led to the destruction of their innate innocence. In the minds of *Menace* writers, this disintegration of innocence followed Catholic children into adulthood as well. The paper argued that "many Romanists, if left to themselves would make good school directors, but the hierarchy are opposed."[80] Even the "slavers" that run convents were not presented as invariably evil. Often they were seen as victims of Rome's corruption, who, because of their debased Catholic mind-sets, placed their "inmates" in harm's way. One report described how two nuns in a Yonkers nursery failed to provide adequate nutrition to a two-year-old boy, who subsequently died. The article stated, "Without papal training they [the nuns] would have been more zealous of the welfare of the inmates than of the profits of the business."[81] Thus Catholics, both children and adults, were often described as literally "pathetic" and, like their Protestant neighbors, victims of clerical schemes and papist ignorance.[82]

On the other hand, however, anti-Catholic journalists occasionally depicted Catholic children as naturally violent, subversive, and dangerous—exactly the opposite of their Protestant counterparts. One *Menace* article reported that the young generation of Catholic children "is like a nest full of cockatrice eggs. When hatched their venomous sting means death to the republic."[83] While this sort of sentiment seems to be the exception, rather than the rule, it does illustrate a contradiction in anti-Catholic attitudes toward and perceptions of Catholic children. As Nandy argues, childhood becomes a way of embodying conflicting adult desires and fears—in this case, desires of ridding the United States of a Catholic peril and fears of Catholics' increased presence and authority in America. Catholic children simultaneously (and paradoxically) represent a tabula rasa that, if stripped of its links to Roman decadence, could be redeemed and the next wave of Catholic assaults on American institutions and freedoms.

"This Crime against Childhood": The Genre of Children's Imprisonment

In order to explore further the ways in which *The Menace* articulated its defense of childhood innocence, it is important to place the paper's message within the broader context of Catholic captivity narratives. As several historians have pointed out, the imprisonment and torture of young children has stood as one of the most significant and powerful tropes in American anti-Catholic literature. For instance, in his study of eighteenth-century Massachusetts, John Demos describes how French and Indian soldiers captured Reverend John Williams and his family in Puritan New England, forcing them to march to French territory. Being forced into captivity was a "deeply shocking inversion" for Williams and his family, both because their new masters were "savage Indians" (and, in the minds of the English, nearly as savage Frenchmen) and because their captors were Roman Catholic. Demos suggests that Williams felt tempted to "turn" to Catholicism and saw the French language, "popish religion," and "Indian savagery" as a single chain of barbarity and danger. While Williams and his son were eventually able to return to Massachusetts, his daughter, Eunice, renounced Puritanism and accepted the "savages" and their Catholic faith, marrying an Indian soldier and living out her life in New France. She thus exemplified the "Unredeemed Captive," representing the danger felt by eighteenth- and nineteenth-century Americans who believed that their children would, like Eunice, be seduced into accepting alien Catholic beliefs and descend into savagery.[84]

Likewise, Franchot demonstrates that America's anti-Catholic captivity genre merged Old World fears of popery with New World anxiety over Native aggression, transporting captivity tales "from the forest to the parochial school, the nunnery and the confessional."[85] Catholic captivity was, in a sense, more dangerous than Native slavery because Catholic institutions were more immanent, physically present in the antebellum landscape. In

Franchot's analysis, Catholic captivity became "a drama, not of being kid-napped into the American wilderness, boundless and frightening, but of being entrapped by built spaces—cathedral, confessional, and convent."[86]

Franchot's study also illustrates that the imprisonment of girls and young women within Catholic prisons was also a means of expressing antebellum concerns for womanhood and femininity. Anti-Catholic leaders frequently perceived priests' and nuns' celibacy as "a sentimental competitor to the Protestant family."[87] Other scholars have echoed Franchot's assertion that convents were believed to "seduce" girls away from their families and their proper roles as daughter, wife, and mother. Both Maureen McCarthy and Joseph Mannard have demonstrated that convent schools, nunneries, and celibacy threatened the nineteenth century's feminine ideals, notably what Linda Kerber's classic study has termed "Republican Motherhood." Mannard points out, "By renouncing marriage and motherhood for themselves, by allegedly proselytizing Protestant children and attempting to enlist Protestant daughters into their ranks, nuns appeared to endanger the essential links between family, church, and state enunciated in the ideology of domesticity."[88]

Nativist papers were quick to criticize their Catholic opponents on this charge. *The Yellow Jacket,* for instance, argued that Protestant daughters and mothers were far more virtuous than their convent counterparts. In describing Catholic nuns, the paper stated, "Doubtless there are virtuous ones among them just as there are virtuous women everywhere else in the world, but they have no monopoly on the cherished social sesame, and they are not one whit better nor more virtuous than tens of millions of good women who never incarcerate themselves behind rock walls and barred windows. . . . Nuns are not half as sacrificing as the true heroines of humanity, the mothers who are willing to go down into the valley of the shadow of death, the hour of travail, and beget offspring to supply the citizenship of this great republic."[89] *The Peril* evoked similar sentiment, insisting, "The strength and glory of this American nation rests for security upon the homes of its people. The strength and power of the homes of a people are measured by the character of the women who preside in them."[90] While asserting that Protestant families formed the bedrock of American nationalism, nativist journalists also criticized Romanists for destroying familial bonds, as nuns and priests turned their backs on parents and siblings to live a cloistered existence, causing once loving homes to be "Rift asunder by Papal Tragedy."[91]

Although Progressive-Era nativism was a later development in America's anti-Catholic history, the anti-Catholic papers of the 1910s exhibited the same concerns for protecting Protestant family life and femininity as witnessed in Demos's and Franchot's studies of the eighteenth and nineteenth centuries. Throughout the myriad of episodes of American anti-Catholicism, opponents accused Catholic institutions of specifically targeting girls and young women, enslaving them in celibate convent life when Protestant worldview dictated that they should be brought up to be wives and mothers. In fact, throughout the nativist press reports of convent captivity nearly always focused on abuse of girls. In part, this seems to be because girls were presented as more fragile and thus more easily injured than boys. Furthermore, many cities and town had few resources available to house women convicted of crimes or left as orphans, forcing civil authorities to send women and girls to Catholic institutions. This practice, of course, only fueled anti-Catholic claims that crooked politics was what sent girls to Rome's institutional "slave pens."

This is not to say, however, that journalists paid no attention to reports of boys held captive by Catholic "jailers." On the contrary, the anti-Catholic press included several descriptions of "a child slave industry" that exploited boys as well. One *Menace* article charged that the St. Joseph Protectory, a Catholic orphanage for boys, subjected inmates to inhuman conditions and worked them nearly to death in exchange for profits. The article illustrated the deplorable working conditions at the orphanage and described a typical scene, with boys "seated six on a side, at power driven sewing machines, each little boy bending over his machine as if for dear life, while the ever present priest or sister stands on guard." The article went on to compare these boys' horrific experiences with girls in the Houses of the Good Shepherd, insisting that both claim to "Christianize" their inmates but actually use children as cheap sources of labor.[92] Likewise, *The Menace* reported on horrendous conditions in a Quebec orphanage for boys, in which boys were repeatedly beaten, forced to sleep on boards, deprived of food and medicine, and forbidden to contact family members.[93] A similar article claimed that a ten-year-old boy was beaten with a club by a mother superior in a Catholic orphanage. In reporting the assault, the author insisted, "The unwarranted cruelty in this case may be due to the absolute lack of motherly instinct . . . but whatever the case, it is surely a crime against childhood, and one too frequently perpetuated against the helpless inmates of Rome's institutions."[94] This "crime against childhood" thus had two facets: the unjust imprisonment of helpless, innocent children and the sweatshop environment that generated huge sums of money for the Catholic hierarchy at the expense of children.

Thus, like other tropes of defending the weak and unfortunate, anti-Catholic crusaders' treatment of children explicitly implicated Catholic leaders in graft and deception. One edition of *The Menace,* for instance, included a cartoon of a young woman bending over a washtub with a priest on one side of her and a nun on the other. The two dark figures each hold a chain in front of the "inmate." Out of the washtub flows not soapsuds but money (with a label on it that reads "For Father"). The sinister-looking priest is also pictured saying to himself, "The Girls work for me." This image suggests that, while children toil in Catholic prisons, the clergy enjoy the fruits of their labors.[95] One article made this point explicitly, insisting that children were pushed through "a Romanized court to be held there in slavery for priestly profit."[96] Calling Catholicism "The Devil's Church," *The Silverton Journal* lamented, "after being persuaded or forced to take the horrible oaths of a nun the poor girl is as a rule, lost to the world. . . . She is a prisoner whose whole life must be used in the priesthood's service."[97] A similar story in the pages of *The Menace* presented the case of a Memphis House of the Good Shepherd that conducted fundraising to cover its expenses. The writer insisted that the institution would "send the dollars it should use to pay its bills into the various sub-treasuries of the papacy and then calls on you to pay its bills."[98] Likewise, a *Menace* writer argued that Catholic convents had "existed for ages on the profits wrung from slave labor, walled in from the world" and were "being fed daily with innocent girls . . . by the modern Romish white slavers who preside over the juvenile courts of this country."[99]

This language of slavery formed yet another overlap between anti-Catholicism and the prevailing rhetoric of patriotism and Americanism in the anti-Catholic press. While several articles echoed the warning issued by *The Silverton Journal* that "The Catholic Slavers are Everywhere," many drew on examples of American iconography and public memory to elicit support for their defense of vulnerable girlhood.[100] *The Menace,* for instance, reported girls' capture and slavery in Cincinnati convents, claiming that "youth and innocence are hounded from city to city by the tools of Rome," much like pre–Civil War slave catchers chased fugitive slaves.[101] *The Peril* likewise warned, "We in America boast today that this is indeed a land of liberty. But is it? What about the slaves that are still in our midst?"

Explicitly linking the anti-Catholic crusade of the twentieth century to the Civil War struggle of the nineteenth, *The Peril* pointed out, "When Lincoln struck the shackles from the limbs of the negroes in this country, he dealt human serfdom a blow that paralyzed it all over the world. . . . But the slaves that are now in our midst are of a different class. They are educated and accomplished. What can be worse than mental slavery—putting shackles on the intellect?"

This article evoked both sympathy for enslaved girls in "Romish Prisons" as well as the common trope of intellectual degeneracy and complicity among Catholic opponents—the ideological nativism that formed the core of Progressive-Era anti-Catholicism. Catholic convents, the writer was careful to point out, are dangerous because they "shackle" the intellect of America's prisoners. Just as nativists often acknowledged that Catholic children and the nuns who instructed them could be virtuous Americans in the absence of corrosive and destructive papal teachings, so too *The Peril* asserted that convent confinement chained and tormented both body and mind. Likewise, the article began by asking, "Are the legislative representatives of a great free people wearing the ball and chain of the chief of white slavers in the Vatican?"—accusing Rome's agents of stymieing state legislatures and preventing governmental inspection of Catholic facilities. The writer concluded by asserting that Catholics' torturous prisons, conspiratorial political manipulation, and "mental slavery" amounted to "a blotch on the fair name of America."[102] *Watson's Magazine* employed similar language to link convent "slavery" to discussions of patriotism and intellectual malfeasance, asking, "What are the privileges of this country worth if children yet unborn are doomed to be cursed with the yoke of papal slavery? Protestant parents had better see their sons and daughters in their grave rather than barter away their rights of liberty of soul and intellect." The writer again illustrated the frequent connection between children's actual, physical confinement in Catholic institutions and America's ongoing threat of mental stagnation and loss of independent will exhibited by Catholic duplicity, trickery, and conspiracy.[103]

Anti-Catholic writers insisted that the only antidote to this pattern of clerical graft and children's exploitation was government inspection of all Catholic charities. One account of children's slavery in Montana, for instance, called for "inspection of these ecclesiastical sweatshops which are run in the name of religion but which actually present only a mockery of true philanthropy and compassion."[104] A similar article asked, "What is the matter with Uncle Sam that he stands outside the convent door and is refused admission?"[105] Catholics' bogus claims of charity and kindness, the paper insisted, were simply ploys to rob Protestant taxpayers of their money. A report of a Pittsburgh House of the Good Shepherd, for instance, instructed *Menace* readers to be wary of nuns using stories of needy children to solicit donations. The writer maintained that "the little children are only used as the pitiful plea to touch sympathetic people" and went on to say, "*Refuse to give a penny!*"[106] Ironically, this message ran contrary to nativists' own strategy of presenting accounts of child abuse to elicit sympathy and support on the part of readers. Apparently, anti-Catholic journalists judged their own use of the rhetoric of childhood as acceptable, since the paper's own actions benefited the security of the American republic, whereas Catholics' motives were corrupt and underhanded.

The duplicity highlighted by accusations of Catholic sham charities and convent depravity stands in contrast to the early twentieth century's prevailing journalistic demands for enlightenment and dissemination of information to a reading public. As I outlined in chapter 2, nativist writers espoused the Progressive-Era ideals of publicity and openness, making their accusations of Catholic secrecy, confinement, and conspiracy particularly acute. As Maureen McCarthy points out, "It is this dichotomy, between what the convent appears to be and what its opponents say it actually is, that stands at the center of this and other nun tales. . . . The crime of the Catholic Church is that it hides the true identity of its institutions. Convent narratives unmask alleged secrets."[107] *The Yellow Jacket* expressed this criticism, saying bluntly, "The Roman Catholic Church is an ordinary aggregation of deceivers, humbugs, crooks, and grafters on a widely organized scale."[108] A subsequent article asserted, "The holy humbuggers have always told their dupes that the Romish Church was the greatest charitable institution in the world. . . . There is more material charity done outside the Catholic Church than in it—ten times more."[109] Likewise, in reporting on "Two Recent Romish Slave Pen Tragedies," *The Peril* remarked on the secretive and close-minded nature of American Catholics, stating, "There are all over this free country Convents and Houses of the Good Shepherd, with high walls around them, and with their doors and windows bolted and barred. . . . The great majority of the American people believe that these walls, bolts and bars are for a double purpose: to keep the prisoners in and the world from going in and finding out what is going on in there. The American people have a right to know what is going on . . . and they are rapidly getting in a temper to find out."[110]

Investigating a Catholic "prison" in New York, *The Peril* claimed that girls were "the victims of the conspiracy" that enriched the clergy at the risk of children's lives.[111] Illustrating that slavers would stop at nothing to wring money from convent prisoners, *The Yellow Jacket* lamented that priests mercilessly cut girls' hair and sold it in the pages of the Sears and Roebuck catalog. The paper began by asking readers, "Have you a daughter . . . ? Do you remember when she was a little baby, just growing into dimpled childhood . . . ? That picture has never faded from your memory. You cherish still its precious recollections." Following this idealized depiction of innocent, normal childhood, *The Yellow Jacket* contrasted appropriate childhood with convent life, illustrating a scene in which "the priests and Mothers Superior line up the helpless Nuns like sheep at a shearing fest." Again, the paper drew the conclusion for readers that Catholic convents required secrecy since they corrupted the natural innocence and purity of childhood—actions that had to be exposed by diligent readers.[112]

Although reports of children's convent captivity follow nativist journalists' emphasis on protecting weak and vulnerable individuals, in some respects their assessment of childhood was remarkably different from attention to other defenseless individuals, such as the sick or the elderly. In its treatment of children, the anti-Catholic press implicated civil authorities— police officers, judges, juvenile welfare agents, and probation officers—as accountable for childhood imprisonment. By making these governmental authorities, alongside sinister Catholic leaders, jointly responsible for convent abuse, the anti-Catholic movement invested Catholic captivity narratives with political meaning. Readers were told not simply to steer clear of convents but to take direct political action against Rome's co-conspirators. One irate *Menace* writer denounced nunneries and asked, "Can anyone tell why the police forces of various cities feel called upon to constitute themselves slave catchers for these black robed pirates . . . ?"[113] *The Yellow Jacket,* (evoking a theme of apathetic or naïve Protestants who enable Catholic atrocity, which I will discuss in greater detail later in this chapter) denounced "those blind Protestant easy-going dupes who are tools for the priests that oppose any exposure to [the Pope's] holy farce."[114] Likewise condemning Protestant "traitors" for "giving aid and comfort to the enemy," *The Silverton Journal* criticized evangelical newspapers who refused to print the "truth" about Catholic convents.[115] *Watson's Magazine* feared that, relying on Rome's "political machine" for votes, public officials turned a blind eye to Catholic depravity and left convent slavery intact and unchecked.[116]

When duping Protestant officials proved insufficient, nativist journalists argued, Catholics would slyly pack city courts and school boards with Catholics or Romanist sympathizers. As *Watson's Magazine* commented, "Why do the Papists get the Juvenile Courts? Simply to control the children; spirit them into 'Houses of the Good Shepherd,' and the like for their Romish purposes."[117] Ultimately, however, nativist writers seemed to have little concern for whether "slave catching" police officers were Catholic or Protestant; both were violating children's innocence and betraying the American nation by delivering young girls into "private prisons" and into the clutches of fiendish nuns.[118]

In a similar vein, anti-Catholic writers attacked "Romanized" judges, who bent to the will of the Catholic hierarchy by acquiescing to political pressure, naïvely believing the words of a charismatic priest, or simply taking a bribe. Corrupt judges and juvenile authorities who sent children to horrific convents were often presented as little better than the priests and nuns who directly administered torture to young boys and girls. One *Menace* article described how a girl was incarcerated in a nunnery against her will, and it condemned the complacent judge as a "hideous monster which seeks to rob us of our children."[119] Another article reported the imprisonment, escape, and eventual recapture of two girls in a Toronto nunnery. In denouncing the judge who placed the girls under such confinement and the police who repeatedly hunted them down to be re-punished, the author virtually taunted readers: "Think of it, a Protestant in a Catholic institution."[120]

While the trope of childhood captivity hinged on the complicity, if not outright participation of civil authorities, it also drew its attraction from accounts of children's injury and death. In fact, within the pages of anti-Catholic periodicals, harm inflicted upon imprisoned children stood as one of the ultimate symbols of Catholics' barbarity, ferocity, and danger to America. Being responsible for a child's death was the ultimate affront to human life and innocence itself and therefore the ultimate indication of Catholics' inhumanity. In the frequent and sensationalized reports of child captivity, imprisonment and death were often intimately linked. As an indication of their unhappiness under Catholic domination, their refusal to comply with Romanists, and their yearning for the family they left behind, children were often willing to sacrifice their bodies, in fact their very lives, for an opportunity to regain their freedom. One *Menace* story describes how three girls made ropes by tying together their bedsheets and attempted to climb out of the convent windows in a Dayton House of the Good Shepherd. While two escaped, one girl fell while halfway down, breaking her ankle. She was therefore recaptured by her slave masters.[121] In an even more extreme example, the paper reported the case of a sixteen-year-old Newark girl who fell four stories out of a convent window while making her escape. The girl hit her head on the hard pavement below and died, to which the writer responded, "NOTHING WILL BE DONE ABOUT IT. The girl will be buried and forgotten, and the slave drivers and kidnappers will replace her with another victim."[122] When describing another girl's death in a Toronto nunnery, one *Menace* writer, in recounting the horrors of convent captivity and their toll on young children, concluded, "it is hardly to be wondered at that a three story jump proved a temptation."[123]

As Anne Higonnet has pointed out, this emphasis on children's death is a crucial component of the modern conception of childhood innocence. Higonnet goes so far as to state that "the image of the Romantic child is haunted by death" and suggests that innocence and death are synonymous features of post-Enlightenment conceptions of childhood.[124] Higonnet also insists, "Every sweetly sunny, innocently cute Romantic child image stows away a dark side: a threat of loss, of change, and, ultimately, of death."[125] This link between innocence and death was a prominent feature of anti-Catholic captivity narratives. Captivity was often invested with the language and rhetoric of death. Articles emphasizing captivity and death behind convent walls thus presented a sharp juxtaposition between girlhood's natural, sensual beauty and the austerity, unnaturalness, and death of convents, underscoring the need to protect femininity and innocence from papal threats. Likewise, a subsequent article reported that children imprisoned in Catholic institutions "wither and die under the heartless routine of drudgery and destitution,"[126] while still another author lamented that convents offered "no promise of liberty or release but through the tomb."[127]

These accounts investing convent life with the language of death are brought into even shaper relief by stories of children who attempted to take their own lives in order to avoid the fate of forced imprisonment.

The Peril reported the harrowing story of a girl in Washington, D.C., who "in an attempt to escape from the House of the Good Shepherd . . . was so badly injured that she died the same day."[128] *The Jeffersonian* described how a girl in a House of the Good Shepherd in Cincinnati broke both ankles jumping from a window in a successful escape attempt. The newspaper went on to state, "Her agony must have been very great as she lay in the hospital, but so hideous had been her treatment in the 'House of the Good Shepherd,' that she was not sorry to escape, even at such a fearful price."[129] Likewise, a *Menace* article entitled "Saved for a Worse Fate" described how a teenage girl in Philadelphia was released from a House of the Good Shepherd, only to be recommitted by the juvenile authorities. Rather than serve in the convent again, the girl swallowed a bottle of iodine, trying to commit suicide. She was sent to a hospital, where she recovered, and was later sent to the convent, where, the author predicted, "this time will witness her complete demoralization."[130] Likewise, *The Menace* described the case of a fourteen-year-old girl who drank a vial of poison in the courtroom just as the judge was pronouncing her sentence to serve in a Catholic nunnery.[131]

Furthermore, the pages of *The Menace* are teeming with accounts of children's literal deaths while trapped in Catholic prisons. One particularly striking article described a Montreal convent adjacent to the St. Lawrence River. One summer, the author maintained, the river dried up "and what a horrible sight was there to behold; for in the sewer, and in the deep mud . . . around its mouth were the dead bodies and the skeletons of hundreds of infants that had been thrown into the vaults of the nunnery and washed down through the river." In describing the location (a Montreal convent) and scene of entombed infant corpses, this article borrowed heavily from images and themes from the horrific accounts of nineteenth-century "escaped nun" stories, particularly *The Awful Disclosures of Maria Monk*. This suggests that descriptions of imprisoned and endangered children were equally effective among early twentieth-century audiences. Children prisoners were often killed by neglect or poor sanitation or by lack of nourishment or ventilation in nunneries, adding to the convents' image as hellish, sinister, and dangerous.[132] As this article suggests, nunneries were conceived as even more deranged because they were places where innocent and unfortunate children were murdered outright.

As if to make this point even more explicit, *The Menace* positioned an illustration just above the article's headline. The image showed an old and hunched-over nun pointing a girl or young woman toward a nunnery. Above the nunnery are the words "abandon hope all ye who enter here" and the figure of a human skeleton.[133] Likewise, *The Silverton Journal* reported the story of an architect "who was employed to build a new Catholic structure in Cleveland, Ohio, and in digging up the foundations of the old convent he found the skulls and skeletons of babes literally saturating the soil."[134] The message sent by these and other accounts of convent captivity was that nunneries signified death not just to an individual but to the notion of childhood innocence.

Childhood and Manhood: The Goals of the "Menace Army"

In a striking article calling on readers to join "The World's Great Fight," *The Silverton Journal* lashed into Roman Catholicism, demanding to know why "that church tells the girl of sixteen or eighteen years of age, with eyes like dew and light" to "put on the veil, woven of death." Yet the article went on to reassure angry readers: "We have a weapon that compared with 'a lie' is like a gattling gun beside an old flintlock musket—'the truth.' Hi there, soldier on the firing line, lend a hand. Help swing this machine gun's muzzle toward the enemy. Pop it to 'em you fellows on the right! Advance those on the left! Give 'em 'hell and repeat' until their every 'lie' is spiked, their every prisoner set free."[135] The article's dual focus—illustrating both the dangers convent life inflicted upon innocent girls while simultaneously stimulating a militaristic and bold response by masculine defenders—demonstrates the overlapping agendas of nativist writers in the 1910s. Furthermore, the writer explicitly equated the influence of truth and the journalistic output of information with military weaponry and violence. Dismantling Rome's prisons and infrastructure, nativists assumed, would therefore rely on courageous writers, loyal readers, and growing subscription lists. But it also employed a language of heroic, vigorous, and strengthened masculinity, one that would seem far more common in a discussion of artillery bombardments than in describing newspaper sales. In fact, the frequent descriptions of manly duty and the need for military maneuvers in retaliation for Catholic atrocities toward children mirrored broader cultural trends in the Progressive Era, which underscored the nation's manliness and presented the rhetoric of masculinity as a powerful agent within America's cultural landscape.

As this article makes clear, nativists' discussion of the trope of the child and the concomitant concern for childhood under attack serves to inform our understanding not only of how the Progressive-Era anti-Catholic movement perceived children but how its members perceived adult men. While Protestant children were described as embodying positive traits of innocence and purity, their adult fathers and brothers were generally condemned as ignorant about or complicit in Catholic aggression. Anti-Catholic writers nearly always contrasted Catholic vigilance with Protestant indifference. The anti-Catholic mission, in fact, seemed to be awakening America's readers to the real threat of Catholic power, intent on destroying America's families, schools, and the nation as a whole.

Children were an essential component of this wake-up call to apathetic Protestants. A frantic article on children's capture and imprisonment in Catholic convents asked readers, "What assurance have you that your own flesh and blood may not be caught in the net of the holy slavers and railroaded to misery and death?" The writer went on to demand, "If there is any manhood . . . left among the American people, the time has come to assert it and stop this illegal, as well as unhuman traffic in the lives of American girls."[136] The thought of innocent girls held prisoner by a foreign power ought to "make the very blood of an American father or brother boil with indignation," another *Menace* writer insisted.[137] Chronicling the degeneracy and neglect faced in Catholic convents, *The Yellow Jacket* asked, "Fellow Americans who have sisters and daughters, don't you think this has been allowed to go on long enough?"[138] Saying that Uncle Sam "let the Romanists catch him asleep," *The Jeffersonian* urged immediate action against Romanist foes.[139] Likewise, a *Menace* writer detailed the tragic case of Irene Bateman, a seventeen-year-old girl who fell from a window while escaping a New York City House of the Good Shepherd and was continually chased by the city's corrupt police force until she was recaptured. The writer warned, "Your daughter or your sister may be the next Irene Bateman. Crush the political aspirations of every Catholic . . . as you would crush a serpent!"[140]

A similar theme permeated another *Menace* article, describing how a thirteen-year-old girl was abused by her stepfather. Later, in order to cover up his crime, the stepfather placed the girl in a House of the Good Shep-

herd, where she had been held in captivity against her will ever since. The
paper reported that "the Menace Army has responded nobly to this twentieth century call to arms and from every nook and corner of the United
States have come the answering words of encouragement . . . in this battle
to free this little girl-child from the iron grip of the blood stained hands
of the Romans."[141] This frequently evoked phrase, "the Menace Army," attached a masculine response and sense of mission to the paper's agenda,
but the militaristic tone and mobilization of readers intent on carrying
out the nativist mission was not limited to *The Menace* itself.

In fact, nearly every extant anti-Catholic periodical of the early twentieth century proscribed the formulation of a group of enthusiastic, supportive men who were called on to hustle for subscriptions, improve the
papers' circulation, and spread the word about Romanist aggression. *The
Peril* urged readers to "become a Minute Man!" and formed a "Firing Line"
similar to those of *The Silverton Journal* and *The Menace*.[142] One particular
article extended this rhetoric, goading readers by announcing, "Your
duty is to help in the fight. If you cannot man a cannon or be a general,
you can be a private. After all, it is the privates who win the victories."[143]
Likewise, *The Woman's Witness* called for the formation of "Bush Beaters"
who would publicize reports listed in the paper and hustle for subscriptions.[144] Issuing a warning call "To the Men of Silverton," *The Silverton Journal* printed the story of an escaped girl from a nearby convent, who reported the horrific abuses within its walls. Illustrating the necessity for
masculine action to protect victimized children, the article called the incident "an appeal for help that stirs us mightily," and continued, "Here
is a case which involves the safety of our country and our homes. Where
the liberty and life of one citizen is in danger of destruction, a principle
is involved which places all of us under obligation to defend her."[145]

Other writers also made use of this intensely masculine rhetoric in calls
for child protection and attacks on convent cruelties. Providing yet another
example of the rhetoric power of "slavery" and reference to American historical memory, one *Menace* writer proclaimed, "Our forefathers—yes,
and many brave men still living, have spilt their blood on the battlefield,
fighting for the great cause of freedom." In contrast, the next generation
of men "have allowed and still allow these institutions of the worst kind
of slavery" to proliferate on American soil.[146] Likewise, an even more direct article condemned Protestant manhood's inability to contend with

Rome and wondered "if it will take another war to free the white girls—as it once did the blacks." The author concluded by saying to Protestant men, "Wake up! *Wake up!* WAKE UP!"[147]

At stake, then, in *The Menace*'s portrayal of children was more than a simple reaffirmation of the virtues and sentiments of childhood innocence. Rather, the paper and its many imitators explicitly linked the language of childhood innocence with a masculine rhetoric of militarism and an ennobled defense of childhood. Nativist writers employed accounts of child abuse in general and convent captivity in particular to illustrate the horror of Catholicism and its un-American, even "un-human" character. But deliberately demonstrating Catholics' abuses upon weak and defenseless children also served as a critical rallying cry for Protestant men to take direct action against Romanism's perceived aggressions.

As earlier chapters mentioned, one of the most plausible reasons for the striking popularity of anti-Catholic periodicals in the early and mid 1910s was their ability to synthesize several of the most salient features of Progressive-Era culture while relying on the rhetoric and imagery of America's long-standing anti-Catholic traditions. Nowhere was this more apparent than in the movement's depiction of valiant masculine readers bravely defending the nation's children from Catholic adversaries. Anti-Catholic writers tapped into classic tropes of children's imprisonment by sinister priests and nuns, forming the basis of antebellum "escaped nun" narratives. Their emphasis on masculinity, warfare, and forceful attacks on Catholic enemies suggests that journalists also drew inspiration from the prevailing ethos of "muscular Christianity" and rugged masculinity that had emerged as powerful cultural stimuli by the early twentieth century.

Recently, historians have sought to explore the causes and effects of this increased emphasis on American masculinity during the Gilded Age and Progressive Era. Gail Bederman's analysis of manhood and American Protestantism indicates that the drive to "masculinize" American Protestant culture sprang from a breakdown of Victorian gender conventions and the limitations of nineteenth-century entrepreneurism brought on by industrialized corporations. Bederman maintains that, although women had constituted the majority of American churchgoers since the mid seventeenth century, "The feminine church only became a problem after 1880, when the Victorian gender system had begun to lose coherence in the face of a cultural reorientation connected to the growth of a consumer-oriented corporate order."[148] Seeking to infuse what had previously been "the 'female' sphere of religion and morality," white, native-born, middle-class Protestant men launched "The Men and Religion Forward Movement," a revival movement designed "to masculinize the Protestant churches by getting as many men as possible active in religion," along with more familiar groups such as the YMCA, Boy Scouts, and, as Bederman puts it, "widespread cries for a muscular Christianity as an aspect of a larger cultural transformation during the years 1880–1920."[149]

As clearly illustrated by Anthony Rotundo's survey of professional sports at the turn of the century, David MacLead's analysis of American boyhood, Donald Hall's treatment of body image in American evangelicalism, and seminal writings from the Progressive Era itself (including those by Theodore Roosevelt and Bruce Barton), the ethos of assertive, rugged masculinity gained enormous cultural currency in the first two decades of the twentieth century.[150] Arriving on the scene as the "masculinization" movement crested, twentieth-century anti-Catholicism quickly incorporated this message, linking anti-Catholicism together with the valiant masculine struggle to defend America from Catholic aggressors. The anti-Catholic crusade, writers insisted, was predominantly a masculine movement, much like the Men and Religion Forward Movement Bederman describes. The role nativist journalists ascribed to women and, tellingly, children was that of victimized innocent, saved by alert masculine readers.[151]

Nativists' insistent rhetoric of manhood's defense of children is in keeping not only with popular notions of childhood innocence but with American men's greater interest in and involvement with the lives of children. As Margaret March's insightful article on Progressive-Era manhood has shown, "masculine domesticity," with its greater emphasis on companionate marriage and child raising (though stopping well short of supporting gender equality or equal sharing of household tasks), emerged alongside contemporaneous developments of overtly "rugged" masculinity, the "strenuous life," and "muscular" Christianity. In part, nativists' rhetoric can be understood as a merger of traditional masculine and domestic imagery. Anti-Catholic writers used militaristic labels and calls for battle but, in an important sense, did so primarily to safeguard the home and family. Whereas scholars have often cast American masculinity as a "flight from commitment," Progressive-Era manhood iconography in general, and early twentieth-century nativism in particular, viewed familial commitments as the apex and raison d'être of the nation's manly "army."[152]

Even this phrase, "the Menace Army," suggests that nativist producers sought to tap into masculine rhetoric in order to stimulate circulation and awareness of Catholic schemes. As a symbol of protecting childhood innocence, the Menace Army and its contemporaries illustrate the overlap of two prominent tropes within anti-Catholic literature: the unjustly suffering child and the "awakened" Protestant man, intent on overcoming the "Romanist peril." One of the important ways in which this reading of anti-Catholic newspapers informs our discussion of twentieth-century nativism is by illustrating how, within their pages, childhood and masculinity become codependent categories. The papers' militaristic rhetoric in describing their crusade against children's convent captivity suggested that "real" men were enlightened about Rome's sinister plots and were actively fighting to stop its exploitation of children. In this way, the anti-Catholicism's descriptive analysis of children's captivity led to a proscriptive account of manhood's defensive response. Although the Menace Army and its numerous imitators proved short-lived, their example of the overlapping features of masculinity and childhood tropes provides an important perspective on the study of anti-Catholic and nativist movements prior and since.

CHAPTER FOUR

"The Slime of the Serpent"

ARTICULATING A COUNTERRESPONSE
TO AMERICAN NATIVISM

Catholics and Protestants together settled America. Together, they laid the
forests, drained the swamps and plowed the land. They fought together
in the battles of the Revolution. They stood side by side in the conventions
and congresses that secured the liberties of the people. Why should they
now suffer self-seeking men to betray them into hatred for one another?
When America outgrew her Colonial limits, Catholics and Protestants,
side by side, faced the toil and danger of pioneer life. State after State
was carved out of the great West. City after city arose. Railroads crossed the
broad wastes and bridges spanned the deep streams. And all was the joint
work of Catholics and Protestants. There is no State but where they live
together, do business together, vote together; no city but where their
churches together lift their spires toward the same heaven; no railroad,
telegraph, express and hardly a mill, factory or mine but where their
moneys and their interests are joined hand in hand. Then, why should
Catholics and Protestants not continue to live together in peace? . . .
Tomorrow, as today, and for generations to come, Catholics and Protestants must live together as neighbors. Shall it not be also as friends?

—Knights of Columbus, Commission on Religious Prejudices,
Second Report (1916)[1]

Although, as the previous chapters have illustrated, the 1910s
represented an immense watershed of hostility and xenophobia toward
the American Catholic Church and its members, these years also witnessed
a vigorous denunciation of nativist anti-Catholic sentiment and a concomitant mobilization of Catholic supporters. In particular, as the above
quotation illustrates, Catholic writers (along with their allies of various

stripes) embraced a language that simultaneously urged national unity and pointed out Catholic contributions to America's development, history, and progress. The prior three chapters have outlined how anti-Catholic nativists worked to present their movement and its leaders as arbiters and defenders of the nation's public good and the safeguards of genuine national traditions that were endangered by modernity and Romanism alike. Like their nativist opponents, however, writers active in the Catholic defense used nationalistic imagery to bolster their arguments about Catholics' place in the nation and the proper behavior of their Protestant neighbors.

While anti-Catholics insisted that Americans should unite as a powerful "army" to oppose the pope's minions, Catholic writers challenged their fellow citizens to do just the opposite, joining together to combat nativist bigotry itself—a force, they argued, that was destructive of the social fabric of American cooperation and unity. Moreover, to carry out their respective crusades, both "Romanists" and nativists relied on a civic construction of nationalism predicated on citizens' acceptance and understanding of historical figures, common political instructions, and belief in a shared symbolic past, rather than overtly racialized or "ethnic" dimensions of national belonging. For both Catholics and xenophobes alike, the measure of Americanism and "popery" and the compatibility of these terms rested not in Catholics' appearance, language, or how they traced their genealogy. Rather, the battle between nativists (who advocated a restrictivist approach to nationalism) and Catholics (who embraced a more liberal, tolerant understanding of Americanism) emphasized whether Catholics had made sufficient contributions to the nation's historical development in the past and how they would continue to benefit the nation in the present and future.

The Knights of Columbus text quoted above foregrounds this ideological assertion of Catholic national contribution. Emphasizing Catholics' wartime service, their labor on behalf of national progress, and their camaraderie with Protestant counterparts, this text stands in direct contrast to the nativist texts already presented, which contradict Catholic claims of patriotism and denounced Protestants who worked alongside the papist "enemy." While Catholics had remained comparatively silent during the nativist outbreaks of the nineteenth century, by the mid 1910s, organizers had begun to mount a vocal counterattack against the latest wave of anti-Romanist periodicals that sought to question Catholic Americanism. The quoted text was drawn from one of the most effective architects of "anti-nativism," the Commission on Religious Prejudices, organized and financed by the Catholic fraternal organization, the Knights of Columbus, in 1914 to curb the proliferation of anti-Catholic periodicals and stem the rising tide of America's nativist xenophobia. The Knights and other defenders of American Catholicism turned to courts, political leaders, even the postal system itself to hamstring the growth of nativist newspapers. But their most direct attack, as their statement above demonstrates, came in the form of written response, urging readers to accept Catholic patriotism and renounce divisive and meddlesome nativist propaganda that turned Americans against one another. Genuine nationalism, they asserted, was based on standing "side by side" with "neighbors" and "friends" to embrace a national ethos of pro-Catholic accommodation and liberalism that made room for America's loyal Catholic citizens.

This is not to say, of course, that the rhetoric of American Catholic nationalism on the part of the Knights of Columbus and their allies necessitated wholesale egalitarianism on the part of their coreligionists. In fact, as Noel Ignatiev and Iver Bernstein demonstrate, several antebellum Irish Catholics exhibited a remarkably close-minded and occasionally violent attitude toward other ethnic or racial groups, exacerbating racial tensions to facilitate their own assimilation, and, as John McGreevy and Thomas Sugrue likewise point out, this pattern extends well into the twentieth century. Catholic laborers were among the most vocal opponents of Chinese immigrants on the West Coast, and, as figures like Charles Coughlin illustrate, Catholics often vigorously opposed inclusion and open-mindedness in American society.[2] While an examination of Catholics' interethnic animosity goes beyond the scope of this book, it is worth noting that Catholic opposition to Progressive-Era nativism virtually always came in the form of calls for greater openness, liberalism, and, specifically, insistence that readers recognize Catholics' contributions and sacrifices in the past and present that made them eligible for full citizenship and invalidated nativist claims to the contrary. Catholics' strenuous insistence that they should be viewed as citizens on equal footing with their Protestant peers obviously did not preclude their simultaneous marginalization of others. But it does illustrate that Catholic demands for accommodation and respectability served to contradict and, Catholic leaders hoped, neutralize

anti-Romanist strategies of pinpointing Catholic conspiracy and disloyalty, while entrenching Catholics in the mainstream of national participation and recognition.

While prior chapters have outlined anti-Catholic claims, I will now turn
to what might be called Catholics' "anti-nativism"—that is, their condemnation of anti-Catholics' xenophobia and exclusivist visions of citizenship
that questioned Catholic national contribution. This chapter explores how
lay and clerical leaders within Catholic organizations articulated a deliberate and vigorous counterresponse to the proliferation of anti-Catholic
texts and the nativist message itself. In several respects, this is a huge
project. How can historians effectively examine an exceptionally prolific
Catholic press that included hundreds of diocesan and national periodicals, growing philanthropic and social organizations, an effective hierarchical structure, and a large and growing voice in national concerns? From
a researcher's perspective, Catholic media and writers were fundamentally different from their anti-Catholic opponents. Whereas only a fraction
of nativists texts have survived, many in fragments, Catholic diocesan and
national periodicals are readily available to historians. While there are virtually no extant business records of the nativist press, careful archival plan-
ning has preserved large amounts of Catholic works.[3] And while nearly all
anti-Catholic papers vanished in the late 1910s or shortly thereafter, their
opponents continued to print throughout the mid twentieth century or
beyond. This situation raises the question of how to delineate a study of
Catholic texts in the late Progressive Era.

Because of the significant volume of Catholic publications and in the
hopes of capturing Catholics' efforts to rebut and counteract the influence of nativism, this chapter seeks to limit its investigation to those works
that arose explicitly in response to the rising tide of anti-Romanist literature in the early to mid 1910s. This approach will, admittedly, exclude
diocesan papers, but it has the advantage of exploring the most direct and,
in many cases, the most confrontational and influential works in Catholics' attempts to confront nativist propaganda.

Although Catholic works and nativist periodicals proved quite different from a logistical and research-oriented point of view, examining their
"war of words" reveals not merely conflict, but, in some respects, striking similarity. Prior chapters have asserted that nativists' successes in the
1910s stemmed from their ability to intertwine traditional anti-Catholic
tropes within three central themes that proved salient to early twentieth-

century readers: gendered expectations of proper manly roles of vigilance and military mobilization in defense of women and children; progressivist language that emphasized the power of facts, investigation, and information to uncover and undo deception; and outward expressions of nationalism and public memory to differentiate genuine from false patriotism. Nativist writers, I argue, tapped into these resonant rhetorical streams to guide and build their movement. What is even more telling is that their Catholic rivals used the very same topics and emphases to mount counterattacks against nativists and to express Catholics' proper place within American society. This chapter uses this frame of reference to explore the direct opposition Catholics manufactured to combat the flood of anti-papal literature through 1910, when the latter had slowed to a mere trickle.

"TRUE AND FALSE AMERICANISM": ANTI-CATHOLICISM MEETS ANTI-NATIVISM

This chapter draws its title—"The Slime of the Serpent"— from a pamphlet of the same name written in 1912 to combat the growing encroachment of nativism. Printed in St. Louis and circulated widely, the pamphlet attacked *The Menace* as a "journalistic reptile" that poisoned the minds of readers, spreading blatant lies for the profit of its editors. Unable to find honest work, the pamphlet insisted, *The Menace* staff resorted to pure fiction and malice, duping readers into accepting its hurtful falsehoods out of their "mercenary" desires.[4] One of the most prevalent nativist arguments was that Catholic opponents were intellectually, mentally, and ideologically unfit to understand and carry out the responsibilities of American citizenship. Although *The Slime of the Serpent* and similar examples of Catholic defense relied on similar "civic" understandings of nationalism—rooted in intellectual and ideological comprehension of American values—they turned nativist arguments on their head. Just as nativists accused Catholics of using superstition and "stunted intellect" to promulgate Romanism, so too "anti-nativist" writers retorted that xenophobia is unpatriotic and bred of ignorance and bigotry. In condemning Wilbur Phelps, the self-serving *Menace* founder, *The Slime of the Serpent* argued, "He finds a market for his wares chiefly in parts of the country where the Catholics are few. Naturally, the Catholics being little known, are misunderstood. To such regions he sends all the lies that a depraved imagination can invent; and to give plausibility to his lies, he gives names of persons that do not exist. . . and sells these lies to you for the nominal sum of 50c a year. It is a bad bargain; because, if you wished to, you could sit down and manufacture all these lies for nothing."[5]

Catholic defenders frequently evoked this line of reasoning, arguing that they, and not their misguided opponents, understood the responsibilities of patriotism, upheld American values of reasoned, independent thought, and uncovered dangerous deception and ignorance that threatened national unity. If anti-Catholic arguments aimed at excluding Romanists from national belonging might be termed "ideological nativism," Catholics' response and their insistence upon the congruity of Catholic behavior and national ideals might be termed "ideological patriotism." One of the most explicit examples of Catholic civic identity and ideological patriotism was printed in a Catholic newspaper aptly titled *The Antidote,* because of its efforts to remedy and counteract nativists' venom. *The Antidote* began publication in 1912, as the anti-Catholic crusade began to gain momentum, and was edited, printed, and distributed by Father J. A. Campbell in the small hamlet of Hereford in rural northern Texas. Like several of its anti-Catholic counterparts, *The Antidote* was a small-scale operation, it was released monthly, and carried out its printing and business operations in a relatively remote rural community, and, unfortunately for subsequent historians, the number of issues that survived in the historical record is rather limited.[6] Also like its anti-Romanist opponents, *The Antidote* maintained that Americanism must be based on shared values, institutions, and beliefs, rather than a common ancestry. In an article titled "True and False Americanism," for instance, *The Antidote* argued, "It is a mistake . . . to think that Americanization consists only in teaching foreigners how to speak our language and how to vote. To be an American requires much more than this, and there are among us native-born Americans who stand just as much in need of Americanization as any foreigner who flies here to escape European oppression." "True independence," the article continued "means a correct sense of liberty" and the willingness to stand up to bigots and close-minded zealots "who misuse liberty in order to attempt to set up a social order entirely un-American in its conception and in its essence."[7]

This article illustrates a common inversion of anti-Catholic claims that appeared frequently in the anti-nativist press. In particular, defenders of

American Catholicism challenged the bigoted claims that *The Menace* and similar newspapers were upholding American traditions and patriotism, arguing that, instead, such papers were the antithesis of American freedom and responsible citizenship. Perhaps the most colorful expressions of Catholic anti-nativism during the Progressive Era came in the form of a short book written by Elihu S. Riley entitled *The American Satyr,* which compared nativist journalists to a mythical beast—half man, half goat—that lurked in forests and preyed on the unsuspecting. Living in darkness on the outskirts of society, the "satyr" represented a dangerous converse of all civility and a fundamental threat to the nation itself. The book outlined the unnatural and un-American views of the satyr, asserting, "Still the American satyr shuts his ears to these pleasant sounds from the voice of profound patriotism and shakes his shaggy locks in token of his utter disbelief in their fraternal tones."[8] Moreover, the book juxtaposed the "satyr" with true Americanism, represented by a simple dove who understands that tolerance and liberalism are the foundation of nationalism. Virtuous and pure, the dove respects the spirit of American brotherhood and liberalism, understanding that "while there may be righteous and material differences in their religious affiliations . . . there is still room enough in the grand Union of States and the household of God to severally maintain these principles and enjoy our rights and privileges in a spirit of affectionate fraternity."[9] Underscoring the distinction between tolerance and bigotry (and sincere and false nationalism, respectively), the book concluded with a direct comparison between these forces, stating, "The American Satyr hates the American dove of peace. Their lives, their callings and their habitats are the opposite each of the other. One seeks to injure and destroy—the other to aid and enlarge all that is pure and lovely and of good report. Inspiring it is to know that the species of the Satyr are few in number compared with the great and innumerable multitude of patriotic Americans who delight in the fraternal coo of the dove of peace."[10]

Anti-nativism, while upholding the value of civic constructions of American nationalism, thus represented a significant inversion of xenophobic exclusivity. Elsewhere, however, Catholic apologists articulated a more straightforward contradiction to nativist claims. Whereas anti-Catholic journalists frequently challenged the morality of the confessional, for instance, *The Antidote* countered that the practice was not a "fountain of vice" but rather an instrument of "high morality."[11] Likewise, *The Antidote* chided *Menace* writers for an article on the illiteracy rates of Catholic European countries, asking, "Will The Menace please explain to its readers why those sections of the United States . . . which have the fewest Catholic in their population, have the largest percentage of illiteracy?"[12] This quip is typical of anti-nativist texts, which included countless assertions designed to contradict anti-Catholic attacks, but the article is also telling because it illustrates how Catholics read, scrutinized, and denounced nativist documents. In fact, one of the most prevalent traits shared by anti-Catholics and their anti-nativist rivals was that they were avid readers of one another's works, scouring the pages of competing arguments to find ammunition for propaganda and legal battles—a point I address in more detail later in this chapter.

While Catholic and nativist writings shared a concern for civic nationalism and an abiding interest in each other's works, they likewise exhibited similar marketing and promotional practices. Like their anti-Catholic counterparts, anti-nativists engaged in cross-promotion, praising like-minded writers and directing readers to examine and support friendly publications. Moreover, like several successful anti-Romanist sheets, Catholic supporters could boast of the wide distribution and extensive circulation of many pro-Catholic media outlets, including a highly successful lecture series and a tremendous proliferation of newspapers, pamphlets, and flyers—including one booklet printed by the Knights of Columbus that reached well over half a million readers.[13]

The tremendous influence, popularity, and scope of anti-nativism in the 1910s stood in stark contrast to American Catholics' reaction to earlier outbreaks of anti-Romanist propaganda, in which the Church and its members made only muted efforts to respond to attacks. In part, the latter intensity of Catholic rebuttal suggests that Progressive-Era nativism was more pervasive and effective than its antebellum antecedents, demanding a more concerted and widespread response. But the volume and expense of Catholic counter propaganda (which cost the Knights of Columbus alone tens of thousands of dollars in a three-year period) also indicates ways in which Catholic organizations had become more vocal, influential, organized, and efficient by the early twentieth century. *The Slime of the Serpent* began by acknowledging the long tradition of American anti-Catholicism, asserting, "The Catholic Church is used to such attacks as 'the Menace' makes. In every generation they had their little day, and died." Whereas bigoted political and journalistic movements such as the Know-

Nothings and the APA flourished briefly but quickly faded to obscurity, the writer noted with pride how the Catholic Church prospered in America: nativists "died away, and the Church became better known." In fact, it was the historical durability of American Catholicism and the ephemeral nature of its opponents, the pamphlet insisted, that prevented a quicker response to Progressive-Era anti-popery. Noting that "in every generation they had their little day and died," *The Slime of the Serpent* dismissed anti-Catholic agitators and their movement, claiming that "the Church hates to bother with it." Only when the extent of nativist falsehood had grown to epidemic degrees and their message had become rife with "such obscenities, blasphemes and libels," the author continued, did Catholics seek to mount an effective counterattack.[14]

The vigor and scope of Progressive-Era nativism, then, mobilized Catholics to abandon a laissez-faire attitude toward anti-Romanism and apply their growing resources to what was fast becoming a prominent nativist threat. In fact, the proliferation of nativist texts and efforts to combat American xenophobia jump-started the formulation of several effective Catholic organizations in the 1910s. One such group was the Catholic Press Association (CPA), which had undergone numerous efforts at forming a "bureau of correspondence" aimed at disseminating information among Catholic journalists and periodicals. In 1890, a group of Catholic editors met in Cincinnati to establish the first CPA, providing channels of communication and sharing noteworthy news items with one another. Funding difficulties and internal conflicts overwhelmed the nascent organization, and it disbanded a few months later. Likewise, a movement to form a CPA at the turn of the twentieth century quickly failed. However, interest in the CPA revived in August 1911, a few months after *The Menace* began publication. Responding to the spread of nativism across the American cultural landscape, Reverend Peter E. Blessing, editor of the Catholic newspaper *The Providence Visitor,* delivered an address at the opening of the CPA's first assembly of Catholic editors. Emphasizing the need both to combat the growth of anti-Catholic periodicals and maintain cohesion within the Catholic press, Blessing began the CPA conference of Catholic journalists and editors by noting, "The question before this assembly is whether through association we can achieve that which for us, as units, is impossible. Throughout the length and breadth of the land there is resounding a clarion call from an interested and intelligent laity for greater knowledge of what the Church is doing and why she is being persecuted.

They want facts and their interpretation. The world is girded with the means of information and in every place there are to be found men well equipped to find and send to us the truth."[15] Blessing's speech illustrates several critical points in assessing the spread of anti-Catholic journalism and the Catholic counterresponse. First, it illustrates how anti-Catholicism stimulated the formation of the CPA: prior to the wave of nativism that swept the 1910s, efforts to galvanize Catholic writers and editors together into a stable body proved short-lived. In the wake of anti-Catholic aggression, however, the organization's mission and necessity became more apparent, making it a viable component of Progressive-Era Catholicism.

Second, the CPA's formation in general and Blessing's comments in particular demonstrate the extent to which Catholic organizers, like their nativist counterparts, emphasized the critical themes of progressivism in articulating their journalistic message. Attention to "facts and their interpretation," "greater knowledge," providing "truth," and especially the image of a "world girded with information" all underscore an investigatory and information-driven model that was consistent with prevailing progressive themes. Just as nativists depended on an ethos of exploration, investigation, and enlightenment aimed at uncovering and rooting out deception, so too anti-nativists espoused a "faith in information" and embrace of factuality, truth, and "light," to combat what they saw as anti-Catholic bigotry and falsehood.

"A VULGAR ASSASSIN OF TRUTH": ANTI-NATIVISM AND THE PROGRESSIVE ETHOS

The expression of CPA goals, then, coincided with a broader anti-nativist agenda of contradicting anti-Catholics' claims of progressivism by casting Catholic defenders as the true arbiters of progressive ideals. Nowhere was this attitude more prevalent than in the most vocal defender of Catholicism during the 1910s, the Knights of Columbus's Commission on Religious Prejudices. Established in 1914 and disbanding with America's entry into World War I in 1917, the commission waged a series of legal and propaganda battles against nativist print culture, basing its arguments on a call for fairness, tolerance, and recognition of Catholic national contributions. Grounding its mission in "the broadminded attitude of the representative American," the commission "appealed to [Americans'] fairmindedness . . . with neither an outburst of indignation nor a whine of complaint, but just as one business man appeals to another, in a considerate, compelling show of the broad principle of a square deal." "Businesslike" in its motives, organization, and efficiency, the commission exemplified the progressive concern for organization and rationality, stressing an appeal to logic and reason. This is particularly apparent in the commission's initial report, which documented its goals and objectives. After acknowledging the Knights of Columbus's appropriation of fifty thousand dollars to cover its first year of operation, the commission pledged "to study the causes, investigate conditions and suggest remedies for the religious prejudice that has been manifest through press and rostrum in a malicious and scurrilous campaign that is hostile to the spirit of American freedom and liberty." Vowing "to conduct such an investigation" in an effort "to ascertain exactly who are the persons behind these movements and who are financing them," the commission's chairman, Patrick Henry Callahan, used similar rhetoric to that of both mainstream progressive texts and nativist rivals.

The commission's anti-nativist progressivism was notably apparent not only in its rhetoric but in its methods and publication strategy as well. During its initial meeting in January 1915, for instance, the commission pledged "to conduct an education campaign by informing and correcting editors and journalists who allowed religious prejudice to surface in their newspapers," stressing the importance the organization placed on circulating and rectifying information to guard against nativism.[16] One of the commission's first orders of business was to undertake a survey of nearly two thousand councils that constituted the entire body of the Knights of Columbus to determine how they were addressing the troubling proliferation of nativist texts on a local level. They also printed hundreds of thousands of copies of pamphlets and booklets lauding Catholic service to America and quoting liberally from Protestant clergy and public officials that upheld Catholic respectability. Commission organizers urged the removal of anti-Catholic language from public school texts and wrote columns in local newspapers explaining the Catholic position on contemporary public issues. Furthermore, Callahan met personally with representatives of *The Menace* and other anti-Catholic newspapers, as well as editors of the metropolitan daily newspapers, to encourage fairness and promote "goodwill" toward Catholics (efforts that proved futile in easing tensions with virulent nativists, but significantly more effective in illustrating the

Catholic perspective to more mainstream media outlets). This use of surveys, letters, and popular media points to a typically progressive reliance
on the power of information and its ability to transform the way readers thought about and behaved toward their Catholic neighbors. It also
demonstrates Callahan's hope that the Commission on Religious Prejudices would serve as a "clearinghouse" of information and resources that
could be used by local councils and the public press in combating anti-
Catholicism, just as nativists hoped that their conglomeration of periodicals would serve as a repository for anti-Romanism.[17]

Throughout their reports, the commission repeatedly announced that
its primary mission was education. Concluding the second report in 1916,
for instance, Callahan noted that "the entire subject to our minds settles
down to one proposition, and that is education. . . . We firmly believe that
social prejudice will yield to a systematic and persevering treatment aim-
ing to correct the misinformation, causes and influence. . . . Catholics and
Protestants alike need proper education, an education that will deal with
broad principles of justice, brotherly love, liberty, and patriotism."[18] Likewise, at the first organizational meeting in 1915, Callahan issued a press release stating, "The commission will endeavor, after learning the facts . . . to
conduct a campaign of education," asking nothing but "the fair-minded
participation of all citizens."[19]

Along with surveys aimed at ascertaining "the activities, plans, and projects proposed or being carried out for the improvement of their members"[20] and calls for greater education and understanding between Catholics and Protestants, Callahan distributed several thousand personal letters
and appeals (by the commission's official count, over a thousand such letters per month) to members of the press, business and community leaders, and political officers, "answering inquiries, noting newspaper items
and editorials, replying to attacks made through press, pulpit and by letters and to various other ends," communicating the Catholic position on
issues, and discrediting nativist propaganda.[21] The intensity and scope of
anti-nativism speaks to the expansive growth and reach of Catholic defenders during the Progressive Era, their great organizational efficiency,
and the considerable resources at their disposal. In his exceptional study
of the Knights of Columbus, Christopher Kauffman outlines how "the
Knights militantly defended the Catholic presence in America" at the dawn
of the twentieth century and "emerged from these battles as a kind of
Catholic anti-defamation league." Looking to their namesake as an arche-

typal Catholic-American, the Knights expressed a "citizen culture," imply-
ing "that those who formed their lives according to the principles of Columbian Knighthood derived their civic virtues from their patron's heroic
deed" of founding and settling the American continent.[22] The Knights'
patriotism (along with the pragmatic appeal of insurance policies and fraternalism) sparked an intense following; in just over a decade, from 1892
to 1905, the Knights of Columbus spread from a small initial base in Connecticut to include councils in every state of the union as well as international locations in Mexico, Canada, the Philippines, and beyond. The fact
that the Commission on Religious Prejudices commanded a considerable
budget and staff speaks to the success and strength of the Knights' organizational and recruitment efforts and the vigor with which they opposed
challenges to Catholic nationalism.[23]

Nativist opponents, not surprisingly, were quick to target the Catholic
Press Association and the Commission on Religious Prejudices as up-and-
coming rivals in a crucial battle over journalism and public opinion. *The
Menace* denounced the highly organized CPA for corrupting and vilifying
the public press, abridging the Bill of Rights, and brainwashing citizens
in the process. In headlines blaring, "Catholic Editors Emit Inky Slime,"
the paper condemned this brain-trust of Romanist writers for producing
"Romanized secular newspapers" that refused to recognize or challenge
papal conspiracy.[24] Likewise, *The Yellow Jacket* attacked the Commission on
Religious Prejudices as a front for dangerous militarism, covering up secret Catholic drill maneuvers as Romanists plotted to take over the country. Singling out Callahan himself as a liar, the paper called him "a nice,
domesticated, tame-looking young man" who was nonetheless championing a violent coup against the nation.[25]

Perhaps the most salient source of friction between the commission
and nativist foes centered on meetings between Catholic organizers and
the popular press. Shortly after its formation in 1914, the commission recognized the limitations of attacking papers of "exclusive anti-Catholic
character." Such direct confrontations with outlets such as *The Menace,
Watson's Magazine,* and other publications, organizers realized, would only
fuel the flames of nativism and provide visibility to the Knights' enemies.
Moreover, nativist papers themselves proved ephemeral: by the time Callahan's commission had issued their second report, for instance, several
had already fallen into journalistic oblivion. While the Commission on Religious Prejudices did not entirely abandon its crusade against the most

blatant anti-Catholic periodicals (in fact, Callahan and his commission played a crucial role in civil and criminal prosecutions of anti-Catholic publishers during the 1910s), the commission also dedicated attention to more productive ends. In particular, the Knights circulated extensive amounts of pro-Catholic propaganda to counteract nativist acrimony and organized a series of meetings with the Associated Press to persuade American journalists to adopt a more accommodating and positive stance toward the nation's Catholic citizens.

The commission admonished the Knights of Columbus as a body to take a more active role in shaping journalism and public opinion, drafting press releases, and even writing movies and plays that presented their coreligionists in a positive light. In March 1915, the commission met with representatives of the Associated Press (AP), expressing Catholics' initial concerns that the AP was staunchly in the anti-Catholic camp, dismissing Catholic achievements and refusing to print articles on the commission's successful prosecution of libelous nativists. Nevertheless, through the Knights' diligence, the commission later argued, this mood changed to one of more optimism and favor in the press's treatment of Catholic issues, a shift, Callahan insisted, that was one of the commission's lasting successes.[26] In closing the meeting, Callahan and the other members of the commission reported progress and applauded the AP's pledge to give more favorable treatment to Catholics. Noting that the commission's own efforts "have been cheerfully carried by the Associated Press on all of its trunk lines and in all of its districts," they reported, "From editorial expression and news items, coming from every part of the country, it seems that the object of the Commission, its policy and its work are endorsed by practically every newspaper of note."[27]

Anti-Catholic foes, however, were far less hopeful in their outlook toward the secular press. *The Yellow Jacket* noted with disdain the "pow wow" between Callahan and prominent publishers and went on to accuse the "jack associated press" of "Just Plain Lying" in their treatment of Catholic positions on public education and American politics. Criticizing opponents for meddling in the press, the article continued, "If the Knights of Columbus think they can pull that over the American people, they are a set of stupid, ignorant fools. It is a plain, deliberate, premeditated lie, and the Knights know it."[28]

Along with influencing the daily press, anti-nativists began an active campaign to print and distribute their own literature, criticizing their opponents as nothing more than self-serving, narrow-minded bigots. The most prolific source of anti-nativism was *The Antidote*, which, like the Commission on Religious Prejudices, emphasized key progressive concepts of fact-gathering, publicity, and investigation. In particular, *The Antidote* reached out to non-Catholic readers, hoping to present facts and statements by supportive Protestant officials to illustrate the falsehood of xenophobic arguments. Although *The Antidote* acknowledged that many of its readers were Catholic, it offered extra low subscription rates to non-Catholics (half the price charged to Catholic readers) and a series of articles aimed at attracting the attention of nativists themselves. One such series, "Talks with Readers of The Menace," insisted, "It is to these we wish to address ourselves in the spirit of fairness and patriotic fellowship and we have not the slightest doubt that we shall succeed after a time in winning from this jury of honest men a verdict that the Catholic Church is NOT the Menace to our free American Institutions. . . . The Aurora Menace is *itself* a Menace."

Nativist papers were particularly dangerous, the article argued, because of their efforts "by false witness and other shyster methods, to dupe a lot of people." In contrast to nativist deception, *The Antidote* maintained that its pages were rooted in truth, accuracy, and fairmindedness. "The only purpose of The Antidote . . . is to address to those who have been misled by this false and suicidal propaganda, an earnest appeal to abandon the malice of fratricidal war, and to join hands with their fellow citizens who happen to be Catholics, in a united stand against the common foe."[29] Likewise, a subsequent installment in the "Talks with Readers of the Menace" series maintained that nativist periodicals were "willfully carrying on a propaganda of malice and false witness with the intention of dividing into hostile camps the Christian forces which have made this Republic what it is" asking sympathetic Protestant readers "How long will honest American Protestants swallow such devilish lies against their fellow Christians?"[30]

Outreach to non-Catholic readers, particularly those supportive of the nativist agenda itself, suggests that *The Antidote* expected its array of facts and arguments would sway even the most stubborn opponent. Thus, in a typical appeal to readers' sense of honesty and factuality, *The Antidote* lashed out at anti-Catholic rivals for exhibiting the opposite traits— poisoning minds and causing division based on falsehood and deception. Just as anti-Catholic periodicals prided themselves on uprooting Catholic conspiracy, their opponents frequently insisted that their mission was to counteract the deceit and trickery of anti-Romanism. One of the most effective weapons in the anti-nativist arsenal, then, was supportive statements by non-Catholics, which would appear disinterested and objective, that discredited the anti-Romanist agenda. One such writer was C. A. Windle, an avowed "independent and free-thinker" but nonetheless a prolific opponent of Progressive-Era xenophobia. Windle's contribution to the anti-nativist movement included a pamphlet, "Straight Talk to Non-Catholics," which counteracted claims of Catholic intolerance, and a provocatively titled booklet replying to accusations by Thomas Watson called simply, "Is the Catholic Church the Deadliest Menace to Our Liberties and Our Civilization?" Windle begins the latter text by answering the question posed in its title with a resounding no. Rather, he asserts, "Mr. Watson is guilty of fomenting a religious conflict, and trying to resurrect animosities that have slept in their graves for decades. . . . He merits a stern rebuke from every patriotic publication in the country."[31]

Moreover, like *The Antidote*, Windle stated that inequality and bigotry were themselves the great menace to American institutions. While nativists presented themselves as model progressives and the defenders of genuine historical interpretation, Windle argued that nothing could be further from the truth. In fact, "Mr. Watson distorts the facts of history in order to place the Church in the worst possible light. He misrepresents Catholicism, past, present, and future. No man ever wrote on the subject with less fairness or more prejudice. . . . Instead of proof, Mr. Watson has given us a lot of bigoted rot born of prejudice and ignorance." Interreligious conflict, Windle asserted, served as nothing more than a smokescreen, a way of distracting readers from the nation's true evil—the growth and power of corporations. Noting that "graft is a cancer gnawing at the vitals of our Republic," Windle critiqued the "trust system" that operated with impunity from legal restraint while nativists bickered over illusionary Catholic conspiracy.[32] Like other anti-nativist texts, Windle's account insisted that anti-Catholic works, despite their veneer of progressive concern, were actually anti-progressive, distorting, manipulating, and derailing the mission of true reform and investigation. Ultimately, Windle concluded, "A careful reading of preceding chapters will show that I have appealed only to truth, reason and logic, and these have been sufficient to utterly refute Mr. Watson's charge against the Catholic Church."[33]

Windle's subsequent publication, *Straight Talk to Non-Catholics,* carried a similar contempt for nativists' claims of investigation, facts, and fairness. Windle began by noting, "I have known supposedly intelligent men to believe the most absurd statements regarding the Catholic Church when the slightest investigation would have shown the fallacious character of the charges," and continued, "We do want to arouse in our non-Catholic readers an intense desire to investigate for themselves. No statement in anti-Catholic papers can be accepted at face value. There is too much invention, fraud, exaggeration in them for anyone to place credence in sheets like the Menace [sic]."[34] Turning nativist appeals to progressivism on their head, The National Catholic Welfare Council likewise voiced contempt for Watson's unfounded accusations. Circulating a brief pamphlet titled simply "Senator Thomas E. Watson's Slander against the Good Shepherd Sisterhood," the organization cited Watson's suggestion that convents in Savannah served as "bawdy houses for the priesthood." Next, the writers proposed to "analyze these statements" so that "all may understand clearly and fully the cowardly evasion of the subtle slanderer."[35] To minimize charges of libel, the pamphlet continued, Watson alluded to or hinted at Catholic crimes, delivering his venom to Catholic foes, while avoiding culpability for his actions: "Like the coward that his is, he insinuates, he shirks the responsibility of his own words."[36] This tactic proved effective because Watson "was not writing for the intelligent and educated, but for the ignorant and prejudiced" living in areas of low culture and high illiteracy. In concluding the pamphlet, the National Catholic Welfare Council insisted "let us give heed to a fact that puts the vilification in the light of the preposterous," noting that the illicit convent Watson demonized must be a falsehood, since there was no House of the Good Shepherd ever established in Savannah.[37]

Like the Commission on Religious Prejudices, this pamphlet demonstrates the insistence with which Catholic organizations scrutinized, examined, and refuted nativist publications. In fact, the Knights of Columbus issued a similar pamphlet defending Catholic convents, entitled "A Protest and a Plea," which asked readers: "Whenever you hear any of these harrowing tales about the sinister and sanguinary plots of the Roman Catholics, never let one go unchallenged. Insist that the narrator give his authorities and furnish his evidences. See that the matter is thoroughly investigated and publish the facts with the names of those who have reported the charges."[38] Moreover, analysis, understanding, fact, and the "responsibility" of the written media stand as emblematic concerns in the progressive "Information Age" as Catholics applied these timely themes to their defense of convents and Catholic institutions. The emphasis on these issues was particularly prominent in *The Slime of the Serpent*, which discussed governmental investigations ordered by the state of Illinois and the city of Las Vegas in two different accusations of priestly complicity in murders and abductions. In describing the investigations, the pamphlet began by contending that Theodore Walker, editor of *The Menace*, "is a vulgar assassin of truth" and his publication "is the cheapest exhibition of cowardice and putrid perfidy on record."[39]

Whereas nativist opponents repeatedly charged civil officials as negligent in their pursuit of accused Catholic criminals, *The Slime of the Serpent* retorted that fraudulent charges were frequently brought against Catholic priests and that such trumped-up accusations virtually always illustrated the innocence and good works of Catholic clergy, while underscoring their opponents' treachery. In these specific instances, readers of *The Menace* accused a Nevada priest of killing an innocent boy, while police investigations and coroner's reports proved conclusively that the boy died of natural causes. In Illinois, sensationalized periodicals prompted the governor to order a thorough state inspection of all Catholic convents, which highlighted the erroneous accusations of the nativist press: "It would be difficult to gather more falsehoods and more malicious statements into one single case than has been done in this instance. The investigations ordered by Governor Deneen have proven that practically each and every one of the assertions made were false or contained an element of falsehood."[40] While "these self-styled patriots at Aurora, Mo., pretend to be fostering and defending" the nation, the author concluded, "In the face of such facts one feels tempted to exclaim: There's the enemy not here. It's the people that are doing the maligning, the slandering, the lying that need watching, not the Church and its priests."[41] Whereas nativists chided governmental agents to enforce inspection of church property, particularly convents, defenders rallying around the Catholic defense insisted that such actions only proved Catholic patriotism and their opponents' malice.

Like its counterparts, Riley's *The American Satyr* derided bigoted xenophobes for corruption, falsehood, and deceit. It argued that "before a marshaled array of facts, invincible in proof, that the American Catholic is the

peer of any other American patriot in love of our country and its institutions, the American satyr still remains a stealthy and suspicious hybrid."[42]
Riley was quick to label false those accusations of Catholics' undue political influence, illicit power, or mysterious conspiracy to grasp the reins of
power in their American homeland, and he condemned "baseless insinu-
ations against the good faith of American Catholics." As Progressive-Era
writers underscored their thirst for information and facts through the
rhetoric of "light," this trope proved popular in the anti-nativist camp as
well. Catholics and their supporters argued that, rather than promoting
progressive enlightenment, nativist opponents resorted to "the most shad-
owy of phantoms" to sell newspapers—feeble arguments that fell utterly
flat "in the light of facts."[43]

Like the Knights of Columbus, *The Slime of the Serpent,* and other anti-
nativist outlets, however, *The American Satyr* reserved its most vocal indictments of xenophobic deception for the vicious and "baseless" attacks
on the nation's Catholic convents. While accusations of Catholic political machinations are bad enough, Riley insisted, "In the charges against
the American convents, no absolute credible proof has ever been given to
show that the cloisters of American Catholicism are dens in iniquity. The
arraignment has, therefore, to be met in reverse order, for these baseless
denunciations go on and on forever without a scintilla of fact to sustain
them. They have to be overhauled on the highway of truth and downed in
their consciousless tracks."[44] Thus, like periodicals penned by their anti-
Catholic foes, Catholic apologetic works often fused prominent Progressive-
Era themes and concerns together, demonstrating, for instance, both the
efficiency and the factuality of Catholicism, while vindicating Catholic convents and attitudes toward femininity. Just as Catholics turned the tables on
nativists by illustrating how narrow-minded bigots, and not their Romanist challengers, violated progressive values, so too Catholic writers emphasized how their coreligionists embraced and upheld gendered expectations, despite anti-Catholics' claims to the contrary.

"GENTLE AND WOMANLY, YET WITH THE COURAGE OF SOLDIERS": CATHOLIC MASCULINITY AND FEMININITY

Throughout the Progressive Era, the pages of the nativist press
were replete with urgent demands calling for readers to mobilize into

manly "armies" to meet and combat the Romanist presence in the nation and defend society's weak and vulnerable individuals from an impending Catholic onslaught. Catholic organizations, however, were quick to point out that the concern and labor they exhibited on behalf of their community and nation aptly demonstrated their true values and discredited vile nativist slander. In particular, Catholic men insisted that they understood and upheld the true meaning of American manhood—rooted in the values of honor, strength, and masculine duty. Lambasting "slimy sheets, published for revenue only" that spin tales "of rifles hidden in the churches—of plans to capture the country—of schemes to murder our neighbors who differ from us," the Knights of Columbus contrasted nativists' "filthy lies" of Catholics' cowardice and deception with examples of genuine Catholic masculinity. In particular, they argued, "every man knows that if the nation was assailed by any power on earth, Catholic or non-Catholic, that the Catholic manhood of the nation would shed the last drop of its blood in her defense." Moreover, the Knights continued, American Catholics had exhibited remarkable restraint, facing the anti-Catholic assault with dignity and respect: "And oh, what splendid self control the Catholics of the state and nation have submitted to the vile abuse which has been heaped upon them. . . . Men have stood with clenched fists and set teeth, and white faces, listening to insults hurled at themselves and at their wives and daughters, and their dead mothers, but they have restrained themselves, but oh, the struggle has been hard."[45]

In *The Slime of the Serpent,* anti-nativists likewise contradicted anti-Catholic arguments. While anti-Romanists contended that the shackles of priestcraft and debauchery prevented Catholic men and women from living up to the example of their Protestant counterparts, Catholics responded by stressing the toughness, professionalism, and respectability of Catholic laymen, along with the bravery and selflessness of Catholic priests and the tenderness and maternity of Catholic women. In particular, the pamphlet dismissed nativist contentions about the immorality of confessionals, pointing out "there are as many men as women that go to confession, and bring their wives, sons and daughters with them; they are doctors, lawyers, bankers, judges . . . hard-fisted businessmen, big-fisted policemen: do you think that you could get 2,000,000 American men allowing their wives and children to resort to a custom that is dangerous to morals?"[46]

Both of the above texts insisted that Catholic men were both physically strong (evoking images of "clenched fists" or "hard fisted businessmen") and reasoned or restrained (emphasizing Catholics' "restraint" or position in professional or public life). Alongside their defense of Catholic men's mental and physical potency, however, anti-nativist texts also sought to counter attacks on the Catholic priesthood. Nativists frequently lobbed attacks at clerical targets, calling priestly celibacy a ruse to mask sexual promiscuity or condemning priests' attire, speech, or religious ritual as a sign of their diminutive, effeminate nature. Celibacy, argued *Watson's Magazine,* amounted to "the unnatural crime of depriving males of their manhood," and priests' acceptance of Mary idolatry and pagan ritual (based on worship of Isis and Venus) was a renunciation of Judaic traditions of "robust manliness."[47] *The Antidote,* however, catechized ignorant and malicious nativist reports about priestly character, pointing out priests' heroic activities during World War I. In spite of nativist attacks, the article insisted, "During the war and at the battle front the Priests of the Catholic Church proved in the eyes of the whole world what manner of men they were in reality. Their brave, unselfish and heroic deed thunder so loud in the ears of enlightened American that by contrast the malignant slanders of the Menace sink to the dimensions of the serpent's hiss." Priests' work in occupied France on behalf of refugees, along with their constant support of allied troops, provided a "tribute to the unselfish conduct of the priests," which was officially noted by Red Cross relief workers.[48]

This vocal defense of Catholic masculinity and manhood is consistent with both the broader Progressive-Era cultural emphasis on militarism and masculinity endemic of the cultural landscape as a whole and the Catholic Church's own specific emphasis on Catholic social organization in general and fraternalism in particular during the early twentieth century. As Kauffman's study points out, "The Knights' rendering of 'masculinity' and 'manhood' was characteristic of gilded-age rhetoric," particularly in its emphasis on "brotherly love," "fraternalism," and the neighborhood meetings of "the Knights of Columbus council, where masculinity flourished."[49] According to one of their earliest leaders, Supreme Knight Thomas Cummings, the Knights represented a "new type of Catholic manhood," emphasizing the dual forces of patriotism and camaraderie that held both local councils and the national organization together.[50] However, Kauffman also notes that the Knights exhibited the same attention to masculine domesticity as their nativist counterparts. Kauffman argues, "the Knights' manliness . . . also evoked a feminized domesticity" and "a strong relationship

between domesticity and fraternalism," in which fraternal ritual and organizations paralleled the close-knit bonds of familial life.[51]

Just as Catholic writers denounced nativists' appeals to progressive
ideals, they also contradicted opponents' assertions of proper masculinity,
happily noting that The Men and Religion Foreword Movement refused
to endorse *The Menace* despite its request ("further proof," announced
Catholic authors, that it is "a vulgar, lying, obscene sheet").[52] While insisting on the congruity between Catholic manliness and national masculine
roles (and emphasizing Catholic men's strength, camaraderie, and professionalism), anti-nativists were even more insistent that Catholic women,
thoroughly misrepresented and slandered in the anti-Catholic press, were
actually the epitome of national femininity. The National Catholic Welfare Council, for instance, argued that Watson's scathing indictments
against the Houses of the Good Shepherd in Georgia were an insult to
the South—disgracing Georgia's men and women alike. The Council
insisted that Watson's despicable lies "stabbed the South in the back," by
tainting the region's heritage of ennobled women and courteous and protective men. As a result, "Southern chivalry assuredly will respond to its
obligation and repudiate the Senatorial slanderer who has ignored the
South's traditions and befouled its good repute for safeguarding virtuous
womanhood from dishonor."[53] While nativists contended that celibacy
and convents stood as dire threats to the nation's femininity (and to the
stability of the nation itself), anti-nativists argued just the opposite, asserting that Watson and his fellow slanders were the true culprits. While
their opponents insisted that vigilant men should oppose priestcraft
and convent cruelties, anti-nativists urged readers to challenge and pun-
ish Watson and his like-minded imitators for their "crime against good
women."

Likewise, while nativists condemned Catholic charity as a conspiratorial sham, Windle's book retorted that the "Little Sisters of the Poor"
and similar agencies were "doing more to quench the fires of hell in this
world than any other agency in society. . . . At this moment thousands of
these consecrated women are busy in hospitals of pain . . . wiping away
tears of sorrow. . . . These brave women are found on every battlefield ad-
ministering to the dying, and nursing back to life and love the fallen heroes of nations."[54] Noting the tremendous charitable work of the Catholic Church, which greatly outshone that of Protestants, Windle challenged
Watson to imitate, rather than assault, the philanthropic work undertaken

by nuns and sisters. Rather than promoting vice and immorality, Windle insisted, celibacy and confessionals were "a safeguard of virtue and the medium by which tens of thousands have been saved from evil deeds and lives of sin."[55] Readers were led to think otherwise by tremendous lies, which misrepresented sisters' true charity and the humble femininity of Catholic nurses and convent workers. Like Windle, the Knights of Columbus spoke with contempt toward nativist lies that "poison the minds of youth" and "cast odium upon the Sisters . . . who are bending night and day over the sick and dying upon the white cots in the hospitals, whose doors are ever open to the suffering of every race, and color, and creed . . . the sisterhood who in every war of the republic, spent their lives upon the battle field, binding the wounds of the fallen, and listening to the last messages of the dying, never asking were they friend or foe, Catholic or Protestant."[56]

The tremendous and beneficial contributions made by nuns and sisters in the service to their nation and the common good, the Knights argued, illustrated their compassion, humility, and gentle nature, while underscoring the extent of nativist misrepresentation and slander. Frequently, anti-nativist publications appealed to readers' logic and common sense. How could the practice of alleged confessional immorality continue for nearly two thousand years, they asked, without arousing the ire of women and their strong fathers, husbands, or brothers? Similarly, why would Catholic parents allow their daughters to enter convents, if they truly contained the horrid tortures anti-Catholics described? This latter point demonstrates a fundamental element of anti-nativists' critique of xenophobic propaganda. While their enemies charged Catholic women with distorting national law and endangering the health of the nation, anti-nativists responded that Catholic women actually represented the pinnacle of enlightened femininity—both as self-sacrificing nuns and in their roles as diligent wives and mothers.

In this latter capacity, writers argued, Catholic women were just as virtuous and compassionate as their Protestant counterparts. Challenging anti-Catholic reports, Riley in *The American Satyr* wrote bluntly, "The Catholic fathers and mothers of America are a perpetual contradiction to these deadly slanders."[57] Anti-nativists repeatedly praised Catholic mothers as "virtuous young women, coming from Christian homes, reared with exalted views and sentiments of personal chastity and sacred virtue," and "holy women, reared under the auspices of the Christian Church, coming from homes of chastity."[58] How, then, could "Christian fathers and mothers—themselves the repository of all that is womanly and virtuous—messengers of truth and piety" turn over their offspring to "lives of hypocrisy and immortality?"[59] *The American Satyr* continued by asking readers to put themselves in the shoes of Catholic parents in considering the logic and believability of nativist claims. "It is beyond belief that chaste fathers and mothers would, for an instant, look with the faintest forbearance on an organization which not only deprived them of the society of their fair daughters and beloved children, but which, besides, transformed them into dishonored lepers."[60]

Catholic writers likewise pointed out that nearly sixty thousand nuns operated and administered hundreds of hospitals, schools, orphanages, and other institutions that prepared young women—Catholic and Protestant—to join the company of "respectable women of the world." Catholic defenders proudly noted that respectable Protestants (including the avowed nativist Thomas Watson himself!) trusted their children to the care of Catholic schoolteachers. In fact, the grounding in Catholic values, writers insisted, did not transform girls into horrendous wretches or heartless villains, as anti-Catholics loudly claimed. Rather, as *The Antidote* maintained, Catholic women were among the noblest citizens of the nation: "Their honesty, their purity, their piety are easily recognized as the outcome of their religion. The church's sanctity is manifested through the sanctity of her children."[61] Ultimately, while nativists condemned nuns as the antithesis of true womanhood, Catholics upheld sisters as diligent, even heroic. In one particularly telling article, *The Antidote* reported that seven daring sisters helped dozens of orphan children escape from a convent when an accidental fire set the building ablaze. Risking their own lives for the safety of the children in their care, the nuns exemplified the courageous attitude that illustrated their true nurturing and self-sacrificing nature.[62]

Writers frequently illustrated how Catholics exhibited similar feats of bravery on the nation's battlefields—a point that anti-nativists frequently capitalized on to underscore the true valor and respectability of Catholic manhood and womanhood. While their opponents scoffed at Catholic contributions or, worse, invented lies about the actions of Catholic priests, nuns, and laity, pro-Catholic publications pointed to their wartime service as the ultimate illustration of the compatibility of Catholic and American attitudes and a further demonstration of their coreligionists' masculine vigor and feminine compassion. *The Slime of the Serpent* exclaimed that, in the face of crisis, Catholics demonstrated their true devotion to their nation, community, and compatriots. Such was the case when priests accompanied American troops to Tripoli, Gettysburg, and the high seas of the Philippine-American War to administer last rites, care for the sick, and comfort the combatants, with "soldier boys kneeling for absolution before they made their final charge." Enduring enemy "volleys" to hear confessions and climbing through minefields and burning buildings to reach the dying, Catholic priests epitomized the same heroism as the numerous lay Catholics that swelled the nation's military forces. In underscoring priests' manly courage and sense of responsibility, the pamphlet asked readers, "Were they all the actions of immoral, intriguing men wishing to gain political control of a country, or were they not the actions of men trying to save souls . . . ? Have you ever known a priest placed suddenly in such a danger that played the coward?"[63]

Like their manly priestly counterparts, the bravery and patriotism of American nuns, along with their truly nurturing and compassionate nature, were explicitly displayed in wartime service, providing ample opportunity to refute nativist remarks. *The Antidote* noted how Abraham Lincoln himself admired the nuns' service to the Union cause during the Civil War, calling them "Angels of Mercy" to fallen troops. The paper proudly reprinted Lincoln's praise: "More lovely than anything I have ever seen in art, so long devoted to illustrations of love, mercy and charity, are the pictures that remain of those modest Sisters going on their errands of mercy among the suffering and dying. Gentle and womanly, yet with the courage of soldiers leading a forlorn hope, to sustain them in contact with such horrors."[64] Subsequent articles reprinted this glowing endorsement, even noting that the words would be inscribed in public monuments. Using the words of one of the nation's most prominent and influential leaders, in effect, killed two birds with one stone. Through Lincoln's speech, *The Antidote* could contradict nativist contentions of sham charities and dangerous nunneries on one hand and accusations of Romanists' insincere or duplicitous patriotism on the other. While Catholics repeatedly pointed to their contributions to the nation's industrial, economic, or social development, it was through wartime service that Catholic Americanism was most visibly demonstrated and the conflicting arguments of nativists and Catholics were brought into the broadest relief.

"THE GREATEST NATION AMONG NATIONS":
CATHOLIC PUBLIC MEMORY AND
AMERICAN DEMOCRACY

While Catholics were quick to address numerous rhetorical quips and foils launched by their anti-Romanist foes, they reserved their most concerted and vocal anti-nativist challenge to accusations of insincere patriotism (or, worse, overt rebellion) directed at their American homeland. Anti-Catholic periodicals were rife with allusions to Catholic revolutionaries, "papal" political parties bent on installing the pope as a monarch over North America, weapons stockpiled in Catholic church basements, and infiltration of police and military forces aimed at securing a Catholic stranglehold on America's public defense. Catholic apologists were equally prolific in their denunciation of such claims and expressions of their genuine Americanism. The reprinting of Lincoln's speech demonstrates the zeal with which Catholic writers showcased their patriotism, but it likewise illustrates the remarkably conservative nature of Catholic nationalist ideology. *The Antidote*'s reference to Civil War nurses has as much to do with venerating and endorsing Lincolnian democratic ideals and the privileged place Lincoln himself enjoyed in national consciousness as it did with praising compassionate nuns. While some Catholic writers did occasionally stop to highlight the actions of heroic priests or kindhearted nuns, their words were frequently drowned out by louder cheers celebrating the path-breaking accomplishments of noteworthy Catholic leaders such as Columbus, Commodore Perry, or Revolutionary-Era generals, making Catholic public memory a largely top-down ideology.

Moreover, whether Catholic journalists were describing recognizable leaders or, less frequently, heroic priests and laymen or humble nuns, their accounts were largely a Whiggish enterprise, one steeped in glorification and veneration of American traditions, praising America's progress completely and unquestioningly. At the most important and essential level, the goal of all anti-nativist texts during the Progressive Era was to urge the reader to accept Catholics as loyal and beneficial members of American society and renounce claims to the contrary. Using Whiggish images and metaphors, such as the one that introduced the chapter (which maintained that Catholics worked shoulder-to-shoulder with Protestants in advancing America's territorial development, ensuring material progress, fighting to defend the nation in wartime, and ushering in technological and economic advancement), served to fulfill this goal in three critical ways. First, and perhaps most obvious, Catholics embraced a glorified and conservative outlook of national progress because such arguments contradicted opponents' ideological nativism. The early twentieth century witnessed a dramatic intensification of nationalistic public memory and pageantry that revered the nation's Founding Fathers and attempted to instill a progressive vision of national development. Catholic nationalism was therefore something of a "fight fire with fire" strategy: while rival journalists argued that Catholics were mentally out of sync with (and thus disqualified from) the American citizenry, Catholics hoped that vocalizing their acceptance of prevailing attitudes toward America's historical development would move them closer to the mainstream.

Second, the Knights of Columbus and other pro-Catholic writers in the 1910s imagined America's history as a linear account of uninterrupted national success in order to highlight Catholics' own role in facilitating and maintaining American prosperity. Jonathan Zimmerman's recent study of early twentieth-century history textbooks, for instance, notes that several immigrant groups and Catholic societies—particularly the Knights of Columbus—worked to stress the triumphalism of the American Revolution and subsequent expansion.[65] The Knights of Columbus, Zimmerman illustrates, were among the most vocal critics of attempts by so-called New Historians such as Charles Beard and David Muzzey to challenge the altruistic impetus and self-sacrificing aims of the revolutionary generation, insisting that any diminution of America's grand national story would erode—not enhance—Catholics' special contributions to it. In effect, Catholics' nationalism prompted them to became ardent defenders of Protestant and Catholic heroes alike, arguing that one's success would not have been possible without the other. Zimmerman quotes an outspoken Catholic writer from Newark who reasoned that any textbook that downplayed or questioned George Washington's heroic deeds would effectively discount the Catholic soldiers and officers from France, Poland, Germany, and other regions that assisted him in securing American independence. Zimmerman points out that Catholic organizations, along with other ethnic or fraternal organizations, did manage to insert new "heroes" such as Crispus Attucks and Thaddeus Kasciusko, adding a few fresh biographies into the straightforward, Whiggish story of American exceptionalism. But the Knights and similar societies also reinforced a simplistic, triumphal message of English tyranny and American righteousness.

The result, Zimmerman concludes, was a history of "many colors, but one idea, culturally diverse, yet intellectually static."[66]

Zimmerman's study highlights the ethos of "contributionism" that pervaded Catholic ideological patriotism throughout the Progressive Era, which also proved an effective means of galvanizing Protestant support for Catholic inclusion. The third element in this strategy of Whiggish nationalism, therefore, was the portrayal of Catholics as good-natured neighbors and coworkers who were effective and stalwart partners with Protestant counterparts in advancing the nation's development. This emphasis, in turn, allowed Catholics to present a nationalistic framework that made room for themselves alongside Protestant neighbors, one that they hoped would attract non-Catholic supporters, winning friends from within the ranks of prominent journalists and Protestant clergy. Catholic writers quoted liberally from non-Catholic supporters, many of whom lambasted the nativist agenda and urged greater cooperation between Catholic and non-Catholic citizens.

Catholics' public nationalism, then, was predicated on ecumenical and public relations efforts aimed at swaying American opinion away from nativist leanings and toward a greater recognition of Catholics' benefits to American society, past and present. Scholars of American Catholicism are correct to assert that the institutional Catholic Church was influenced, in the words of Jay Dolan, by a "fortress mentality" and devotional style that emphasized an insular and separatist mentality, distinguishing Catholics from broader American culture during the bulk of the twentieth century. Nevertheless, the actions of Callahan, his fellow Knights, and like-minded supporters illustrate a competing public-spirited agenda among influential elements of American Catholic leadership.[67]

One of the leading supporters of Catholic engagement with American institutions, and perhaps the Catholic Church's most visible leader in ecumenical outreach during the Gilded Age and Progressive Era, was Cardinal John Ireland, the outspoken Archbishop of St. Paul, Minnesota, who vocally maintained the compatibility of American and Catholic ideologies. *The Antidote*, for instance, reprinted one of Ireland's speeches, which bluntly asserted "Next to God is country, and next to loyalty to God is loyalty to country. . . . To speak of America is to speak of the greatest nation among nations; to defend America is to defend not only the nation that protects you, that nurtures you, but the nation that stands in the universe for the highest ideals, the noblest principles of governing mankind."[68]

Seeking to rebuff nativist attacks, highlight Catholic contributions, and generate goodwill with sympathetic Protestants, Catholic activists espoused an Americanism that mapped onto prevailing conventions of national glorification and challenged nativist understandings of impending Catholic threats. While their anti-Romanist rivals broadcast alarmist messages of Catholic rebellion, anti-nativists pointed out that Masons, Methodists, and other Protestant denominations or organizations contributed far more representatives to Congress than their Catholic peers and that allegations of Catholic coups or conspiratorial rebellion had been repeatedly proven false in American courts. Reports of a Catholic cabal, writers contended, was "a fabrication of enemies of the Church," which insulted Catholic and Protestants alike, threatening to replace Americans' trustfulness and openness with fear and antagonism. While nativists argued that priestcraft and ignorance prevented Catholics' independence and political autonomy—making them pliable drones in the hands of manipulative priestly officials—anti-nativists pointed to the diversity of Catholic voting patterns and political affiliations, suggesting that they had already embraced the obligations of respectable citizenship.[69]

Just as anti-nativist writers inverted xenophobes' claims of manhood and progressivism to show that their bigotry counteracted, rather than supported, these ideals, Catholics and their supporters juxtaposed their "sincere" patriotism against their rivals' narrow-mindedness. *The American Satyr,* for instance, remarked that "the American Catholics have shown a far more loyal respect for the genius of our government than many of their foes" and went on to point out, "Injustice of one to the other weakens the ties of patriotism."[70] Arguing that nativist division curtails authentic American ideals, *The American Satyr* traced the history of anti-Catholic xenophobia from the Ursuline convent riots through the Know-Nothing crisis, concluding with the APA and its twentieth-century manifestations in the form of *The Menace, Watson's Magazine,* and other texts. All told, Riley's work contended, the history of American nativist foment served as a blot on national liberties, "a menace to the peace and harmony of the country, without one redeeming element; but fraught with disregard of the rights of fellow citizens to life and property."[71]

To counteract and dismiss anti-Catholic claims, the Knights of Columbus led the way in demonstrating and articulating a fervently patriotic and nationalistic rhetoric aimed at demonstrating Catholics' rightful place as champions of Americanism. The Knights' leaders, Kauffman notes, "viewed

Catholicism and American democracy as dwelling in a complementary, almost symbiotic, relationship."[72] The Knights' Commission on Religious Prejudices likewise announced, "It is a cruel and offensive thing to question the loyalty of Catholics when both past history and living example show them as true as the truest and as brave as the bravest in the service of their country."[73] The commission illustrated Catholic heroism and dedication to America by noting that their coreligionists "are always ready to make a full measure of sacrifice in time of war and to give a full measure of devotion in time of peace."[74] Emphasizing Catholic wartime service, in fact, was one of the most frequent arguments in demonstrating Catholic loyalties and patriotism. *The Antidote,* for instance, dedicated a full front-page article to demonstrating that the French general Ferdinand Foch, commander of Allied forces in Europe, was a practicing Catholic, contradicting opposite claims made by *The Menace.*[75] Catholics routinely asserted that their efforts as workers, voters, philanthropists, and good neighbors illustrated that their values and mind-set were in sync with their Protestant counterparts, thus demonstrating their "ideological patriotism." Catholics' service in America's ongoing participation in World War I provided a timely and especially compelling indication of the need for national cohesion on the one hand and Catholic Americanism on the other (see chapter 5).

However, just as Catholic defenders were quick to point out how military service in World War I nullified anti-Catholic claims of Catholic depravity and disloyalty in the present, anti-nativist publications also hoped to retroject examples of patriotism and wartime sacrifice to demonstrate Catholic loyalties throughout the nation's historical development. The Knights of Columbus, fittingly, chose their patron as the archetypal Catholic-American, representing the concomitant forces of Catholic patriotism on the one hand and national progress and development on the other. Illustrating Catholic public memory and ideological patriotism, the Knights drafted a pamphlet entitled "A Protest and a Plea," which urged readers to dismiss allegations of Catholic disloyalty and insincere patriotism. The Knights began the publication by insisting:

Ever since that far off day when Columbus, the Catholic, planted the cross, the emblem of Christianity, upon American soil, people of that faith have stood side by side with men of every creed in every human effort to make this the grandest and most free nation in the world.

Catholic and Protestants builded [*sic*] the colonies side by side—
they fought in the battles of the Revolution. Catholic explorers first
traveled the untrod forests, and first explored the great rivers of the
west. Side by side Catholics and non-Catholics cut down the forests
and plowed up the prairies. In the log huts of pioneer days, they laid
the foundation of our present civilization, and no one asked at what
alter he knelt. . . . When the flag was fired upon at Sumpter, and Lincoln called for troops, the fathers and sons from Catholic homes,
bade good-bye to the loved ones, caught step with the drumbeat, and
beside their non-Catholic neighbors, they followed the flag to the
field of battle. . . . Side by side they died in the trenches, and their
dust is mingled upon many a southern battlefield.[76]

This account of Catholics' role in Americanization and the nation's
geographic and material expansion was an exceedingly popular trope in
Catholic publications of the Progressive Era. The Knights' chronicle of
American history, like similar surveys in *The American Satyr*, and the Commission on Religious Prejudices reports presented snapshots of Catholic
contributions to formative events in distinct phases within the nation's
history—exploration, settlement, Revolution, westward expansion, and
the Civil War and its aftermath. In fact, with the notable exception of Columbus himself, Catholics and their supporters generally cited the same
national symbols, the same historical pantheon of American heroes, and
the same pivotal events in American history as displays of Catholic courage and republican sacrifice as their nativist rivals did to signal Catholic disloyalty and cupidity. Both Catholics and their opponents looked to
glorified, almost mythical, archetypes in national public memory to bolster their claims of authenticity and legitimize their assessment of Catholics' proper role in American society.

OUTLETS OF CATHOLIC COUNTERRESPONSE

Basing their claims of patriotic nationalism on Catholics' contribution to and embrace of America and its most salient values, then, required a similar celebration of a conservative and traditional chronologi-
cal outline of America's enlightened progress. Demonstrating Catholic
contributions (and soliciting respectable non-Catholic allies to vouch for

their Catholic neighbors' respectability), then, became one of the most pervasive and rhetorically powerful weapons in anti-nativists' arsenal. While
Catholics and their supporters attempted several methods aimed at shutting down their nativist foes, few met with any long-standing success. When
tactics of direct repression of anti-Romanist periodicals fell short, Catholic apologists turned to a more nuanced approach in reversing nativist
advances—generating propaganda to convince individual readers to turn
away from nativism and recognize Catholics as patriotic and friendly neighbors. Anti-Catholics, not surprisingly, denounced both Romanists' efforts
at direct suppression and the more long-standing proliferation of Catholic publications. The result was a consistent and circular battle of contrasting arguments and counterarguments that influenced both nativist and
anti-Catholic propaganda in the Progressive Era.

One of the boldest, though least successful, efforts by Catholic supporters in the fight to stop the spread of popular nativist periodicals was
barring them from the U.S. mail. Catholics sent letters to postal officials,
including the Postmaster General, asking them to revoke second-class
mailing privileges from *The Menace, Watson's Magazine,* and other prominent anti-Catholic sheets on the grounds that they represented vile and
indecent matter and therefore postal executives should execute their right
to ban their circulation in the public mail. While Canada had barred *The
Menace* from its mail by 1914, similar efforts to oust the paper from circulation in the United States were dismissed by postal officials.[77] These efforts received an even more rigorous rebuttal in the pages of the nativist
press, which accused Catholics of abridging the freedom of speech and
the press, nullifying the Bill of Rights, and suppressing the truth about
Catholic conspiracy revealed in anti-Catholic papers. Anti-Catholic papers
charged that Catholic postal officials and letter carriers deliberately destroyed or misrouted offensive books and periodicals, preventing them
from reaching readers, and anti-Catholic journalists frequently contacted
postal officials to ensure that they would not fall victim to Catholic cen-
sors' schemes.[78]

Ultimately, the suppression effort played right into nativist hands—
underscoring their claims of Catholic conspiracy mongering and antipathy for American freedoms and values. Anticipating nativists' attacks and
recognizing the futility of direct mail suppression, the Commission on Religious Prejudices quickly urged Catholic sympathizers to abandon this
strategy by the mid 1910s.[79] Recognizing that suppression efforts invariably

generated "advertising" for nativist papers and their agenda, the commission instead began a more subtle tactic of informing public opinion, using secular periodicals and the words of non-Catholic supporters to instill in readers a more positive and accepting attitude toward Catholics. In their second report in 1916, for instance, the commission noted with pride the efforts of Protestant, Masonic, and secular organizations to discredit and discourage anti-Catholic speakers and periodicals. Their cooperation, the commission remarked, served as "ample proof, if we were not already convinced, that we should have an abiding faith in the liberality and fair-mindedness of the American people, for we had the same spirit of co-operation against this common enemy of our country."[80] Within its first year of operation, Kauffman notes, the commission "had successfully re-cruited several Protestant clergymen" as well as "secular" periodicals (such as *Harper's* and *The Century*) to discredit, denounce, and repudiate the anti-Catholic message.[81]

Perhaps the commission's most compelling and successful maneuver in generating opposition to Progressive-Era anti-Catholicism was a series of meetings with journalists and publishers from the Associated Press in March 1915. Callahan and his coworkers impressed upon AP reporters that many of their coreligionists believed that America's Associated Press was staunchly in the nativist camp and presented one-sided treatments of events and individuals that painted Catholics in an unfair and uncompli-mentary manner. Moreover, they insisted, the AP paid little or no atten-tion to pivotal lawsuits in which anti-Catholic publishers were convicted of libel and forced to recant their harsh criticism of America's Catho-lic organizations and their membership. As a result of the meeting, the Associated Press pledged to present more positive treatments of Catho-lics and increase its coverage of anti-Catholic legal setbacks. While influ-encing the treatment of Catholics in the national news, the commission urged individual councils of the Knights of Columbus to work on a local level as well, nominating members to submit articles presenting Catholic opinions or teachings on "matters of interest to the public."[82] Catholic writers noted with intense optimism the widespread approval their move-ment against nativist bigotry was creating among their non-Catholic coun-terparts of all stripes, citing supportive newspapers from large cities and far-flung regions such as Bismarck, North Dakota, as proof that public opinion had shifted away from anti-Catholic hostility and toward a recog-nition of Catholic respectability. Toward the end of the 1910s, *The Antidote* called the supportive writings of Protestant leaders toward their Catholic neighbors "a straw on the waters to indicate how the tide of reactionary Protestantism is turning toward the Catholic Church."[83]

Anti-Catholic papers, of course, objected vehemently to this development and the alliance their rivals forged with non-Catholics in general and with supportive journalists and editors in particular. Whereas Catholics urged the daily press to exhibit greater fairness and sensitivity to the Catholic perspective, nativists retorted that the popular press was already "muzzled" and thoroughly "Romanized." Perhaps in response to opponents' efforts to put a Catholic "spin" on public issues, anti-Catholic papers lambasted periodicals that were out of sync with their nativist agenda. Though anti-Catholic papers occasionally reprinted articles from likeminded mainstream papers that expressed criticism toward the Catholic Church, they more often printed scathing indictments of "Romanized" dailies and denounced the Church for meddling in the public press. In light of the high-profile meetings between Associated Press leadership and the Knights' Commission on Religious Prejudices, anti-Catholic accusations in this regard seem at least somewhat germane. Nevertheless, anti-Catholic sheets frequently stretched their claims to extreme lengths to illustrate how their movement represented the only genuine source of journalistic "truth" and legitimize the nativist mission while denouncing publications from the mainstream and Catholic press alike. In describing the press's treatment of the ordination of three cardinals in the United States, for instance, *The Menace* announced that "the daily press of this country, the growing readiness of which to acclaim whatever Rome desires acclaimed and relate to oblivion whatever Rome wants so relegated, is one of the most sinister items in the situation. . . . The Catholics have put their finger on the press in America in order to juggle with fairness and gain advantage for themselves."[84]

Condemning the Commission on Religious Prejudices, *The Peril* dismissed Catholics' efforts to curry favor with non-Catholics, who should instead embrace the nativist cause. The article began in a chastising tone: "The Roman hierarchy of the United States sent out last month a pitiful appeal to the secular daily papers of the country, and to the Protestant church papers, begging these non-Catholic publications to protect the Roman Catholic church" against the "onslaughts" of nativist periodicals. While Catholics applauded these efforts for their success, *The Peril* called such ecumenism "a losing cause" and warned readers in characteristic

hyperbole, "Does the Roman hierarchy of the United States deserve protection at the hands of our loyal people? Yes, if the ghouls that fed upon
human corpses and the devilfish that crush their victims to death with
their tentacles deserve any protection."[85]

Elsewhere, papers such as *The Liberator* warned that "Romanism has
been trying to corner the daily press," while *The Yellow Jacket* bluntly accused metropolitan daily papers, jealous of its circulation, of spreading
deliberate lies about nativist papers and their editors.[86] *The Silverton Journal* argued, "The press of the United States is muzzled," and turned its
critique of the Romanized press into a marketing campaign, insisting that
"the great daily newspapers do not dare to publish" accurate facts about
Rome's depravities, "so our only hope is to build up the circulation of the
Silverton Journal and such other papers as dare tell the truth."[87] Tom Watson and his periodicals joined the fray as well, condemning the "Cathedral
influence" and the power of Catholic boycotts and deception.[88] Asking,
"Will the religious press of this country remain silent?" *Watson's Magazine*
challenged Protestant ministers to chastise Catholic aggressors from the
pulpit and non-Catholic editors to do so in their newspapers. Attacking
the duplicitous Catholic Church and its secular cronies, Watson argued,
"Will the American press lay down and be used by Rome to destroy the
American constitution and political liberty?"[89]

Throughout the nativist press, assertions of collusion between the
Catholic hierarchy and its secular agents in the publishing industry was
a poignant and consistent form of attack. *The Menace* argued that "Romanism manages to monopolize the big head lines in the daily papers,"
and warned nativist supporters "how to proceed to counteract this dangerous condition."[90] Demonstrating its disdain for "Romanized" metropolitan papers, *The Yellow Jacket* likewise unleashed a brutal critique of the
daily press in Chicago. Condemning "the Pope-pandering Tribune," one
of Chicago's leading newspapers, *The Yellow Jacket,* argued that the paper
and its staff delivered "the latest papal lie" to American readers and
printed interviews that were "a pure fake." Suggesting that Chicagoans
should stick to genuine reports from the anti-Catholic press, the article
concluded, "The Yellow Jacket reminds its Chicago readers that, once
again, it is compelled to put history straight."[91]

The Yellow Jacket's assessment of Chicago's daily newspapers illustrates a
compelling point about journalistic developments during the Progressive
Era. Catholics and their nativist foes alike took great pains to illustrate

how metropolitan daily newspapers were providing unfair and biased treatment against their constituents and agenda. Both sides expressed skepticism about the secular press and drafted extensive correspondence aimed at demonstrating the daily press's bias, hoping that it would change its tune. David Nord's examination of Chicago newspapers during the mid 1910s demonstrates that *The Yellow Jacket* was not alone in its condemnation of the expansive dailies in the Windy City. Nord begins his article by citing a customer's letter to James Keeley, editor of *The Chicago Herald*, which chastised the paper for its favoritism and preferential coverage of Catholic issues, a transparent attempt at winning over Catholic readers. But Nord immediately contrasts this letter with a nearly identical one from a subscriber wondering why Keeley's paper shows unwarranted criticism and contempt for the city's Catholics.

In attempting to reconcile these opposing conclusions about the *Herald*'s pro- or anti-Catholic stance, Nord argues that, despite movements toward journalistic objectivity and impartiality, reading the newspaper was, and continues to be, a "transaction between text and reader."[92] In particular, Nord's research of early twentieth-century Chicago papers found that some readers objected to their overt praise and kowtowing to Romanism, while, paradoxically, Catholic readers condemned the very same papers for being "down on us Catholics" and unfairly criticizing Catholic citizens and officials.[93] Nord points out that the Progressive Era ushered in a new trend in American journalism—"an embrace of impartiality and facticity."[94] Sometimes confused and often skeptical, however, readers and petitioners of Chicago papers "wanted their newspaper to tell the truth—that is, *their* truth," and, moreover, "they understood that modern journalistic objectivity meant balance, they just wanted more of it for their side."[95]

Ultimately, then, pro- and anti-Catholic forces both saw the emerging influence of the metropolitan daily press as a potential ally, if it could be convinced of the veracity of each side's claims, and a potent adversary if it could not. Drawing attention to the anti-nativist movement was therefore a plausible and, in the end, viable strategy in Catholicism's battle against the spread of anti-Romanist propaganda. But Catholics and their supporters explored other avenues as well. One less visible maneuver was to arrange boycotts of products and companies that advertised in anti-Catholic periodicals. This strategy proved relatively unsuccessful because nativist papers were small (generally only four pages) and therefore dedicated limited space to advertising. What little space was reserved for advertising generally contained testimonials for other anti-Catholic products or calls for "job" printing at anti-Catholic plants (asking loyal readers to support nativist publishers by sending printing jobs to their press). Moreover, as outlined in chapter 2, nativist enterprises likely relied primarily on incoming new subscriptions to support their operations, meaning that circulation rolls, not advertising dollars, fueled anti-Catholic expansion.[96]

One of the most alluring, though least tenable, nativist claims was that frustrated Romanists often relied on violence to retaliate against the anti-Catholic crusade. Progressive-Era nativists repeated tried-and-true anti-Catholic tropes, accusing opponents of stockpiling weapons and arms in church basements, plotting assassination attempts, and conspiring to bring about national revolution.[97] Where twentieth-century arguments were innovative was in asserting that Catholics were actively seeking to conspire against anti-Romanist papers themselves. Nativist papers insisted that Rome's minions were attacking anti-Catholic sales agents, lecturers, and publishers to curtail the spread of the nativist message. Writers insisted that alleged escaped nuns were frequent targets of violent Catholic mobs, who attempted to kill the unfortunate women before they could reveal their powerful secrets of Catholic depravity. And nativists reprinted threatening letters they claimed to have received from angry Catholics, vowing to murder the editor and destroy the paper if it continued to spout anti-Catholic venom.[98]

Although it is unclear whether such threats and attacks were genuine and, if so, how often they were carried out, one report does seem particularly salient. On the morning of July 29, 1916, *The Menace*'s printing plant was damaged by dynamite explosives, which required one thousand dollars in repairs. The paper concluded that it was the work of Catholic opponents, seeking to destroy the most successful anti-Catholic printing enterprise. Damage to the paper's production seemed limited; the paper continued printing and experienced no noticeable delays in its publication or distribution schedule. Although the paper's editors posted a significant reward, no clues or suspects were identified. In fact, given the paper's extreme drive for subscribers and the frequency with which its other anti-Catholic accusations were disproved in court, it even seems possible that *The Menace* arranged the explosion as a publicity gimmick, although it's just as plausible that outraged Catholics carried out the subterfuge.[99] Regardless of the culprits, the scope and frequency of violence directed at anti-Catholic publishers seems to have been relatively limited and flies in the face of the Progressive Era's most notable examples of pro-Catholic propaganda, which instead cultivated alliances with non-Catholics and urged readers to accept facts and rational arguments to counteract nativist slander. Moreover, isolated examples of violence pale in comparison to the damage inflicted in the nation's courtrooms, where anti-Catholics faced mounting legal bills, and more so in American public opinion, which rapidly abandoned the anti-Catholic message as the 1910s drew to a close.

Legal battles between Catholic and nativist foes were commonplace throughout the late Progressive Era, representing a new strategy in Catholic efforts to combat American nativism. While American Catholics had remained remarkably close-mouthed during prior outbreaks of anti-Catholic nativism, their Progressive-Era counterparts vigorously and vocally challenged anti-Romanist journalists. Turning to the courts to curb nativist influence also speaks to the significant human resources and financial capital at Catholic leaders' disposal and their willingness to dedicate these resources to combat the nativist threat. Mounting successful anti-defamation lawsuits in several states required an organized structure, deep pockets, and powerful allies. The Knights provided these on a scale and national scope that were previously unavailable.

By the mid 1910s, anti-Catholic papers had become mired in legal battles orchestrated by the Knights of Columbus and Catholic individuals. Charged in criminal and civil proceedings in several states, nativist publishers increasingly shifted their attention to their own legal woes, adopting a somewhat narcissistic and self-referential perspective, dedicating substantial space in their columns to dramatic accounts of pending trials, and bombarding readers with almost ceaseless appeals for new subscribers and cash donations to fund their legal defense. *The Silverton Journal*, for instance, printed a front-page article entitled "Romanists on War Path" and cautioned readers, "This issue of the Silverton Journal may appear to be all about itself and the editor, and no wonder." After detailing pending legal action against the paper (including both criminal and civil cases, which would cost the paper tens of thousands of dollars or land the editor in jail for printing scathing critiques of a nearby Catholic convent), the article told readers, "we'll be crippled so that it will need some kind of doctor to arouse our spirits and our finances to a point of operation. You are the doctor, dear reader, and we'll have to take our medicine."[100] This article, and dozens like it throughout the anti-Catholic press, admonished supporters to rally around anti-Romanist periodicals under siege from numerous lawsuits. All told, the Knights of Columbus, their supporters, and civil authorities brought well over a dozen cases to trial during the 1910s. While significant, this number would probably have been greater were it not for nativists' successful brandishing of First Amendment rights and creative use of loopholes in prevailing libel laws.[101]

Nevertheless, Catholics and their supporters scoured nativist papers to identify possible avenues for legal action and exploited these to the fullest. On June 1912, Thomas Watson was arrested in Georgia and subsequently indicted in Federal District Court in Augusta, Georgia, on the charge of sending obscene material through the mail, for printing a series of articles outlining the perversion and vice in Catholic confessionals.[102] John E. Hosmer, editor of *The Silverton Journal,* was convicted on June 16, 1914, on charges of criminal libel for printing a series of false statements against the Mount Angel convent. The *Journal* had claimed that Mary Lasenan served as a novice in the nearby convent and had escaped, revealing to Hosmer and his staff the horrendous atrocities and tortures that had taken place at Mount Angel. When the nuns challenged Hosmer in court, the editor claimed that he could not produce Lasenan as a witness because conspiring Catholics had kidnapped her, intercepted telegrams, and detained her to keep her from testifying. With Hosmer unable to produce a single witness in his defense, the court sided with the Mount Angel convent, and Hosmer, unable to pay court costs and a substantial fine, was forced to spend several months in prison. The nuns also secured a two-hundred-dollar judgment in a civil case against Hosmer.[103] Likewise, William Lloyd Clark, editor of *The Rail Splitter,* was convicted on two counts of criminal libel in 1911 and was ordered to pay four hundred dollars plus court costs, prompting several anti-Catholic papers to conduct fundraising efforts on his behalf.[104]

While several anti-Catholic publishers found themselves in court during the 1910s, anti-nativist organizers launched their most concerted legal attacks at *The Menace,* which, since it reached over 1.5 million subscribers and sparked a series of imitators, was a natural target for Catholics and their supporters. The earliest lawsuits brought in conjunction with *The Menace* occurred in Philadelphia in January 1914, when a Knight of Columbus named Charles Dowd brought a criminal libel suit against Charles Megonegal and Clarence Stage for printing and circulating an alleged Knights of Columbus Oath. The oath, which was later shown to be a complete fabrication, asserted that the Knights' Fourth Degree members pledged to disavow civic allegiances and dominate Protestants in an all-out effort to make America a Catholic nation. Megonegal and Stage claimed to have received the oath from *The Menace* and appealed to the paper for help. *The Menace* staff initially obliged and praised the men as defenders of the free press. Soon, however, paper's staff relented, urging the defendants to plead guilty and suggesting in letters to their attorney that the oath was a fake, admitting that its publication was "something of a bluff." Megonegal and Stage pleaded guilty and were charged a fine plus court costs.[105]

Despite its inauthentic origins, the "bogus" oath had a wide circulation, and the Knights scrambled to persecute those who spread its false message. Following the Philadelphia trial, the Knights aided prosecutors in Santa Cruz, California, in charging a Socialist paper with criminal libel in 1914, and similar convictions, upheld on appeal, were secured in Minnesota in July 1915.[106] These cases illustrate both nativists' proclivity to invent and fabricate sources and reports as well as Catholic organizations' effective mobilization in their own defense. While the Philadelphia case provided an initial black eye to *The Menace*, subsequent trials attacked the paper more explicitly, naming *The Menace* and its staff as defendants. In 1914, F. P. Rossman, a Catholic priest from West Virginia, secured a $1,500 judgment in federal court against the Menace Publishing Company for an article attacking his morality and accusing him of licentiousness. A similar case brought by a Missouri candidate for county sheriff, who contended that a 1912 *Menace* article had spread rumors about him and cost him the county election, was settled by both parties out of court in 1914.[107]

Despite these initial victories, the most vigorous persecution of anti-Catholic publishers came in January 1916, when *The Menace* staff stood trial in Federal Court in Joplin, Missouri, for seven counts of sending obscene material through the mail. The prosecution's witnesses at the trial were primarily high-ranking officials in the Knights of Columbus and the American Federation of Catholic Societies, who had furnished prosecutors with newspaper clippings, copies of books, and other *Menace* publications for the purpose of securing indictments and convictions. Ultimately, their efforts fell short, and the jury acquitted the publishers of all counts—largely, it seems, based on concerns of First Amendment rights and the defendants' argument that the questionable content of their paper was drawn largely from readily available sources, already in circulation in the public mail.[108] *The Menace* trilled in its its defeat of Catholic foes, calling its vindication "a victory of great significance and interest to all present day patriots, and will take its place with other historic cases in the people's warfare throughout the ages in defense of their vital freedom from the assaults of despotic rulers."[109] Linking the acquittal with patriotic victories in the Revolution, and the paper's persecution of innocent martyrs in the Reformation, *The Menace* elevated its trial to the level of moral crusade, and accounts of the trial swelled with patriotic fervor. Ultimately, in highlighting Catholics' concerted campaign of conspiracy and corruption, the paper assessed the trial by remarking, "Thus in this great battle in Rome's campaign against the constitutional guarantees, of freedom of religious discussion and freedom of the press, the cause of democracy triumphed over the papal forces."[110]

One of the most intriguing aspects of *The Menace* trial, suggested by the quotation above, was that the *Menace* defendants were less concerned with asserting their own innocence than with demonstrating how the trial itself was part of a Romanist conspiracy to limit Americans' constitutional rights and railroad the paper itself out of business, so that Catholic encroachment in America's institutions could continue unabated. *Menace* attorneys were quick to point out that similar claims of Catholic immorality and insistences that priests posed lewd and vulgar questions to women in the confessional were made by several other sources, including metropolitan dailies throughout the country. Rather than persecuting these papers, however, Catholic authorities lashed out at the *Menace*, whose only crime, publishers insisted, was printing the truth about Catholic depravity.[111] In one particularly telling portion of the trial, *Menace* attorneys cross-examined officials of Catholic organizations, particularly the Knights of Columbus, who admitted that they constructed files of *The Menace* and other anti-Catholic publications and handed these over to state and federal prosecutors to file indictments and formulate strategies in prosecuting anti-Catholic editors. Fortunately, *Menace* publishers and their anti-Catholic allies maintained, Catholic conspirators faltered in the face of "red-blooded American" jurors, who valued their freedoms and despised Romanism.[112]

A War of Propaganda:
Response and Counterresponse

Just as Catholic leaders compiled evidence of nativists' writings, as illustrated by the proceedings at *The Menace* trial itself, nativist writers frequently cited Catholic documents and welcomed readers to send clippings from Catholic papers to showcase Romanist wrongdoing. While the Knights of Columbus gathered evidence, surveyed members, and served as a repository for the study and exploration of nativist foes, anti-Catholic agitators adopted a similar strategy, compiling records from Catholics themselves and circulating them in the nativist press to demonstrate Catholicism's duplicity and danger to fellow readers. *The Peril*, for instance, reported that its staff "wants loyal citizens in every part of the country to report to it facts regarding the outrageous doing of local priests" and send "proof" and "facts" to contradict Catholic apologists.[113] *Watson's Magazine* likewise encouraged readers to keep a detailed file on Catholic periodicals and circulate Catholic efforts to refute or rebut the nativist message to daily papers as well as the anti-Catholic press.[114]

In a subsequent article titled "A Sample of the Style and Spirit of a Roman Catholic Controversialist," *Watson's Magazine* reprinted a clipping from *The Marian*, a Catholic newspaper from Alabama, which attempted to contradict Watson's "slimy lies" about the temporal authority of the pope and the licentiousness of Catholic confessionals. *The Marian* lambasted Watson for "nauseating" falsehoods, adding, "no educated man would believe them, no educated man does believe them. But we have found many of the ill-educated in little towns and through the woods who actually thought them true." Attempting to set the record straight and explain away Watson's criticism, the clipping from *The Marian* is typical of antinativist critiques that sought to invert nativist attacks and educate non-Catholic readers on Catholics' genuine character. In this rebuttal, however, Watson engaged and editorialized *The Marian*'s own attacks. Watson wrote that *The Marian* neglected to point out that bishops individually own all diocesan property and are under the supervision and watchful eye of the pope himself—in effect securing American land and riches for the pontiff. Moreover, Watson asserted that the confessional is a relic of indulgences and materialistic Catholic ritual, a distortion of genuine Christianity, and a threat to the women who submit to priests' wantonness. Concluding with the comment, "I am almost ashamed to waste time on such an ignoramus," Watson's article typifies the Progressive-Era exchange between nativist and Catholic writers. Both the Catholic and the anti-Catholic press undoubtedly scrutinized one another's periodicals with great enthusiasm and eagerness in order to refute each other's arguments and evidence. In fact, pro- and anti-Catholic agitators were likely some of the most avid readers of each other's work, frequently citing, assessing, and contradicting opposing viewpoints.[115]

Perhaps the most vocal clash in this nativist and Catholic "war of words" arose when anti-Romanist papers challenged the Knights of Columbus, the Commission on Religious Prejudices, and anti-nativist publications themselves, which, in turn, challenged and chastised nativist rebuttals. *The Silverton Journal* devoted a scathing article to attacking *The Slime of the Serpent,* whose purpose, the *Journal* insisted, was to "attempt to stem the tide of American sentiment that is very liable to soon swamp the old pirate ship of Romanism." After quoting extensively from the pamphlet, the *Journal* replied in the typical militaristic fashion of anti-Catholic crusaders. Pledging "to use the sharp two-edged sword of truth on your old licentious anatomy to its utter death and destruction," the *Journal* responded to Catholic accusations of nativist slander and falsehood, noting "'The Menace' . . . is telling the truth about your institution and your priests, and the half has not yet been told."[116] Emphasizing the righteousness and patriotism of the nativist mission, *The Yellow Jacket* likewise questioned the Knights of Columbus, its publications, and, in particular, the Commission on Religious Prejudices. Arguing that the Knights were "frantically" organizing meetings and publications "to eliminate from the minds of American citizens the belief that the Knights are an oath-bound, anti-American organization," the article went on to suggest that the Knights fabricated reports and perjured themselves in their eagerness to indict nativist opponents and conceal their anti-American sentiments.[117]

Likewise, *Watson's Magazine* contained a poignant illustration of the circular pattern of response and counterresponse in nativist and anti-Catholic texts. As the Progressive-Era anti-Catholic publishing craze was beginning in 1911, *The Catholic Union and Times* of Buffalo, New York, printed an article accusing Watson of "fir[ing] his filth-filled popgun at everything of a Catholic character." Watson, in turn, reprinted a portion of this article in his August 1911 issue, countering that it "shows the venom and the vindictiveness of the Pappycrat priesthood." Moreover, Watson concluded, "it is a national calamity that these Mary-worshipping idolaters were ever allowed to set up their heathenish church in this Protestant country. Not a single one of these priests is or can be a loyal citizen."[118] A year later, however, in his defense of American Catholicism, Charles Windle cited Watson's contention, noting, "What a pity Washington and Jefferson could not have the benefit of Watson's advice! Had Jefferson been imbued with the Tom Watson spirit, the Declaration of Independence would have been made to read: 'All men—except Catholics—are created equal.' Yet Watson calls his publication 'The Jeffersonian Magazine!'"[119]

As the circular debate pitting Watson against Catholic authors illustrates, both nativists and their opponents evoked similar nationalistic themes, alarmist tones, and, in particular, identical goals of winning public approval by discrediting rival writers. Just as Catholics and their allies considered it essential to demonstrate their genuine acceptance of American values, so too nativists fought to uphold their message of Catholic depravity and insincerity. One *Silverton Journal* article expressed this view in no uncertain terms, vowing that the paper's mission was "nothing less than entirely destroying the Roman Catholic hierarchy root and branch." Articulating the means to bring about the incapacitation of Romanist foes, the article continued, "To this end we call on every true American patriot to lend a hand in our propaganda warfare. Help us circulate our paper. Help us build a library of progressive literature. Help us keep up financially to pay out, so as not to have to stop before getting fairly started."[120] In this article and dozens more, nativists responded to Catholic rebuttals by calling for an even wider circulation (and increased revenue) to win the "propaganda warfare" that raged throughout the 1910s.

In carrying out propaganda battles, both nativists and anti-nativists relied on remarkably similar methods—mobilizing speakers, organizing lecture circuits, jockeying for position and respectability in the secular dailies, alternately admiring and chastising publishers and journalists to influence the public press, and, above all, churning out staggering quantities of print material to advance their viewpoint and disarm their opponents. This war of propaganda was waged in America's courtrooms and post offices, but in large part this warfare played out as a fight for circulation. Anti-Catholic papers certainly relied on new subscribers to maintain their operations but also broadcast their rapidly expanding circulation totals as a sign of Protestants' growing awareness of Catholic threats and the growing condemnation of priestcraft. Illustrating their substantial readership, in effect, legitimized and vindicated anti-Romanist papers and their mission from anti-nativist critiques. Catholics, in turn, boasted that the success of the Commission on Religious Prejudice and other organizations in securing non-Catholics' approval and demonstrating Catholic viewpoints through promulgation of facts both facilitated and showcased a shift in American mentalities and attitudes.[121]

At stake in this war of propaganda, was nothing less than the right to articulate Catholicism's place in the American nation, which presented both sides with ample incentive and opportunity to write diligently and prolifically in their own defense. Nativists chided that Catholics' alleged Americanism and pretended civic virtue were deliberate inventions aimed at cloaking their deception in "a veritable fabric of lies." Catholics' "Patriotism Begets Heresy," argued *Watson's Magazine,* insisting that readers "question whether there can be patriotic loyalty in the bosom of a loyal Catholic."[122] In contrast, the Knights of Columbus authors reversed Watson's claims. Nativists, the Knights argued, betrayed America's sacred traditions and values: "They stain the flag with their dirty fingers, and as they wave it aloft, pour forth their foul abuse of every Catholic, charging that they are disloyal to their country, heedless of the fact that oceans of Catholic blood have been shed in its defense." Citizens of the Catholic faith, the Knights respond, are quite deserving of both titles—Catholic and American, as demonstrated by their religious faith and their patriotic service. Contrasting nativists' depravity with their own Catholic loyalty, the Knights maintained, "For more than a century now, Catholics have served the nation and the state . . . and no one yet has been able to point out a single act done, nor a single word uttered by any one of the thousands who have thus been called to service, which could be construed as unpatriotic or lacking in loyalty to the nation or its flag."[123]

CATHOLIC AMERICANISM AND
THE RISE OF WORLD WAR I

This emphasis on Catholic contributions and their role in substantiating claims for citizenship underscores an important distinction between Progressive-Era expressions of Catholic Americanism and those of subsequent decades. One of the most insightful and informative accounts of post–World War I Catholic nationalism is Garry Gerstle's book, *Working Class Americanism,* which examines the activities of French-Canadian

Catholics and their participation in Connecticut textile factories and labor unions. Gerstle argues that the rhetoric and malleability of the term "Americanism" proved a powerful and highly successful ideology in unifying both leftist organizers and traditionalist French-Canadian workers into a potent labor union during the 1930s. Noting patriotism's enduring influence on working-class Catholics throughout the mid twentieth century, Gerstle argues, "Radicals could express their progressive beliefs in the language of Americanism while ethnics could use the same language to promote traditionalist values. And both could find in their words and ideas of Americanism's democratic dimension a justification for limiting the rights of capital and augmenting the rights of labor." This overlap between nationalism and citizens' "rights" was prominent in the 1930s, particularly in the decade's evocation of public memory, and played a large part in post–World War I popular culture and imagination of the past. Patriotic inheritance, Gerstle illustrates, allowed workers in the post–World War I era to demand the rights due to them by the state and their peers.[124]

This "rights-based" rationality of citizenship in general and Catholics' Americanism in particular was altogether absent or, at most, implicit and severely muted in Catholics' articulation of patriotism during their clash with nativists in the 1910s. During this decade, Catholic and their allies instead articulated a contribution-based understanding of nationalism, one that implored readers to witness the struggles and contributions of Catholic counterparts and consequently recognize their national loyalty. Gerstle's account forecasts the experience of later decades, which witnessed a shift in Catholic consciousness. In particular, while Gerstle suggests that the foundation of Catholics' insistence on "rights-based" citizenship was grounded in the aftermath of World War I in the 1920s, Catholics who actually lived through and reported on the war expressed a different sentiment. Instead of urging Catholic soldiers and workers to demand their appropriate "rights," Catholic observers asked their non-Catholic neighbors, including their nativist opponents, to view Catholic wartime service as a symbol of and call for national unity in a time of significant crisis. Anti-nativists galvanized support for their movement by noting Catholics' honor, heroism, and loyalty to the nation. In demonstrating "The Lesson of Unity," for instance, an outspoken article in *The Antidote* noted, "We have learned many lessons from the war, not the least being the value of unity. How insignificant many things are that we once thought all-important in the light of the supreme sacrifice of men's lives!"[125] Catholics quickly recognized that wartime service heightened and substantiated their claims of bone fide patriotism and national contribution, and as much as opponents tried to discredit and refute such claims, the exigencies of wartime gave greater cultural currency to appeals for national cohesion and inclusion. In fact, America's participation in World War I in 1917 signaled an abrupt decline in Progressive-Era anti-Catholicism, culminating in the virtual disintegration of the anti-Catholic movement by 1919. With national attention directed toward external conflicts overseas, papers had a harder time attracting attention to domestic infiltration and xenophobia. Moreover, Catholic organizations became more focused on wartime relief and mobilization and consequently less attuned to combating anti-Catholic attitudes at home. In effect, actions of military service proved stronger than the words of the Commission on Religious Prejudices and similar organizations in demonstrating Catholic contributions to national well-being.

The Knights of Columbus discontinued the Commission on Religious Prejudices in 1917, hoping to shift their resources to assisting soldiers called to battle overseas and partly as a result of the decline of nativist vigor itself. Patrick Callahan, the commission's chairman, concluded its final report by insisting, "The war will kill bigotry. Not the individual sentiment; but the movement. . . . Jealousies, enmities, bitterness and hate, wholesale inventions of scandal . . . these the war will quiet and the social ferment arising from their systematic exploitation will stagnate and die." By bringing Catholic contributionism to the forefront and cultivating a greater perception of American unity, World War I had made the commission's efforts a foregone conclusion, ending both the attacks of most anti-Catholic groups and the need to defend against the scattered few that remained.

CHAPTER FIVE

World War I and the Anti-Catholic Hiatus

W hile legal maneuvers and propaganda warfare proved somewhat effective in limiting anti-Catholicism's expansion in the late Progressive Era, with America's entry into World War I the already stumbling nativist movement dissolved into obscurity. This disintegration arose in part because the war brought increased production and distribution costs, which put a strain on nativist periodicals, many of which were already feeling the effects of legal expenses and court fees. Wartime anxiety also took a toll on subscribers, the lifeblood of the anti-Catholic crusade, which suddenly had to compete for readers' attention and demonstrate how Catholics posed a greater threat than the German Kaiser. Ultimately, however, World War I facilitated nativists' departure from the American literary spotlight because it legitimated and exemplified Catholic contributionism and, in so doing, made nativists' exclusivist, anti-Romanist nationalism temporarily unpopular. Nativism fell out of vogue in the late 1910s chiefly because wartime exigency made its brand of xenophobia and ideological nativism directed toward the nation's largest religious denomination untenable and gave greater weight to competing claims of national tolerance and unity in general and Catholics' "100 percent Americanism" in particular.

Catholics, for their part, envisioned the Great War as an opportunity to demonstrate their profound national loyalties, enlisting for military duty in the thousands and participating in wartime service in greater proportions than their Protestant counterparts.[1] The Knights of Columbus, for instance, called Catholic military service "an answer to the bigots' erstwhile cry of disloyalty, one more powerful than any words." Suggesting that wartime militarization demonstrated Catholic masculinity as well as patriotism, the Knights' Commission on Religious Prejudices concluded, "Here is living, incontrovertible proof that the loyalty of Catholics to their country, and their love of freedom and right, do not shrink by their comparison with their fellow-citizens, but show up brave and true."[2] Catholic men's heroism, truthfulness, courage, and self-sacrifice, the commission insisted, illustrate the utter falsehood of rival claims, demonstrating how nativists sought to divide American citizens, pitting one segment of the population against the other, when both sides should join together in presenting a united front.

Anti-Catholic periodicals exhibited little support for Catholic visions of national unity and inclusion. Instead, they countered that activities in World War I merely represented a further illustration of and opportunity for Catholic betrayal and deception. While the Vatican officially professed neutrality in the conflict, nativist publications extended their critique of domestic Catholic conspiracy to include wartime sabotage and espionage overseas. Anti-Catholic newspapers asserted that Romanist foes had infiltrated American fighting units and were providing intelligence to German officers, conspiring to influence diplomatic negotiations, formulating secret spy networks that intercepted American radio communications, and delivering vital information on troop placements into the enemy's hands. Catholic spies, nativists maintained, contributed to German naval victories, priestly deception and meddling bolstered the authority of Austrian powers, and, amid American forces, Catholic chaplains and army bureaucrats siphoned money from American forces, shifting it to the papacy or to the enemy's coffers.

In several respects, nativists' arguments during World War I were remarkably similar to their prewar contentions—Catholics could not be trusted to uphold the nation or its values and must be diligently scrutinized and monitored for the public welfare. The wartime environment, however, heightened these claims and raised anti-Catholic arguments to a feverish, almost paranoiac pitch. By the late 1910s, anti-Romanist papers insisted that Catholic "skullduggery" animated wartime conflicts and that backroom deals, Catholic assassins, and political machinations aimed at instituting papal sovereignty over all of western civilization had precipitated the war itself. *The Menace* warned Americans that the conflict had become "Jesuitized" and that the German enemy had been "aided and abetted by all the chicanery and villainy" of the merciless "Black Pope."[3]

While Catholics' international intrigue and espionage were destructive enough, nativist publications maintained that Catholics constituted an even more dangerous and conspiratorial influence on the American home front. Nativists recycled long-familiar assertions that Catholics were hiding weapons in churches, using parochial schools to train paramilitary forces, and entering governmental and police forces with the intent of toppling the American government itself. Nativists argued that Catholics intended to form a domestic "fifth column" and were receiving guidance and cryptic instructions from American enemies abroad to corrode the nation's military and political rigor from within. *The Menace* cautioned readers that claims of Catholic patriotism, which might seem genuine, were actually dangerous weapons, designed to lure Americans into accepting Romanist propaganda and inviting subterfuge into the nation's war effort. The paper argued, "The gravest element of danger confronting the government at this very hour" consisted of Catholic infiltration, "the powerful and efficient spy system built up with the very borders of our country." Concluding with the warning "the destructive power of Rome will show its hand with a boldness that none can fail to see," *The Menace* pleaded with readers to fight Catholic encroachment by purchasing additional copies of the newspaper, which would expand its reach, spread enlightenment, and preserve the nation itself.[4]

The Nativist Decline

By the late 1910s, however, fewer readers bought into these contentions of Catholic conspiracy, and fewer still actually bought nativist periodicals themselves. Nativists insisted that wartime concerns must not distract readers from the more long-standing and salient threat to American stability posed by popery and its followers, but few seemed to listen, and circulation rolls plummeted by 1919. *The Menace* complained about "shifting events of the time," which motivated readers to focus on other concerns, and the Commission on Religious Prejudices noted that nativism continued to be eclipsed by reports from overseas, stating that newspapers were "flooded with war 'stories' and other articles bearing on the war which operates against the publication of matters of lesser interest."[5] John Higham's survey of American nativism likewise points out how wartime concerns precipitated nativism's decline by the late 1910s. Higham notes that American participation in World War I generated "competing appeals" among anti-Catholic audiences, asserting that "undoubtedly the breakup of Protestant xenophobia also reflected a shift of attention from the Pope to the more substantial and exciting menace of the Kaiser. Instead of invigorating anti-Catholicism, anti-Germanism stole its thunder."[6] American Catholics of German or Italian descent occasionally experienced resentment in the wake of the nation's wartime mobilization. As Higham's study illustrates, such hostility was generated on the basis of their ethnic "otherness" and therefore represents "ethnic"—as opposed to "ideological"—nativism and, consequently, a departure from the prior modes of Progressive-Era anti-Catholicism.

As readers turned their attention away from explicitly anti-Catholic themes, nativist periodicals that had experienced tremendous growth and influence only a few years earlier began to decline rapidly. A couple of the most notable papers—particularly *The Menace* and *The Rail Splitter*—survived through the end of the 1910s, managing to endure financial difficulties to continue production. Most papers, however, dramatically reduced their output. *The Yellow Jacket* and *The Crusader*, for instance, dropped from weekly to monthly circulation by 1917, after which only scattered issues were released before the papers dropped out of circulation entirely. Numerous periodicals dissolved even more rapidly, disappearing from the historical record entirely by the time American troops began mobilization for war. Still others, such as *The Mountain Advocate*, continued publication into the 1920s but suddenly dropped any mention of anti-Catholicism by the late 1910s, in effect, mirroring the trajectory of metropolitan dailies in their focus on wartime developments. The Knights of Columbus cheered the disintegration of nativist print culture in the wake of World War I, eagerly reporting that the vast majority of anti-Catholic publications had "quit the field" and gone out of business, with "only two or three having any circulation worth mentioning." By their count, rival periodicals had slipped from sixty explicitly anti-Catholic papers in the early part of the 1910s to a mere handful as the decade drew to a close. With the decline of anti-Romanist texts, the Knights maintained, came the end of anti-Catholicism's cultural and political influence in the nation as a whole.[7]

While some nativist papers criticized Catholic opponents for exaggerating their circulation woes, most conceded that subscriptions had experienced a sharp downturn and filled their pages with urgent appeals for new readers and frequent donations to keep the paper afloat. *The Crusader,* for instance, noted that at least half a dozen anti-Catholic papers had gone out of business in less than two years, and added that several more were in real financial trouble. "Even the Old War Horse, The Menace," the article continued, "has seen as much as 40,000 of a deficit in its subscription list in one week," illustrating its quick drop-off in readership.[8] *The Menace* increased the frequency and intensity of its circulation drives, but the paper reported that its stockroom was still littered with "several thousand copies of back issues." Clearly these drives met with limited success as the decade wore on.[9]

Nativist publishers were quick to blame their troubled financial outlook on decreasing supplies (and thus increased prices) of paper and printing materials brought about by the war. Papers also pointed to increased shipping costs as the root of economic hardship.[10] Ultimately, however, these concerns proved trivial in light of the more transformative shifts in American culture that rendered the nativist argument moot—namely, the opportunity for Catholics to locate new outlets in demonstrating their fervent Americanism. Anti-Catholics continued to demonstrate their own patriotic loyalties, but their dwindling voices were drowned out by Catholic vocal assertions of national service in World War I.[11] *The Antidote,* for instance, praised the charitable relief work performed by the Knights of Columbus on behalf of the nation's soldiers, noting that they had collected and distributed over seven hundred tons of food and supplies, valued at nearly three million dollars, to troops at the front. Such devotion, the article concluded, earned the organization the nickname "The Knights of Cooperation." A subsequent article likewise praised the Knights' diligence and charity, arguing that "it is no wonder that the victorious Yankee lads return . . . brimming with gratitude for the genuine patriotism of the Knights."[12] In illustrating the success of a Catholic-led war drive, *The Antidote* noted citizens' remarkable ecumenism and willingness to put aside differences in light of the national crisis. Such openness and cooperation, the paper insisted, demonstrated that "the big majority of the American people are not laboring under the influenza of Romaphobia . . . and are ready to join hand in hand with their Catholic fellow citizens in any patriotic or charitable enterprise of a nation-wide character."[13]

While Catholic writers showcased nurses, relief workers, and charitable contributors as exemplars of their coreligionists' contribution to the nation's war efforts, they focused much of their attention on Catholic soldiers who were battling amid "the blood soaked trenches of suffering France" and fighting for the American cause. Their actions were both "patriotic and inspiring," as they joined the "cry of a nation's heroic army—an army fighting for humanity and freedom." Alongside such examples of Catholic bravery, anti-nativist writers remarked, agents of anti-Romanism seemed utterly impotent and pathetic. While Catholic soldiers and philanthropists were facing the "big task of smoothing the rugged ways for [General John] Pershing's gallant crusaders," their foes were busying themselves dreaming up nonsensical schemes, trying in vain to convince a wary nation that the pope was stealing money from the American war chest "and would convert it into guns and bayonets to aid a march on Washington so as to lock up the President of the United States."[14]

Recognizing that Progressive-Era anti-Catholicism had run its course and lost nearly all of its vitality and support, Catholic organizations quickly shifted their attentions as well. The Commission on Religious Prejudices disbanded in 1917, and, within two years, *The Antidote* had altered its course substantially, moving away from anti-nativist themes to address war developments and the growing power of socialism and bolshevism. By the close of the 1910s, *The Antidote* shifted its focus away from *The Menace* and like-minded periodicals and adopted a new concern for "the Menace of the Servile State" and "The Bolsheviki Menace," emphasizing engagement with new enemies that underscored the demise of anti-Catholic agitation in the first two decades of the twentieth century. As World War I drew to a close, *The Antidote* had discontinued its "Talks with Readers of The Menace," column and in fact provided virtually no mention of anti-Catholicism after its coverage of the Versailles Peace Accords in 1919, suggesting the paper, and possibly its readers, felt the nativist threat was too weak to deserve much journalistic attention.[15]

World War I was, *The Antidote* insisted, a "Knock-Out for the Fanatics," and, indeed, anti-Catholic papers quickly faded away during the war and its aftermath.[16] Thomas Watson's periodicals—*The Jeffersonian* and *Watson's Magazine*—were briefly suppressed by the U.S. Post Office in the late 1910s as a result of Watson's criticism of Wilson and wartime conscription. Watson himself died in 1922. *The Menace* printing plant in Aurora, Missouri, was destroyed by what appears to be an accidental fire on December 11,

1919. Publishers made several attempts to rebuild their movement in following years, achieving only limited success. Internal squabbles among the paper's editorial staff over how and where the paper should be published further threatened the once-prominent movement and jeopardized *The Menace*'s survival. Renamed *The New Menace*, the paper continued publication into the 1920s, with frequent changes in staff and location. *The New Menace*'s earliest issues were printed in Kansas City, before the paper moved to Branson, Missouri, where it remained through 1922. Publication then returned to Aurora briefly, where the paper also launched a variety of spin-off papers (boasting names such as *The Torch* and *The Monitor*), which printed only a couple scattered issues in their short lifetimes. Ultimately, *The New Menace* never achieved the notoriety, financial success, or cultural influence of its predecessor. Moreover, *The New Menace* attracted neither the significant readership nor the attention of rival publishers that characterized the dramatic movement of anti-Catholic print culture witnessed in the Progressive Era.[17]

While most nativist periodicals of the decade abruptly ceased production and *The Menace* struggled on in a fractured state for several years, one of the few Progressive-Era anti-Catholic publications to survive intact through the 1920s was William Lloyd Clark's *The Rail Splitter*. Clark's monthly publication, while it never achieved an extensive readership, continued to extort anti-Catholic themes through the roaring twenties, though only a handful of documents persist in the historical record. Perhaps Clark's paper endured because of its small scale—a one-man operation printed in a remodeled barn with Clark conducting all of the writing, editing, and typesetting himself. In the mid 1920s, Clark went on to champion the cause of the Ku Klux Klan in the upper Midwest, serving as a lecturer and organizer. Subsequent Klan publications praised "Brother Clark" and his efforts at denouncing Romanism, urging loyal Klansmen to buy *The Rail Splitter* and support its efforts. Moreover, the Klan's *KAP Magazine* (which likely evoked the long-standing acronym "Keep America Protestant") dedicated a story in 1926 to Clark's pioneering work in alerting readers to the dangers of Catholic hostilities. Clark's devotion to anti-Catholicism and his path-breaking newspaper, writers insisted, ought to inspire "every Patriot in America" to join the Klan's crusade in preserving American purity.[18] Although the *KAP Magazine* and Clark's latter efforts shared the same crusading tone and alarmist rhetoric as *The Rail Splitter*, Clark's subsequent embrace by the Klan speaks to the divergent directions and shifting message of American nativism following 1919, bringing both continuity and different agendas to post–World War I anti-Catholicism.

In an important sense, the steep downturn in America's anti-Romanist publishing and the concomitant and continued prominence of competing Catholic periodicals speaks to the latter's ability to harness public opinion and support, an opportunity that was enhanced by pointing to Catholic wartime patriotism. Whereas previous attempts to jump-start Catholic public relations campaigns (notably the Catholic Press Association) had proven futile and previous outbreaks of anti-Catholic agitation met with little resistance from lay or clerical organizations, Catholic writers, like their nativist counterparts, were quick to apply the prevailing tone and language of progressivism to their war of propaganda. In doing so, architects of the Catholic defense in the 1910s formed what might be termed America's first lasting Catholic public relations campaign, urging a unified national effort on the part of Knights of Columbus members to guard against emerging enemies by carefully monitoring and influencing other writers and launching extensive media drives of their own. As Christopher Kauffman's study illustrates, the Knights' subsequent mobilization, charitable work, insurance drives, and postwar fraternalism on both the local and the national level demonstrate that the organizational and public relations skills called into service in defense of the Catholic faith in the 1910s continued to motivate and expand the organization's mission in latter decades.[19]

Ironically, however, in guarding against anti-Catholic encroachment, the Knights and their supporters in the Catholic media drive committed many of the transgressions so frequently asserted by the nativist press. Seeking to mollify the influence of nativist ire, for instance, Catholic writers drafted hundreds of letters urging newspaper editors to adopt a more positive stance toward Catholic citizens. The Catholic position in the war of propaganda hinged on convincing secular newspapers and their readers that their Catholic neighbors were fully supportive of America's traditions and values, a position that was enhanced and ultimately triumphed over rival arguments in the face of World War I. In carrying out their public relations efforts, Catholics sought to influence the American press, convince citizens of Catholic generosity and benevolence, mobilize the courts and postal authorities to silence opposition, and otherwise use their tremendous financial backing and efficient organizational structure to wage war against rival viewpoints. In short, they took the very actions that sparked alarm and consternation from the nativist camp. Of course, these were, in effect, the same actions taken by nativist themselves, as they worked tirelessly to boost circulation, organize lectures, and sway mainstream papers toward the nativist outlook.

At issue, then, in this public relations duel was which view would prove most salient and acceptable to American readers. The rapid disintegration of a once-potent anti-Catholic publishing enterprise suggests, as Catholics themselves cheered at the end of the 1910s, that feelings of wartime loyalty and solidarity trumped nativist xenophobia, at least temporarily, at the close of the decade. In outlining their vindication and triumph over nativist foes, the Knights of Columbus insisted that World War I had shattered the forces of Progressive-Era anti-Catholicism, just as the Spanish-American War decimated the American Protective Association, the Civil War brought an end to Know-Nothingism, and the Mexican-American War cast doubt on the earliest outbreak of the Maria Monk affair.[20] Catholics thus pointed to a long tradition of wartime involvement and sacrifice, in turn bringing about a temporary disruption of the nation's nativist xenophobia. Each of the nation's great military victories, Catholics asserted, also served as an achievement in Catholic patriotism, disrupting the vocal critics of Catholic loyalties while providing yet another illustration of Catholic Americanism. Historian Charles Morris, in addressing Catholicism's place in twentieth-century America, reiterates this point, illustrating the role of wartime involvement in carving out a place for the nation's Catholics within the framework of national respectability. "By the end of World War I," Morris contends, "the loyalty of American Catholics was as unquestioned as it was unquestioning."[21]

Unlike Morris' optimistic observation of twentieth-century Catholic life, the Knights' timeline of Catholic wartime service has a flipside: while national crises temporarily joined together Catholics and the American mainstream, the Knights also recognized that the end of hostilities invariably brought about another episode in the nation's anti-Catholic legacy. In concluding their final report, for instance, the Commission on Religious Prejudices warned readers not to underestimate the durability and longevity of America's anti-Catholic nativism. Americans might be tempted to assume, the commission remarked, that because the most vocal anti-Catholic periodicals had gone out of business, nativism itself had been defeated. "It is not," the commission warned. "Buried in its secret recesses, it is germinating like a fruit that has fallen ripe. . . . These germs [will] slowly spring

into life and in the next generation a new crop of tares will need to be gar-
nered with the wheat of the social harvest."[22]

In several respects, it would be tempting to accept Morris's assertion
at face value and conclude this book on a high note, arguing that the vali-
dation and vindication Catholics experienced during World War I signaled a permanent and consistent shift in America's social attitudes. Such
an assertion would suggest that Catholics had passed their last hurdle
en route to full participation and acceptance in the nation's mainstream
by 1919. But such an argument would also misrepresent the durability
and longevity of America's anti-Catholicism and shortchange subsequent
movements that likewise called Catholic Americanism into question. As
the Knights of Columbus themselves recognized, Progressive-Era nativism
proved a basis for, rather than a conclusion to, the nation's later manifestations of anti-Catholic bigotry.

The Ku Klux Klan and Anti-Catholic Longevity

In fact, while Progressive-Era anti-Catholicism itself proved
short-lived, several of its most salient and essential elements resurfaced
in subsequent decades as anti-popery again intensified. A thorough investigation of these later developments would certainly go beyond the
scope of this study and would duplicate the efforts of some excellent and
extensive works currently in print. Nevertheless, in concluding this assessment of early twentieth-century anti-Catholicism, it is worth mentioning how Progressive-Era nativists' concerns and dominant themes manifested themselves in the mid to late twentieth century. Progressive-Era
nativists' anxieties about the declining influence of rural America and
the corresponding shift in the social prestige of their middle-class community leaders echo later concerns that motivated and guided the second
Ku Klux Klan in the 1920s. Both movements also shared a deep ambiva-
lence toward modernization and a strong desire to preserve conventional
hierarchies in the face of dramatic social change, which increasingly called
the hegemony of white Anglo-Saxon Protestant men into question. In later
decades, anti-Catholic print culture likewise experienced a rebirth, when
writers such as Paul Blanshard penned dramatic and best-selling diatribes
against Catholic priestcraft and its destructive influence on American in-

stitutions. Such works extended both the ideological nativism and the anti-Catholic literary tradition exemplified in Progressive-Era periodicals.

While the Progressive-Era anti-Catholic movement was still reaching the height of its influence and popularity in the early 1910s, *The Jeffersonian* published an article fittingly titled "A Letter from an American Patriot," which argued, "A greater oppression now confronts the American people than did in 1776, and calls for the same united action on the part of the people . . . and nothing short of this will preserve our freedom of speech, press, and liberty of conscience." A vigorous anti-Catholic crusade, the article concludes, serves as the only remaining way "to redeem this country, the glory of the nations and heritage of the sons of the fathers of the revolution of 1776, from the bloodiest and most merciless war that ever disgraced a civilized people—Jesuitical Romanism."[23] Here *The Jeffersonian* suggests that American traditions—embedded in the nation's glorious revolutionary heritage—were in danger of slipping away, usurped by the force of violent social upheavals that threatened American civilization and the birthright of the revolution's heirs.

Calling for readers to "redeem" the nation's virile revolutionary sentiment, this article anticipated many of the motivations and dominant themes exhibited in the more well-known architects of twentieth-century anti-Catholicism—the second Ku Klux Klan, which emerged in the 1920s as a response to growing concerns that America's traditional pastoral social order was breaking down. Like its Progressive-Era anti-Catholic forebears, the Klan, or "Invisible Empire," served, in John Higham's assessment, as an "instrument of modern American nationalism" cloaking its xenophobia in trappings and pageantry that were steeped in American iconography and symbolism. While individual "klaverns" and local organizations adopted remarkably divergent goals and objectives as the 1920s wore on, most shared the concern outlined in the *Jeffersonian* article cited above. "Average white Protestants," Higham notes, "were under attack: their values and traditions were being undermined, their vision of America's natural progress and social order appeared to be threatened, and their ability to shape the course of public affairs seemed to have diminished."[24] By the mid 1920s, the Ku Klux Klan had expanded dramatically (by one estimate, membership topped five million dues-paying members), mirroring the rapid rise of nativist xenophobia in the previous decade. Like the nativist movements that came before it, Klan membership proved popular primarily because it provided an outlet for seething frustrations, as the nation moved uneasily away from conventional social and economic models.[25]

As I outlined in chapter 2, anti-nativists in the 1910s established their anti-Romanist crusade in part as an attempt to retain their privileged positions of leadership in small-town life, roles that were rapidly deteriorating as far-flung communities themselves transformed in the wake of industrialization and mass markets. This likewise proved to be the dominant motivation in Klan activity in subsequent decades. David Chalmers's influential study *Hooded Americanism*, for example, notes that men joined the Klan because they feared that "time was chipping away at the traditional religious and moral values of small-town America."[26] With the erosion of conventional social hierarchies, Chalmers argues, the Klan embarked on the "grim defense of a society under attack in the twentieth century," just as anti-Catholic writers in the Progressive Era mobilized to preserve their "island communities" from external encroachment.[27] In her case study of the Ku Klux Klan in Athens, Georgia, Nancy MacLeon likewise remarks that Klansmen felt trapped in "the vise of modernity," noting that cultural shifts evidenced by women's suffrage, greater black enfranchisement, and the prevalence of divorce and labor unrest "were the birth pangs of a new social order" in which "relations of power and culture differed from those of the nineteenth-century world" and "undercut the kind of hierarchy from which men like themselves had derived security."[28]

Moreover, economic transitions and greater industrialization had stripped American society of the entrepreneurial and advancement opportunities that created at least an outward illusion of rough egalitarianism among white Protestant men. Rural life, Klansmen feared, had become threatened and corrupted (possibly irreversibly) by tenant farming, absenteeism, and megalomaniacal industrialists and railroads. Declining economic opportunities for the Southern white man brought about a concomitant decrease in his social influence and feelings of autonomy. As a result "maintaining his authority over African Americans and immigrants— let alone over his own wife and children—would be more difficult than ever before."[29]

Klansmen's dwindling opportunities to assert and repair their paternalistic influence over other members of society prompted their stark backlash against the representations of modernity and social disintegration. Scholars have noted that the Invisible Empire drew its staunchest supporters from middle- and upper-middle-class men who were leaders in their small-town communities. Klan activism as a whole, MacLeon demonstrates, was motivated by "reactionary populism," in which disenfranchised white men banded together to reconstruct "the provincial, paternalistic world of their dreams."[30]

The Invisible Empire, in effect, mirrored the Menace Army and its Progressive-Era counterparts by acting to enforce rigid and gendered conceptualizations of proper social organization. Like anti-Catholic movements from prior years, Klansmen developed a thoroughly militaristic rhetoric and understood manhood's proper role as upholding national traditions and small-town ways of life. Their desire to cast themselves as chivalrous guardians (and powerful rulers and protectors) of their families and communities informed Klansmen's varied agendas—from their enforcement of prohibition laws to concerns for teenage sexuality and condemnation of birth control. This also resonated with earlier episodes of American xenophobia, in which concerns for the nation's internal degradation overlapped with powerful masculine tropes and expectations of feminine submissiveness, illustrating anther parallel between nativism in the 1910s and 1920s. Ultimately, as Leonard Moore's study of Klan nationalism points out, Klan leaders and their rank-and-file members "seemed unable to adjust to the wider notions of pluralism in an urban-based society," a statement equally true of anti-Catholic editors and much of their readership.[31]

Despite their overarching similarities, however, Klan activists in the 1920s and xenophobic writers of the previous decade were fundamentally different in one key respect. While this book has endeavored to show how Progressive-Era nativists were motivated by a civic or ideological nationalism, the Ku Klux Klan formed, in Moore's words "a temporary, but powerful outpouring of ethnic nationalism," in which "persecuting ethnic minorities" provided a means of "promoting the ability of average citizens to influence the workings of society and government."[32] Both forms of nativism sought to address critical challenges to white Protestant men's sense of power and authority. Whereas Progressive-Era writers contended that their superiority over Catholic adversaries came from nativists' proper understanding of American traditions, values, and institutions (and their opponents' attempts at corrupting and destroying these ideals), Klansmen inserted white supremacist attitudes and rhetoric into their attempts at upholding white society. Both movements singled out Catholics as dangerous to America, but for the Ku Klux Klan, Romanists (among many enemies) were dangerous not only for their alleged inability to understand or uphold American values but because of their immigrant status and ethnic impurities. In essence, anti-Catholic architects in the 1910s and Klan leaders in the 1920s responded to similar social, cultural, and economic concerns and hoped to uphold a similar traditionalist worldview, but they arrived at these objectives by different paths.

PAUL BLANSHARD AND "NEW NATIVISM"

While the Ku Klux Klan in the 1920s exemplified the masculine, conservative, and anti-modernist rhetoric popularized by Progressive-Era anti-Catholic crusaders, the movement's literary outpouring and focus on ideological nativism found support later in the twentieth century, notably in the pages of outspoken author Paul Blanshard. In the early twentieth century, Blanshard worked as a lawyer and labor activist before turning his attention in the post–World War II era to documenting the Catholic Church's destructive activities, dangerous hierarchical power structure, and manipulative influence in political affairs and social policy. In his prolific career, beginning in the late 1940s and continuing well into the 1970s, Blanshard penned nearly a dozen monographs on anti-Romanist themes, emphasizing Catholicism's danger to American institutions and its growing power on the world stage. His first such book, *American Freedom and Catholic Power*, was released in 1949, and in keeping with America's long tradition of popular anti-Catholic diatribes, it met overwhelming and instant acclaim. Blanshard's book quickly became a national best seller, earning rave reviews from public figures, such as Albert Einstein and John Dewey (who praised Blanshard's work as "a necessary piece of work with exemplary scholarship, good judgment, and tact," an endorsement that appeared on the book's front cover).

Central to Blanshard's analysis, as the title suggests, was the familiar claim that Catholicism "is not only a church but a state within a state" and that, consequently, Catholics "were not citizens but subjects."[33] As historian Mark Massa points out, Blanshard's fierce attacks, "like the reports of Mark Twain's death, turned out to be somewhat exaggerated." Massa goes on to illustrate that, ironically, Blanshard's tome, touting what Catholic opponents branded as "new nativism," hit bookshelves at the time that

American Catholics "entered the American middle class with ease, and embraced middle-class values with an enthusiasm that belied Protestant fears." Despite (or, perhaps, because of) Catholics' transition to greater national acceptance, Blanshard's book found a captive audience of American readers.[34] Like Progressive-Era nativists, Blanshard reasoned that the Catholic hierarchy dominated the minds and, more importantly, votes of its millions of congregants "to bring American foreign policy into line with Vatican temporal interests." The Catholic priest, agent of this Vatican power bloc, "is armed with several special and effective devices of control over his people," Blanshard insisted, making the priestly establishment dangerous and foreign-minded resisters to American ways of life. Whereas the Ku Klux Klan emphasized racial divides, Blanshard, like earlier anti-Catholic writers, encouraged tolerance, "charity toward men of all races and creed," and "complete open-mindedness toward all ideas," values he asserted were lacking in the nation's Catholic population.[35]

Like Progressive-Era agents of anti-Romanism, Blanshard insisted that the Catholic Church manipulated the press, suppressing criticism and preventing open dialogue. Catholic leaders likewise limited the free will, academic freedoms, and independence of their own members by promoting intellectually stunting parochial schools, an ethos of separation from Protestants and non-Catholics, and restrictive, dogmatic policy that prevents avenues of scientific research and medical practice. Romanism, in Blanshard's view, "has given many hostages to superstition," "exploits the superstition of the ignorant," and "has not adjusted its teachings to modern knowledge."[36] Blanshard's attacks on the Church's power to preempt civil law in matters of marriage and divorce, his contempt for priestly power mongering, and his similar disdain for political meddling on all levels would be quite similar if read alongside Progressive-Era nativist reporters. In fact, Blanshard concluded his work by referring to *The Menace* explicitly and the question it and similar papers intimated: "What will become of American democracy if the United States is captured by papists?" Blanshard continued by postulating that if the current ignorance toward Catholicism's dire threat to America persisted, Romanists would certainly wield their power to upend the Constitution, make the Catholic Church the state religion, exempt priests from civil law, ban non-Catholics from teaching in public schools, repeal the First Amendment, and restrict marriage and divorce laws to adhere strictly to Catholic doctrine.[37]

This nightmarish scenario outlining Catholics' disintegration of American liberties demonstrates Blanshard's extension of Progressive-Era anti-Catholicism to America's post–World War II society. The extreme popularity of *American Freedom and Catholic Power* likewise speaks to a continued market for anti-Catholic print culture stretching back more than a century and to the prominence of ideological nativism in articulating a Catholic threat. The nation's Catholics, Blanshard insists, could never be truly loyal to America, as they were limited by priestly imposed ignorance and superstition—an argument that would be embraced by anti-Catholic writers in 1911 and in 1949. Taken together, the anti-Romanism exemplified by Paul Blanshard and the second Ku Klux Klan both demonstrate that nationalist and anti-Catholic nativism, while temporarily disrupted by World War I, did not entirely die away. Instead, this icon retained powerful cultural credence, influencing American literature and the broader national culture in successive decades.

AMERICA'S ANTI-CATHOLIC LEGACY

In 1955 Will Herberg published his landmark work, *Protestant, Catholic, Jew: An Essay in American Religious Sociology,* which argued that America's immigrant and ethnic character had become largely supplanted by identification with one of three dominant religious traditions.[38] Herberg asserted that postwar America had set aside the conventional "melting pot" ideology, which imagined that newcomers would blend into the environment of their adopted country, in favor of a "triple melting pot" theory, which assumed that certain religious communities both facilitated and demonstrated acceptance of Americanism by immigrants, their children, and their grandchildren.

Although the extent to which Herberg's thesis accurately portrayed American religious identity is a contentious one, *Protestant, Catholic, Jew* is important for its articulation of the overlapping features of religion and national belonging. Also notable are the religions that Herberg selected to highlight as typically American (as are, one might argue, those he chose to leave out). Since both Judaism and Catholicism experienced intense hostility and persecution on American soil, Herberg's analysis would suggest that these once-persecuted religions had risen to a position of prestige or, at the very least, respectability and security. Several historians, however, have pointed out that the transition from "margins" to "mainstream" was one of considerable unease, inconsistency, and uncertainty.[39]

Nevertheless, Herberg's study serves as a potent reminder of the ways in which Americanism and religion are self-reinforcing concepts, each informing and shaping the other. In particular, if Catholicism, as Herberg asserts, has become emblematic of American culture, so too has its antithesis, anti-Catholic nativism. Just as American Catholics have left an indelible mark on American society, anti-Romanist xenophobia has shaped the contours of the American cultural landscape for centuries, exerting perhaps its most significant influence only a few decades before Herberg's pioneering study was published. Remarking on the enduring influence and profoundly significant legacy of anti-Catholicism, for instance, the noted Catholic scholar Andrew Greeley has termed it "America's ugly little secret" and suggested that academia has overlooked, perhaps even perpetuated, America's anti-Catholic tradition.[40]

In late May 2002, with the maelstrom of the Catholic Church's sexual abuse scandals swirling in the background, Fordham University's Center for American Studies convened a conference entitled "Anti-Catholicism: The Last Acceptable Prejudice." In beginning his discussion of the topic, Greeley noted that "Anti-Catholicism is as American as Thanksgiving, apple pie à la mode, and chocolate malts with two butter cookies."[41] Reading Greeley's remarks in light of Herberg's conclusions suggests the true malleability and expansive power of nationalism in general and Americanism in particular. As their comments and this book demonstrate, American nationalism is pervasive and flexible enough to accommodate, even legitimate, the voices of both anti-Catholic nativists with their restrictivist views of patriotism and their anti-nativist, Roman Catholic opponents, who bring a more tolerant, inclusive vision of American civil participation. In the final analysis, each of these groups and the struggle between them exerted a significant influence on the boundaries of American nationalism during the twentieth century.

Ultimately, anti-Catholic nativism succeeded in the early twentieth century because it sold readers a particular vision of American nationalism. This vision invited them to become partners in exposing and denouncing the secretive, elusive, and palpable threat Catholicism posed to American institutions and, in the process, repel the encroaching forces of modernity that distracted and abridged the authority of rural communities, on which the nation's history and traditions were based. Acting to meet Romanists' conspiratorial and treasonous threats, anti-Catholic writers vigorously mobilized an "army" of readers, investing their movement with a militaristic and masculine appeal that raised the act of reading, writing, selling, and circulating newspapers to the level of a moral and patriotic crusade. The chief weapon in this endeavor was a sense of patriotism that imagined the nation's values as based on and preserved in a rural heartland that cultivated small-town values of independent thought, stable social relations, and familial obligations—the very same ideals undermined and attacked by Catholic opponents, who professed patriotism and benevolence to hide their insidious plots to destroy the nation from within.

Articulating this nightmarish scenario of a divided, embattled nation and calling upon readers to recognize and eliminate America's Catholic threat served as the impetus for Progressive-Era nativism's striking successes. But this worldview also accounted for nativism's significant declines at the end of the decade. Although the nativist message of conspiratorial Romanism was remarkably static, the nationalistic attitudes of Americans at large were not. While the tremendous circulations and revenues enjoyed by several anti-Catholic texts in the 1910s, and those prior and since, attest to the profound durability and popularity of American anti-Catholicism, the tumult of World War I temporarily made this internal dissention impractical and politically infeasible.

Because of the repeated rebirth of American anti-Catholicism, the momentary suspension of anti-Catholic agitation in the wake of World War I should be understood not as a complete abandonment of anti-Romanist ideology but as an illustration of the shifting and intermittent features of American nationalism itself. Despite its short tenure in the nation's cultural and literary spotlight, anti-Catholic nativism succeeded in synthesizing early twentieth-century concerns of modernity, masculinity, and progressivism in a medium that reflected America's long-standing anti-Catholic traditions, which had proven popular and financially lucrative in prior decades. As such, nativism represents a valuable snapshot of Progressive-Era concerns across a wide range of social and cultural issues, informing historians' understanding of an often contentious and oppositional era that eludes easy definition and categorization. Moreover, unifying a broad spectrum of ideas into a single cohesive movement speaks to the utility and cohesive power of a restrictivist and elitist nationalistic ideology, without which anti-Catholicism temporarily lost its support and cultural credence. Empowering their movement with the authority to judge genuine Americans from national traitors and correct sources of American tradition from insincere patriotism, nativists imagined themselves as arbiters and defenders of an idyllic national past, one that was threatened and ultimately supplanted, at least for a moment, by a heterogeneous vision of American national belonging.

Appendix

The following figures are taken from Bruce Phelps, *Menace Cartoons: Some Fun and Facts* (Aurora, Mo.: Menace, 1914), and are reproduced here courtesy of Brown University Library.

These illustrations underscore the central tenets of anti-Catholic nativism during the Progressive Era, its commentary on America's broader print culture, and, in particular, nativists' use of American traditional imagery, patriotic rhetoric, and a glorified interpretation of the nation's past to legitimize and strengthen anti-Catholics' own agenda.

Courtesy of the Religious Telescope

ROMANISM EXTINGUISHING THE LIGHT OF LIBERTY

Figure 1. The Statue of Liberty, portrayed in these next four illustrations, proved an immensely popular trope within the pages of the nativist press. In particular, this archetype of American freedoms served to highlight anti-Catholics' understandings of civic nationalism and the juxtaposition between their movements' genuine, heroic vision of Americanism and Catholics' aggression, danger, and hostility toward American traditions and institutions.

A Menace Battle Hymn

Dedicated to the Guardians of Liberty.

Freeborn Americans! Behold!
Within our starry banner's fold
   The Romish viper lurks,
E'en now in Home and School and State,
With secret intrigue born of hate,
   Her deadly virus works.

Scourg'd from the lands beyond the sea,
Her Jesuit minions forced to flee,
   Seek refuge on our shore.
They come to sow the seeds of strife,
To make our land with treason rife
   And Rome our conqueror.

In cloistered hall, beyond the ken
Or watchful eye of fellow men,
   Their cursed plots they brood.
By pope absolv'd their greed for gold
And lust for power have made them bold
   Against the common good.

Rome never sleeps—she changes not,
Her creed has ever been a plot
   'Gainst human Liberty.
She dulls the conscience, dwarfs the mind,
With superstition's fetters binds
   All souls that own her sway.

And shall we craven stand and see
Our native country bow the knee
   To foreign potentate?
Nay! deem not this but idle fear,
Rome's scheming vassals bide the hour
   When she shall rule the state.

Rouse then, ye patriots! front this wrong.
The hour has struck; the battle's on!
   Against this pirate crew.
Be not deceived by false pretense,
The freeman's ballot's your defense,
   Let every vote ring true!

E. A. N., Chicago.

MY FELLOW CITIZEN, WHICH SHALL IT BE;
A STAND FOR LIBERTY OR BOW TO ME?

Figures 2 (above) and 3 (right) likewise demonstrate nativists' critique of Catholic opponents. Contrasting Catholic priestcraft and hierarchy against American individuality and institutions, Figure 2 suggests that priestly control stands opposed to the nation's traditions and institutions. The caption— challenging readers to "stand for liberty" or "bow" to Catholic aggressors, suggests that nationalist imagery served to galvanize readers into an empowered movement to combat Catholic rivals. This point is further reinforced by the adjacent poem, which served as a "Battle Hymn" to the "Menace Army." Figure 3 similarly demonstrates nativist arguments that Romanism's potent political influence corrodes and endangers American liberties—literally choking the life out of American institutions.

Figure 4. This image likewise demonstrates anti-Catholics' use of the Statue of Liberty to underscore their opponents' reliance on priestcraft and hence their un-American ideologies. But this illustration, contrasting national liberties with a tyrannical priest astride a mountain of skulls, also resonates with the potent language of death and priestly endangerment, which formed a powerful dimension of nativist print culture throughout American history, one which Progressive-Era writers frequently evoked. This illustration reflects anti-Catholics' reliance on civic nationalism but also depicts nativists' fascination with tropes of death and decay, which permeate their attacks on Romanism. (See chapters 1 and 3.)

Figure 5. Typical of nativist arguments that praised America's Protestant heroes and minimized Catholic contributions to American development, this illustration contrasts Columbus (portrayed as a pirate and slaver) with Washington and Jefferson (embodying freedom and genuine American values). Nativists' critique of Columbus, John Barry, and other Catholic Americans stems from their understanding of public memory and civic nationalism as distinctly nativist domains. Catholic efforts to justify their place in contemporary society by retrojecting Catholic patriotism were met with fierce resistance in the pages of nativist periodicals. (See chapter 1.)

Figures 6 (above) and 7 (right) illustrate ideological nativism—the belief that Catholics could not become loyal citizens because their values, traditions, and mind-set were out of sync with genuine Americanism. These dangerous thoughts and values, in turn, threatened American institutions from within. While prior and subsequent outbreaks of American nativism relied heavily on racial dichotomies or hierarchies, Progressive-Era anti-Catholicism employed an ideological or  "civic" nationalism, rather than an "ethnic" conception of American belonging rooted in a common language, a common ancestry, or shared biological characteristics. Figure 6 illustrates the danger nativists feared from "priestcraft" and the Catholic hierarchy's undue influence in public affairs. (See chapter 1.)

Figure 7 demonstrates nativists' widespread fears that priestly control and hierarchical influence would undermine the independence and rationality of Catholic voters, making them Vatican pawns capable of corroding American democracy or toppling the republic altogether and installing a Catholic monarch to rule over the nation. Ironically, this Progressive-Era nativist contention also underscored the classic anti-Catholic critique penned by Paul Blanshard in 1949. (See chapters 1 and 5.)

Figures 8 (top) and 9 (bottom) illustrate nativists' thirst for circulation and their conception that reading and promoting anti-Catholic periodicals were necessary political acts that crippled Romanism's encroachment. Figure 8 demonstrates that subscriptions, the lifeblood of the anti-Catholic apparatus, became the tool to uncover and disperse Catholic power. Typically progressive in their faith in the transformative power of information, nativist writers elevated their journalistic mission to the height of a political and moral crusade. Figure 9 foregrounds nativist arguments that Catholicism was dissolving American freedoms and must be met with swift action. (See chapter 2.)

Figure 10. This illustration demonstrates nativist parallels between Catholic foes and typical progressive antipathy for "trusts" and power mongering. Like muckraking critiques in the early twentieth century that condemned oil monopolies, banking conglomerates, or power blocs in other industries, *The Menace* and like-minded newspapers denounced the Catholic Church as a cabal that illicitly accumulated power to fuel dangerous conspiracies. The Church's claim to benevolence and respectability, nativists insisted, was a front to hide its true purpose of destroying and defrauding the American public. As such, Catholicism was a hideous monster that must be destroyed by vigilant readers. Fittingly, the monster's "tentacles" (which represented "ignorance," "superstition," "corruption," and other tools of Romanist aggression) literally squeezed the life out of the values and institutions that strengthened and preserved American society—including public schools, femininity, civil law, and nationalism itself (represented by the American flag in the image's foreground). The Catholic "octopus" likewise grabs greedily at America's public moneys, a common critique among nativist foes, who charged Catholic agents with cheating American taxpayers with false claims of charity and philanthropy. (See chapter 2.)

Figures 11 (top) and 12 (bottom) likewise illustrate nativist contentions of Catholic greed and false philanthropy. Figure 11 clearly contrasts Romanist avarice and materialism with Lincolnian values of freedom and Americanism; the portrait of Lincoln in the image's background stands distinctly apart from the money-grabbing priest in the foreground. (See chapter 2.)

Figure 12 launches an even more explicit attack on Catholic "sham" charity and the pitiful American dupes that unknowingly fuel Catholic enterprises. Lurid stories of Catholic subterranean hideouts, swindling schemes to funnel money into secret coffers, and political bribery (the priests' "Political Correction Fund") demonstrate nativists' efforts to uncover Catholic conspiracy. Moreover, this image also resonates with classic anti-Catholic tropes of entrapment—the same underground channels that hid Catholic con-artists and their "slush fund" away from public scrutiny also shielded Catholic convents and their "prisoners" from an ignorant public. (See chapters 2 and 3.)

Depictions of girls' capture and imprisonment were commonplace in Progressive-Era nativism. Figures 13 (above) and 14 (right) portray Catholic convents as impenetrable fortresses that stand outside the bounds of civil law and American values alike. These illustrations of convents, coupled with the grotesque accounts of life within their walls, fueled nativist charges of Catholic licentiousness and enslavement of innocent girlhood and femininity. (See chapter 3.)

The Confessional has been the means of degrading many an American home. This is but one of Rome's methods of undermining our national life. The blush of shame would mantle the fair face of every true American mother; her heart would stand still with fear should she imagine for one moment that HER daughter would be subjected to the vile and insulting questions asked by designing and immoral priests in the Confessional.

Figure 15. *The Menace*'s critique of Catholic confessionals offered above plays on a double meaning. At first glance, this image appears to show a portly priest leering at an innocent girl. The smirk on the priest's face and his forward-leaning posture suggests he is about to pounce on the girl, who stands helpless within the confessional's walls. A closer look, however, reveals another image entirely—a gestalt in which the room's lone window frames the shape of a white skull. The dual meaning suggests that the confessional is a deadly and dangerous device that destroys the lives of its penitents, particularly the hapless girls who are forced to submit to priestly lust. (See chapter 3.)

Have Your
Wife or Sister
Tell It to Father

Figures 16 (top) and 17 (bottom) likewise illustrate the themes of Catholic licentiousness and its dangers to proper femininity and womanhood. Figure 16 showcases the danger of Catholic confessionals. Figure 17 contrasts images of vitality and life with Catholic deception and death. The figure's left side presents conventional images of domesticity—a tranquil home, a bonnet, a pail and well (representing domestic chores). Images are light and seem to shine in the bright sun. The right side is far darker—with a stone fortress in the background bordered by skeletons and the night sky. The nun in the image's foreground tempts the young woman to enter the nearby convent and sacrifice her vibrant domestic life for one surrounded by death and despair. (See chapter 3.)

ROME'S METHOD
OF INTIMIDATING
NUNS TO OBEDIENCE

HUMAN SKULLS
ARE PLACED
ON THE TABLE
WHERE POOR AND
SCANTY FOOD
IS SPREAD

Figures 18 (above) and 19 (right) underscore a
fundamental contradiction in the nativist press.
On the one hand, as figure 18 points out (along
with prior illustrations, such as Figures 13, 15, and
17 above), nativists presented the Catholic enemy
as medieval; their convent "dungeons" and brutal
treatment of nuns demonstrated that Catholics
were opposed to the values of modern life. But
just as Catholics were depicted as "anti-modern,"
they were also shown to meddle dangerously in
contemporary politics in general and urban life in
particular. Figure 19 asserts that President Woodrow Wilson has become Romanized—showcasing

the reach of Catholic political influence. This influence threatened to contami-
nate and corrupt American traditions, as Catholics embodied the most dangerous
and threatening aspects of the "rising volcano" of modern life. The threat emanating from Catholic-controlled urban centers is also underscored in nativists'
critique of metropolitan daily newspapers, as suggested by Figure 20.

FIGURE 20. This picture illustrates nativist attitudes toward their more main-stream journalistic counterparts. Here, the metropolitan daily newspapers and national periodicals alike are "muzzled"—unwilling to report the truth about Catholic conspiracies for fear of losing Catholic readers. These "Romanized" papers, nativists asserted, simply pandered to priestly autocrats and displayed the Catholic Church in an overly positive light. In contrast to these impotent and puny periodicals (the small dogs that stand idle while the portly Catholic priest walks through the yard), *The Menace* presented itself as a powerful adversary that shed its muzzle to challenge the power of Catholic priestcraft. Ironically, Catholics likewise expressed dismay at their portrayal in the public press and chided reporters and publishers who failed to convey their position on public events. (See chapter 4.)

Notes

ABBREVIATIONS

MtA   *The Mountain Advocate*
SJ   *The Silverton Journal*
TM   *The Menace*
WM   *Watson's Magazine*
YJ   *The Yellow Jacket*

INTRODUCTION. ANTI-CATHOLICISM AND THEORIES OF NATIONALISM

1. On *The Menace*'s acquittal see Benjamin O. Flowers, *The Story of the Menace Trial: A Brief Sketch of This Historic Case, with Reports of the Masterly Addresses by Hon. J.L. McNatt and Hon. J.I. Sheppard* (Aurora, Mo.: United States Publishing, 1916).

2. Though much of the debate and implications of the clerical abuse scandal in the Catholic Church is still unfolding, several noted historians have addressed the issue of priestly sexual abuse. Two useful studies are Philip Jenkins, *Pedophiles and Priests: Anatomy of a Contemporary Crisis* (New York: Oxford University Press, 2001), and Jason Berry and Andrew M. Greeley, *Lead Us Not into Temptation: Catholic Priests and the Sexual Abuse of Children* (Urbana: University of Illinois Press, 1995). The most recent study on the subject (and the first to treat the latest developments in allegations of Catholic conspiracy) is Investigative Staff of the Boston Globe, *Betrayal: The Crisis in the Catholic Church* (Boston: Little, Brown, 2002). For an example of the illiberal vision of America, see Patrick Buchanan, *The Death of the West: How Dying Populations and Immigrant Invasions Imperil Our Country and Civilization* (New York: St. Martin's, 2002).

3. Charles R. Morris, *American Catholic: The Saints and Sinners Who Built America's Most Powerful Church* (New York: Times Books, 1997), quote on p. vii, emphasis in original.

4. Some excellent studies on Catholic Americanism include Andrew M. Greeley, *The Catholic Myth: The Behavior and Beliefs of American Catholics* (New York:

Scribner's, 1990); Mark S. Massa, *Catholics and American Culture: Fulton Sheen, Dorothy Day, and the Notre Dame Football Team* (New York: Crossroad, 1999); Christopher Lynch, *Selling Catholicism: Bishop Sheen and the Power of Television* (Lexington: University Press of Kentucky, 1998); and the excellent anthology by Thomas J. Ferraro, ed., *Catholic Lives, Contemporary America* (Durham, N.C.: Duke University Press, 1997).

5. See Ernest Gellner, *Nations and Nationalism* (Ithaca: Cornell University Press, 1983). For a more thorough exploration of ethnicity and its role in shaping nationalism, see Michael Ignatieff, *Blood and Belonging: Journeys into the New Nationalism*, rev. ed. (New York: Farrar, Straus, and Giroux, 1994).

6. Miroslav Hroch, "From National Movement to the Fully-Formed Nation: The Nation-Building Process in Europe," in Gopal Balakrishnan, ed., *Mapping the Nation* (London: Verso, 1996), pp. 78–97, quotes on p. 79.

7. Rogers Brubaker, *Nationalism Reframed: Nationhood and the National Question in the New Europe* (New York: Cambridge University Press, 1996).

8. Liah Greenfeld, *Nationalism: Five Roads to Modernity* (Cambridge, Mass.: Harvard University Press, 1992). A similar conception of the role of ethnicity in shaping, though not solely determining, nationalism can be seen in Adrian Hastings's 1996 lecture, subsequently republished as *The Construction of Nationhood: Ethnicity, Religion, and Nationalism* (New York: Cambridge University Press, 1997).

9. Michael Hechter, *Containing Nationalism* (New York: Oxford University Press, 2000), p. 15.

10. For a discussion of nationalism and its implications for toleration and interreligious conflict in Britain and France, see Richard Dees, "Establishing Toleration," *Political Theory* 27, no. 5 (October 1999): 667–93. I discuss Dees's work in greater detail in chapter 2.

11. Eric Foner, "Who Is an American? The Imagined Community in American History," *The Centennial Review* 41, no. 3 (1997): 425–38, quote on 427.

12. For a classic analysis of the tenacity and abiding presence of liberalism in America, see Louis Hartz, *The Liberal Tradition in America: An Interpretation of American Political Thought since the Revolution* (New York: Harcourt Brace, 1955). In contrast, see Rogers Smith's *Civic Ideals: Conflicting Visions of Citizenship in U.S. History* (New Haven, Conn.: Yale University Press, 1997), which argues that liberalism, while influential, was but one of a competing series of political philosophies and often competed with illiberal or "inegalitarian ascriptive" traditions.

13. For the 1910s, the combined circulation of Chicago's largest daily, *The Chicago News* (or, for 1913, *The American*) and New York City's largest daily, *The Journal* (or, for 1911, *The World*) never topped 1.2 million, whereas *The Menace* boasted a greater circulation as early as 1913. See *Newspaper Annual and Directory: A Catalogue of American Newspapers* (Philadelphia: N.W. Ayer and Sons, 1911–19).

14. "The Roman Hierarchy: The Deadliest Menace to Our Liberties and Our Civilization," *WM,* January/February 1911, p. 11; "Cry for Help from Convent

Walls," *WM*, May 1913, pp. 42–43; "Rome's Inquisition at Work Again," *The Jeffersonian*, June 13, 1912, p. 8; "Roman Catholic Designs on the American Nation," *WM*, August 1912, p. 278; "Military Maneuvers Start," *The Peril*, March 5, 1914, p. 1.

15. A complete lack of existing business records, reporters' notes, and other correspondence makes it difficult to corroborate anti-Catholic writers' articles or determine their intent, since many of the sources sited to support anti-Catholic claims are no longer extant. However, several anti-Catholic papers, notably *The Menace*, did make use of mainstream, secular newspapers still in the historical record, such as large urban daily newspapers (currently available on microfilm) to substantiate their claims of Catholic abuses. I was frequently unable to locate the articles cited in anti-Catholic papers, suggesting that anti-Catholic journalists either noticed news clippings in minor news outlets and attributed them to more prestigious newspapers to make them seem more tenable or completely fabricated these stories. The success of numerous Catholic lawsuits charging criminal libel also suggests that anti-Catholic writers used more than a little artistic license in their columns. More important, anti-Catholic papers put a pejorative spin on nearly every facet of Catholic activity—even interpreting expressions of Catholic pride and loyalty as proof of Romanist subversion. I address this point in greater detail in subsequent chapters.

16. Robert Wiebe, *The Search for Order, 1877–1920* (New York: Hill and Wang, 1967). Wiebe addresses similar concerns in his previous work, *Businessmen and Reform: A Study of the Progressive Movement* (Cambridge, Mass.: Harvard University Press, 1962). For commentary on Wiebe's analysis of "island communities" and their place in shaping Progressive-Era discourse, see Kenneth Cmiel, "Destiny and Amnesia: The Vision of Modernity in Robert Wiebe's *The Search for Order*," *Reviews in American History* 21, no. 2 (June 1993): 352–68. I will discuss Wiebe's interpretation of Progressive-Era history in greater detail in chapter 2.

17. On post–World War II American anti-Catholicism, see Paul Blanshard, *American Freedom and Catholic Power* (Boston: Beacon, 1949); *God and Man in Washington* (Boston: Beacon, 1960); and *Communism, Democracy, and Catholic Power* (Boston: Beacon, 1951). On the role of intellectuals in American anti-Catholicism following World War I, see, for example, Robert Westbrook, *John Dewey and American Democracy* (Ithaca, N.Y.: Cornell University Press, 1991).

18. Benedict Anderson, *Imagined Communities: Reflections on the Origins and Spread of Nationalism* (London: Verso, 1983). Anderson suggests that the Protestant reformation signaled "the dawn of the age of nationalism but the dusk of religious modes of thought" (p. 11).

19. While Anderson's analysis of nationalism rests on the emergence of print culture and constructed national identity, other scholars present competing interpretations, such as Ernest Gellner's study linking nationalism to the emergence of industrialization and urbanization in British cities. See Gellner, *Nations and Nationalism*. Likewise, Joe Cleary's recent interpretation of "partitioned" nations in

Europe and Asia argues that Anderson's broad definition of nationalism is simplistic and insufficient to explain "loyalist" or sub-nationalist movements in former colonial regions. In *Literature, Partition, and the Nation State: Culture and Conflict in Ireland, Israel, and Palestine* (Cambridge: Cambridge University Press, 2002), Cleary writes, "Anderson's *Imagined Communities* neither invites us to ask nor provides us with theoretical equipment to consider why territorial cleavages of this kind should have happened in some colonies and not others" (p. 16).

CHAPTER ONE. "UTTERLY INCOMPATIBLE ARE ROMANISM AND AMERICANISM"

1. "Knights of Columbus Storm Washington," *TM,* June 22, 1912, p. 1. For an analysis of the roots of antebellum anti-Catholic rhetoric and violence, see the classic text by Jenny Franchot, *Roads to Rome: The Antebellum Protestant Encounter with Catholicism* (Berkeley: University of California Press, 1994). For an in-depth discussion of the Ursuline convent riots and nineteenth-century anti-Catholicism, see Nancy Lusignan Schultz, *Fire and Roses: The Burning of the Charlestown Convent, 1834* (New York: Free Press, 2001); idem, ed., *Fear Itself: Enemies Real and Imagined in American Culture* (West Lafayette, Ind.: Purdue University Press, 1999); and idem, ed., *Veil of Fear: Nineteenth-Century Convent Tales* (West Lafayette, Ind.: Purdue University Press, 1999). An excellent discussion of the political climate of anti-Catholicism can be found in Tyler Anbinder, *Nativism and Slavery: The Northern Know-Nothings and the Politics of the 1850s* (rev. ed.; New York: Oxford University Press, 1994).

2. On the Catholic emphasis on Columbus Day, see Roger Abrahams, "The Eighteenth-Century Discovery of Columbus: The Columbian Tercentenary (1792) and the Creation of American National Identity," in William Pencak, Matthew Dennis, and Simon P. Newman, eds., *Riot and Revelry in Early America* (University Park: Pennsylvania State University Press, 2002); Claudia Bushman, *America Discovers Columbus: How an Italian Explorer Became an American Hero* (Hanover, N.H.: University Press of New England, 1992).

3. John Higham, *Strangers in the Land: Patterns in American Nativism* (New Brunswick, N.J.: Rutgers University Press, 1955), p. 4. Numerous subsequent historians have commented and elaborated on Higham's work. For an insightful retrospective analysis of Higham's work, see the panel discussion in *American Jewish History,* June 1986, which includes the essays "*Strangers in the Land*: Then and Now," by Leonard Dinnerstein and David Reimers (pp. 107–16), "The Concept of Nativism in Historical Study since *Strangers in the Land*," by James Bergquist (pp. 125–41), "Silent Strangers: Germs, Genes and Nativism in John Higham's *Strangers in the Land*," by Alan Kraut (pp. 142–58), and Higham's own reflections, "The Strange Career of *Strangers in the Land*" (pp. 214–26).

4. Higham, *Strangers in the Land,* p. 5.

5. Ibid.

6. Ibid.

7. Ibid., p. 13. For a recent elaboration of Higham's discussion of immigration restriction movements in the early twentieth century and a useful discussion of restrictionists' legacy in contemporary immigration policy, see David Reimers, *Unwelcome Strangers: American Identity and the Turn Against Immigration* (New York: Columbia University Press, 1999).

8. John Higham, "Another Look at Nativism," *Catholic Historical Review* (July 1958): 147–58, quote on 150–51.

9. Ibid., 151.

10. Noel Ignatiev, *How the Irish Became White* (New York: Routledge, 1996); Matthew Frye Jacobson, *Whiteness of a Different Color: European Immigrants and the Alchemy of Race* (Cambridge, Mass.: Harvard University Press, 1999). For an overview of recent historiography on "whiteness" and the social construction of race, see, for instance, David Roediger, *The Wages of Whiteness: Race and the Making of the American Working Class* (London: Verso, 1991); Michael Rogin, *Blackface, White Noise: Jewish Immigrants in the Hollywood Melting Pot* (Berkeley: University of California Press, 1996); George Lipsitz, *The Possessive Investment in Whiteness: How White People Profit from Identity Politics* (Philadelphia: Temple University Press, 1996); and Karen Brodkin, *How Jews Became White Folks and What That Says about Race in America* (New Brunswick, N.J.: Rutgers University Press, 1998).

11. David Brion Davis, "Some Themes of Counter-Subversion: An Analysis of Anti-Masonic, Anti-Catholic, and Anti-Mormon Literature," *The Mississippi Valley Historical Review* (October 1960): 205–24, quote on 207. Davis continues: "If Masons, Catholics, and Mormons bore little resemblance to one another in actuality, as imagined enemies they merged into a nearly common stereotype" (207). Davis's essay was subsequently reprinted in David Brion Davis, ed., *The Fear of Conspiracy: Images of Un-American Subversion from the Revolution to the Present* (Ithaca, N.Y.: Cornell University Press, 1971), pp. 9–22. By the twentieth century, links among Catholic, Mormon, and Masonic conspiracy were extremely sparse. In my study of several hundred anti-Catholic articles, I noticed only one reference connecting Catholic and Mormon hierarchies as similarly threatening institutions; see "Shall the People or Shall Rome Rule," *WM,* December 1912, p. 91.

12. Davis, "Some Themes of Counter-Subversion," 213.

13. Ibid.

14. Ibid.

15. Ibid., 215.

16. Ibid., 217, 219. Davis continues, "We should recall that this literature was written in a period of increasing anxiety and uncertainty over sexual values and the proper role of women," but he also points out that "the imagined enemy might serve at first as an outlet for forbidden desires, but nativist authors escaped

from guilt by finally making him an agent of unmitigated aggression" (219, 221). On the concept of sexualized conspiracies in general and their application in the study of American anti-Catholicism in particular, see John Demos, *The Unredeemed Captive: A Family Story from Early America* (New York: Knopf, 1994), for an exploration of Colonial-Era anti-Catholic anxiety. For an examination of subsequent antebellum notions of Catholic illicit sexuality and captivity, see Franchot, *Roads to Rome*. I discuss the issue of convent captivity, Catholic licentiousness, and nativist anxiety in much greater detail in chapter 3.

17. Davis, "Some Themes of Counter-Subversion," 223, 224.

18. "By Their Fruits Shall Ye Know Them," *The Peril*, March 5, 1914, p. 4.

19. "Romish Immigration," *The Liberator*, October 2, 1914.

20. "What it Takes to be a Good Catholic," *WM*, January 1913, pp. 148–51, quotes on pp. 150 and 151.

21. "Open Letter to Cardinal Gibbons," *WM*, August 1913, p. 197, emphasis in original.

22. "Nature vs Nurture," *SJ*, June 12, 1914, p. 2.

23. "Roman Catholic Designs on the American Nation," *WM*, August 1912, pp. 276–79, quotes on pp. 276–77.

24. "No True Catholic Can be a True American," *YJ*, May 11, 1916, p. 4.

25. Stuart McConnell, "Reading the Flag: A Reconsideration of the Patriotic Cults of the 1890s," in John Bodnar, ed., *Bonds of Affection: Americans Define their Patriotism* (Princeton, N.J.: Princeton University Press, 1996), quote on p. 103. In introducing this volume, Bodnar echoes McConnell's contention that the twentieth century signaled a heightened importance and increased visibility for variegated expressions of nationalism and public memory in which "the articulation of specific goals became more pronounced" (p. 4).

26. McConnell, "Reading the Flag," p. 105.

27. Ibid., 112.

28. See Cecilia Elizabeth O'Leary, "'Blood Brotherhood': The Racialization of Patriotism, 1865–1918," in Bodnar, ed., *Bonds of Affection*, esp. p. 53. O'Leary makes a similar point in her subsequent and more detailed account of American nationalism; see idem, *To Die For: The Paradox of American Patriotism* (Princeton, N.J.: Princeton University Press, 1999). Other scholars of Civil War memory and postbellum patriotism likewise point to masculinity and heroism as the root causes for abandoning racial concerns following Reconstruction and a valorized interpretation of wartime experience. See, for instance, Gerald Linderman, *Embattled Courage: The Experience of Combat in the American Civil War* (New York: Free Press, 1987), and Mark Kann, *On the Man Question: Gender and Civic Virtue in America* (Philadelphia: Temple University Press, 1991). For a generalized study of the Civil War's influence on American public memory, see David Blight, *Race and Reunion: The Civil War in American Memory* (Cambridge, Mass.: Harvard University Press, 2001).

29. For an insightful and comprehensive analysis of American public memory, see Michael Kammen, *The Mystic Chords of Memory: The Transformation of Tradition in American Culture* (New York: Vintage Books, 1993). Ironically, Kammen notes, corporate titans sought to memorialize quaint images of American nationalism, even as their products and business practices threatened and transformed America's small-town and parochial traditions. Kammen also addresses these themes in his subsequent volume, *In the Past Lane: Historical Perspectives on American Culture* (New York: Oxford University Press, 1997). On the use of public memory and the early preservationist movement to substantiate Yankee culture and temper the effects of immigrant ethnic culture in early twentieth-century Massachusetts, see James Lindgren's excellent study, *Preserving Historic New England: Preservation, Progressivism, and the Remaking of Memory* (New York: Oxford University Press, 1995).

30. For an overview of twentieth-century nationalism, see David Glassberg, *American Historical Pageantry: The Uses of Tradition in the Early Twentieth Century* (Chapel Hill: University of North Carolina Press, 1990). For a description of official and vernacular culture, see John Bodnar, *Remaking America : Public Memory, Commemoration, and Patriotism in the Twentieth Century* (Princeton, N.J.: Princeton University Press, 1992). For other perspectives on public memory and its influence on American culture, see Albert Boime, *The Unveiling of the National Icons: A Plea for Patriotic Iconoclasm in a Nationalist Era* (New York: Cambridge University Press, 1998); Mike Wallace, *Mickey Mouse History and Other Essays on American Memory* (Philadelphia: Temple University Press, 1996); and my essay "Public Memory and Popular Culture: The Erie Canal in the Imagination of the 1920s," *New York History* (October 1999): 423–54. On contemporary issues related to public memory, see Kristin Haas, *Carried to the Wall: American Memory and the Vietnam Veterans Memorial* (Berkeley: University of California Press, 1998), and Marita Sturken, *Tangled Memories: The Vietnam War, the AIDS Epidemic, and the Politics of Remembering* (Berkeley: University of California Press, 1997).

31. Eric Hobsbawm and Terence Ranger, eds., *The Invention of Tradition* (New York: Cambridge University Press, 1984).

32. On the endurance of "vernacular" culture, see Kathleen Neils Conzen, *Immigrant Milwaukee, 1836–1860: Accommodation and Community in a Frontier City* (Cambridge, Mass.: Harvard University Press, 1976); Jon Gjerde, *From Peasants to Farmers: The Migration from Balestrand, Norway, to the Upper Middle West* (New York: Cambridge University Press, 1985); and Roy Rosenzweig's classic study, *Eight Hours for What We Will: Workers and Leisure in an Industrial City, 1870–1920* (New York: Cambridge University Press, 1983). On the persistence of localized celebrations and public commemoration, see Thomas Spencer, *The St. Louis Veiled Prophet Celebration: Power on Parade, 1877–1995* (Columbia: University of Missouri Press, 2000). On the growing Catholic embrace of American nationalism, see Jay Dolan, *Catholic Revivalism: The American Experience* (Notre Dame, Ind.: University of Notre Dame

Press, 1978); David O'Brien, *Public Catholicism* (2nd ed.; Maryknoll, N.Y.: Orbis Books, 1996); Christopher Kauffman, *Faith and Fraternalism: The History of the Knights of Columbus, 1882–1982* (New York: Harper and Row, 1982); and Robert Orsi's exceptional studies, *The Madonna of 115th Street: Faith and Community in Italian Harlem, 1880–1950* (New Haven, Conn.: Yale University Press, 1985), and *Thank You, St. Jude: Women's Devotion to the Patron Saint of Hopeless Causes* (New Haven, Conn.: Yale University Press, 1996).

33. Franchot, *Roads to Rome,* p. 88.

34. Ibid., p. 20.

35. Richard Slotkin has written several definitive volumes on the American frontier and its lingering mythic values and place in American historical memory. See Slotkin, *Gunfighter Nation: The Myth of the Frontier in Twentieth-Century America* (Norman: University of Oklahoma Press, 1998), and idem, *Regeneration through Violence: The Mythology of the American Frontier, 1600–1860* (Norman: University of Oklahoma Press, 2000).

36. Demos, *Unredeemed Captive,* p. 37.

37. Franchot, *Roads to Rome,* p. 99.

38. For an in-depth elaboration of the influence of anti-Catholic literature, see Franchot, "Unseemly Commemoration: Religion, Fragments, and the Icon," in Larry J. Reynolds and Gordon Hunter, eds., *National Imaginaries, American Identities: The Cultural Work of American Iconography* (Princeton, N.J.: Princeton University Press, 2000). Here, Franchot reiterates the central themes of *Roads to Rome,* but also delves into the cultural meanings of Catholic "contamination" in the minds of Protestants. Franchot maintains that for nineteenth-century nativists, "Catholic culture was denigrated into the seen in order to establish the purified precincts of Protestant spirituality" (p. 213). Catholicism's sensuousness contrasted with and contaminated Anglo-Saxon Protestantism, and Catholic iconographic imagery bespoke "loss and ruin" (p. 214) and needed to be tamed and contained by mindful Protestants.

39. Nancy Lusignan Schultz, ed., *Veil of Fear: Nineteenth-Century Convent Tales by Rebecca Reed and Maria Monk* (West Lafayette, Ind.: NotaBell Books, 1999), quote on p. 5. Schultz's account contains an excellent introduction to *Six Months in a Convent* and *The Awful Disclosures* and represents the only academic texts in print that reprints these essential anti-Catholic texts in full. For an elaboration of Reed's account, see John Regan, "'There Are No Ranks among Us': The Ursuline Convent Riot and the Attack on Sister Mary Ursula Moffatt," in Schultz, ed., *Fear Itself.* Regan argues that nativism alone is insufficient to explain the Charlestown riots, and historians have under-examined the category of class and the convent's role in cementing upper-class respectability in addressing rioters' motives. For an exploration of the Ursuline convent riots and their aftermath, see Nancy Lusignan Schultz, *Fire and Roses: The Burning of the Charlestown Convent, 1834* (New York: Free Press, 2000).

40. Schultz, *Veil of Fear,* quotes on pp. 5, xii, and xxi, respectively.

41. Schultz, *Veil of Fear,* p. xxii. For an elaboration of the Maria Monk story and its appeal to American readers, see also Barbara Welter, "From Maria Monk to Paul Blanshard: A Century of Protestant Anti-Catholicism," in Robert N. Bellah and Frederick E. Greenspahn, eds., *Uncivil Religion: Interreligious Hostility in America* (New York: Crossroad, 1987).

42. The Maria Monk story continued to fascinate readers well into the twentieth century. As late as 1936, the story was still a topic of discussion among American readers and critics. See Allen Churchill, "The Awful Disclosures of Maria Monk," *The American Mercury,* January 1936, pp. 94–98. Churchill points out that Monk's story was completely untenable and was refuted by Monk's own mother and Quebec doctor, and he blames the gross fabrication on Monk's editor, W. K. Hoyt, who falsely posed as a Catholic priest. Churchill reports that the Maria Monk story, in various editions, sold over one hundred thousand copies during the early nineteenth century. Nancy Shultz echoes these figures, adding that "escaped nun" literature from Reed and Monk proved enormously successful and sold over a half million copies since their initial publication. See Schultz, *Veil of Fear,* p. vii.

43. Franchot, "Unseemly Commemoration," p. 216. See also Franchot, *Roads to Rome.*

44. Tyler Anbinder, *Nativism and Slavery: The Know Nothings and the Politics of the 1850s* (New York: Oxford University Press, 1992). On nativism in antebellum politics, see also John Mulkern, *The Know-Nothing Party in Massachusetts: The Rise and Fall of a People's Movement* (Boston: Northeastern University Press, 1990). Scholars have also investigated the political elements of anti-Catholicism outside of America. For an insightful reader of popular literature denouncing the "dual allegiance" to the British crown on the one hand and Catholic influence on the other, see E. R. Norman, *Anti-Catholicism in Victorian England* (New York: Barnes and Noble, 1968).

45. For an illustration of the influence and motivations of the American Protective Association (APA), see Donald Kinzer, *An Episode in Anti-Catholicism, The American Protective Association* (Seattle: University of Washington Press, 1964). Kinzer points out that the APA's motivation was primarily to garner political influence for Bowers and the movement's other leaders, who chose Catholics as a highly visible enemy. For an overview of the APA's growth and use of pageantry to attract members, see Higham, *Strangers in the Land,* esp. pp. 80–86.

46. Les Wallace, *The Rhetoric of Anti-Catholicism: The American Protective Association, 1887–1911* (New York: Garland, 1990), quotes on pp. 55 and 84–85, respectively. Wallace also points out that the APA began a successful publishing campaign that sparked over a dozen newspapers throughout the country. Though none would survive to join the ranks of Progressive-Era anti-Catholicism, several of the themes espoused by APA newspapers continued into the twentieth century, particularly their vehemence toward the Houses of the Good Shepherd and

illicit Catholic sexuality. Kinzer illustrates these themes in some detail, see *Episode in Anti-Catholicism,* esp. pp. 95–96.

47. Higham, *Strangers in the Land,* p. 79. For a discussion of the overlapping agendas of anti-Catholic groups in the nineteenth century, see David Bennett, *The Party of Fear: From Nativist Movements to the New Right in American History* (Chapel Hill: University of North Carolina Press, 1988), and Jay P. Dolan, *The American Catholic Experience: A History from Colonial Times to the Present* (Notre Dame, Ind.: University of Notre Dame Press, 1992).

48. "Maria Monk Story Confirmed," *TM,* February 8, 1919, p. 2.

49. "Unexpected and Powerful Corroboration of Maria Monk," *The Jeffersonian,* September 15, 1912, p. 6.

50. Thomas Watson, *Maria Monk and Her Revelation of Convent Crimes* (Thompson, Ga.: Jeffersonian, 1917), see especially pp. 4–5. On continued Catholic abuses as corroboration of Monk's antebellum accounts, see "Open Rome's Prison Houses in America," *TM,* December 2, 1911, p. 1.

51. "What Maria Monk Said," *YJ,* November 25, 1915, p. 1. A similar example of links between Monk's account of nineteenth-century captivity and continued Catholic cruelties in the twentieth century can be seen in "Convents Need Inspection: Revelations of a Census in Great Britain," *The Rail Splitter,* February 1934, p. 2, and M.R. Grant, *Americanism vs. Roman Catholicism* (Gulfsport, Miss.: n.p., 1923). Grant includes as one of his "indictments" against Catholicism "the forcible incarceration of women," which, he says, is nothing less than "a blot on the civilization of the Twentieth Century" (p. 4). Grant draws heavily from *The Menace* in outlining his depiction of convent abduction; see esp. pp. 126–61. Both Grant's book and William Lloyd Clark's edition of *The Rail Splitter* also show how forms of anti-Catholic journalism that developed in the 1910s linger on in some fashion in the decades thereafter, though, as I show in chapter 5, they carry a much more limited message to an increasingly shrinking audience following World War I.

52. "The A.P.A." *TM,* January 6, 1912, p. 4. On the links between the APA of the nineteenth century and *The Menace* and similar newspapers in the early twentieth century, see, "A.P.A.ism Is Not Dead," *TM,* March 16, 1912, p. 3.

53. On Thomas Nast and references to earlier anti-Catholic writers and artists, see "A Divided Allegiance," *The Crusader,* May, 1914, p. 1.

54. On Catholic convents as "institutional slave pens," see "Let's Open Rome's Prisons and Free the Slaves!" *TM,* January 27, 1917, p. 4. On the danger and tortures facing girls in Catholic institutions, see "Mystery as to Fate of Nun Clarified," *TM,* March 8, 1919, p. 4; "5 Kansas City Girls Escape Convent," *TM,* July 5, 1913, p. 4; "Police, Popery, Prisons," *TM,* March 18, 1916, p. 1. The latter article is informative for illustrating how Rome's slave catchers use dupes or bribes to get police or judicial authorities to send children to Catholic convents. I will discuss these points in greater detail in chapter 3.

55. "Open Letter to Cardinal Gibbons," *WM*, September 1913, quotes on pp. 249 and 248, respectively. Watson wrote an intermittent series of these "open letters" during 1913 and thereafter.

56. "Cry for Help From Convent Walls," *WM*, May 1913, pp. 42–43.

57. "Statement of Miss Lasenan," *SJ*, August 22, 1913, p. 1. This article describes the experiences of an alleged "escape nun" near Mount Angel, Oregon, in much the same language as Maria Monk's sensationalized account.

58. Anti-Catholic papers frequently carried such disclaimers, asserting that their articles upheld, rather than contradicted, the First Amendment. The quotes are taken from "The Roman Catholic Hierarchy: The Deadliest Menace to Our Liberties and Our Civilization," *WM*, October 1912, p. 414, and "Roman Catholic Designs on the American Nation," *WM*, August 1912, p. 277, respectively, emphasis in original.

59. "Churches in Politics," *MtA*, May 8, 1914, p. 1. For a relatively rare example of nativist papers eulogizing a practicing Catholic for resisting the influence of the Church, see "A Bad Catholic but a Real Good Citizen," *TM*, July 27, 1918, p. 3.

60. Quotes are from "Patriotic Meeting Called," *The Liberator*, October 16, 1913, p. 2, and "There Is a Modern Inquisition," *WM*, August 1912, p. 212, respectively. The *Watson's Magazine* article goes on to call for "the defense of our blood-bought legacy of liberty, our government of the people, by the people, and for the benefit of the people." The article concludes by pledging "support of the undefended victims of the modern inquisition."

61. "What We Are Fighting," *The Peril*, March 5, 1914, p. 1. For threats to the United States from Catholicism and its unity of temporal and religious power, see "Papal Supremacy," *Crusader*, July 1914, p. 1. On the disloyalty of Catholics to the American republic, see "Are the Men Who Take These Oaths Loyal Citizens?" *TM*, November 25, 1911, p. 3.

62. *The Menace* first used the headline "Rome Never Sleeps" on March 30, 1912, p. 4, and employed it frequently thereafter.

63. "Silence Is Treason," *SJ*, December 12, 1913, p. 3.

64. "American Pope Is Probable," *SJ*, January 9, 1914, p. 1. "The Danger Signals," *SJ*, October 10, 1913, p. 2.

65. "The Fruits of Four Hundred Years of Catholic Rule in Puerto Rico," *WM*, October 1913, p. 335.

66. Ibid. For a similar discussion of the "dark day ahead of America" if Romanism goes unchecked, see "Immigration Bill," *The Liberator*, October 16, 1913, p. 2; "Do We Need Them?," *The Liberator*, October 2, 1913, p. 2.

67. "Lincoln's Life an Inspiration," *MtA*, February 13, 1914, p. 8.

68. Anti-Catholic newspapers attempted to both magnify and personalize the lives of influential Protestant historical figures to make them exemplars of American nationalism. For a description of both Lincoln's genius and his willingness to help a woman move her piano, for instance, see "Ever Ready to Do Kindly Act,"

MtA, February 13, 1914, p. 8. On his personal character, see "The Personal Side of Lincoln," *MtA*, February 6, 1914, p. 9. In contrast, contemporary political leaders, particularly President Taft, were depicted as complicit with the plans of Rome. See Crowley, *Romanism*, esp. pp. 189–96.

69. "Lying on George Washington," *YJ*, November 23, 1916, p. 2.

70. Ibid.

71. "Praising Lincoln," *TM*, March 2, 1912, p. 1.

72. "Who Assassinated Abraham Lincoln?" *SJ*, February 20, 1914, p. 2. On the Catholic Church's culpability in Lincoln's death, see also, "The Roman Catholics Have Another Reformer Killed," *WM*, December 1912, p. 2.

73. "The Battle Ship Maine," *TM*, June 22, 1912, p. 2.

74. "Columbus Day Might Suffer Competition at Hands of Chinese," *TM*, April 4, 1917, p. 2.

75. "Governor Wilson Joins the Knights of Columbus," *The Jeffersonian*, October 24, 1912, p. 11.

76. "The Name of America," *WM*, September 1911.

77. "The Real Christopher Columbus," *WM*, June 1911, pp. 194 ff., quotes on pp. 194, 194, and 199, respectively. On Columbus's "real" nature as a pirate and slave trader, see, for instance, "More Columbus History," *TM*, March 2, 1912, p. 2.

78. "The Pope Didn't Believe in Columbus," *YJ*, February 4, 1915, p. 4.

79. Crowley, *Romanism*, p. 145.

80. Ibid., p. 146.

81. "Commodore John Barry to Have Monument, Founded on False Claim," *WM*, October 1912, p. 474.

82. "Barry Statue Unveiled," *TM*, June 6, 1914, p. 4.

83. On Galileo and other Catholic contributors to western traditions, see "A Sample of Romanist Mendacity," *Jeffersonian*, February 1, 1912, p. 12. On Lafayette, see George Watson Brown, *Roman Catholics in America: Falsifying History and Poisoning the Minds of Protestant School Children* (Thompson, Ga.: Tom Watson Book, 1928), esp. pp. 10–11. Brown, whose book was financed and distributed by Watson's publishing enterprise after Watson's two largest anti-Catholic organs had gone out of print, continued to rail against Columbus and other prominent Catholic historical figures as well, stating, "No good in this country is traceable to Columbus" (p. 11) and endeavoring to prove that other individuals were Catholic in name only.

84. On the egregious use of public funds in Catholic public memory projects, see "Erecting Monuments to the Catholics," *TM*, June 7, 1913, p. 1; untitled article, *TM*, March 23, 1912, p. 2.

85. "The Washington Monument and the Pope," *TM*, June 13, 1914, p. 2.

86. On the Statue of Liberty, see "A Real Statue of Liberty," *YJ*, November 25, 1915, p. 2. On Catholic cowardice and desertion in American wars, see untitled article, *YJ*, February 4, 1915, p. 2. Nativists also countered Catholic claims to patriot-

ism in other ways. When a Catholic wrote to *The Peril*, asserting that the patriotism of his coreligionists was responsible for American freedoms, the paper retorted, "You state that Catholic money, Catholic blood and Catholic lives paid for all the liberties your people now enjoy in this country. Look over the list of the 57 signers of the Declaration of Independence and you will find only one of the Roman Catholic faith." See "Patriotism vs Catholicism," *The Peril*, March 5, 1914, p. 2.

87. "We Hand Jack Noll a Few Facts," *The Peril*, March 5, 1914, p. 2.

88. "We Keep History Straight," *YJ*, May 13, 1915, p. 1.

89. "Patriotism Begets Heresy," *WM*, October 1912.

90. "Shall the People or Shall Rome Rule?" *WM*, December 1912, pp. 89−93, quote on p. 90. On priestly control of political elections, see also "Catholic Dogma," *TM*, December 9, 1911, p. 4. On Catholic meddling in American politics, civil marriage, and legal doctrine, see "Papal Infallibility, and the Great Problems Growing Out of It for America," *The Jeffersonian*, February 16, 1914, p. 2. On the potential conflicts resulting from political and economic entanglements with Catholic countries overseas, see "Romanism Showing Its Hand in This Country," *The Jeffersonian*, October 28, 1915, p. 1.

91.. "The Political Leaders and the Catholic Vote," *WM*, July 1912, p. 183.

92.. "The Ballot Box vs. the Confessional Box," *The Liberator*, October 16, 1913, p. 4.

CHAPTER TWO. "HELP US TO TURN ON MORE LIGHT"

1. Two excellent studies of progressivism and America's shifting understanding of the press include Leon Fink, *Progressive Intellectuals and the Dilemmas of Democratic Commitment* (Cambridge, Mass.: Harvard University Press, 1997), and Steven J. Diner, *A Very Different Age: Americans of the Progressive Era* (New York: Hill and Wang, 1998). Diner emphasizes the progressive rationale: "Struggling to redefine the meaning of American democracy in the age of corporate capitalism, Americans of diverse backgrounds asked how government could protect its citizens against the negative effects of industrialism and economic concentration and how the polity could sue government to regain control of the nation's destiny" (p. 12).

2. On the ongoing debates over the relative longevity of progressivism, see Eldon Eisenach, *The Lost Promise of Progressivism* (Lawrence: University Press of Kansas, 1994), and Bill Kaufman, *With Good Intentions? Reflections on the Myth of Progress in America* (Westport, Conn.: Praeger, 1998). Eisenach argues that progressivism was "lost" with Wilson's election in 1914, replaced by an intellectual and political "stagnation" brought on by a new political paradigm of "liberalism" that remained dominant through the late twentieth century. Kaufman notes that much Progressive-Era philosophy was rooted in instilling white Anglo-Saxon, Protestant virtues on America at large, a strategy that became less tenable at the close

of World War I. In contrast, see Louis Filler, *Muckraking and Progressivism in the American Tradition* (rev. ed.; New Brunswick, N.J.: Transaction, 1996). Filler chastises historians for underestimating Progressivism and takes a sweeping view of reform from the colonial era through the late twentieth century. Filler concludes that the perceived disintegration of progressivism in the twentieth century is rooted in the fragmenting of historical study itself, not historical subjects per se.

3. Robert Miraldi, "Charles Edward Russell: 'Chief of the Muckrakers,'" *Journalism and Mass Communication Monographs* 150 (April 1995): 1–27, quote on p. 2. On the conservative nature of muckraking and progressive approaches to business, see Richard McCormick's influential essay, "The Discovery that Business Corrupts Politics: A Reappraisal of the Origins of Progressivism," *American Historical Review* 86, no. 2 (April 1981): 247–74, reprinted in Glenda E. Gilmore, ed., *Who Were the Progressives?* (Boston: Bedford, 2002), pp. 103–40.

4. Colin Gordon, "Still Searching for Progressivism," *Reviews in American History* 23, no. 4 (1995): 669–74.

5. Gilmore, *Who Were the Progressives?*

6. Circulation figures for anti-Catholic papers and other periodicals are from *Newspaper Annual and Directory: A Catalogue of American Newspapers* (Philadelphia: N.W. Ayer and Sons, 1911–19).

7. Richard Hofstadter, *The Age of Reform: From Bryan to F.D.R.* (New York: Knopf, 1955). For a concise depiction and contextualization of Hofstadter's study, see Gilmore, *Who Were the Progressives?* For a rebuttal to Hofstadter's depiction of "Mugwump" Progressivism, see Robert Wiebe, *The Search for Order, 1877–1920* (New York: Hill and Wang, 1968). For a useful corollary to Wiebe's approach, see Kenneth Cmiel, "Destiny and Amnesia: The Vision of Modernity in Robert Wiebe's *The Search for Order,*" *Reviews in American History* 21, no. 2 (June 1993): 352–68. Cmiel praises Wiebe's book for its broad and ingenious synthesis—"the history of a civilization"—but also warns that it is a "grim, even bleak, picture of life in the twentieth century" (p. 352). Other works commentating on the Wiebe-Hofstadter debate include Kenneth Finegold, *Experts and Politicians: Reform Challenges to Machine Politics in New York, Cleveland, and Chicago* (Princeton, N.J.: Princeton University Press, 1995), which adopts a Wiebian analysis of "organizational" structures and the progressive thirst for efficiency, but dismisses Wiebe for overlooking electorate politics in his "search for order," and Sean Dennis Cashman, *American in the Gilded Age: From the Death of Lincoln to the Rise of Theodore Roosevelt* (2nd ed.; New York: New York University Press, 1988), which adopts the arguments mustered by Hofstadter and Wiebe to describe early twentieth-century professionalization and middle-class bureaucracy.

8. Several recent studies illustrate historians' elaboration of the term "progressive," to include the actions of women and the influence of gender ideology, such as Katherine G. Aiken, *Harnessing the Power of Motherhood: The National Florence Crittenden Mission, 1883–1925* (Knoxville: University of Tennessee Press, 1998);

Camilla Stivers, *Bureau Men, Settlement Women: Constructing Public Administration in the Progressive Era* (Lawrence: University of Kansas Press, 2000); Rebecca Edwards, *Angels in the Machinery: Gender in American Party Politics from the Civil War to the Progressive Era* (New York: Oxford University Press, 1997); and Maureen Flanagan, "Gender and Urban Political Reform: The City Club and the Woman's City Club of Chicago in the Progressive Era," in Gilmore, *Who Were the Progressives?* On the role of class and ethnic attachments in developing Progressive reform, see James Connolly, *The Triumph of Ethnic Progressivism: Urban Political Culture in Boston, 1900–1925* (Cambridge, Mass.: Harvard University Press, 1998); Shelton Stromquist, "The Crucible of Class: Cleveland Politics and the Origins of Municipal Reform in the Progressive Era," in Gilmore, *Who Were the Progressives?*; and Elizabeth Sanders, *Roots of Reform: Farmers, Workers, and the American State, 1877–1917* (Chicago: University of Chicago Press, 1999). Sanders also makes important points about the overlap between rural and urban progressivism, arguments echoed by Mary Neth, *Preserving the Family Farm: Women, Community and the Foundations of Agribusiness in the Midwest, 1900–1940* (Baltimore: Johns Hopkins University Press, 1995), and an insightful study of Progressivism and reform in the southwest by David Berman, *Arizona Politics and Government: The Quest for Autonomy, Democracy, and Development* (Lincoln: University of Nebraska Press, 1998). On the role of race and Progressivism, see Jacqueline Moore, *Leading the Race: The Transformation of the Black Elite in the Nation's Capital, 1880–1920* (Charlottesville: University Press of Virginia, 1999), and Glenda Gilmore, *Gender and Jim Crow: Women and the Politics of White Supremacy in North Carolina, 1896–1920* (Chapel Hill: University of North Carolina Press, 1996). On transatlantic progressive impulses and international reform influences, see Daniel Rogers, *Atlantic Crossings: Social Politics in a Progressive Age* (Cambridge, Mass.: Belknap, 1998).

9. "Open Letter to Cardinal Gibbons," *WM*, June 1913, p. 77, emphasis in original; Watson elaborates on this point in a subsequent "Open Letter," arguing that the Catholic Church attacks the most sacred American institutions—it had "fulminated savagely against liberty of speech, and of conscience" and points out that Pope Gregory XVI "denounce[d] all those who maintained the liberty of the press." The message in these and numerous other articles is that "Romanism" was incompatible with the basic freedoms of Americanism and, moreover, that Catholics were thus incapable of independent thought. See "Open Letter to Cardinal Gibbons" *WM*, Sept. 1913, p. 250.

10. Higham, *Strangers in the Land: Patterns in American Nativism* (New Brunswick, N.J.: Rutgers University Press, 1955), p. 181. Higham also points out "[Wilbur] Phelps' paper [that is, *The Menace*] shared with *Watson's Magazine* a second characteristic that defines the sources of the new religious nativism. Both were published in country towns with a population of four thousand or less. So also were a number of other nativist sheets that sprang up in their wake. From 1912 through 1914 a score of less successful imitators appeared" (pp. 180–81).

11. On the role of violence and urban conflict in antebellum nativism, see Iver Bernstein, *The New York City Draft Riots: Their Significance in American Society and Politics in the Age of the Civil War* (New York: Oxford University Press, 1990). On nativism as manifested in antebellum political conflict, see Tyler Anbinder, *Nativism and Slavery: The Northern Know-Nothings and the Politics of the 1850s* (New York: Oxford University Press, 1992). Nancy Lusignan Schultz has written extensively on the issue of antebellum vigilantism in American cities. See her excellent study, *Fire and Roses: The Burning of the Charlestown Convent, 1834* (New York: Free Press, 2001). On antebellum anti-Catholicism and its new forms in the twentieth century, see also Higham, *Strangers in the Land.*

12. Higham, *Strangers in the Land,* p. 181.

13. The 1910 and 1920 Census also reveal a similarly low rate of foreign-born residents in counties in which extant anti-Catholic texts were produced. Though some population rates of foreign-born residents were extremely low (zero percent in Knox County, Kentucky, where *The Mountain Advocate* was printed), on the whole, the median foreign-born population in counties producing nativist texts was 8.5 percent in 1910 and only 7.4 percent in 1920. As I've argued earlier, Progressive-Era anti-Catholicism had less to do with eugenics, ethnic nationalism, or racially based arguments of national purity. This assertion is strengthened by the fact that counties with the most vocal nativism in the 1910s actually experienced a decline in their foreign-born populations. See Bureau of the Census, *1910 Federal Population Census* and *1920 Federal Population Census* (Washington, D.C.: Bureau of the Census, 1913 and 1923, respectively).

14. The 1920 Federal Census measured population in residents per square mile, which precludes the direct urban/rural comparison available in previous censuses. See *1920 Federal Census.*

15. Bureau of the Census, *1916 Census of Religious Bodies* (Washington, D.C.: Bureau of the Census, 1919). The growing Catholic population and its influence were noted in nativist texts themselves. One article even employed the Census itself to show naïve Protestant readers that Catholics had become a majority of the population in eighteen states. See "Making America Catholic," *YJ,* March 18, 1915, p. 4.

16. Jane Adams, *The Transformation of Rural Life: Southern Illinois, 1890–1990* (Chapel Hill: University North Carolina Press, 1994), p. 68. On the influence of machinery and technology in rural life, see also Sanders, *Roots of Reform.*

17. David Danborn, *Born in the Country* (Baltimore: Johns Hopkins University Press, 1995); David Blanke, *Sowing the American Dream: How Consumer Culture Took Root in the Rural Midwest* (Athens: Ohio University Press, 2001); Mary Neth, *Preserving the Family Farm: Women, Community and the Foundations of Agribusiness in the Midwest, 1900–1940* (Baltimore: Johns Hopkins University Press, 1995). For an analysis of nineteenth-century connections between cities and outlining rural communities, see Paul Johnson's classic study, *A Shopkeeper's Millennium: Society*

and Revivals in Rochester, New York, 1815–1837 (New York: Hill and Wang, 1978), which illustrates not only commercial and economic connections between urban and rural life but self-reinforcing networks of communication, religious practice, and social interaction.

18. Robert G. Barrows, "Urbanizing America," in Charles Calhous, ed., *The Gilded Age: Essays on the Origins of Modern America* (Wilmington, Del.: Scholarly Resources, 1996).

19. "Adventists Have Squabble," *SJ*, October 3, 1913, p. 1.

20. "Fresh Air Kiddie," *SJ*, July 10, 1914, p. 2.

21. "Silver Stream," *SJ*, March 20, 1914, p. 1.

22. "My Southland," *WM*, August 1909, p. 653.

23. "The Mountains," *MtA*, October 2, 1914, p. 3.

24. Adams, *Transformation of Rural Life*, p. 41.

25. "The Country Library, A Clearing-House of Books," *WM*, April 1912, p. 14.

26. "Common Sense and Love of Right Needed: Every City a Battle Field with Crime," *SJ*, March 20, 1914, p. 1.

27. "Silverton, Happy Homes with No Saloons," *SJ*, July 18, 1913, p. 1.

28. "The Athens of the Mountains," *MtA*, January 17, 1908, p. 2. *The Mountain Advocate* repeatedly attempted to undo the image of rural Kentuckians as crude and ignorant. For a discussion of the "feudists of the Kentucky mountains," see "Our Mountain People," *MtA*, April 11, 1913, p. 2.

29. On boosterism in the early twentieth century in general, and the use of historical imagery to promote Progressive-era values in American cities in particular, see David Glassburg, *American Historical Pageantry: The Uses of Tradition in the Early Twentieth Century* (Chapel Hill: University of North Carolina Press, 1990). For the role of city promotion in boosterism, see also an excellent anthology edited by Dennis Judd and Susan Fainstein, *The Tourist City* (New Haven, Conn.: Yale University Press, 1999).

30. "A Scene in Silverton," *SJ*, March 27, 1914, p. 1.

31. "Silverton, Not Now a Country Town; Is Up-To-Date Business-Like City," *SJ*, February 27, 1914. A prior article boasted similar progress and efficiency in the once-small town, noting that Silverton had "solid banks, Two newspapers, a large gristmill, a large opera house, a good sewer system, many beautiful homes," and so forth—in short, was a locus of culture, natural beauty, and effective businesses. See "Silverton Has. . ." *SJ*, July 25, 1913, p. 2.

32. "Silverton and Progress," *SJ*, October 17, 1913, p. 2.

33. "Remarkable Productive Country Is Appalachia," *MtA*, September 30, 1910, p. 1. On promotion of Barbourville and the Appalachian region of Kentucky as the site for abundant resources and the draw of businesses to the region, see also "Location Is an Ideal One," *MtA*, September 30, 1910, p. 1.

34. "A Receipt for a Good Town," *MtA*, April 15, 1910, p. 1. On boosterism and business efficiency in Barbourville, see also "Factories Assured: For the Flourishing

City of Bartlesville, Oklahoma," *MtA*, April 15, 1910, p. 1. The latter article compares Bartlesville, Oklahoma, favorably with Barbourville—particularly since both communities have a corps of "business and professional" men who will insist that their towns receive excellent economic direction and will ensure the production of new factories and businesses. These articles suggest that *The Mountain Advocate* was looking to other smaller communities as sources of direction and inspiration in promoting its own Progressive-Era mission.

35. "Silverton and Progress," *SJ*, October 17, 1913, p. 2.

36. "Freedom of the Press Sustained," *YJ*, January 20, 1916, p. 1.

37. Untitled article, *YJ*, August 17, 1911, p. 2.

38. "Present Day Emancipation," *MtA*, February 7, 1913, p. 4.

39. "The Romanists Begin a Criminal Prosecution of Mr. Watson," *WM*, July 1912, pp. 196–98.

40. "City Congestion and Farm Desolation," *WM*, July 1912, p. 186.

41. "The Human Fool Mule," *SJ*, June 20, 1913, p. 1.

42. "Modern Witchcraft," *SJ*, June 20, 1913. On nativists' condemnation of novel forms of entertainment and recreation, see also "Exit Roller Skates," *MtA*, June 13, 1913, p. 1; "Our Moving Picture Show," *MtA*, February 28, 1913, p. 1. On the corrupting effects of smoking or chewing tobacco by children, see "Fanaticism's Latest," *YJ*, April 1920, p. 1.

43. "Hogs and Boys," *YJ*, September 18, 1913, p. 1.

44. On modernism, anti-sabbatarianism, and popular entertainment, see "Romish Church a 'Movie,'" *YJ*, January 17, 1915, p. 4.

45. "Fool Fashion," *SJ*, December 12, 1913, p. 3.

46. "The Jazz Age," *YJ*, May 1923, p. 6.

47. On the proliferation of entertainment in the late nineteenth and early twentieth centuries, see, for instance, Roy Rosenzweig, *Eight Hours for What We Will: Workers and Leisure in an Industrial City, 1870–1920* (New York: Cambridge University Press, 1983); Kathy Peiss, *Cheap Amusements: Working Women and Leisure in Turn-of-the-Century New York* (Philadelphia: Temple University Press, 1986); Michael Kimmel, *Manhood in America: A Cultural History* (New York: Free Press, 1996). On anti-Catholics' treatment of modern entertainment, and their rhetoric of safeguarding children from its corrosive effects, see "To Boys and Girls," *SJ*, February 20, 1914, p. 1.

48. "Christ's Gospel Misrepresented," *MtA*, April 11, 1913, p. 4. On overspending and consumer debt, see "Buying on the Installment Plan," *YJ*, April 17, 1913, p. 1.

49. "Old Time Religion," *YJ*, April 3, 1913, p. 1.

50. "Going Too Far," *YJ*, April 29, 1915, p. 3. On the error and corruption of Darwinism, see also "Was His Grandpaw a Monkey?" *YJ*, August 5, 1915, p. 4.

51. Richard Dees, "Establishing Toleration," *Political Theory* 27, no. 5 (October 1999): 667–93. Dees likewise points out that anti-Catholicism formed a po-

tent ingredient in establishing toleration between England's competing Protestant denominations, effectively minimizing denominational differences in the face of more salient Catholic foes.

52. Benjamin O. Flowers, *The Story of the Menace Trial: A Brief Sketch of This Historic Case, with Reports of the Masterly Addresses by Hon. J. L. McNatt and Hon. J. I. Sheppard* (Aurora, Mo.: United States Publishing, 1916), p. 8. The account goes on to describe the town of Aurora's jubilant response to the verdict, suggesting that the entire community shared in the fortunes of the newspaper. Residents organized prayer meetings and vigils, hoping to secure an acquittal, and formed an ad hoc parade when the verdict was announced and the defendants returned home. See p. 15 ff.

53. "My Barbourville," *MtA,* January 17, 1908, p. 1.

54. On veneration of Lincoln as a backwoods folk hero and exemplar of national greatness, see "Lincoln," *MtA,* February 11, 1910, p. 1; "Lincoln Day," *MtA,* February 18, 1910; "Memorial Day," *MtA,* May 27, 1910, p. 1.

55. "The Story of the Y. J.," *YJ,* February 18, 1915, p. 1.

56. "The Rural Church," *SJ,* October 23, 1914, p. 1. On the importance of rural culture and the need to preserve backwoods tradition and history, see "Important Work Is Being Done by Kentucky Folklore Society," *MtA,* May 23, 1913, p. 1.

57. "The Rural Press," *MtA,* January 15, 1915, p. 4.

58. "A Visit to The Menace Office," *TM,* September 26, 1914, p. 1.

59. "Priest and Catholic Teacher as Home Breakers," *The Peril,* March 5, 1914, p. 1. Several examples of editorials or letters supporting other anti-Catholic works abound in nativist literature; see, for instance, "Letters of Encouragement," *SJ,* August 29, 1913, p. 3. On advertisements for other anti-Catholic literary sources, see "The Menace," *WM,* April 1912, n.p. On cooperation as opposed to competition within anti-Catholic ranks, see "Deliverance, Is It at Hand?" *The Crusader,* August 1915, p. 1. This article points out that "petty jealousies and even animosities existing among the several patriotic societies" must be sidestepped to further the anti-Catholic movement. On the cooperation between anti-Catholic publishers, see also "Is There Any Danger? Are We Too Radical?" *The Crusader,* February 1915, p. 1.

60. "Shall the People or Shall Rome Rule?" *WM,* December 1912, p. 89.

61. On the origin of the name "The Menace" and its roots in Watson's periodicals, see "Brother Scarboro Talks Straight from the Shoulder in The Liberator," *The Jeffersonian,* October 24, 1912, p. 15. Ironically, this article, which reprises several episodes of American anti-Catholicism, is itself a reprinted essay from *The Liberator,* illustrating once again the exchange of material and information among several anti-Catholic sources.

62. "Who Is Headed for Hell? The 'Kentucky Irish American' Takes Another Fit," *MtA,* April 3, 1914, p. 1. For a further example of the desire of newspapers to venerate and assist *The Menace,* see "The Menace Shut Out of the Canadian

Mails," *The Peril* April 2, 1914, p. 1. Here news of the censorship of *The Menace* is reported in an entirely different periodical, urging readers to stop Rome's "muzzle on their free press."

63. "Let Minnesota Patriots Get Busy," *The Peril*, April 2, 1914, p. 2.

64. Cross-promotion by anti-Catholic authors abounds in Progressive-Era nativist texts. See, for instance, "Silverton Escaped Nun," *TM*, September 6, 1913, p. 3, and "Dealers in Human Flesh and Blood," *TM*, October 24, 1913, p. 3. Compare these with "This Attempted Murder Ought to Arouse Every Patriot," *SJ*, April 24, 1914, which urges patriotic readers to consult *The Menace*. *The Silverton Journal* also promoted the writings of William Lloyd Clark, editor of *The Rail Splitter*. See "A Book for Protestants," *SJ*, October 3, 1913, p. 7. For other promotion of *The Silverton Journal*, see "Nun Flees from Oregon Convent and Tells Horrible Story," *The Peril*, March 5, 1914, p. 2, and "Hans Schmidt—The Roman Priesthood; Once a Priest, Always a Priest," *The Liberator*, October 16, 1913, p. 1.

65. The praise to an "elder brother" in the anti-Catholic movement is from "What They Say of Us," *The Crusader*, March 1914, p. 4; the "warm welcome" extended by like-minded journals is from "What Watson Says of The Crusader," *The Crusader*, March 1914, p. 2. Other efforts to promote *The Crusader* can be seen in "The Crusader," *The Peril*, March 5, 1914, p. 2.

66. For examples of reprinting *The Liberator* in other anti-Catholic sources, see "Romanism in Mexico," *WM*, January 1913, p. 164. On shared advertising between *The Liberator* and *The Menace*, see "Cures Blood Poison" and "Sore Teeth," *The Liberator*, October 2, 1913, p. 1. On the shared admiration for James Crowley, well-known anti-Catholic writer, whose works were subsequently syndicated and reprinted in book form by the Menace Publishing Company, see "Crowley Hits Romanism," *The Liberator*, October 2, 1913, p. 2. Similar enthusiasm for Crowley's work can be seen in "Pastor Myers' Reply to the Priest," *SJ*, August 29, 1913, p. 1.

67. On the longevity of anti-Catholic networks in the early twentieth century, see, for instance, "A Slippery Priest and the Yellow Preacher," *The Rail Splitter*, February 1934, p. 2, which reprints an article from *The Yellow Jacket*.

68. During the numerous legal battles in which anti-Catholic writers found themselves as defendants during the 1910s, like-minded newspapers often printed advertisements and fund-raising notices to generate donations to pay for legal defense. See "Are the Dark Ages Coming Again?" *SJ*, October 9, 1914, p. 1, which excerpts an article written in *The Rail Splitter* asking readers to support the imprisoned editor of the *Silverton Journal*, J. E. Hosmer. *The Liberator* likewise denounced the persecution of Thomas Watson; see "Watson's Trial," *The Liberator*, October 16, 1913, p. 2. *The Menace* likewise drew connections between the legal difficulties of its own editors and the experiences of Thomas Watson, both sued in federal court for criminal libel. See Flowers, *Story of the Menace Trial*, p. 11. Anti-Catholic writers reported weekly on the developments of one another's trials, suggesting that readers kept themselves informed about the proceedings (or, at least, that

editors hoped these issues would interest readers). Writers also made explicit links between the trials of different periodicals.

69. "What about It?" *SJ*, June 13, 1913, p. 5. For other early discussions on Catholicism in *The Silverton Journal*, see "Father Moore Answers Charges," *SJ*, July 25, 1913, p. 1, and "The Lying, Malignant Menace," *SJ*, August 1, 1913, p. 1. Compare with "Reply to Father Moore's Letter," *SJ*, July 25, 1913, p. 1. On the preservation of a slightly localist outlook in treatment of the anti-Catholic crusade, see "God's Children at War," *SJ*, August 8, 1913, p. 1.

70. "The Blatt Calls Us 'The Journal-Menace Clique,'" *SJ*, October 17, 1913, p. 1. This article superficially rejects identification with *The Menace*, but it also emulates the latter paper in its condemnation of the priesthood and fierce attacks on critics. See also "Journal Menace Pipe Dream," *SJ*, March 13, 1914, p. 1.

71. "Stickers," *SJ*, August 9, 1915, p. 1. These pithy sayings proliferated in the pages of *The Silverton Journal* from 1913 on. For a discussion of *The Appeal to Reason* and its journalistic conventions, see David Nord, "The Appeal to Reason and American Socialism," *Kansas History* 1, no. 2 (Summer 1978): 75–89, and Elliot Shore, *Talkin' Socialism: J. A. Wayland and the Radical Press* (Lawrence: University Press of Kansas, 1988), esp. pp. 193–94.

72. Untitled article, *SJ*, August 1, 1913, p. 1.

73. "Wonderful Demand," *SJ*, August 8, 1913, p. 1.

74. Untitled article, *SJ*, August 8, 1913, p. 4.

75. The first anti-Catholic article in *The Mountain Advocate* was "The Black Nunnery," on January 9, 1914. By April 3, 1914, the paper's masthead reported that circulation had grown from 1,000 to 1,800.

76. "To the Readers of the Crusader," *The Crusader*, March 1914, p. 4. A similar example of patriotic rhetoric can be seen on that issue's masthead, which boasts: "We are not Anti-Catholic as to the religious opinions of Catholics, but we are American, and whenever any party, sect, or organization is un-American, we are fighting anti-Americanism."

77. See "The Crusader's First Anniversary," *The Crusader*, January 1915, p. 1, which outlines the beginning stages of the paper's early decline. Unlike its contemporaries, *The Crusader* was almost exclusively a monthly newspaper.

78. "A Million in 1914," *The Peril*, March 5, 1914, p. 2. The paper never approached the lofty goal of a million readers; see its masthead for April 2, 1914, for the peak of its circulation at just under 35,000. Similarly, *The Yellow Jacket*, which began in the late nineteenth century, released only scattered issues from mid 1919 through the early 1920s.

79. Readership among anti-Catholic papers differed in terms of overall circulation and in the region and location of subscribers. While there are no extant subscriber lists or business correspondence, the papers themselves offer several clues as to the location of their primary audiences. *The Liberator* indicated that "we go all over the United States but our special field is the great South and West,

the strongest Protestant country in the World." See "Our Helpers," *The Liberator,* October 2, 1913. This is reinforced by the paper's publication of new subscribers by location, which indicate that most readers lived in the paper's home state of Arkansas and nearby states like Texas and Oklahoma, with only a handful of readers in various Western and Midwestern states and virtually none in the Northeast. See "New Subscribers by States," *The Liberator,* October 16, 1913, p. 1. Likewise, *The Yellow Jacket* reported a circulation that was strongest in the Midwest and upper South with far fewer readers in New England and the Northeast. See "How the Yellow Jacket Circulates in the States," *YJ,* May 12, 1910, p. 2. In contrast, *The Menace* published a series of articles called "The Big Twelve" early in its publication, showing which cities witnessed the greatest number of subscribers. See, for instance, "The Big Twelve," *TM,* November 11 and 18, 1911, p. 4. While the newspaper discontinued the column after 1911 (and thus only reported circulation figures early in the decade), it illustrated that industrialized sections of the Northeast, particularly New York and Ohio, expressed an early interest in the paper. By the middle of the decade, *The Menace* reported that, with the exception of the paper's home state of Missouri, states in the Northeast and upper Midwest held the highest circulation. See "Circulation by States," *TM,* November 15, 1913, p. 1.

80. Nord, "Appeal to Reason"; Shore, *Talkin' Socialism*; Aileen S. Kraditor, *The Radical Persuasion, 1890–1917: Aspects of Intellectual History and the Historiography of Three American Radical Organizations* (Baton Rouge: Louisiana State University Press, 1981). Wayland and other leaders of *The Appeal* frequently attempted to sidestep or deny accusations of owning *The Menace.* See "Ownership of The Menace," *Appeal to Reason,* December 28, 1912; "Facts about The Appeal," *Appeal to Reason,* July 5, 1913. Yet evidence shows that leaders of *The Appeal* followed the workings of *The Menace* and provided legal and financial help to the paper. See Flowers, *Story of the Menace Trial.*

81. Nord, "Appeal to Reason," 86. Nord also illustrates the anti-Catholic inclinations of *The Appeal*'s editor, J. A. Wayland; see p. 84.

82. Nord, "Appeal to Reason," 86.

83. "Bundle Brigade," *TM,* December 9, 1911, p. 4. Another, more indirect source of support for *The Menace*'s subscription campaigns came from Catholic attention, which allowed *The Menace* to draw publicity from its critics. See "A Loathsome Sheet," *TM,* December 9, 1911, p. 4. I will address this point in greater detail in chapter 4.

84. "Live Wire! Don't Tire!! Fire!!!" *SJ,* January 9, 1914, p. 2.

85. "The Journal in Danger," *SJ,* October 24, 1913, p. 1. The *Journal*'s adoption of club-based subscriptions is another illustration of its adoption of the practices of anti-Catholic counterparts, suggesting that transition in the paper's rhetoric carried with it a shift in circulation, commercial, and distribution practices. In its quest to secure 10,000 subscribers, the *Journal* outlined how subscriptions could easily multiply: "Here is the simple method by which it can be done: Get a

subscriber, give him a subscription blank, and tell him to get another, giving him a blank also with the same instructions. . . . When we reach the 5000 mark we will double the size of our paper and this will help us all to get the other 5000." See "10,000 Subs for Journal," *SJ*, November 21, 1914, p. 1.

86. "Spreading the Jeffs Circulation Is the Best Way to Aid in Fight," *The Jeffersonian*, July 18, 1912, p. 11.

87. C. Vann Woodward, "Tom Watson and the Negro in Agrarian Politics," *Journal of Southern History* 4, no. 1 (February 1938): 14–33, quote on p. 23.

88. For a discussion of this term, see C. Vann Woodward's classic text *Tom Watson: Agrarian Rebel* (New York: Rinehart, 1938). Several subsequent articles address Vann Woodward's portrayal of Watson, particularly Watson's shift from racial solidarity to segregation and hate-mongering. See, for instance, the recent essay by the eminent historian Bertram Wyatt-Brown, "Tom Watson Revisited," *The Journal of Southern History* 68, no. 1 (February 2002): 3–30. For a discussion of Catholics' response to Watson's nativism, see Felicitas Powers, "Prejudice, Journalism, and the Catholic Laymen's Association of Georgia," *U.S. Catholic Historian* 8, no. 3 (Summer 1989): 201–12. I offer a more complete discussion of Catholics' response to Watson and anti-Catholic journalism writ large in chapter 4.

89. On the growth of newspaper technology and circulations in the late nineteenth and early twentieth centuries, see William Thorn and Mary Pat Pfiel, *Newspaper Circulation: Marketing the News* (New York: Longman, 1987), and Harold Wilson, *McClure's Magazine and the Muckrakers* (Princeton, N.J.: Princeton University Press, 1970). For a survey of publishing innovation and its influence on "investigative" reporting from the eighteenth century through the Pentagon Papers scandal of the late twentieth, see Edd Applegate, *Journalistic Advocates and Muckrakers: Three Centuries of Crusading Writers* (Jefferson, N.C.: McFarland, 1997).

90. "Troubles of the Editor," *TM*, August 9, 1913, p. 1. On the commonality of the anti-Catholic message as a barrier against Romanist corruption of American institutions, see also "Cathedral in Washington," *TM*, January 27, 1912, p. 2; "Make America Yellow Jackety," *YJ*, January 7, 1915, p. 1.

91. S. S. McClure, "Editorial," in *McClure's Magazine*, January 1903, reprinted in Arthur Weinberg and Lila Weinberg, eds., *The Muckrakers: The Era in Journalism that Moved America to Reform* (New York: Simon and Schuster, 1961), quote on p. 4.

92. Ibid., p. 5.

93. Lincoln Steffens, "The Shame of Minneapolis," *McClure's Magazine*, January 1903, reprinted in Weinberg and Weinberg, *The Muckrakers*, quote on p. 10. For a useful comparison and overview of muckraking, "machine" politics, and municipal graft, see Jerome Krase and Charles La Cerra, *Ethnicity and Machine Politics* (Lantham, Md.: University Press of America, 1991).

94. Steffens, "The Shame of Minneapolis," p. 21.

95. Ida M. Tarbell, "The History of the Standard Oil Company," in *McClure's Magazine*, January 1903, reprinted in Weinberg and Weinberg, *The Muckrakers*,

quote on p. 22. For a complete account of Tarbell's treatment of Standard Oil, see her mammoth and path-breaking exposé, *The History of the Standard Oil Company*, 2 vols. (New York: Macmillan, 1925).

96. Tarbell, "The History of the Standard Oil Company," p. 28.

97. Ibid.

98. Ray Stannard Baker, "The Right to Work," in *McClure's Magazine*, January 1903, reprinted in Weinberg and Weinberg, *The Muckrakers*, quote on p. 40.

99. Ibid., p. 46.

100. "Romanism Ruling and Ruining," *WM*, August, 1911, p. 323.

101. "Is Popery in Power in Washington?" *MtA*, October 22, 1915, p. 8.

102. "Get Busy! Get Awake! Get Alive," *The Peril*, April 2, 1914, p. 3.

103. "Patriotic Meeting Called," *The Liberator*, October 16, 1913, p. 2.

104. "Joseph Pulitzer," *The Jeffersonian*, November 16, 1911.

105. "The Crime of the Age," *TM*, December 9, 1911, p. 1. On patriotic sacrifice as the price of a free press, see "On the Firing Line," *TM*, February 10, 1912, p. 2, and May 31, 1913, p. 4.

106. "The Roman Catholic Political Machine," *The Crusader*, March 1914, p. 4.

107. On favoritism in New Orleans, see "Open Letter to Cardinal Gibbons," *WM*, October 1912, pp. 480–82; in Chicago, see "Knows Romanism System from Inside," *The Jeffersonian*, July 18, 1912, p. 2; on Catholic bribery, duplicity, and political monopoly in New York City, see "How the Knights of Columbus Tried to Bribe a Congressman to Betray His Country," *The Jeffersonian*, November 7, 1912, p. 5. On Catholic political influence, see "Do the Knights of Columbus Own the Democratic Party?" *The Crusader*, August 1915, p. 1. On nativists' call to improve urban efficiency and stem the growth of Catholic influence, see "The Growth of the Office-Holding Class," *WM*, March 1913, p. 107 ff.; "The Political Power of Romanism in America," *YJ*, July 22, 1915, p. 4.

108. "America's Danger," *SJ*, May 22, 1914, p. 2. *The Menace* called pro-Catholic sympathizers "cringing cowards in the reputed land of the free and home of the brave." See "Political Rome, the Nation's Peril," *TM*, May 24, 1913, p. 1.

109. "Knows Romanist System from the Inside," *The Jeffersonian*, July 18, 1912, p. 2. On Catholic urban graft, corruption, and infiltration of the police and legal system, see also "Catholic Abuses Must Be Stopped," *SJ*, December 11, 1914, p. 2.

110. "Catholics Control Large Cities," *SJ*, March 13, 1914, p. 1.

111. On arguments against Catholic progressivism, see "Non-Partisan Democracy: Direct Legislation," *WM*, August 1911, p. 301. On anti-Catholic texts questioning the alleged "progressivism" of their opponents while reserving the mantle for themselves, see also "Another Governor Submerges Himself," *The Jeffersonian*, November 16, 1911, p. 3. On Catholic dismissal of progressive politics in favor of vigilantism, see "Read This and Think," *YJ*, May 29, 1915, p. 4; "As the Haverstraw Knights Do It," *YJ*, June 24, 1915, p. 4.

112. "A Catholic Sheriff," *TM*, September 28, 1912, p. 4.

113. "Booze and Vice Over-run [*sic*] at Terre Haute," *The Woman's Witness*, February 23, 1914, p. 1.

114. "Help Us Turn on the Light," *SJ*, October 24, 1913, p. 2;

115. "Good Catholics in Spite of Their So-Called Church," *SJ*, September 18, 1914, p. 1. On the rhetoric of "light" in anti-Catholic texts, see also, "More Light on the Friars of the Philippine Islands," *The Jeffersonian*, November 16, 1911, p. 7, and "Let a Little Light Shine In," *TM*, May 16, 1914, p. 3.

116. "The Crusader Is One Year Old, Do You Know What That Means?" *The Crusader*, February, 1915, p. 1

117. "Do Not Elect Catholics!" *TM*, November 1, 1913, p. 1. On the role of Catholicism in civil power, see also "Roman Catholic Party," *TM*, November 25, 1911, p. 2.

118. On Catholic philanthropy as a front for priestly deception, see "Sisters Hospital Graft Is Rejected," *TM*, June 21, 1919, p. 2, and untitled cartoon, *TM*, May 24, 1913, p. 1.

119. See David Brion Davis, "Some Themes of Counter-Subversion: An Analysis of Anti-Masonic, Anti-Catholic, and Anti-Mormon Literature," *The Mississippi Valley Historical Review* 47, no. 2 (October 1960): 205–24, and Jenny Franchot, *Roads to Rome: The Antebellum Protestant Encounter with Catholicism* (Berkeley: University of California Press, 1994).

120. "Rome's Ripening Conspiracy," *SJ*, February 6, 1914, p. 1. Like Tarbell's depiction of Standard Oil, anti-Catholic newspapers occasionally pointed to Catholic manipulation of and profits from the railroad industry; see "The Modern Triumvirate; Combined to Ruin America," *TM*, November 21, 1914, p. 2; "Papal Encroachment," *TM*, January 27, 1912, p. 1.

121. "Are There Arms Secured in the Catholic Churches?" *The Crusader*, February 1915, p. 3. On Catholicism's use of military maneuvers and threats of a Catholic coup, see "Is There a Catholic Menace?" *The Jeffersonian*, July 18, 1912, p. 15.

122. "What of the War," *The Crusader*, September 1915, p. 1. On Rome's involvement in the "Triple Conspiracy" and European espionage, see "Pope's Secretary Caught Red Handed Directing Three Plots of Intrigue," *TM*, May 12, 1917, p. 1.

123. "There Is a Modern Inquisition," *WM*, July 1912, p. 211.

124. "Is a Conspiracy Possible? Did You Get Your October Magazine?" *The Jeffersonian*, November 16, 1911, p. 1. Watson edited both *The Jeffersonian* and *Watson's Magazine* and frequently promoted one periodical in the pages of the other.

125. "Watch Your Catholic Postmasters," *YJ*, May 11, 1916, p. 4. *The Yellow Jacket* also dedicated a great deal of publicity to the case of F. C. Seibengartner, the postmaster of Bettendorf, Iowa, who admitted to stealing and destroying copies of *The Yellow Jacket* and other anti-Catholic periodicals. Despite his own confession, *The Yellow Jacket* maintained, Seibengartner was acquitted by a "Romanized" grand jury

and continued to hold his job at the post office. See "Couldn't Be Guilty If He Was," *YJ,* June 10, 1915, p. 4.

126. "Where Is the Book?" *TM,* February 10, 1912, p. 1. On nativists' claims that opponents sabotaged or stole anti-Catholic books, see also "Mysterious Disappearance of My Books," *WM,* February 1913, n. p.

127. "Is the American Press to Be Muzzled?" *The Crusader,* February 1915, p. 2.

128. On other Catholic strategies to dismantle anti-Catholic circulation, see "Another Stab at Free Speech," *YJ,* January 6, 1916, p. 1; "To Exclude Critics," *TM,* December 9, 1911, p. 4; "Roman Catholic Legislation," *YJ,* October 14, 1915, p. 2; "Evidently, Romanists Bought Up All the May Issues of Our Magazine," *The Jeffersonian,* June 13, 1912, p. 7; "This Man Wants to See Watson's on Newsstand," *The Jeffersonian,* November 16, 1911, p. 3.

129. Thorn and Pfiel, *Newspaper Circulation.* In examining Joseph Pulitzer's victory in America's circulation wars, Thorn and Pfiel assert, "Pulitzer's genius, in part, lay in his recognition of constant self-promotion as a circulation tool of broad reach" (p. 55).

130. "The Modern War," *SJ,* September 26, 1913, p. 2.

131. On nativist condemnation of Catholics' misrepresenting and distorting sources of information, see "We Keep History Straight," *YJ,* May 13, 1915, p. 1; "Rome and the Government Print Shop," *TM,* May 31, 1913, p. 3; "The Juvenile Court at the National Capital, a State Institution, Converted into a Roman Catholic Institution," *WM,* August 1912, p. 308; "Important Notice to All Patriots by Father Jones," *The Crusader,* April 1915, p. 2.

132. "Poisoning the Wells," *TM,* December 2, 1911, p. 4.

133. Kevin Mattson, *Creating a Democratic Public: The Struggle for Urban Participatory Democracy during the Progressive Era* (University Park: Pennsylvania State University Press, 1998), quote on p. 7. For another Progressive-Era text that echoes anti-Catholicism's concern for accuracy and fidelity in the spread of information, see Mark Sullivan, "The Patent Medicine Conspiracy against the Freedom of the Press," *Colliers,* November 4, 1905, reprinted in Weinberg and Weinberg, *The Muckrakers.*

134. Gilmore, *Who Were the Progressives?* quote on p. 4. Louis Menand's Pulitzer Prize–winning discussion of American pragmatism likewise argues that the emergence of pragmatism, the thirst for ideas, and the grounding of social theory in material realities rather than abstract or objective theory contributed to and was reinforced by Progressive rationality. See Louis Menand, *The Metaphysical Club: A Story of Ideas in America* (New York: Farrar, Straus, and Giroux, 2002).

135. "Read This for Our Plan," *The Woman's Witness,* February 23, 1914, p. 2.

136. McCormick, *The Discovery that Business Corrupts Politics,* p. 260.

137. Ibid., p. 272.

138. "The Political Leaders and the Catholic Vote," *WM,* July 1912, p. 177.

139. Untitled article, *TM,* February 10, 1912, p. 1.

CHAPTER THREE. "ROME IS THE JAILER OF YOUTH"

1. "Girls Hunted by Slave Catchers," *TM*, April 15, 1914, p. 1. This chapter was published in a more condensed form in *U.S. Catholic Historian* 20, no. 1 (Winter 2002): 57–82.

2. On *The Menace*'s support of Maria Monk, see "Maria Monk Story Confirmed," *TM*, February 8, 1919, p. 2; "Open Rome's Prison Houses in America," *TM*, December 2, 1911, p. 1.

3. "A.P.A.ism [*sic*] Is Not Dead," *TM*, March 16, 1912, p. 3. On the American Protective Association, see also "The A.P.A.," *TM*, January 6, 1912, p. 4.

4. Maureen McCarthy, *The Rescue of True Womanhood: Convents and Anti-Catholicism in 1830s America* (Ann Arbor, Mich.: UMI Dissertations International, 1996), p. 97.

5. Ibid., p. 99.
6. Ibid., p. 2.

7. For analysis of the APA's political agenda, its brief rise to prominence, and its eventual collapse, see Donald Kinzer, *An Episode in Anti-Catholicism: The American Protective Association* (Seattle: University of Washington Press, 1964), and Les Wallace, *The Rhetoric of Anti-Catholicism: The American Protective Association, 1887–1911* (New York: Garland, 1990).

8. Kinzer, *An Episode in Anti-Catholicism*, p. 96.

9. APA organizations published over a dozen different anti-Catholic newspapers in the course of the 1890s in large cities, such as Denver and Los Angeles, and small towns such as Butte, Montana, and Lansingburg, New York. See ibid., p. 95.

10. Sarah H. Hatch, *A Woman's Plea for Her Country* [broadside] (Everett, Mass.: n.p., 1894).

11. Margaret L. Shepherd, *Two Great Lectures on Romanism* (Providence, R.I.: A.P. Young, 1893). Similar concerns over priests' sexual abuse of women and girls can be found in the writings of Georgia populist and anti-Catholic author Thomas Watson. See, for instance, Thomas Watson, *What Goes On in the Nunneries?* (Thompson, Ga.: Jeffersonian, 1917), and idem, *Maria Monk and Her Revelation of Convent Crimes* (Thompson, Ga.: Jeffersonian, 1917).

12. W.H. Carlisle, *Raise a Flag o'er Every Schoolhouse* (Pittsburgh: n.p., 1915).

13. McCarthy, *The Rescue of True Womanhood*, p. 51. See also Jenny Franchot, *Roads to Rome: The Antebellum Protestant Encounter with Catholicism* (Berkeley: University of California Press, 1994), pp. 137–54.

14. Untitled article, *TM*, March 30, 1918, p. 1.

15. On Catholics as subversives see "Preparedness as a Prevention of a Calamity," *TM*, May 5, 1917, p. 1; "Does the Church Have Guns?" *TM*, May 4, 1918, p. 1; "The Pope and the Kaiser," *TM*, May 12, 1917, p. 2; "America," *TM*, May 19, 1917, p. 3.

16. "The 'Little Red Schoolhouse,'" *YJ*, April 27, 1916, p. 3.

17. "Watch the School Elections," *TM*, March 30, 1918, p. 4. On *The Menace's* claims of Catholic graft in public education, see also "Rome's Late Attack on Godless Schools," *TM*, October 6, 1917, p. 3; "Put No Free School Enemy in Office," *TM*, June 14, 1913, p. 2; "Bushwacking Our Public Schools," *TM*, January 25, 1919, p. 3; "Public or Parochial Schools," *TM*, May 4, 1912, p. 2; "Rome Gets School Funds in Canada," *TM*, June 22, 1918, p. 3; "The Difference in Educational Ideals," *TM*, August 18, 1917, p. 1; "Papal Traitors to the Public School," *TM*, September 14, 1918, p. 1; "School Troubles Ahead," *TM*, January 20, 1912, p. 3. Similar condemnation was launched in *The Silverton Journal*. The paper chastised Catholics for seeking nothing short of "absolute control of the public schools of Greater New York." See "Largest City in America in Hands of Romans," *SJ*, June 12, 1914, p. 1. The paper made a similar point in "Catholics Responsible for Fight," *SJ*, January 2, 1914, p. 1.

18. "Popery Gassing the Public Schools," *TM*, November 9, 1919, p. 2.

19. "Roman Catholic Designs on the American Nation," *WM*, August 1912, p. 279.

20. Ibid. For another example of the dangers of Catholic attacks on public school boards, see untitled article, *The Liberator*, October 2, 1913, p. 1.

21. "League Is Determined to Stop Forever Rome's Deadly War on Public Schools," *TM*, March 24, 1917, p. 1.

22. "Parish vs. Public Schools in Court," *TM*, November 30, 1918, p. 2. For fears of Catholic influences on Protestant students, see also "Nun Principal of a Public School," *TM*, June 29, 1918, p. 4; "Popery Admits It Doctors School Texts," *TM*, December 28, 1918, p. 1; "Papalized Books in Public Schools," *TM*, February 22, 1919, p. 1; "Cloistered Education," *TM*, February 22, 1913, p. 2.

23. "Women and the Catholic Priest," *TM*, March 23, 1912, p. 1.

24. "Woman's Position in the Catholic Church," *WM*, December 1912, p. 78.

25. "Suffrage Movement Causes Organization of Roman Catholic Women into a Solid Body," *The Peril*, March 5, 1914, p. 2.

26. "The Deadly Parallel," *The Woman's Witness*, February 23, 1914, p. 2. On women's economic and political marginalization and exploitation, see also "Romish Immigration," *The Liberator*, October 2, 1913, p. 2.

27. On priests' physical and sexual abuse of women, see "Priests Bind, Gag, Blindfold and Rape Nun," *TM*, September 20, 1913, p. 1; "Rome's Appreciation of Women," *TM*, October 17, 1914, p. 3; "The Priest The Woman & The Confessional," *TM*, December 7, 1918, p. 1; "Heart to Heart Woman to Woman," *TM*, May 3, 1919, p. 2.

28. "Nun Flees from Oregon Convent and Tells Horrible Story," *The Peril*, March 5, 1914, p. 2. This article recounted the harrowing story of a woman escaping the Mount Angel convent near Silverton. Interestingly, the article illustrates the intra-journalistic borrowing that occurred between anti-Catholic texts,

since *The Silverton Journal* first reported on depravity at Mount Angel, and shortly thereafter, several other anti-Catholic periodicals had picked up the story. For a more in-depth illustration of the networks of anti-Catholic readers and writers, see the discussion in chapter 2.

29. "Women and Priestcraft," *TM*, June 26, 1915, p. 1. On support of women in the nativist press, see also "Women's Suffrage a Live Issue," *The Woman's Witness*, February 23, 1914, p. 1.

30. "To the Women of America—A Message," *TM*, September 21, 1912, p. 3. On women's political role in stopping Catholic aggression, see "Women and Popery," *TM*, March 29, 1919, p. 1; "Women and Democracy," *TM*, May 3, 1919, p. 1; "The Women on the Firing Line," *4* February 1, 1919, p. 4; "Will Michigan Women Vote?" *TM*, February 8, 1919, p. 4; "Ladies, This Is Your Hour," *TM*, January 11, 1919, p. 1; "Even Nuns Vote for Catholic Governor," *TM*, January 4, 1919, p. 2.

31. On the late treatment of women readers, see "Ladies, This Is Your Hour"; "Women and Democracy," *TM*, May 3, 1919, p. 1 (this article was part of a special "women's issue" published by *The Menace*).

32. On women and reports of convent abuse, see, for instance, "Ana Lowry at Winona," *The Peril*, April 2, 1914, p. 2.

33. Ryan's studies of architecture, arts, and public pageantry demonstrates that women served as symbols of liberty and national, local, and ethnic pride long before suffrage. See Mary Ryan, *Women in Public: Between Banners and Ballots, 1825–1880* (rev. ed.; Baltimore: Johns Hopkins University Press, 1992); and "'A Laudable Pride in the Whole of Us': City Halls and Civic Materialism," *The American Historical Review* 105, no. 4 (October 2000): 1131–70. Rebecca Edwards's study of Progressive-Era politics suggests that women exerted a substantial role in political campaigns. See Edwards, *Angels in the Machinery: Gender in American Party Politics from the Civil War to the Progressive Era* (New York: Oxford University Press, 1997).

34. "Hospital Graft in Mich.," *TM*, March 25, 1916, p. 2. On Catholic philanthropy as financial and political corruption, see "The Awakening in Oregon," *TM*, January 20, 1917, p. 4; "Catholic 'Charities' in Bad Light in N.Y.," *TM*, January 6, 1912, p. 1; "Building Catholic Hospitals with Protestant Money," *TM*, September 21, 1912, p. 2; "Papal Hospital at Jackson Michigan," *TM*, December 27, 1913, p. 1; "A Government Hospital?" *TM*, March 8, 1919, p. 1; "Maine Asked to Aid Catholic 'Charity'," *TM*, February 8, 1919, p. 1.

35. "Experience at a Non-Sectarian (?) Hospital," *TM*, September 13, 1913, p. 1. On Catholic hospitals' maltreatment of Protestant patients, see also "Catholic Hospital Defies the Court," *TM*, December 28, 1918, p. 1. For Catholic hospitals' abuse and torture of the insane, see "Abuse Soldiers in Papal Hospital," *TM*, February 15, 1919, p. 2.

36. "Catholic Hospitals," *TM*, January 20, 1912, p. 1.

37. "Proselytizing among the Sick and Dying," *TM*, November 23, 1918, p. 1.

38. "Declare Priest Influenced Will," *SJ*, October 17, 1913, p. 1.

39. On Jesuit trickery toward widows, see "The Secret Instructions of the Jesuits," *WM*, October 1912, pp. 465–72. On deathbed conversion and kidnapping of children, see "Romanists Rob Father of Children," *The Jeffersonian*, July 18, 1912, p. 3. For a similar story of an Australian woman who was misled by a priest into giving donations she believed would help her dead father's soul escape purgatory (but which the priest spent on drinking), see "Bridget's Money," *SJ*, January 23, 1914, p. 2.

40. "Tortured in a Catholic 'Home'," *TM*, November 22, 1913, p. 1. On Catholic political corruption in elderly homes, see "Pasadena Wants Non-Catholic Home," *TM*, March 16, 1918, p. 1. On Catholic treatment of the poor and insane, see "A Reply to Rev Lucian Johnson, Catholic Priest, and Author of The Shame of It," *WM*, August 1911. *The Crusader* insisted that, rather than treat patients who truly needed care, Catholics hauled healthy people into insane asylums as a way of silencing critics. See "Conspiracy to Send Father Jones to the U.S. Government Insane Asylum," *The Crusader* August 1915, p. 2.

41. For statistics and a helpful overview of Catholic charitable work in the early twentieth century, see Jay P. Dolan, *The American Catholic Experience: A History from Colonial Times to the Present* (Notre Dame, Ind.: University of Notre Dame Press, 1992), esp. p. 329 ff. Large-scale Catholic charitable bodies experienced tremendous growth during these years, as well. For an insightful investigation of the St. Vincent de Paul Society and its philanthropic efforts, see Deirdre M. Moloney, "Divisions of Labor: The Roles of American Catholic Lay Women, Lay Men, and Women Religious in Charity Provision," *Catholic Historian* 20, no. 1 (Winter 2002): 41–56. For an elaboration of nuns' roles in shaping Catholic charity and American philanthropy at large, see Barbara Mann Wall, "'We Might as Well Burn It': Catholic Sister-Nurses and Hospital Control, 1865–1930," *U.S. Catholic Historian* 20, no. 1 (Winter 2002): 21–40.

42. Several studies of Catholic history and historiography have illustrated the divide between Catholic and Protestant reform and social ideology. See, for instance, John E. Tropman, *The Catholic Ethic in American Society: An Exploration of Values* (San Francisco: Jossey-Bass, 1995), which presents a Weberian-styled examination of Catholic values as distinct from the American public at large. Other works include Peter Steinfels, "The Failed Encounter: The Catholic Church and Liberalism in the Nineteenth Century," in R. Bruce Douglass and David Hollenbach, eds., *Catholicism and Liberalism: Contributions to American Public Philosophy* (New York: Cambridge University Press, 1994), and Andrew M. Greeley, *The Catholic Myth: The Behavior and Beliefs of American Catholics* (reprint ed.; New York: Collier, 1997). Yet other writers have demonstrated Catholicism's appeal to American policy makers in general and Protestants in particular, noting how high-profile Catholic leaders made excellent use of popular media to generate interest in Catholicism. See Christopher Owen Lynch, *Selling Catholicism: Bishop Sheen and the Power of Television* (Lexington: University Press of Kentucky, 1998; and Donald

Warren, *Radio Priest: Charles Coughlin, the Father of Hate Radio* (New York: Free Press, 1996). For a useful overview of American Catholicism and its relationship to American society and culture, see Charles R. Morris, *American Catholic: The Saints and Sinners Who Built America's Most Powerful Church* (New York: Times Books, 1997).

43. Although some scholars, such as Joseph Varacelli, question the extent to which American Catholics were able to affect significant change prior to the mid twentieth century, most see the Progressive Era as a watershed moment in which Catholics began to vocally participate in and affect the contours of American society. Varacelli contends that Catholics should be commended for opposing American liberalism prior to the Second Vatican Council in the 1960s, distancing themselves from mainstream America. See Varacelli, *Bright Promise, Failed Community: Catholics and the American Public Order* (Lanham, Md.: Lexington Books, 2000). Most researchers disagree, however, pointing to the church's changing position on social justice and greater lay and clerical involvement in social issues. On the church's initial reluctance to pursue an agenda of reform and subsequent entrée into Progressive-Era reform, see Joseph M. McShane, *"Sufficiently Radical": Catholicism, Progressivism, and the Bishops' Program of 1919* (Washington, D.C.: Catholic University Press, 1986). McShane discusses the influence of Progressive-Era reform in shaping Catholic hierarchical attitudes and motivations and addresses the Church's transition from opposing to accepting social and political reform. Other works exploring the overlap between Catholicism and Progressivism include Deirdre M. Moloney's dissertation, *Reclaiming Reform: Catholic Lay Groups and American Society, 1880–1925* (Ann Arbor, Mich.: UMI International, 1996), recently revised and published as *American Catholic Lay Groups and Transatlantic Social Reform in the Progressive Era* (Chapel Hill: University of North Carolina Press, 2002), and Mary J. Oates, *The Catholic Philanthropic Tradition in America* (Bloomington: Indiana University Press, 1995). For an analysis of more recent Catholic approaches to reform and political activism, and the seemingly contradictory nature of Catholic attitudes, which seem to defy conventional "conservative" and "liberal" dichotomies, see John Coleman, "American Catholicism, Catholic Charities USA, and Welfare Reform," *Journal of Policy History* 13, 1 (2001): 73–108.

44. Dolan, *American Catholic Experience*, p. 350. On the establishment of the American Federation of Catholic Societies and its influence on organized Catholic philanthropy, see Philip Gleason, "American Catholics and Liberalism, 1789–1960," in Douglass and Hollenbach, *Catholicism and Liberalism*. For recent studies on the intellectual contributions of American Catholics in the early twentieth century, see Peter A. Huff, *Allan Tate and the American Catholic Revival* (Mahwah, N.J.: Paulist, 1996); and Ross Labrie, *The Catholic Imagination in American Literature* (Columbia: University of Missouri Press, 1997).

45. Mary J. Oates, *The Catholic Philanthropic Tradition in America* (Bloomington: Indiana University Press, 1995).

46. "Brutal Assault on an Innocent Child," *TM*, August 17, 1918, p. 1.

47. "Catholic Priest Cripples Milwaukee Boy for Life," *TM*, November 18, 1911, p. 1.

48. "A Priest Wrongs His Housekeeper," *TM*, January 3, 1914, p. 3.

49. "Priest Accused of Seduction," *TM*, June 28, 1913, p. 4. On Catholic sexual and physical abuse, see also "Another 'Holy Roman' Seductionist Goes Free," *TM*, February 14, 1914, p. 1.

50. "Let's Open Rome's Prisons and Free the Slaves," *TM*, January 27, 1917, p. 4.

51. "How Long Will These Prison Houses Run?" *SJ*, February 6, 1914, p. 2.

52. "Convent Cruelty," *TM*, December 30, 1911, p. 4. On abuse in convents, see also, "What Became of This Child?," *TM*, September 6, 1913, p. 1; "Don't Imprison Girls, Eh," *YJ*, February 4, 1915, p. 1.

53. "The Same Old Story, Skeleton in Basement [of] Catholic Home," *The Jeffersonian*, October 28, 1915, p. 7.

54. "H.O.G.S. and State Institutions," *TM*, July 10, 1915, p. 2. ("H.O.G.S." was the abbreviation used for Houses of the Good Shepherd.)

55. "Roman Catholic Designs on the American Nation," *WM*, August 1912, p. 278.

56. "The Roman Catholic Hierarchy: The Deadliest Menace to Our Liberties and Our Civilization," *WM*, September 1912, p. 331.

57. "The Truth, the Whole Truth, and Nothing but the Truth," *The Liberator*, October 16, 1913, p. 3.

58. "The Roman Catholic Hierarchy: The Deadliest Menace to Our Liberties and Our Civilization," *WM*, March 1911, p. 105, emphasis in original.

59. Nancy Lusignan Schultz, ed., *Veil of Fear: Nineteenth-Century Convent Tales by Rebecca Reed and Maria Monk* (West Lafayette, Ind.: Purdue University Press, 1999), p. xxiv.

60. Franchot, *Roads to Rome*, p. 185.

61. Ann Douglas, "Soft Porn Culture," *The New Republic*, August 1980, pp. 25−29, quotes on p. 26.

62. Janice A. Radway, *Reading the Romance: Women, Patriarchy, and Popular Literature* (rev. ed.; Chapel Hill: University of North Carolina Press, 1991), quote on p. 45. For more discussion of twentieth-century mass marketing of novels and print literature and its commentary on broader American society, see Janice A. Radway, *A Feeling for Books: The Book-of-the-Month Club, Literary Taste, and Middle-Class Desire* (Chapel Hill: University of North Carolina Press, 1997).

63. Chris Jenks, *Childhood* (London: Routledge, 1996), p. 10.

64. Ibid., p. 8.

65. Ibid., p. 3.

66. Ashis Nandy, "Reconstructing Childhood: A Critique of the Ideology of Adulthood," in idem, *Traditions, Tyranny and Utopias: Essays in the Politics of Awareness* (Delhi: Oxford University Press, 1992 [1987]), p. 56.

67. Ibid., p. 63.

68. Philip J. Greven, *The Protestant Temperament: Patterns of Child-Rearing, Religious Experience, and the Self in Early America* (New York: Knopf, 1977).

69. See Philip Greven, *Spare the Child: The Religious Roots of Punishment and the Psychological Impact of Physical Abuse* (New York: Vintage Books, 1990), especially Part II, pp. 11–42.

70. Philippe Ariès, *Centuries of Childhood: A Social History of Family Life*, trans. Robert Baldick (New York: Random House, 1965). For discussions of childhood that respond to and attempt to refute Ariès, see Steven Ozment, *Ancestors: The Loving Family in Old Europe* (Cambridge: Harvard University Press, 2002), and Nicholas Orme, *Medieval Children* (New Haven, Conn.: Yale University Press, 2002). Other scholars discussing the role of social change on childhood and family life in the United States include Vivian Zelizer, *Prizing the Priceless Child: The Changing Social Value of Children* (rev. ed.; Princeton, N.J.: Princeton University Press, 1994), and Paula S. Fass and Mary Ann Mason, eds., *Childhood in America* (New York: New York University Press, 2000).

71. Anne Higonnet, *Pictures of Innocence: The History and Crisis of Ideal Childhood* (New York: Thames and Hudson, 1998), p. 8.

72. Ibid., p. 15.

73. "Rome Robbing Chicago of Thousands through Merciless Child Traffic," *TM*, February 24, 1917, p. 1.

74. "Conserve the Girls, Too," *TM*, March 28, 1914, p. 2.

75. "H.O.G.S. Wants Prostitutes," *TM*, July 9, 1913, p. 4.

76. "White Slavers Busy," *TM*, March 1, 1913, p. 3.

77. "Is $30,000,000 to Enslave Protestant Children?," *TM*, January 4, 1919, p. 3.

78. "Innocent Girl Committed to Roman Prison," *TM*, September 23, 1916, p. 1. See also "Georgia Editor Lambasts Inspection," *TM*, August 14, 1915, p. 1.

79. Untitled article, *TM*, March 4, 1916, p. 1.

80. "Public School Boards," *TM*, March 9, 1912, p. 1.

81. "Heads of a Roman Nursery Arrested," *TM*, November 10, 1917, p. 1.

82. On Catholics as pathetic, see "The Pathetic Side," *TM*, February 23, 1918, p. 3, and "The Houses of the Good Shepherd," *TM*, November 16, 1912, p. 3. On Catholics as victims of the hierarchy, see "A Bad Catholic but a Real Good Citizen," *TM*, July 27, 1918, p. 3.

83. "Romanizing the Children," *TM*, February 2, 1912, p. 1.

84. John Demos, *The Unredeemed Captive: A Family Story from Early America* (New York: Vintage Books, 1994). On the notion of the white captive held by savages as an ongoing American myth, see Richard Slotkin, *Gunfighter Nation: The Myth of the Frontier in Twentieth-Century America* (Norman: University Oklahoma Press, 1998), and idem, *Regeneration through Violence: The Mythology of the American Frontier, 1600–1860* (rev. ed.; Norman: University of Oklahoma Press, 2000). For a recent study linking whiteness and its link to captivity and danger, see Louis Warren,

"Buffalo Bill Meets Dracula: William F. Cody, Bram Stoker, and the Frontiers of Racial Decay," *The American Historical Review* 107, no. 4 (October 2002): 1124–57.

85. Franchot, *Roads to Rome,* p. 99.

86. Ibid., p. 112.

87. Ibid., p. 117.

88. Joseph Mannard, "Maternity . . . of the Spirit: Nuns and Domesticity in Antebellum America," *U.S. Catholic Historian* 5, nos. 3 and 4 (1986): 305–24, quote on pp. 306–7. McCarthy echoes this sentiment, noting that convents "took young girls out of their homes and placed them under the supervision of women who provided a false image of nunnery life." See McCarthy, *Rescue of True Womanhood,* p. 51. For a classic discussion of "Republican Motherhood," see Linda K. Kerber, *Women of the Republic: Intellect and Ideology in Revolutionary America* (Chapel Hill: University of North Carolina Press, 1980). For more recent studies on the overlap between gender and republicanism in America, see Angela Vietto, *Sisters and Citizens: Women Writing Identity in the Early American Republic* (Ann Arbor, Mich.: UMI Microfilms, 2000), and Shirley Samuels, *Romances of the Republic: Women, the Family, and Violence in the Literature of the Early American Nation* (New York: Oxford University Press, 1996).

89. "Roman Catholic Nuns," *YJ,* June 27, 1916, p. 3.

90. "A Tribute to American Womanhood," *The Peril,* March 5, 1914, p. 2.

91. "Family Ripped Asunder by Papal Tragedy," *TM,* March 16, 1918, p. 1. On how Catholic institutions corrode American families, see also "Too Much Popery Breaks Up Family," *TM,* December 6, 1919, p. 1; "Meddling Priest Breaks Up Family—Home Wrecked in the Clash of American Law with Rome," *TM,* March 4, 1916, p. 1. On how Catholic convents lead to children's abandonment and neglect of parents, see "Third Sister Takes Veil," *TM,* November 18, 1911. On *The Menace*'s claim that Catholics influence the courts to disrupt family life, see "Mother and Child Separated," *TM,* January 30, 1914, p. 3; "Robbed of Her Children," *TM,* January 4, 1913, p. 2; "See How Priestcraft Broke Up This Home," *TM,* September 27, 1919, p. 4.

92. "Shortage of Girl Slaves," *TM,* March 8, 1919, p. 4.

93. Untitled article, *TM,* October 25, 1913.

94. Untitled article, *TM,* April 20, 1918, p. 1.

95. "Pittsburgh's Good Shepherds Again," *TM,* April 19, 1913, p. 4.

96. "An Inspection Bill for Georgia," *TM,* August 12, 1916, p. 4.

97. "The Devil's Church," *SJ,* October 17, 1913, p. 2.

98. "Feeding the H.O.G.S.," *TM,* November 16, 1918, p. 4.

99. "Roman Catholic Slave Pens Are Hard Up for Funds," *TM,* September 12, 1914, p. 1.

100. "The Catholic Slavers Are Everywhere," *SJ,* April 3, 1914, p. 1.

101. "Police, Popery, Prisons," *TM,* March 18, 1916, p. 1.

102. "Are Legislative Representatives of a Great Free People Wearing the Ball and Chain of the Chief of the White Slavers in the Vatican?" *The Peril*, March 5, 1914, p. 1. For a much later discussion of the threat of child captivity and its implications for American society at large, see "One Hundred Fifty School Girls Prostituted in Beer Dives," *The Rail Splitter*, February 1934, p. 1.

103. "The Roman Catholic Church, Divorce, and the Home," *WM*, June 1913, p. 101. For a discussion of the Catholic Church as a "white slave dealer," see also "Dealing in Human Flesh," *TM*, December 7, 1912, p. 1.

104. "Slave Illegally Held Freed by the Court," *TM*, February 10, 1917, p. 4.

105. "Papal Abduction of Women for Nuns," *TM*, March 28, 1914, p. 3.

106. "Tag Day for Pittsburgh Convent," *TM*, September 21, 1912, p. 2. For more on Catholic graft and corruption in convent "enslavement," see "Catholic Charity Cuts Queer Capers," *TM*, July 3, 1915, p. 1; "Another Catholic Orphan Asylum," *TM*, November 15, 1913, p. 1; "What Are Nunneries For?," *TM*, March 16, 1912, p. 1; "H.O.G.S. Story from Chicago," *TM*, March 3, 1917, p. 1.

107. McCarthy, *Rescue of True Womanhood*, p. 189. *The Peril* illustrated a similar sentiment, highlighting the secrecy inherent in convent captivity. In a cartoon ridiculing Catholic conspiracy, the paper showed a nun in full habit writing a scroll that reads "Oh! If you only knew—Open these vile dens of shame." See *The Peril*, March 5, 1914, p. 1.

108. "An Outrageous Swindle," *YJ*, October 29, 1915, p. 1.

109. "How Do You Like This, Catholics!" *YJ*, March 16, 1916, p. 3.

110. "A Review of Two Recent Romish Slave Pen Tragedies," *The Peril*, March 5, 1914, p. 2.

111. "Priest and Catholic Teacher as Home Breaker," *The Peril*, March 5, 1914, p. 1.

112. "First Cut Convent Hair," *YJ*, May 13, 1915, p. 4.

113. Untitled article, *TM*, July 5, 1913, p. 4.

114. "Republican Patriots, How Do You Like This?" *YJ*, May 13, 1915, p. 4.

115. "Aid and Comfort to the Enemy," *SJ*, October 17, 1913, p. 1.

116. "Romanism Ruling and Ruining," *WM*, August 1911, p. 324.

117. "Some Significant Facts in Regard to Conditions in Washington City," *WM*, December 1912, p. 106. Interestingly, *Watson's Magazine* and other anti-Catholic sheets routinely termed the nation's capital "Washington City" as a way of avoiding the link between Columbus and the Capital District. On the use of courtroom manipulation and judicial tampering to send innocent children to Catholic convents, see also "The Juvenile Court of the National Capital, a State Institution, Converted into a Roman Catholic Institution," *WM*, August 1912.

118. On authorities' complicity with Romanists, see, for example, "Romish Slave Catcher Sued," *TM*, May 31, 1913, p. 2; "Six Months in a H.O.G.S. Laundry," *TM*, September 5, 1914, p. 4; "State Inspection the Crucial Test," *TM*, February 15, 1919,

p. 4; "Strange Story from Omaha H.O.G.S.," *TM*, October 30, 1915, p. 2; "Another Escape from H.O.G.S.," *TM*, November 7, 1914, p. 2.

119. "Silverton Escaped Nun," *TM*, September 6, 1913, p. 3.

120. "A New House of Good Shepherd Story," *TM*, September 13, 1913, p. 1.

121. "The Same Old Story," *TM*, April 5, 1919, p. 1.

122. "The Same Old Story," *TM*, October 11, 1913, p. 4.

123. "It Should Have Been Called Murder," *TM*, March 8, 1919, p. 1. On convent escapes leading to children's injury or death, see also, "Mystery in Woman's Fall From Roof," *TM*, April 11, 1914, p. 2; "Mother Seeks Girl Lost in the H.O.G.S.," *TM*, March 24, 1919, p. 2; "Priest and Sisters Guilty," *TM*, October 12, 1912, p. 2.

124. Higonnet, *Pictures of Innocence*, p. 30.

125. Higonnet, *Pictures of Innocence*, pp. 28–29.

126. "Is $30,000,000 to Enslave Protestant Children?" p. 3.

127. "Reported Dead—Found in Convent," *TM*, September 2, 1916, p. 4.

128. "Innocent Girl Loses Her Life in Attempting to Escape the Confines of a Romish Slave Pen," *The Peril*, March 5, 1914, p. 3.

129. "Who Is This 'Girl from Georgia?'" *The Jeffersonian*, September 5, 1912, p. 8. This article is largely a reprint of a similar story in *The Menace* with additional commentary by *The Jeffersonian*'s writers and Thomas Watson.

130. "Saved for a Worse Death," *TM*, September 4, 1915, p. 4.

131. "Preferred Death to H.O.G.S. Slavery," *TM*, March 24, 1919, p. 2. On suicide as an alternative to Catholic captivity, see also, "Risks Death to Escape H.O.G.S.," *TM*, November 15, 1919, p. 3.

132. See "The Demoralizing Advice of a Priest to Young Girls of Panama," *TM*, January 12, 1918, p. 1; "Girl Kidnapped to Slave for Popery," *TM*, March 1, 1919, p. 4; "Courts Furnish Slaves for H.O.G.S.," *TM*, October 23, 1915, p. 1; "Papal Deathtrap Kills and Mangles," *TM*, May 17, 1919, p. 2; "Some More H.O.G.S.," *TM*, May 16, 1914, p. 3; "Roman Catholic H.O.G.S. Defies the Law," *TM*, February 16, 1918, p. 1.

133. "Open the Nunneries and Free the Slaves!" *TM*, February 3, 1912, p. 4.

134. "Charges Romish Priests with Most Fiendish Crimes," *SJ*, September 26, 1913, p. 1. *The Silverton Journal* also spoke of imprisoned and imperiled nuns who wished "to hunt for the instruments of torture for bringing sisters to a submissive frame of mind. I want to hunt for lime pits for obliterating the remains of the ill-begotten offsprings of the institution." See "Would Like to Quiz Nuns," *SJ*, September 19, 1913, p. 2.

135. "The World's Great Fight," *SJ*, November 14, 1913, p. 2.

136. "Why Papal Prisons in America?" *TM*, November 28, 1914, p. 1.

137. "Open Rome's Prison Houses in America!," *TM*, December 2, 1911, p. 1. *Watson's Magazine* chides readers for apathy and indifference: "Why are *you* so blind and indifferent . . . ?" See "The Fruits of Four Hundred Years of Catholic Rule in Puerto Rico," *WM*, October 1913, p. 335, emphasis in original.

138. "Religious Lice," *YJ*, March 2, 1916, p. 2.

139. "Ludicrous the Way Uncle Sam Did It," *The Jeffersonian*, July 11, 1912, p. 6. For a further discussion on "sleeping" or apathetic readers, see "Catholicism vs. Our Public Schools," *SJ*, October 24, 1913, p. 2. The article states flatly "We are asleep" but writes hopefully, "Some of our liberty loving people are waking up."

140. "Out of the H.O.G.S. into Hospital," *TM*, December 4, 1915, p. 2. On the use of militaristic rhetoric, see also "The Political Leaders and the Catholic Vote," *WM*, July 1912, p. 185.

141. "Viola—The Girl in Bondage!," *TM*, November 22, 1912, p. 1.

142. Untitled article, *The Peril*, April 2, 1914, p. 4. For a discussion of *The Peril*'s use of the imagery of a "firing line," see "The Army at the Front," *The Peril*, March 5, 1914, p. 2.

143. "Don't Be a Drone," *The Peril*, March 5, 1914, p. 2.

144. "Subscription Rates," *The Woman's Witness*, February 23, 1914, p. 4. On galvanizing readers' support, see also "A Duty We Must Not Neglect," *The Crusader*, April 1915, p. 2.

145. "Statement of Miss Lesanal," *SJ*, August 22, 1913, p. 1.

146. "Catholicism Murders an Innocent Girl," *TM*, August 23, 1913, p. 2.

147. "The Detroit H.O.G.S.," *TM*, June 3, 1916, p. 2, emphasis in original.

148. Gail Bederman, "'The Women Have Had Charge of the Church Work Long Enough': The Men and Religion Forward Movement of 1911—1912 and the Masculinization of Middle-Class Protestantism," *American Quarterly* 41, no. 3 (September 1989): 432—65, quote on p. 436. Susan Jester's analysis of colonial New England and Ann Douglas's depiction of nineteenth-century Protestantism have likewise demonstrated how masculine anxiety or crisis influence (and are influenced by) religious transformation. See Susan Juster, *Disorderly Women: Sexual Politics and Evangelicalism in Revolutionary New England* (Ithaca, N.Y.: Cornell University Press, 1994), and Ann Douglas, *The Feminization of American Culture* (New York: Bantam Books, 1988). Tony Ladd and James A. Mathisen have likewise illustrated shifts in the meanings ascribed to American manhood in light of cultural and social transformation. See Ladd and Mathisen, *Muscular Christianity: Evangelical Protestantism and the Development of American Sport* (Grand Rapids, Mich.: Baker Books, 1999).

149. Bederman, "The Women Have Had Charge . . . ," quotes on pp. 432 and 434, respectively. For an elaboration of Bederman's use of the "spheres" dichotomy, see Nancy F. Cott, *The Bonds of Womanhood: "Women's Sphere" in New England, 1780—1835* (New Haven, Conn.: Yale University Press, 1977).

150. On the role of "masculinization" in Progressive-Era culture, see E. Anthony Rotundo, *American Manhood: Transformations in Masculinity from the Revolution to the Modern Era* (New York: Basic Books, 1993), and the excellent anthology by Donald Hall, ed., *Muscular Christianity: Embodying the Victorian Age* (New York: Cambridge University Press, 1994). On masculinity and early twentieth-century

264 NOTES TO PAGES 143–147

sports, see Clifford Putney, *Muscular Christianity: Manhood and Sports in Protestant America* (Cambridge, Mass.: Harvard University Press, 2001); and Ladd and Mathisen, *Muscular Christianity.* On masculinity and literature, see Norman Vance, *The Sinews of the Spirit: The Ideal of Christian Manliness in Victorian Literature and Religious Thought* (New York: Cambridge University Press, 1985). On Progressive-Era writings outlining manly ideals, see, for instance, Bruce Barton, *The Man Nobody Knows: A Discovery of the Real Jesus* (rev. ed.; Chicago: Ivan R. Dee, 2000). For a biography of Theodore Roosevelt that also outlines cultural attitudes toward militarism and masculinity, see Kathleen Dalton, *Theodore Roosevelt: A Strenuous Life* (New York: Knopf, 2000).

151. In several respects, this is in keeping with the prevailing rhetoric of captivity, rape, and seduction narratives to which Progressive-Era anti-Catholic writers were heirs. As Sharon Block has recently pointed out, whereas eighteenth-century accounts of rape removed women's voices and emotions from their descriptions, by the nineteenth century, women factored prominently in graphic accounts of rape and violence, which invested their stories with greater meaning and power. See Sharon Block, "Rape without Women: Print Culture and the Politicization of Rape, 1765–1815," *Journal of American History* 89, no. 3 (December 2002): 849–68.

152. On the domestic features of Progressive-Era masculinity, see Margaret Marsh, "Suburban Men and Masculine Domesticity," *American Quarterly* 40, no. 2 (June 1988): 165–86. On competing notions of men's "flight from commitment," see Barbara Ehrenreich, *Hearts of Men: American Dreams and the Flight from Commitment* (rev. ed.; New York: Doubleday, 1984).

CHAPTER FOUR. "THE SLIME OF THE SERPENT"

1. Commission on Religious Prejudices, *Second Report* (Davenport, Ia.: Knights of Columbus, 1916), pp. 48–49. On the Knights' emphasis of cooperation and Catholics' joint settlement, progress, and innovation alongside Protestants, see also Commission on Religious Prejudices, *Initial Report* (Seattle: Knights of Columbus, 1915).

2. On Catholic racism and tensions between Catholics and other ethnic groups, see Noel Ignatiev, *How the Irish Became White* (New York: Routledge, 1996); John McGreevy, *Parish Boundaries: The Catholic Encounter with Race in the Twentieth-Century Urban North* (rev. ed.; Chicago: University of Chicago Press, 1996); Iver Bernstein, *New York City Draft Riots: Their Significance for American Society and Politics in the Age of the Civil War* (New York: Oxford University Press, 1989); Thomas Sugrue, *The Origins of the Urban Crisis: Race and Inequality in Postwar Detroit* (Princeton, N.J.: Princeton University Press, 1996). On Chinese exclusion, see George Peffer, *If They Don't Bring Their Women Here: Chinese Female Immigration before Exclusion*

(Urbana: University of Illinois Press, 1999), and Andrew Gyory, *Closing the Gate: Race, Politics, and the Chinese Exclusion Act* (Chapel Hill: University of North Carolina Press, 1998). For a thorough analysis of Charles Coughlin and his agenda of exclusion, see Donald Warren, *Radio Priest: Charles Coughlin, the Father of Hate Radio* (New York: Free Press, 1996).

3. Several exceptional archivists and librarians proved immensely helpful in conducting research for this chapter. I am particularly thankful to Sister Hildegard Varga, OSB, of the Diocese of Amarillo, Texas, and Father Walter Gagne and Barbara Martire, of the Atonement Friars of Graymoor, New York, for their help in locating copies of *The Antidote,* a prominent newspaper founded to combat American nativism. The University of Notre Dame has a very accessible archive of American nativism and counter-nativism. For their help in researching and providing copies of Progressive-Era texts in the Catholic defense, I am grateful to Kevin Cawley, University Archivist and Curator of Manuscripts. In writing this chapter, I also benefited from the suggestions and advice of Christopher Kauffman, editor of *U.S. Catholic Historian.*

4. *The Slime of the Serpent: The "Menace," A Journalistic Reptile, an Appeal to Fairminded Americans* (St. Louis: Central Bureau, 1912).

5. Ibid., p. 3.

6. *The Antidote* began publication in 1912, but an extensive search of public, diocesan, and monastic archives has failed to turn up any issues prior to January 1919. For more information on *The Antidote* and J.A. Campbell, see Diocese of Amarillo, *West Texas Register: Anniversary Issue* (Amarillo, Tex.: n.p., 1956).

7. "True and False Americanism," *The Antidote,* August 1919, p. 118.

8. Elihu S. Riley, *An American Satyr: The Morbid Misconstruction and Malevolent Misrepresentation of American Catholics Are a Menace to the Public* (Annapolis, Md.: Daily Record Press, 1916), quote on p. 49 (copy furnished by University of Notre Dame Archives, Folder 8).

9. Ibid., p. 63.

10. Ibid.

11. "Protestant Testimony to the Influence of the Catholic Confessional upon Morals," *The Antidote,* April 1919, p. 63. As the title suggests, *The Antidote* paid particular attention to the opinion of non-Catholics who were supportive of its ideals of inclusivity and tolerance.

12. "It Is Easy to Ask Questions," *The Antidote,* February 1919, p. 19.

13. On the proliferation of anti-nativist reading material, particularly Knights of Columbus pamphlets, see Commission on Religious Prejudices, *Second Report,* p. 6. On Catholic cross-promotion and the spread of Catholic documents, see also *Slime of the Serpent,* pp. 5 and 8 (which reference *The Antidote* and C.A. Windle, respectively). For other cross-promotion of Windle's works and non-Catholic defenders of American Catholicism, see also Riley, *American Satyr,* p. 61.

14. *The Slime of the Serpent,* p. 1.

15. "An Associated Catholic Press," paper delivered by Monsignor Peter Blessing at the Catholic Press Association Meeting, August 24, 1911. Quoted in Mary Lonan Reilly, *A History of the Catholic Press Association* (Metuchen, N.J.: Scarecrow, 1971), p. 35.

16. Christopher J. Kauffman, *Faith and Fraternalism: The History of the Knights of Columbus, 1882–1982* (New York: Harper and Row, 1982), quote on pp. 182–83. Kauffman provides an excellent overview of the Knights in general and the commission in particular, emphasizing the influence of nationalism on their activities. In addressing the Knights' patriotic nationalism, for instance, Kauffman points out, "reference to anti-Catholic bigotry as un-American was not, in itself, distinctly Columbian. . . . However, when patriotism was linked with the Catholic heritage of America, including Catholic respect for freedom of worship . . . the notion that anti-Catholicism was un-American meant that the former was viewed as a distortion of the historical events in which Catholics and Catholicism had played such significant roles" (p. 86). For an analysis of Catholic organizations' patriotism, see also Kauffman's later study, *Patriotism and Fraternalism in the Knights of Columbus: A History of the Fourth Degree* (New York: Crossroad, 2001).

17. On Patrick Henry Callahan's use of survey data and the commission as an anti-nativist clearinghouse, see Kauffman, *Faith and Fraternalism,* pp. 185–87.

18. Commission on Religious Prejudices, *Second Report,* p. 44.

19. Commission on Religious Prejudices, *Initial Report,* p. 4.

20. Commission on Religious Prejudices, *Second Report,* p. 14.

21. Commission on Religious Prejudices, *Initial Report,* p. 6.

22. Kauffman, *Faith and Fraternalism,* quotes on pp. 83 and 80, respectively.

23. On the spread of the Knights of Columbus, see Kauffman, *Faith and Fraternalism,* pp. 72–94.

24. "Catholic Editors Emit Inky Slime," *TM,* September 28, 1912, p. 2.

25. "Don't Drill, Eh?" *YJ,* February 18, 1915, p. 3.

26. On the success in galvanizing public and journalistic opinion in support of the commission and American Catholicism more generally, see Commission on Religious Prejudices, *Initial Report,* p. 26.

27. Ibid., p. 17.

28. "Just Plain Lying," *YJ,* June 1914, p. 3.

29. "Talks with Readers of The Menace," *The Antidote,* February 1919, p. 21.

30. "Talks with Readers of The Menace," *The Antidote,* March 1919, p. 36.

31. C. A. Windle, *Is the Catholic Church the Deadliest Menace to Our Liberties and Our Civilization? A Reply to Thomas E. Watson* (2nd ed.; Chicago: Iconoclast, 1912), p. 2. Windle makes similar points in a subsequent publication, *Straight Talk to Non-Catholics: Is the Catholic Church Intolerant?* (Chicago: Iconoclast, 1923[?]).

32. Windle, *Deadliest Menace,* p. 8.

33. Ibid., p. 21.

34. Windle, *Straight Talk*, pp. 2 and 13, respectively.

35. National Catholic Welfare Council, *Senator Thomas E. Watson's Slander against the Good Shepherd Sisterhood* (n.p.: National Catholic Welfare Council, 1918), p. 2.

36. Ibid., p. 2.

37. Ibid., p. 3.

38. Knights of Columbus, *A Protest and a Plea* (Sioux City, Ia., 1914), pp. 18–19.

39. *Slime of the Serpent*, p. 6. Elsewhere, the pamphlet critiques Walker again, noting that his motive for printing deliberate falsehood against the Church "is either hatred or hunger,—maybe a little of both" (p. 12).

40. Ibid., p. 24.

41. Ibid., p. 24.

42. Riley, *American Satyr*, p. 59.

43. Ibid., quotes on pp. 50 and 35, respectively.

44. Ibid., p. 60.

45. Knights of Columbus, *Protest and a Plea*, p. 7.

46. *Slime of the Serpent*, p. 15.

47. "The Roman Catholic Hierarchy: The Deadliest Menace to Our Liberties and Our Civilization," *WM*, July 1911, p. 202. On Catholic celibacy, see also, "The Roman Catholic Hierarchy: The Deadliest Menace to Our Liberties and Our Civilization," *WM*, April 1911, p. 944. On priestly masculinity, see "Open Letter to Cardinal Gibbons," *WM*, February 1913, p. 186 ff.

48. "Red Cross Workers and The Menace Differ about the Character of Catholic Priests," *The Antidote*, December 1919, p. 182.

49. Kauffman, *Patriotism and Fraternalism*, quotes on pp. 13, 14, and 15, respectively.

50. Kauffman, *Faith and Fraternalism*, p. 167.

51. Kauffman, *Patriotism and Fraternalism*, p. 14. On ritualism, solidarity, and masculinity in turn-of-the century pageantry, see also Mark C. Carnes, "Middle Class Men and the Solace of Ritual," in Mark C. Carnes and Clyde Griffen, eds., *Meanings for Manhood: Constructing Masculinity in Victorian America* (Chicago: University of Chicago Press, 1990).

52. On the cold-shoulder treatment nativists received at the hands of the Men and Religion Forward Movement, see *Slime of the Serpent*, p. 16.

53. Catholic Welfare Council, *Watson's Slander*, p. 7.

54. Windle, *Deadliest Menace*, p. 25. Windle also argues that "The infernal charges against Catholic sisters are almost wholly built upon imagination" (p. 4).

55. Windle, *Deadliest Menace*, p. 5.

56. Knights of Columbus, *Protest and a Plea*, p. 5.

57. Riley, *American Satyr*, p. 60.

58. Ibid., pp. 61, 62.

59. Ibid., p. 61.

60. Ibid., p. 61.

61. "The Catholic Working Girl and Her Inspiration," *The Antidote,* January 1919, p. 13. The article continued that Catholic women's labor and hard-working attitude are further indications of her trustworthiness and effectiveness as a mother and a citizen. On Protestant enrollment in Catholic institutions and Watson's daughter's participation in convent education, see *Slime of the Serpent,* p. 12.

62. "Happenings of Interest to the Sisterhood," *The Antidote,* January 1919, p. 14.

63. *Slime of the Serpent,* p. 14.

64. "Lincoln Praised Sisters as Angels of Mercy," *The Antidote,* April 1919, p. 64. On the battlefield monuments as immortalization of Lincoln's praise, see "President Lincoln's Tribute to Heroic Nuns of the Battlefields Inscribed on Capitol Monument," *The Antidote,* June 1919, p. 85.

65. Progressive-Era Catholics' public memory of diverse facets of American history meshes unevenly with historians' subsequent analysis of these eras and the scholarly analysis of American public memory. For a study outlining Civil War public memory, see, for instance, David W. Blight, *Race and Reunion: The Civil War in American Memory* (Cambridge, Mass.: Belknap, 2001); Tony Horwitz, *Confederates in the Attic: Dispatches from the Unfinished Civil War* (rev. ed.; New York: Random House, 1999); Jim Cullen, *The Civil War in Popular Culture: A Reusable Past* (Washington, D.C.: Smithsonian Institution, 1996). Cullen is one of only a few scholars to treat the overlap between Catholic public memory and the broader national memory with more than passing interest. For his insightful study, see Cullen, *Restless in the Promised Land: Catholics and the American Dream: Character Studies of a Spiritual Quest from the Time of the Puritans to the Present* (New York: Sheed and Ward, 2001). See also Mark Massa, *Catholics and American Culture: Fulton Sheen, Dorothy Day, and the Notre Dame Football Team* (New York: Crossroads, 1999).

66. Jonathan Zimmerman, "'Each 'Race' Could Have Its Heroes Sung': Ethnicity and the History Wars in the 1920s," *Journal of American History* 87, no. 1 (June 2000): 92–111, quote on p. 94. Catholics' conservative historiography can be witnessed in Riley, *The American Satyr,* pp. 36–37, and Commission on Religious Prejudices, *Initial Report,* pp. 3–4, both of which present traditional chronologies with Whiggish themes of American expansion and independence.

67. On Catholics' "fortress" mentality and the separatism in devotional Catholicism in the early twentieth century, see Jay P. Dolan, *The American Catholic Experience: A History from Colonial Times to the Present* (Notre Dame, Ind. Notre Dame University Press, 1992). Dolan makes a similar point about Catholics' insular mind-set in a subsequent, exceptionally written text. See Dolan, *In Search of American Catholicism: A History of Religion and Culture in Tension* (New York: Oxford University Press, 2002).

68. "Archbishop Ireland's Idea of Patriotism," *The Antidote,* March 1919, p. 48.

69. On the contradiction of Catholic rebellion and anti-Americanism, see, for instance, Windle, "Straight Talk to Non-Catholics," pp. 9–10. Windle points out the diversity of Catholic voting patterns and political affiliation as a refutation of nativists' claims of priestcraft and its homogenizing effect on the Catholic voting block.

70. Riley, *American Satyr,* quotes on pp. 33 and 72, respectively.

71. Ibid., frontispiece, emphasis in original. On the misrepresentation and malicious nature of nativist texts, see also Kauffman, *Faith and Fraternalism,* p. 87, which quotes from prominent Knights in their articulation of nativist denunciation. See also "The Merry Side of the Menace," *The Antidote,* November 1919, p. 168, which asserts that the newspaper misrepresents Catholic history to a completely comical degree.

72. Kauffman, *Faith and Fraternalism,* p. 167. Kauffman goes on to note that the Knights' Americanism carried a strong anti-socialist stance as well and involved organizing lectures and public relations campaigns to promote an understanding of Catholic patriotism among non-Catholics. See pp. 187 ff.

73. Commission on Religious Prejudices, *Second Report,* p. 39.

74. Commission on Religious Prejudices, *Initial Report,* p. 29.

75. "General Foch Undoubtedly a Catholic," *The Antidote,* February 1919, p. 18.

76. *Protest and a Plea,* pp. 1, 3. The Whiggish accounts that begin with Columbus's exploration of the Americas, trace Catholic involvement in American settlement and warfare, and end with contemporary progress proliferate in Catholic texts in general and the Knights of Columbus's pageantry and promotional materials in particular. Kauffman outlines how the Knights' publications from the Gilded Age through the twentieth century carried a remarkably conservative outlook on American history. See Kauffman, *Faith and Fraternalism,* p. 80 ff.

77. On efforts to remove *The Menace* from the U.S. mail, see Paul Bakewell, "Open Letter to W. H. Lamar, Esq., Solicitor to the Post Office Department," n.p., 1915 (?).

78. On nativist retaliation against Catholics for mail tampering, censoring, and suppression, see "Shall the Menace Be Suppressed?" *TM,* February 17, 1912, p. 1, which outlines an exchange between postal officials and Catholic organizers, and comments on how Catholic correspondence demonstrates their conspiratorial intentions. See also "Letter from Father Jones," *The Crusader,* June 1914, p. 3.

79. For anti-nativist criticism of suppression campaigns, see Commission on Religious Prejudices, *Initial Report,* esp. pp. 21–22.

80. Commission on Religious Prejudices, *Second Report,* p. 29.

81. Kauffman, *Faith and Fraternalism,* p. 183.

82. For treatment of Catholics' influence on the public press, see Kauffman, *Faith and Fraternalism,* p. 184.

83. "Free Catholicism," *The Antidote,* June 1919, p. 89. On the far-flung geography of anti-nativist support, see, for instance, "Sam Clark Castigates The Menace," *The Antidote,* August, 1919, p. 134.

84. "The Catholic Menace," *TM,* January 27, 1912, p. 2. I found very few examples of anti-Catholic citations of supportive journalists from the mainstream press, one being, "Papal Infallibility," *SJ,* October 10, 1913, p. 2, which reprinted an article from *Harper's Weekly* criticizing Catholics' inability to Americanize on the basis of papal loyalty.

85. "The Howl of the Wolves," *The Peril,* March 5, 1914, p. 2.

86. Untitled article, *The Liberator,* October 16, 1913, p. 1. For further critiques of secular dailies, see "The Lying Charlotte Observer," *YJ,* January 6, 1916, p. 1; "Kissing the Hand," *TM,* March 2, 1912, p. 2; "Another Stale Egg," *TM,* February 24, 1912, p. 4. *The Yellow Jacket* likewise insisted that the press waged war on nativist papers by corrupting governmental investigations and postal regulations. See "State Government Officially Lies," *YJ,* January 6, 1916, p. 1.

87. Two quotes are from "Silence of the Press," *SJ,* April 24, 1914, p. 1, and untitled article, *SJ,* October 10, 1913, p. 2, respectively.

88. "The Roman Catholic Hierarchy Prosecuting Me, For Telling the Truth," *The Jeffersonian,* June 13, 1912, p. 1. On the Catholic manipulation of news agencies and "the Catholic muzzled daily press of the country," see also "Father Harrington 'Calls' the Menace and Peril," *The Peril,* March 5, 1914, p. 2.

89. "Romanism Ruling and Ruining," *WM,* August 1911, p. 326.

90. "Romanizing the Press," *TM,* March 23, 1912, p. 2.

91. "Chicago Tribune Caught Again," *YJ,* September 2, 1915, p. 3.

92. David Nord, "Reading the Newspaper: Strategies and Politics of Reader Response, Chicago, 1912–1917," *Journal of Communication* 45, no. 3 (Summer 1995): 66–93, quote on p. 67.

93. Ibid., p. 67.

94. Ibid., p. 76.

95. Ibid., quotes on pp. 79 and 78, respectively; emphasis in original.

96. For an examination of Catholics' attempted boycotts, see Commission on Religious Prejudices, *Second Report,* passim.

97. On Progressive-Era nativism's use of classic tropes of Catholic warfare and rebellion, see "The Jesuitical Oath, the Knights of Columbus Oath, and Comment Theron," *The Jeffersonian,* July 18, 1912, pp. 12–13, which argued that the Knights of Columbus and other Catholic organizations stockpiled weapons in Church basements; "Rome's Army," *TM,* February 24, 1912, p. 4, which compared Catholic societies to paramilitary organizations; "Rome Never Changes," *SJ,* April 24, 1914, p. 2, which demonstrated that Catholics had long plotted to assassinate American presidents; and "Neither Guns, Nor Swords, Nor Pistols," *TM,* May 12, 1917, p. 1, which took a somewhat different approach, arguing that Catholics, though

possibly hording weapons, were likely to use their infiltration of police and military forces to assault American institutions from within.

98. On accusations of Catholic attacks against nativist enemies, see "Make the Priests Answer for It," *YJ*, July 22, 1915, p. 3, which insisted that Catholic priests incited a mob, and "Unless . . . ," *SJ*, August 22, 1913, p. 2, which printed a threatening letter. See also, "A.O.H., 'Molly Maguires,' Celebrate," *The Peril*, April 2, 1914, p. 1; "Murder of Miss Lasenan Attempted at Portland," *SJ*, September 23, 1913, p. 1.

99. On the dynamiting of *The Menace* plant, see "Romish Church Backing Scheme to Suppress The Menace," *TM*, April 14, 1914, p. 1; "Try to Blow up The Menace Presses," *TM*, August 1916, p. 4.

100. "Romanists on War Path," *SJ*, August 22, 1913, p. 1.

101. Unfortunately for pro-Catholic organizers, accusations of libel could only be made in reference to false statements directed toward individuals, not entire groups. Nativists' condemnation, therefore, against the Catholic clergy or religious orders, for instance, would be protected under libel law, a point noted by the Commission on Religious Prejudices as a stumbling block to criminal prosecution of anti-Catholic writers. See Commission on Religious Prejudices, *Initial Report*, pp. 23–24, and idem, *Second Report*, pp. 33–35.

102. On criminal proceedings against Watson, see "The Watson Indictment," *The Jeffersonian*, July 11, 1912, p. 16; "Mr. Watson Defended," *The Jeffersonian*, July 11, 1912, p. 16; "Yep, the Arrest Occurred All Right," *The Jeffersonian*, July 11, 1912, p. 15; "The Indictment against Thomas E. Watson," *WM*, March 1913, pp. 256–58; "The Knights of Columbus Endeavoring to Destroy Thos. E. Watson," *WM*, December 1912, pp. 94–95; "The Romanists Begin Criminal Prosecution of Mr. Watson," *WM*, July 1912, pp. 196–98.

103. On John E. Hosmer's conviction, see "Hosmer Convicted of Criminal Libel," *SJ*, June 19, 1914, p. 1; "A Fight to the Finish," *SJ*, June 19, 1914, p. 1; "To Our Readers," *SJ*, September 25, 1914, p. 1; "Editor of the Journal Indicted," *SJ*, October 10, 1913, p. 2. On the civil case by the Mount Angel Convent against Hosmer, see "Sued for $50,000," *SJ*, August 15, 1913, p. 2; "The Father Brags Loud," *SJ*, November 21, 1913, p. 1; "The Silverton Journal Sued for $50,000," *SJ*, August 22, 1913; "A False Report Nailed—Mary Lasenan's Friend's True Blue," *SJ*, July 17, 1914, p. 1; "Tickled to Death," *SJ*, November 14, 1913, pp. 1, 4.

104. On William Lloyd Clark's conviction, see "Clark Is Convicted in Federal Court in Peoria," *TM*, October 28, 1911, p. 1. *The Menace* asked readers to send money for Clark's legal defense. See "To Clark's Rescue," *TM*, November 25, 1911, p. 4, and "The Clark Fund," *TM*, December 2, 1911, p. 1.

105. Kauffman, *Patriotism and Fraternalism*, p. 43. Kauffman's prior book covers the "Bogus Oath" in much greater detail. See Kauffman, *Faith and Fraternalism*, pp. 173–74. The Knights addressed the "Bogus Oath" trial in detail. See

Knights of Columbus, *Protest and a Plea*, pp. 9 ff. For the nativist response, see also "The K. of C. Stage Stunt Falls," *The Peril*, March 5, 1914, p. 2.

106. On subsequent persecution of "bogus oath" circulators, see Kauffman, *Faith and Fraternalism*, pp. 173–74.

107. On the Rossman trial, see "Rossman vs. The Menace," *TM*, June 20, 1914, p. 2. This case was also followed with great interest by the Commission on Religious Prejudices; see Commission on Religious Prejudices, *Initial Report*, p. 22. On a *Menace* case settled out of court, see "Libel Suit of P. E. Burress against the Publishers of The Menace Settled," *TM*, June 13, 1914, p. 2.

108. On *The Menace*'s acquittal, see Benjamin O. Flowers, *The Story of the Menace Trial: A Brief Sketch of This Historic Case, with Reports of the Masterly Addresses by Hon. J. L. McNatt and Hon. J. I. Sheppard* (Aurora, Mo.: United States Publishing, 1916), esp. pp. 28–29. For an illustration of the support generated by other nativist texts, see "Freedom of the Press Sustained," *YJ*, January 20, 1916, p. 1; "Watch The Menace Trial," *YJ*, January 6, 1916, p. 2.

109. Flowers, *Menace Trial*, frontispiece.

110. Ibid., p. 29.

111. On the charge that Catholics singled out *Menace* publishers to hamstring the paper's proclamation of truth, see ibid., p. 58.

112. "Notes on The Menace Trial," *YJ*, January 20, 1916, p. 2.

113. "Facts Wanted," *The Peril*, April 2, 1914, p. 2.

114. On files kept to search Catholic papers for errors and attacks, see "Kissing the Pope's Foot," *WM*, July 1910, pp. 544–45.

115. For Watson's critique of *The Marian*, see "A Sample of the Style and Spirit of a Roman Catholic Controversialist," *WM*, October 1911, pp. 474–81, quotes on pp. 475, 477, respectively. Watson continued to chastise *The Marian* in a subsequent article, "The Romanists Cannot Afford to Fight Fair," *WM*, September 1912, p. 355.

116. "The Slime of the Serpent," *SJ*, February 6, 1914, p. 1.

117. "They Have Been Reading The Yellow Jacket," *YJ*, May 29, 1915, p. 3. The article's title demonstrates that nativist periodicals understood that Catholic foes were scouring their pages.

118. "How the Roman Catholic Societies Are Fighting This Magazine," *WM*, August 1911, p. 299. On Watson's condemnation of Catholic apologists, see also "A Reply to Rev. Lucian Johnson, Catholic Priest, and Author of 'The Shame of It,'" *WM*, August 1911, pp. 292–99.

119. Windle, *Deadliest Menace*, pp. 14–15.

120. "Democratic," *SJ*, November 14, 1913, p. 2.

121. On propaganda warfare and the use of lecturers and public information, see, for instance, Jeremiah Crowley, *Romanism: A Menace to the Nation* (Aurora, Mo.: Menace, 1915), which outlines Crowley's career as lecturer and author intent on exposing Catholicism's duplicity and treachery. See also "Our Patriotic

Lecturers and What they are Doing," *SJ*, November 27, 1914, p. 1. On the importance of circulation rolls in substantiating and legitimizing the anti-Catholic message, see, for example, "On the Firing Line," *The Peril*, April 2, 1914, p. 2.

122. "Patriotism Begets Heresy," *WM*, October 1912, p. 451.

123. Knights of Columbus, *Protest and a Plea*, quotes on pp. 4 and 5, respectively.

124. Gary Gerstle, *Working-Class Americanism: The Politics of Labor in a Textile City, 1914–1960* (New York: Cambridge University Press, 1989), quote from pp. 194–95. Moreover, Gerstle notes that French-Canadian Catholics, while openly patriotic, would simultaneously "insist that their new American identity serve their economic and cultural needs" (p. 60); moreover, embracing the rhetoric of "Americanism" served as a means of enhancing "power in the real world of politics" (p. 87). This understanding of nationalism, Gerstle contends, was facilitated and made possible by a greater homogeneity of Americanism during the 1920s and Catholics' continued participation in American society as soldiers and workers.

125. "The Lesson of Unity," *The Antidote*, March 1919, p. 39.

CHAPTER FIVE. WORLD WAR I AND THE ANTI-CATHOLIC HIATUS

1. On Catholics' pride in enlistment and their participation in military enrollment campaigns in greater proportion than their population, see National Catholic Welfare Council, *Senator Thomas E. Watson's Slander against the Good Shepherd Sisterhood* (n.p.: National Catholic Welfare Council, 1918), p. 4.

2. Commission on Religious Prejudices, *Final Report* (Chicago: Knights of Columbus, 1917), p. 14.

3. "The Pope and the Kaiser," *TM*, May 12, 1917, p. 2. On anti-Catholic reports of Catholic sabotage and spying to aid enemy forces, see "We Pay for Priests' Prayers," *SJ*, May 29, 1914, p. 2; "An Example of How They Do It," *The Crusader*, November 1914, p. 2; "The Revival of Popery," *YJ*, January 4, 1917, p. 1; "Something Significant," *The Crusader*, January 1915, p. 2; "War, What For?" *SJ*, April 24, 1914, p. 2; "Alliance between Germany and the Pope," *YJ*, January 1916, p. 1; "When the Soldiers Come Marching Home," *MtA*, April 21, 1916, p. 2. "Und Now We Haf War," *SJ*, January 20, 1914, p. 4. See also "The Roman Catholic International Political Conspiracy," *The Crusader*, August/September, 1914, p. 1; "Is Vatican Aiding the Teutonic Powers?" *YJ*, February 1918, p. 1.

4. "Preparedness as a Prevention of a Calamity," *TM*, May 5, 1917, p. 1. For other assertions of Catholic domestic aggression and duplicity, see "What about the Enemy within Our Borders?" *YJ*, January 6, 1916, p. 1; "Newspaper Pirates and Traitors," *YJ*, March 2, 1916, p. 1; "The Pope's Spy at the White House, Standing between our People and the President," *The Jeffersonian*, February 26, 1914, p. 1;

"Pope's Parochial Schools Made Military Academies," *TM*, April 19, 1919, p. 2; "Our Papal Military Schools," *TM*, April 19, 1919, p. 2.

5. Quotes are from "Firing Line," *TM*, April 24, 1917, p. 1, and Commission on Religious Prejudices, *Second Report*, p. 36, respectively. On the war as a distraction from nativists' anti-Catholic agenda, see also "And Now We'll Have War," *YJ*, April 15, 1915, p. 1; and "The Papal Grafters Are Elated over the War," *YJ*, May 11, 1916, p. 4. The latter article maintains that Catholics will use the distraction offered by wartime pursuits to bilk the government out of tax dollars and funnel these into the pope's treasury.

6. John Higham, *Strangers in the Land: Patterns in American Nativism* (New Brunswick, N.J.: Rutgers University Press, 1955), p. 201.

7. Commission on Religious Prejudices, *Second Report*, p. 27. For a further illustration of anti-Catholicism's decline, see Christopher J. Kauffman, *Faith and Fraternalism: The History of the Knights of Columbus, 1882–1982* (New York: Harper and Row, 1982), pp. 188–89, and Commission on Religious Prejudices, *Final Report*, pp. 3, 9. One anti-Catholic paper, *The Liberator*, conceded that it was experiencing significant circulation declines, though it insisted that Catholics exaggerated the extent of its decline. See untitled article, *The Liberator*, October 2, 1913, p. 1.

8. "Two Moves Are as Bad as a Fire," *The Crusader*, November 1915, p. 2.

9. "The Firing Line," *TM*, March 24, 1917, p. 2.

10. On increases in printing and shipping costs as an explanation for nativists' economic woes, see "Firing Line," *TM*, April 24, 1917, p. 1; "The World Confronting a Paper Famine," *MtA*, May 5, 1916, p. 4. *The Mountain Advocate* also suggested that regional economic hardship contributed to a decline in its circulation base. See "European War Shatters King Cotton's Throne," *MtA*, December 4, 1914, p. 4.

11. On nativists' persistent use of nationalistic themes and iconography, see, for instance, "What Is Our Americanism?" *The Crusader*, April 1915, p. 4; "Patriotism and the War Dogs," *MtA*, May 19, 1916, p. 2; "This Is the War Edition," *The Crusader*, November 1915, p. 1. While embodying the themes of wartime patriotism, nativists also used militaristic imagery in its depictions of battles with Romanists. See "Popery Gassing the Public Schools," *TM*, November 9, 1919, p. 2, which argues that Catholics were attacking public schools—"bombarding them with gas shells" and exposing them to "the danger of Vatican submarines."

12. Quotes are from "Knights of Columbus War Work," *The Antidote*, February 1919, pp. 23–24, and "Men and Events of the Time," *The Antidote*, May 1919, p. 69, respectively.

13. "The United War Drive and Religious Bigotry," *The Antidote*, January 1919, p. 2.

14. Ibid.

15. On *The Antidote*'s abandonment of anti-Catholic concerns in favor of anti-socialism, see "The Menace of the Servile State," *The Antidote*, July 1919, p. 98;

"The Bolsheviki Menace," *The Antidote*, March 1919, p. 34; "Socialism is Bolshevism," *The Antidote*, February 1919, p. 32; "Those Who Support Socialism Support Atheism and Divorce," *The Antidote*, March 1919, p. 34; "The Bolshevik Propaganda in Our Own Land," *The Antidote*, April 1919, p. 51; "Hell Reigns in Russia," *The Antidote*, April 1919, p. 55; "Socialism in Theory and Practice: Two Examples from Real Life," *The Antidote*, June 1919, p. 88; "Communization of Women," *The Antidote*, June 1919, p. 96. On the paper's coverage of war issues, see, for instance, "War's Own Horrors May End All Wars," *The Antidote*, January 1919, pp. 10–11.

16. "Men and Events of the Time," *The Antidote*, January 1919, p. 3.

17. On *The Menace*'s fire and the rise of *The New Menace*, see Robert Maury, *The Wars of the Godly* (New York: Robert M. McBride, 1928), pp. 261–63. On the collapse of *The Menace* and for an overview of its influence on community life, see Kathleen Van Buskirk, "Historic Buildings of Branson: Keeping Track of the Past," *The Ozark Mountaineer*, July-August 1990, pp. 49–50; "What the Teens Brought to Aurora," in *Aurora Centennial, 1870–1970: Yesterday and Today* (Aurora, Mo.: Centennial Committee, 1970), p. 5; "Marvin Lee Brown," in *The Ozark Region: Its History and Its People*, vol. 2 (Springfield, Mo.: Interstate Historical Society, 1917), p. 211. I am extremely grateful to Mary Strickrodt and Irene Asher of Aurora, Missouri, for their assistance in locating these documents. On Watson's influence on politics and for a brief sketch of his latter life, see Walter J. Brown, *J. J. Brown and Thomas E. Watson: Georgia Politics, 1912–1928* (Macon, Ga.: Mercer University Press, 1994). For a classic study of Watson, see C. Vann Woodward, *Tom Watson: Agrarian Rebel* (New York: Oxford University Press, 1963).

18. On William Lloyd Clark's activity in Klan activity see S. H. Bemendorfer, "Story of Wm. Lloyd Clark and the Railsplitter," in *The KAP Magazine*, May 1926, pp. 20–21, quote on p. 21.

19. On the Knights' post–World War I expansion and role in American media, culture, and philanthropy, see Kauffman, *Faith and Fraternalism*.

20. Commission on Religious Prejudices, *Final Report*, p. 11.

21. Charles R. Morris, *American Catholic: The Saints and Sinners Who Built America's Most Powerful Church* (New York: Times Books, 1997), p. ix.

22. Commission on Religious Prejudices, *Final Report*, p. 20.

23. "Letter from an American Patriot," *The Jeffersonian*, January 16, 1913, p. 16.

24. Higham, *Strangers in the Land*, quotes on pp. 266 and 287, respectively.

25. On the Klan's rapid rise to national prominence, see Nancy MacLean, *Behind the Mask of Chivalry: The Making of the Second Ku Klux Klan* (New York: Oxford University Press, 1994), esp. p. xi.

26. David M. Chalmers, *Hooded Americanism: The History of the Ku Klux Klan* (3rd ed.; Durham, N.C.: Duke University Press, 1987), p. 291.

27. Ibid., p. 2.

28. MacLean, *Behind the Mask*, quotes on pp. 23 and 33, respectively.

29. Ibid., p. 24.

30. Ibid., quotes on pp. xiii, 51.

31. Leonard J. Moore, *Citizen Klansmen: The Ku Klux Klan in Indiana, 1921–1928* (Chapel Hill: University of North Carolina Press, 1991), quote on p. 3. On Klansmen's gendered ideology, see also MacLeon, *Behind the Mask.*

32. Moore, *Citizen Klansmen,* p. 11.

33. Paul Blanshard, *American Freedom and Catholic Power* (Boston: Beacon, 1949), p. 4. On Dewey's perceptions of American Catholicism, see Robert Westbrook, *John Dewey and American Democracy* (rev. ed.; Ithaca, N.Y.: Cornell University Press, 1993). Westbrook's exemplary biography suggests that scholars have overemphasized the extent of Dewey's anti-Catholic leanings. For Blanshard's other works dealing with the threat of American Catholicism, see Paul Blanshard, *Freedom and Catholic Power in Spain and Portugal: An American Interpretation* (Boston: Beacon, 1962); idem, *God and Man in Washington* (Boston: Beacon, 1960); idem, *Religion and the Schools: The Great Controversy* (Boston: Beacon, 1963); and idem, *Personal and Controversial: An Autobiography* (Boston: Beacon, 1973).

34. Mark Massa, *Catholics and American Culture: Fulton Sheen, Dorothy Day, and the Notre Dame Football Team* (New York: Crossroad, 1999), quote on p. 2. For an excellent anthology with an insightful essay on Blanshard's extension of anti-Catholic ideology stretching back to Maria Monk, see Frederick Greenspahn and Robert N. Bellah, eds., *Uncivil Religion: Interreligious Hostility in America* (New York: Crossroad, 1987). On American anti-Catholicism in the twentieth century, see also Robert P. Lockwood, ed., *Anti-Catholicism in American Culture* (Huntington, Ind.: Our Sunday Visitor, 2000).

35. Blanshard, *American Freedom and Catholic Power,* p. 36.

36. Ibid., quotes on pp. 211 and 212, respectively.

37. Ibid., p. 266.

38. Will Herberg, *Protestant, Catholic, Jew: An Essay in American Religious Sociology* (rev. ed.; Chicago: University of Chicago Press, 1983). This revised version also includes excellent introductory remarks by the influential religion scholar Martin Marty.

39. On the study of religious groups' accommodation to or transition into the American mainstream, see an excellent survey by R. Lawrence Moore, *Religious Outsiders and the Making of Americans* (New York: Oxford University Press, 1987); Diane Eck, *A New Religious America: How a "Christian Country" Has Become the World's Most Religiously Diverse Nation* (San Francisco: HarperSanFrancisco, 2001). For a perspective on Catholics' uneasy transition to the nation's mainstream, see, for instance, Robert A. Orsi, *Thank You, St. Jude: Women's Devotion to the Patron Saint of Hopeless Causes* (New Haven, Conn.: Yale University Press, 1998), and *The Madonna of 115th Street: Faith and Community in Italian Harlem, 1880–1950* (New Haven, Conn.: Yale University Press, 1988); John McGreevy, *Parish Boundaries: The Catholic Encounter with Race in the Twentieth-Century Urban North* (Chicago: University of Chicago Press, 1998); and Massa, *Catholics and American Culture.*

40. Andrew M. Greeley, *An Ugly Little Secret: Anti-Catholicism in North America* (Kansas City, Kan.: Sheed, Andrews, and McMeel, 1977). Greeley makes a similar argument about the place of anti-Catholicism in American academia in his article "Anti-Catholicism in the Academy," *Change* 9, no. 6 (1977): 40–43.

41. Andrew M. Greeley, "What Does the Data Show? An Ugly Little Secret: A Pretest on Anti-Catholicism in America," paper delivered at the conference, Anti-Catholicism: The Last Acceptable Prejudice, Fordham University, May 24, 2002. Text available at: http://www.catholicsinpublicsquare.org/papers/anticath52402/greely/greelyprint.htm.

Index

Catholic Union and Times, The, 187–88
Catholic Western Watchman, The, 45
celibacy, 130
Centuries of Childhood (Ariès), 126
Chalmers, David, 204
charitable work, Catholic
    increase in, 117–18
    nativist criticism of, 13, 15, 116,
        117, 221*f*
    —call for investigation of
        institutions, 116, 133–34
    —as phony schemes, 96
    Windle on, 166–67
Charleston, Massachusetts
    burning of the Ursuline convent,
        19, 111, 234n39
Chicago
    The Crusader on police force in,
        99–100
    The Jeffersonian on corruption in, 97
    newspapers in, 180
    The Yellow Jacket on daily press in,
        179
child, trope of the threatened.
    See children, anti-Catholics on
    Catholic threat to
childhood
    depiction by nativist writers, 128–29
    Progressive-Era on, 124–25
    Protestant, 140
    as social construct, 125–26, 128–29
childhood innocence, trope of,
    126–27
    link with death, 137
children, anti-Catholics on Catholic
    threat to, 107–8, 111, 120–21,
    124–29, 140–41, 144
    accounts of injury and death,
        136–37, 138
    and accusation of Catholic graft
        and deception, 132
    child slave industry, articles on, 131

and masculine call to action, 142
and responsibility of civil
    authorities, 135
circulation of periodicals
    anti-Catholic periodicals, 9–10,
        55–57, 56*t1*, 195, 219*f*, 228n13
    Catholic periodicals, 152
    causes of increase in, 53, 89
    mainstream periodicals, 57*t2*,
        228n13
    propaganda war as fight for, 188
cities
    Catholics on city courts, 136
    condemnation of Catholic
        domination of civil servant
        jobs, 96
    depiction by nativists, 72–73
citizenship
    Catholic demand for equal, 147
    Catholics seen as unfit for, 30
    rights-based, 190
civic nationalism. *See also* ideological
        nationalism
    Catholics and, 146
    versus ethnic nationalism, 7, 28–29
    nativism and, 205
Civil War
    The Antidote on nuns as nurses
        during, 169, 170
    masculinity and public memory of,
        32–33
    nativism and, 23
    new perception of, 32, 40
Clark, William Lloyd, 183, 199
Cleary, Joe, 229n19
Coburn, Carol, 118
Collier's, circulation of, 57*t2*
Columbus, Christopher
    Catholics and, 20
    nativist criticism of celebrations
        for, 46
    nativist view of, 48, 217*f*

JUSTIN NORDSTROM
is assistant professor of history at Pennsylvania State University, Hazleton.